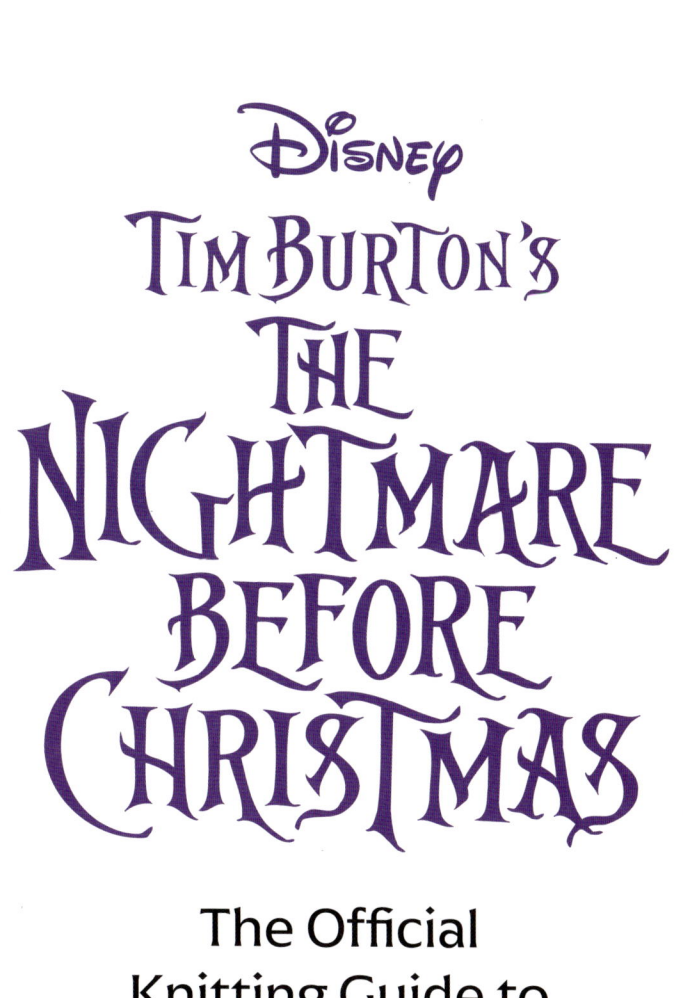

Disney
Tim Burton's THE NIGHTMARE BEFORE CHRISTMAS

The Official Knitting Guide to Halloween Town and Christmas Town

Disney
Tim Burton's
The Nightmare Before Christmas

The Official Knitting Guide to Halloween Town and Christmas Town

By Tanis Gray

INSIGHT EDITIONS

SAN RAFAEL · LOS ANGELES · LONDON

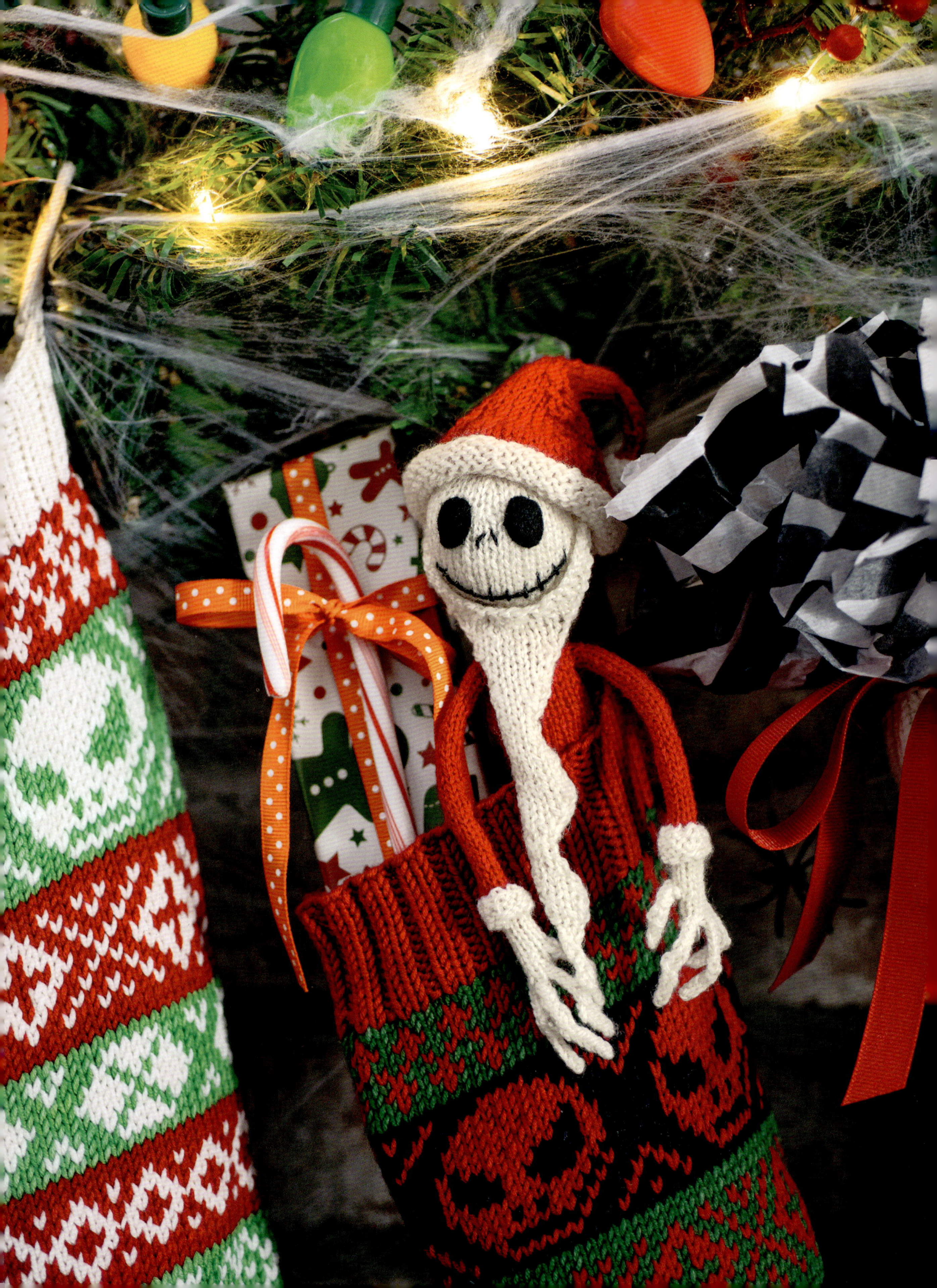

Contents

07 Introduction

09 Terrifying Toys
- 11 Jack Skellington & Santa Jack Toy Figures
- 21 Zero Toy Figure
- 27 Oogie Boogie Toy Figure

33 Creepy Costume Replicas
- 35 The Mayor's Badge
- 39 Sally's Fingerless Mitts
- 45 Harlequin Pullover
- 55 Barrel's Pullover

63 Inspired Apparel
- 65 Skeletal Reindeer Hat
- 69 Oogie Boogie Roulette Cowl
- 75 Sally's Dress Wrap
- 85 Full Moon Oogie Boogie Hat
- 89 Jack's Pinstripe Cowl
- 93 Sally's Shawl
- 99 The Mayor Two-Face Mittens
- 107 Jack's Lament Fingerless Mitts
- 113 Sally's Socks
- 123 Wickedly Cute Pinstripe Socks
- 129 Jack's Tailcoat Cardigan
- 139 Halloween Town Pullover
- 147 Spiral Hill Sweater Vest
- 163 The Nightmare Before Christmas Cowl

169 Horrifying Home Décor
- 171 Jack Skellington Pillow
- 177 Halloween Town Ornaments
- 181 Oogie Boogie Dice Bag
- 185 The Nightmare Before Christmas Throw
- 195 Festive Stockings
- 201 Sally's Potion Jars
- 211 Snake Draft Blocker

214 Glossary and Techniques

222 Abbreviations

223 Yarn Resource Guide

💀💀💀 BEGINNER
💀💀💀 INTERMEDIATE
💀💀💀 ADVANCED

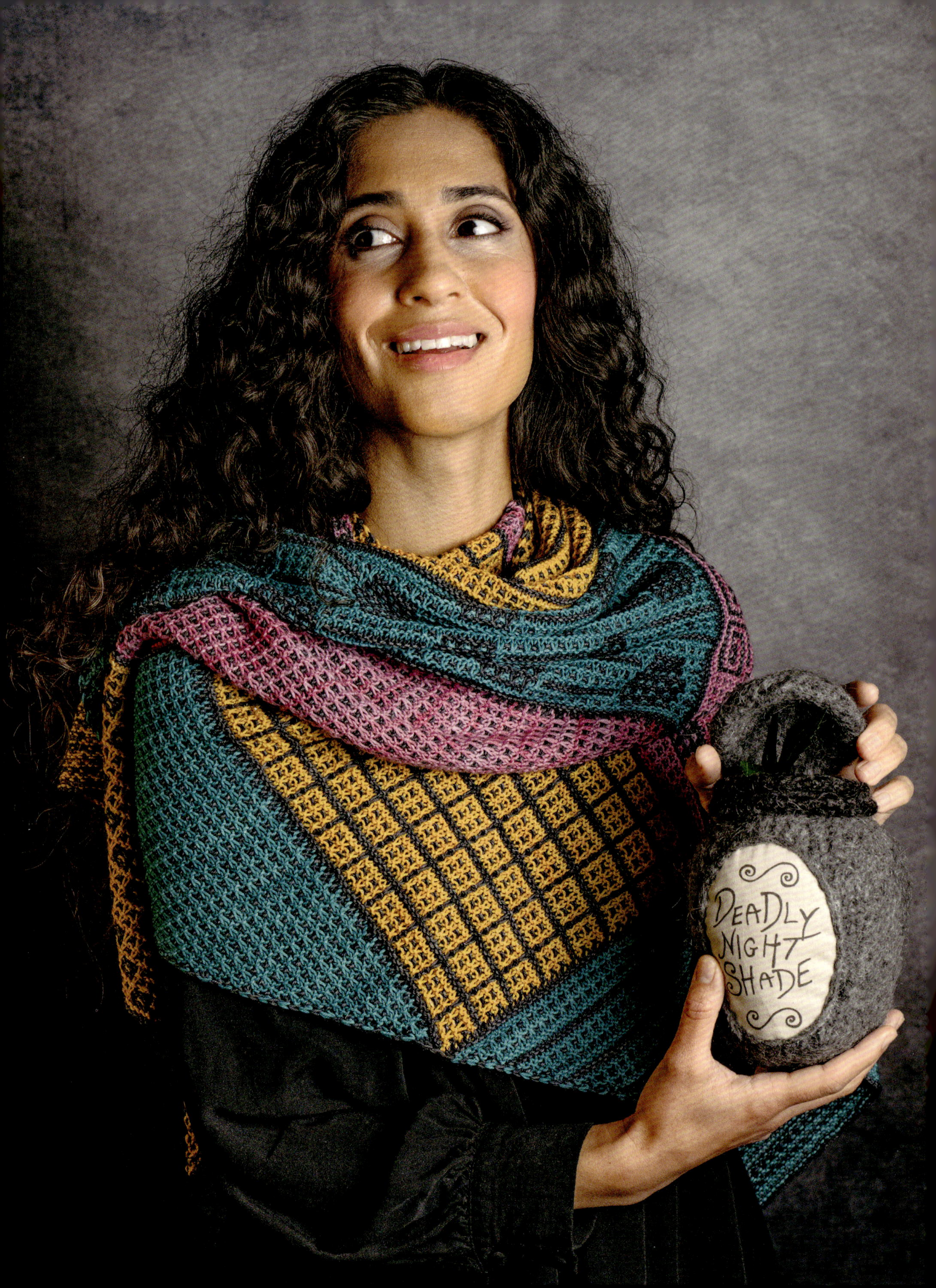
DEADLY
NIGHT
SHADE

Introduction

In 1993, *Tim Burton's The Nightmare Before Christmas* was the first full-length stop-motion animation feature from a major studio to hit theaters in decades. A game changer for both audiences and animation studios—who had never seen anything like it—the film introduced us to the highly stylized, ghostly world of Halloween Town. Puppets walked with elegance and ease, sang haunting songs, danced, and moved in ways so realistic, at times it was easy to forget we were watching animation created a single frame at a time. The story of Jack—who seemed to have it all—wanting something more, and Sally watching him from afar wanting to be his friend, pulled us in. We felt Zero's worry, the Mayor's fear, and Dr. Finkelstein's exasperation. We empathized with the characters and all of Halloween Town, fully invested in their world and goals.

When I watched it again years later while at the Rhode Island School of Design (RISD) for training in animation, I was in awe of the technical aspects and creation of the film. The extraordinarily detailed sets, the exceptional character and costume design, the seamless movement, striking lighting, and camera angles—it was a masterpiece in the medium of stop-motion animation. My fellow animators and I would gather and watch, discussing techniques, aesthetics, storyline, and wonder, "How did they do that?" Even after all these years, this film has lost none of the magic it bestowed on me and audiences long ago.

As time has passed, the popularity and acclaim for *Tim Burton's The Nightmare Before Christmas* have only grown. What was once a cult favorite is now both a Halloween and winter holiday family staple, whether watching by the glow of twinkle lights as the snow falls gently outside or settling in with a candy stash to watch after a night of trick-or-treating. While we aren't stuffed with leaves with sewn-on limbs, or walking skeletons wearing pinstripe suits, we can each relate to one or more of the characters and recognize some of them and their personalities inside of us.

Like many others, this film is one I go back to again and again, singing along with the songs, reciting favorite lines, or settling in with a knitting project to watch for the hundredth time. For many years I have wished to see a book like this out in the world, combining my love of *Tim Burton's The Nightmare Before Christmas* with my love of knitwear design. The result is a chillingly delightful collection of cozy knits with an eerie twist. Cast on for a scraptastic Sally's Shawl (page 93), knit Festive Stockings for the whole family with a hint of creepiness (page 195), make a stunning cabled cardigan inspired by Jack's suit coat (page 129), or create your very own knitted guard dog Zero (page 21). Designers from around the world have channeled their affection and appreciation for this film into lace, cables, stranded colorwork, intarsia, mosaic, and double-knitting projects both in film replica pieces and inspired-by creations.

With a collection of garments covering a wide size range for superfans in addition to those just discovering this timeless classic, there are also spine-chilling accessories, home décor, socks, shawls, and toys. A new knitter? No problem—we've got projects tucked inside these pages for you as well, designed to increase your skill level with each project you begin.

Instead of asking, "What's this?" we say, "Cast on!"

—Tanis

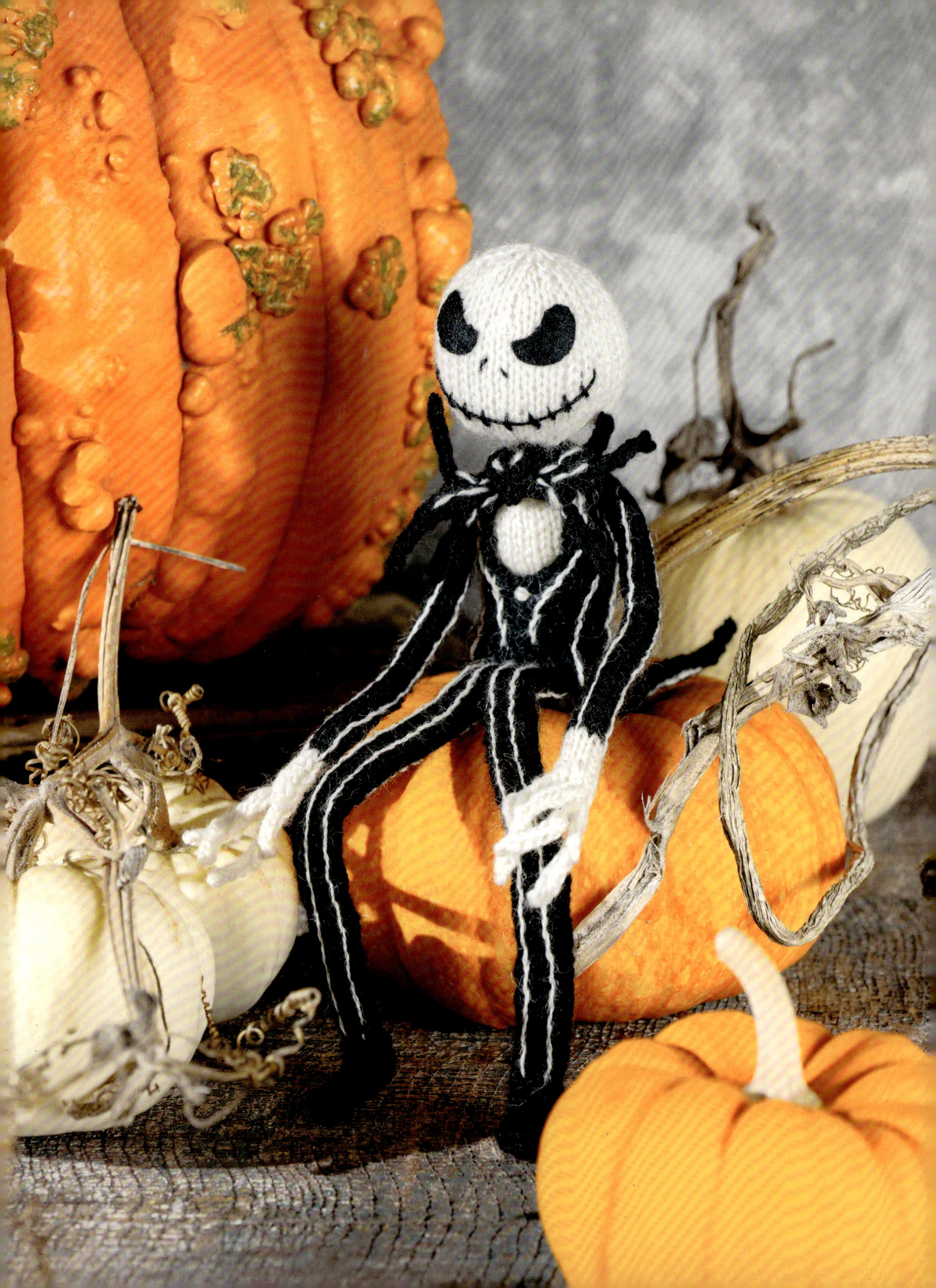

Terrifying Toys

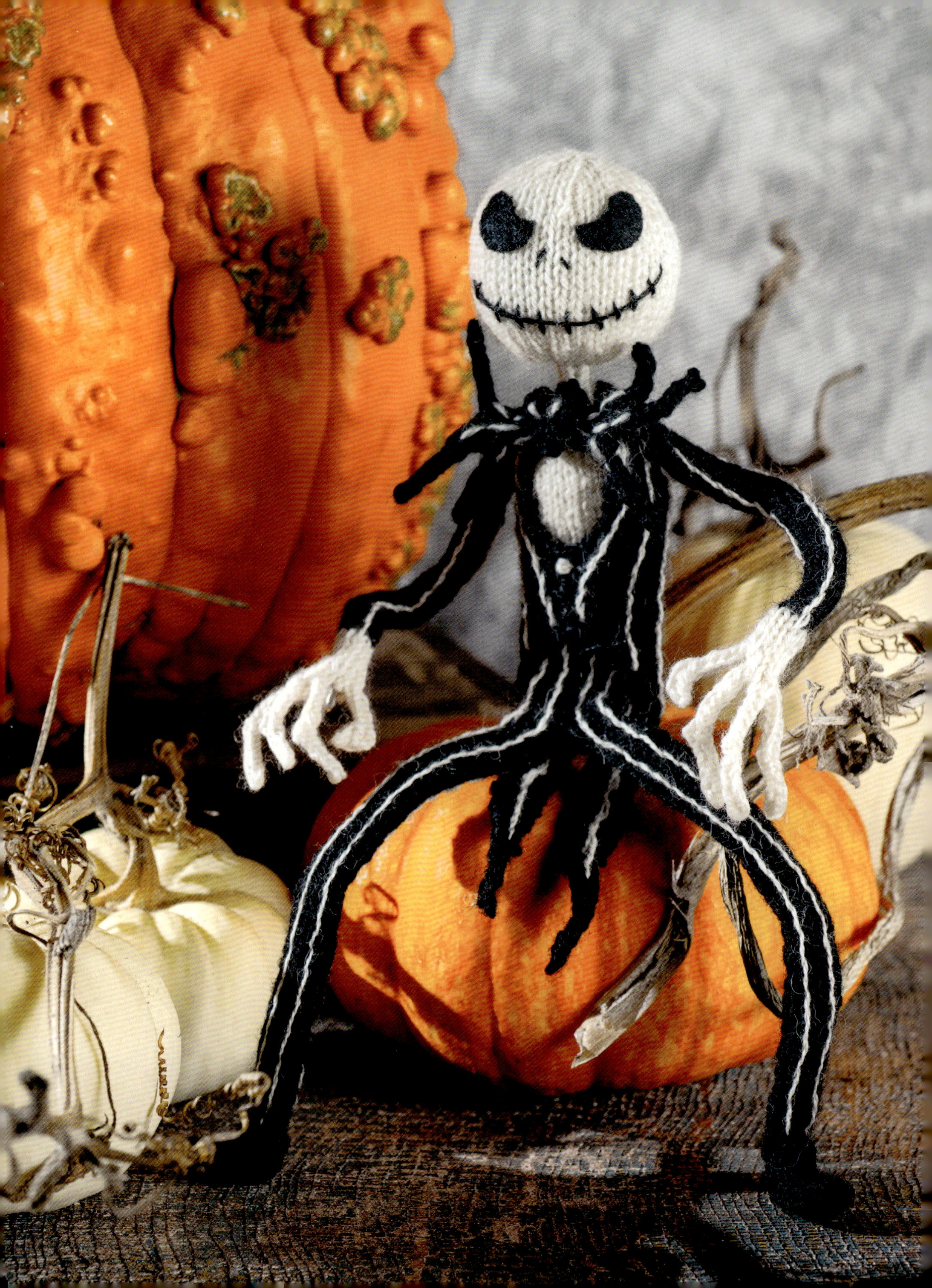

Jack Skellington & Santa Jack Toy Figures

Designed by Jesie Ostermiller

SKILL LEVEL

"Now don't be modest. Who else is clever enough to make my Sandy Claws outfit?"
—Jack Skellington to Sally

As the Pumpkin King of Halloween Town, elegant Jack Skellington wears a sophisticated pinstripe suit with a bat bow tie, and his long, lean body moves like a spider. Although it appears that he has it all and is happy with his eerie existence, Jack longs for something more beyond the monotony of scaring humans and planning the next Halloween. He finds what he thinks is missing from his world in the bright, jolly Christmas Town.

Creator Tim Burton states, "I love Jack. He has a lot of passion and energy; he's always looking for a feeling. That's what he finds in Christmas Town. He is a bit misguided, and his emotions take over, but he gets everybody excited." Set designers wanted to create an obvious shift between the hard angles and limited color palette in Halloween Town and the rounded edges and dazzling tone of Christmas Town. Jack also gets a makeover going from his dark pinstripe suit to the bold red Santa outfit that Sally made.

Bring a bit of Halloween Town into your home with these adorable posable figures of Jack Skellington and Jack in his Sandy Claws costume. Knit from the bottom up, the legs are made separately, then joined at the hips to be worked in the round up through the torso, neck, and head. The doll is fully posable thanks to a wire armature inside (much like the puppets made for the film), which is inserted while working the torso. Arms are attached last. Both figures can be knit from the same pattern with just a few wardrobe changes. Make a Santa suit, hat, and beard like Sally made for Jack, or recreate his dapper tuxedo with embroidered stem stitching and bat bow tie. All hail the Pumpkin King!

SIZES
One size

FINISHED MEASUREMENTS
Height: 10½ in. / 26.5 cm

YARN
Fingering weight yarn, shown in Cascade Yarns *Cascade 220 Fingering* (2-ply; 100% Peruvian Highland wool; 273 yd. / 250 m per 1¾ oz. / 50 g hank)

COLORWAYS:
- Main Color (MC): #8555 Black, 1 hank
- Contrast Color 1 (CC1): #8505 White, 1 hank
- Contrast Color 2 (CC2): #8895 Christmas Red, 1 hank

Lace weight yarn, shown in Cascade Yarns *Alpaca Lace* (100% baby alpaca; 437 yd. / 400 m per 1¾ oz. / 50 g hank)

COLORWAY:
- Contrast Color 3 (CC3): #1405 Ecru, 1 hank

NEEDLES
US 2 / 2.75 mm, set of 5 double-pointed needles

NOTIONS
Stitch markers (locking and fixed)

Tapestry needle

Polyester stuffing (approx. 1 oz. / 29 g per toy)

1/16 in. / 14 AWG armature wire and wire cutter (approx. 1.5yd. / 1¼ m per toy)

Black felt

Black thread and sewing needle

GAUGE
29 sts and 44 rows = 4 in. / 10 cm in stockinette stitch worked in the round using fingering weight yarn, unblocked

PATTERN NOTES

- These figures are worked in the round from the feet up (both legs worked separately), then joined at the hips and worked in the round up through the torso, neck, and head. The armature wire skeleton is inserted while working through the torso.
- The fingers are knit next, then combined into the hands before knitting the lengths of the arms. Arms will be attached to the body after the body is complete.
- Due to the small circumference of stitches, the instructions alternate between working an i-cord with 2 needles and working on multiple dpns in the round.
- Jack Skellington's pinstripes are embroidered onto the arms and legs of the toy with lace weight yarn using a stem stitch when the body is finished. The jacket should be embroidered with the pinstripes separately, before wrapping it around Jack's torso.
- Instructions are provided for the Jack Skellington toy. Variations for the Santa Jack toy will be provided in {braces} where applicable. If only one set of instructions is provided, it applies to both toys.

PATTERN INSTRUCTIONS

PREPARE WIRE SKELETON

Cut two 15 in. / 38 cm lengths of armature wire. Bend one end of each wire approx. 2 in. / 5 cm from the end. Bend this same section again into the rough shape of a paper clip. This double bend will serve as the foot form for both legs after being inserted into the toy. Approx. 6½ in. / 17 cm above the foot form, twist the remaining ends of the wires around each other tightly to create a strong support for the body, neck, and head.

FIRST FOOT AND LEG

Using MC, CO 6 sts using the Long Tail Cast On method. Distribute sts evenly over 3 dpns (2 sts per needle). Pm for BOR and join to work in the rnd, being careful not to twist the sts.
RND 1 (INC): *Kfb, k1; rep from * 2 more times—9 sts.
RNDS 2–6: Knit.
Redistribute the sts so that the first 5 sts of the rnd are on one dpn and last 4 are on a second dpn.
Working flat only on the first dpn:
ROW 7 (RS): K5, turn.
ROW 8 (WS): P5, turn.
ROWS 9–12: Rep [Rows 7 and 8] 2 times.
Resume working in the rnd.
RND 13 (INC): K5, pick up and knit 1 st from the edge of the heel flap (approx. in the middle), k4 across second dpn, pick up and knit 1 st on other side of the flap—11 sts.
RND 14 (DEC): K5, (k2tog) 3 times—8 sts.
FOR JACK: {see **For Santa Jack, below}
RND 15: Knit.
RND 16: Purl (this purl ridge creates the bottom hem of the pants).
RNDS 17–75: Knit.
ROW 76 (RS, PARTIAL ROW): K4, break yarn. Leave sts on dpn or transfer to spare needle / waste yarn if preferred. Do not weave in this end until directed.
Note: When you attach the legs, you will start the new round at this yarn tail.

{**FOR SANTA JACK:
RNDS 15–40: Knit.
The boot is now complete. Break MC; join CC1 and shape fur cuff as follows:
RND 41 (INC): (Kfb) 8 times—16 sts.
RNDS 42–45: Purl.
The cuff is now complete. Break CC1; join CC2.
RND 46 (DEC): (K2tog) 8 times—8 sts.
RNDS 47–75: Knit.
ROW 76 (RS, PARTIAL ROW): K4, break yarn. Do not weave in this end until directed.
Note: When you attach the legs, you will start the new round at this yarn tail.}

SECOND FOOT AND LEG

Work Rnds/Rows 1–75 as for the First Foot and Leg for the toy you are making. Do not break yarn.

JOIN LEGS

Arrange both legs parallel, so the feet are pointing forward. Using the working yarn from the second leg, knit 8 sts of the first leg beginning at the yarn tail from Row 75. Pm for new BOR (located on the center of the back)—16 sts total. Distribute the sts for comfort over dpns.
FOR JACK: {see **For Santa Jack, below}
Knit 12 rnds. Break yarn.
Proceed to Shape Body.
{**FOR SANTA JACK:
Knit 8 rnds.
Place the live 16 sts of the joined legs on waste yarn or spare needle. Break CC2.
Using CC2, work Rows 1–35 of Coattails (page 14). Do not break CC2 when Row 35 is complete. Then return to these instructions to join the tails to the body.
Prepare coattails for joining with the body by knitting the first 8 sts. Slip these 8 sts onto waste yarn

or spare needle and set aside; leave the rem 8 sts on a dpn. The coattails will join to the body at the center back. Break CC2.
Join MC for the belt.

SANTA JACK BELT:

Lay the Coattails piece over the top of the joined legs so that the second half of the coattail (8 sts on a dpn) lines up with the first 8 sts of the live rnd. Hold the two sets of 8 sts on parallel dpns.

With MC, join the two sets of live sts together by knitting together one coattail st with one body st (like a k2tog). Repeat 7 more times until half of the coattail is joined to the body.

Move the rem 8 coattail sts from waste yarn to a dpn. Arrange this dpn with the front of the body so the 8 sts of the coattail line up with the 8 rem sts of the body. Continuing with MC, join the two sets of live sts together by knitting together one coattail st with one body st (like a k2tog). Repeat 7 more times until all the coattail sts are joined to the body—16 sts.
Knit 3 rnds even with MC; break MC. Proceed to Shape Body.}

SHAPE BODY

Join CC1 {CC2}.
RND 1: Knit.
RND 2 (INC): K5, M1L, k6, M1R, k5—18 sts.
RNDS 3–5: Knit.
RND 6 (INC): K5, M1L, k8, M1R, k5—20 sts.
RNDS 7–9: Knit.
RND 10 (INC): K5, M1L, k10, M1R, k5—22 sts.
RNDS 11–13: Knit.
RND 14 (INC): K5, M1L, k12, M1R, k5—24 sts.
RNDS 15–19: Knit.
Redistribute sts over 4 dpns (6 sts per needle).
RND 20 (DEC): K3, k2tog, k2, ssk, k6, k2tog, k2, ssk, k3—20 sts.
Before further shaping, insert prepared wire skeleton by pushing the folded ends into each leg and the foot forms down into each foot. Bend wire to a 90-degree angle at the top of the foot form to create the ankle. The remainder of the project will be worked around the armature wire.
Lightly stuff the body around the armature wire with some of the polyester. The stuffing should not extend into the toy's legs.
RND 21 (DEC): K2, k2tog, k2, ssk, k4, k2tog, k2, ssk, k2—16 sts.
RND 22 (DEC): K1, k2tog, k2, ssk, k2, k2tog, k2, ssk, k1—12 sts.
FOR JACK: {see **for Santa Jack, below}
RND 23 (DEC): K2tog, k2, ssk, k2tog, k2, ssk—8 sts.
RND 24 (DEC): (K2tog) 4 times—4 sts.
Proceed to Neck & Head.
{FOR SANTA JACK:**
Break CC2; join CC1 and shape fur cuff as follows:
RND 23 (INC): (Kfb, k1) 6 times—18 sts.
RNDS 24–26: Purl.
RND 27 (DEC): (K2tog) 9 times—9 sts.
RND 28 (DEC): K3tog, (k2tog) 3 times—4 sts.
Proceed to Neck & Head.}

NECK & HEAD

Cont with CC1.
RNDS 1–5: Work a 4-stitch i-cord around the twisted/doubled wire.
RND 6 (INC): (Kfb) 4 times—8 sts.
RND 7 (INC): (Kfb) 8 times—16 sts.
RND 8 (INC): (Kfb) 16 times—32 sts.
RND 9: Knit.
RND 10 (INC): (Kfb, k3) 8 times—40 sts.
RNDS 11–22: Knit.
Before creating the head shaping with decreases, shorten the rem skeletal wires. Starting with the exposed ends of the wire, and using an object with approx. ¾ in. / 2 cm circumference (like a highlighter or glue stick), roll the ends up into a circle. These rolled ends sit inside the head.
Use a small amount of polyester to stuff the head, around the wire, distributing stuffing evenly so that the head has a nice round shape.
RND 23 (DEC): (K2, k2tog) 10 times—30 sts.
RNDS 24–26: Knit.
RND 27 (DEC): (K1, k2tog) 10 times—20 sts.
RND 28: Knit.
Fill rem area inside the head with polyester.

RND 29 (FINAL DEC): (K2tog) 10 times—10 sts.

Break yarn leaving an 8 in. / 20.5 cm tail. Thread yarn tail into tapestry needle and weave through rem sts. Pull tight to secure and fasten off. The rem tail can be woven inside the head.

FOR JACK: Proceed to Coattails.
{FOR SANTA JACK: Proceed to Right Thumb.**}**

COATTAILS

With MC {CC2}, CO 2 sts using the Long Tail Cast On method. Do not join to work in the rnd.
ROW 1 (WS): K1, p1.
ROW 2 (RS): K1, p1.
ROWS 3 AND 4: Rep [Rows 1 and 2] 1 time.
ROW 5 (INC): Kfb, k1—3 sts.
ROW 6: P1, k1, p1.
ROW 7: K1, p1, k1.
ROWS 8 AND 9: Rep [Rows 6 and 7] 1 time.
ROW 10: P1, k1, p1.
ROW 11 (INC): (Kfb) 2 times, k1—5 sts.
ROW 12: (P1, k1) 2 times, p1.
ROW 13: (K1, p1) 2 times, k1.
ROWS 14–21: Rep [Rows 12 and 13] 4 times.
ROW 22: (P1, k1) 2 times, p1.
ROW 23 (INC): (Kfb, p1) 2 times, k1—7 sts.
ROW 24: (P1, k2) 2 times, p1.
ROW 25: (K1, p2) 2 times, k1.
ROWS 26 AND 27: Rep [Rows 24 and 25] 1 time. This completes the first coattail.

Break MC {CC2} yarn; place live sts on waste yarn or spare needle and set aside.

Make a second coattail by working Rows 1–27 once; do not break yarn.

JOIN COATTAILS

ROW 28 (RS): P1, k2, p1, k2, p1 from the second coattail. Without breaking the working yarn, place the held sts of the first coattail onto the working needle and p1, k2, p1, k2, p1—14 sts.
ROW 29 (WS): (K1, p2) 2 times, k2, (p2, k1) 2 times.
ROWS 30–33: Rep [Rows 28 and 29] 2 times.
ROW 34 (INC): Kfb, k11, kfb, k1—16 sts.
ROW 35: Purl.
FOR JACK: Proceed to Jacket.

JACKET

ROW 36 (RS, INC): Kfb, k13, kfb, k1—18 sts.
ROW 37 (WS): Purl.
ROW 38 (INC): Kfb, k15, kfb, k1—20 sts.
ROW 39: Purl.
ROW 40 (INC): Kfb, k17, kfb, k1—22 sts.

Note: Place a locking stitch marker at each end of the last row. These markers indicate where the front of the jacket will come together to be "buttoned."

ROW 41: Purl.
ROW 42: P2, k18, p2.
ROW 43: Purl.
ROWS 44–47: Rep [Rows 42 and 43] 2 times.
ROW 48 (DEC): P1, p2tog, k16, p2tog, p1—20 sts.
ROW 49: Purl.
ROW 50: P2, k16, p2.
ROW 51: Purl.
ROWS 52–63: Rep [Rows 50 and 51] 6 times.
ROW 64 (DEC): (K2tog) 10 times—10 sts.
ROW 65 (DEC): P1, (p2tog) 4 times, p1—6 sts.

With RS facing, BO all sts and break MC leaving a 10 in. / 25.5 cm tail.

Note: This extra-long tail will be used to sew the jacket to Jack's body.

Use stem stitch and CC3 to embroider pinstripes all over the jacket. Pinstripes will be placed approx. 2 st columns apart.

Proceed to Right Thumb.

RIGHT THUMB

With CC1, CO 2 sts.
RNDS 1–3: Work a 2-stitch i-cord.
RNDS 4 AND 5: Pull the yarn behind like an i-cord, sl1 wyib, k1.

Note: Rnds 4 and 5, with slipped sts, make the i-cord bend like a knuckle.

RNDS 6–11: Work a 2-stitch i-cord. Break CC1, leaving a 2 in. / 5 cm tail. Set aside on dpn.

LEFT THUMB

With CC1, CO 2 sts.
RNDS 1–3: Work a 2-stitch i-cord.
RNDS 4 AND 5: Pull the yarn behind like an i-cord, k1, sl1 wyib.
RNDS 6–11: Work a 2-stitch i-cord. Break CC1, leaving a 2 in. / 5 cm tail. Set aside on dpn.

FINGERS & HAND

Note: Jack has three fingers and a thumb. All three fingers are joined together for the first part of the hand. The thumb, which was knit separately, is joined to the fingers as the hand is finished. Make two sets of fingers the same; each set will be joined to the left or right thumb to complete each hand.

FIRST FINGER

With CC1, CO 2 sts.
RNDS 1–6: Work a 2-stitch i-cord.
RNDS 7 AND 8: Pull the yarn behind like an i-cord, sl1 wyib, k1.
RNDS 9–14: Work a 2-stitch i-cord. Break CC1, leaving a 2 in. / 5 cm tail. Slip sts to a separate dpn.

SECOND FINGER

Work as for the First Finger; transfer the live sts to the same separate dpn as the first finger, to the right of the first finger sts.

THIRD FINGER

Work as for the First Finger. When complete, do not break CC1; transfer the live sts to the same dpn as the first and second fingers, to the right of the second finger sts—6 sts.

Join all three fingers together in the following way:
RND 15: K1 (from third finger), (k2tog) twice, k1—4 sts.
RNDS 16 AND 17: Work a 4-stitch i-cord. Do not break yarn. Proceed to Right/Left Hand.

RIGHT HAND

Join thumb to hand in the following way:
Place 2 right thumb sts onto the LHN tip holding the 4 live sts of the fingers/hand.
RND 18: K2 (from right thumb), k4 (from hand)—6 sts.
RNDS 19–22: Work a 6-stitch i-cord. Do not break yarn; proceed to Arms.

LEFT HAND

Join thumb to hand in the following way:
RND 18: K4 (from hand), k2 (from left thumb)—6 sts.
RNDS 19–22: Work a 6-stitch i-cord. Do not break yarn; proceed to Arms.

ARMS (MAKE 2 THE SAME)

FOR JACK: {see **For Santa Jack, below}
Break CC1, join MC.
Work 6-stitch i-cord for 3¼ in. / 8.5 cm.
With RS facing, BO all sts knitwise. Break MC, leaving a 10 in. / 25.5 cm tail.

Note: This extra-long tail will be used to sew the arm to Jack's body.

Proceed to Assembling Jack.

{**FOR SANTA JACK:
Cont with CC1; shape fur cuffs as follows:
RND 23 (INC): (Kfb) 6 times—12 sts.
RNDS 24–28: Purl.
Break CC1, join CC2.
RND 29 (DEC): (K2tog) 6 times—6 sts.
Work 6-stitch i-cord until arm measures 3 in. / 7.5 cm above fur cuff.
With RS facing, BO all sts knitwise. Break CC2, leaving a 10 in. / 25.5 cm tail.

Note: This extra-long tail will be used to sew the arm to Santa Jack's body.

Proceed to Attaching Arms to Body.}

ASSEMBLING JACK

Wrap finished jacket around Jack's torso, matching up widest jacket points (indicated by locking markers) in the front, at the top of Jack's pants (where the yarn changes from MC to CC1).

Use the extra-long tail from the jacket bind off to stitch down the right front lapel of the jacket to Jack's torso. When you reach the points that meet, use a whipstitch to close the front of the jacket so approx. 1 in. / 2.5 cm is stitched closed right above the pants.

Secure the left front edge of the jacket to the torso. Continue stitching across the back of the jacket to the neck. Secure the yarn tail and weave it inside the torso.

ATTACHING ARMS TO BODY

Cut one 10 in. / 25.5 cm length of armature wire; one long piece will be used to create structure for both arms.

Fold one end of the wire approx. ½ in. / 1.5 cm from the end to create a small loop. Insert the looped end into Jack's {Santa Jack's} left arm, pushing the small loop into the palm of his hand.

Optional: You may tack the loop into the palm of the hand after attaching the arms to the body to ensure it stays in place.

Thread the other end of the wire (the unlooped end) through Jack's jacket/body about ½ in. / 1.5 cm below the base of his neck (approx. where the shoulder decreases start). After wire is threaded through the body, fold over the opposite end of the wire about ½ in. / 1.5 cm (to create a second small loop) and insert it into Jack's {Santa Jack's} right arm, pushing the end loop down into his right palm.

Use the BO tail of each arm to sew the arm to the body, around the wire. *Note: Make sure the arm is oriented the right way, regarding fingers & thumb, before sewing into place.*

Optional: If desired, Jack's {Santa Jack's} fingers can be lightly steam blocked and bent into place to make them more uniform.

FOR JACK: Proceed to Bow Tie.
FOR SANTA JACK: Proceed to Beard.

BOW TIE (JACK ONLY)

Note: The bow tie is constructed of 2 bat wings, each with 3 wing spokes. Make all 3 wing spokes for the first bat wing before making the second bat wing.

FIRST BAT WING

WING SPOKE #1
With MC, CO 2 sts using the Long Tail Cast On method.
RNDS 1–6: Work a 2-stitch i-cord.
Break yarn, leaving a 2 in. / 5 cm tail. Set aside on dpn.

WING SPOKE #2
With MC, CO 2 sts using the Long Tail Cast On method.
RNDS 1–6: Work a 2-stitch i-cord.
RND 7 (INC): Pull yarn behind like an i-cord, kfb, k1—3 sts.
RNDS 8–10: Work a 3-stitch i-cord.
Break yarn, leaving a 2 in. / 5 cm tail. Transfer the live sts to the same dpn as Wing Spoke #1, to the right of the Spoke #1 sts.

WING SPOKE #3
Work as for Wing Spoke #1. When complete, do not break yarn; transfer the live sts to the same dpn as Spokes #1 and #2, to the right of the Spoke #2—7 sts.

JOINING SPOKES FOR BAT WING
Join Spokes #1, #2, and #3 in the following way using the working yarn from Spoke #3:
ROW 1 (RS, DEC): (K1, k2tog) 2 times, k1—5 sts.
ROW 2 (WS): Purl.
ROW 3: Knit.
ROW 4: Purl.
ROW 5 (DEC): K2tog, k1, ssk—3 sts.
ROW 6: Purl.
Break yarn, leaving a 2 in. / 5 cm tail. Set aside on dpn.

SECOND BAT WING

Work as for the First Bat Wing; at completion, do not break MC yarn.

ASSEMBLING BAT WINGS
Arrange the first and second wings RS together. With the working yarn from the second bat wing, join the two sets of live stitches using the Three-Needle Bind Off method. Proceed to Bat Head.

BAT HEAD

With MC, CO 3 sts using the Long Tail Cast On method. Do not join to work in the rnd.
ROW 1 (RS): Knit.
ROW 2 (WS): Purl.
ROW 3 (INC): (Kfb) 2 times, k1—5 sts.
ROW 4: Purl.
ROW 5 (DEC): K2tog, k1, k1, pass first knit stitch over second and off the needle (1 st BO), sl first st on RHN to LHN purlwise, ssk—2 sts.
ROW 6 (INC): P1, yo, p1—3 sts.
ROW 7 (RS): Knit.
ROW 8 (WS): Purl.
With RS facing, BO all sts knitwise. Break MC, leaving a 10 in. / 25.5 cm tail.

Fold the bat head along Row 5 with the WS together (the row where you bound off 1 st in the middle); the resulting shape is a pointed face with two pointy ears. Tie the CO & BO tails together to secure the folded shape.

Use the long tail from the BO to sew and secure the bat head to the center of the wings.

Use a small amount of CC3 to embroider eyes on the bat head and some lines on each spoke of the wings as shown in the photo using stem stitch.

BEARD {SANTA JACK ONLY}

With CC1, CO 25 sts using the Long Tail Cast On method. Do not join to work in the rnd.
ROW 1 (RS, DEC): BO 4 sts knitwise, slide st on RHN back to LHN purlwise, ssk, k5, yo, k3, yo, k5, k2tog, k4—21 sts.
ROW 2 (WS, DEC): BO 4 sts purlwise, slide st on RHN back to LHN purlwise, ssk, p13, k2tog—15 sts.
ROW 3 (DEC): (Ssk) 2 times, k7, (k2tog) 2 times—11 sts.
ROW 4 (DEC): P2tog, p7, ssp—9 sts.
ROW 5: Knit.
ROW 6 (AND ALL WS ROWS UNTIL OTHERWISE NOTED): Purl.

ROW 7 (DEC): Ssk, k5, k2tog—7 sts.
ROW 9: K1, M1L, k4, k2tog.
ROW 11: K1, M1L, k4, k2tog.
ROW 13: Knit.
ROW 15: Ssk, k4, M1R, k1.
ROW 17: Ssk, k4, M1R, k1.
ROW 19: Knit.
ROW 21: K1, M1L, k4, k2tog.
ROW 23: K1, M1L, k4, k2tog.
ROW 25 (DEC): Ssk, k3, k2tog—5 sts.
ROW 27: Knit.
ROW 29: Ssk, k2, M1R, k1.
ROW 31: Ssk, k2, M1R, k1.
ROW 33: Knit.
ROW 35 (DEC): Ssk, k1, k2tog—3 sts.
ROW 37: Knit.
ROW 39 (DEC): K1, k2tog—2 sts.
ROWS 40–42: K1, p1.
ROW 43 (DEC): Ssk—1 st.
With WS facing, fasten off rem st.
Wet block beard by soaking in water, squeezing it dry with a towel, and then pinning the edges out to emphasize the curves created by the shaping. Be fairly aggressive in blocking the CO row so that each end of the row comes up as points on each side, creating a half-moon shape. This will allow the fake beard to hang nicely below Santa Jack's skull.
Proceed to Santa Hat.

SANTA HAT {SANTA JACK ONLY}

With CC1, CO 44 sts using the Long Tail Cast On method. Pm for BOR and join to work in the rnd, being careful not to twist the sts.
RNDS 1–7: Purl.
Break CC1, join CC2.
RNDS 8–16: Knit.
RND 17 (DEC): (K20, k2tog) 2 times—42 sts.
RND 18 (DEC): (K1, k2tog) 14 times—28 sts.
RNDS 19–21: Knit.
RND 22 (DEC): K5, k2tog, ssk, k10, k2tog, ssk, k5—24 sts.
RND 23: Knit.
RND 24 (DEC): K4, k2tog, ssk, k8, k2tog, ssk, k4—20 sts.
RNDS 25 AND 26: Knit.
RND 27 (DEC): K3, k2tog, ssk, k6, k2tog, ssk, k3—16 sts.
RNDS 28–30: Knit.
RND 31 (DEC): K2, k2tog, ssk, k4, k2tog, ssk, k2—12 sts.
RNDS 32–34: Knit.
RND 35 (DEC): K1, k2tog, ssk, k2, k2tog, ssk, k1—8 sts.
RNDS 36–40: Knit.
RND 41 (DEC): (K2tog, ssk) 2 times—4 sts.
RNDS 42–49: Knit.
Note: These 8 rnds can be worked as a 4-stitch i-cord if preferred.
Break CC2, join CC1.
RND 50 (INC): (Kfb, M1L) 4 times—12 sts.
RNDS 51–55: Purl.
Break yarn. Thread yarn tail into tapestry needle and weave through rem sts. Pull tight to secure and fasten off.

17

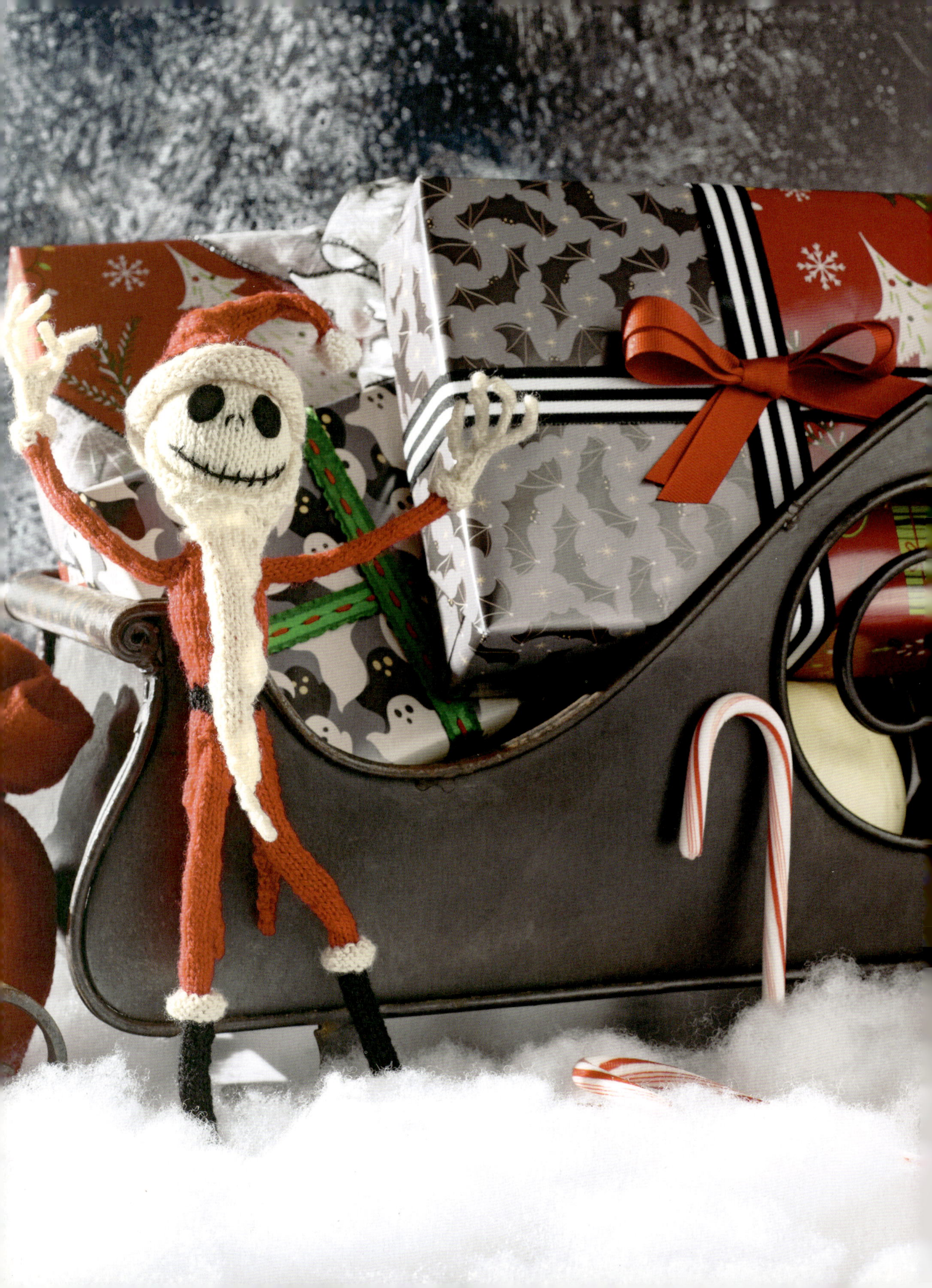

JACK SKELLINGTON EYE TEMPLATE

FINISHING

FOR JACK: [see **For Santa Jack, below]. Use CC3 to embroider pinstripes on Jack's suit in vertical straight lines. Create lines that are approx. 2 sts apart.

CC1 to embroider a "closure button" on the front of Jack's jacket.

Use MC to attach bow tie to the front of Jack's jacket, right at the base of the neck.

{**FOR SANTA JACK**, use CC1 to attach fake beard to each side of Jack's head so that the beard hangs slightly below his skull. Place the Santa Jack hat on his head.}

FACE

Use the Jack Skellington Eye Template to cut shapes out of black felt. Use black thread to stitch eyes to head using the photos as inspiration for placement.

Divide strands of MC yarn so you're only working with one ply of yarn. Thread a tapestry needle with one ply of MC and use it to embroider a mouth and nostrils onto Jack's face using the photos as inspiration for placement.

FRIGHTENING FACT

When Lock, Shock, and Barrel are using a plunger to try to push the kidnapped Santa Claus down the metal tube connecting their tree house to Oogie Boogie's lair, viewers can see Santa's mistletoe underpants.

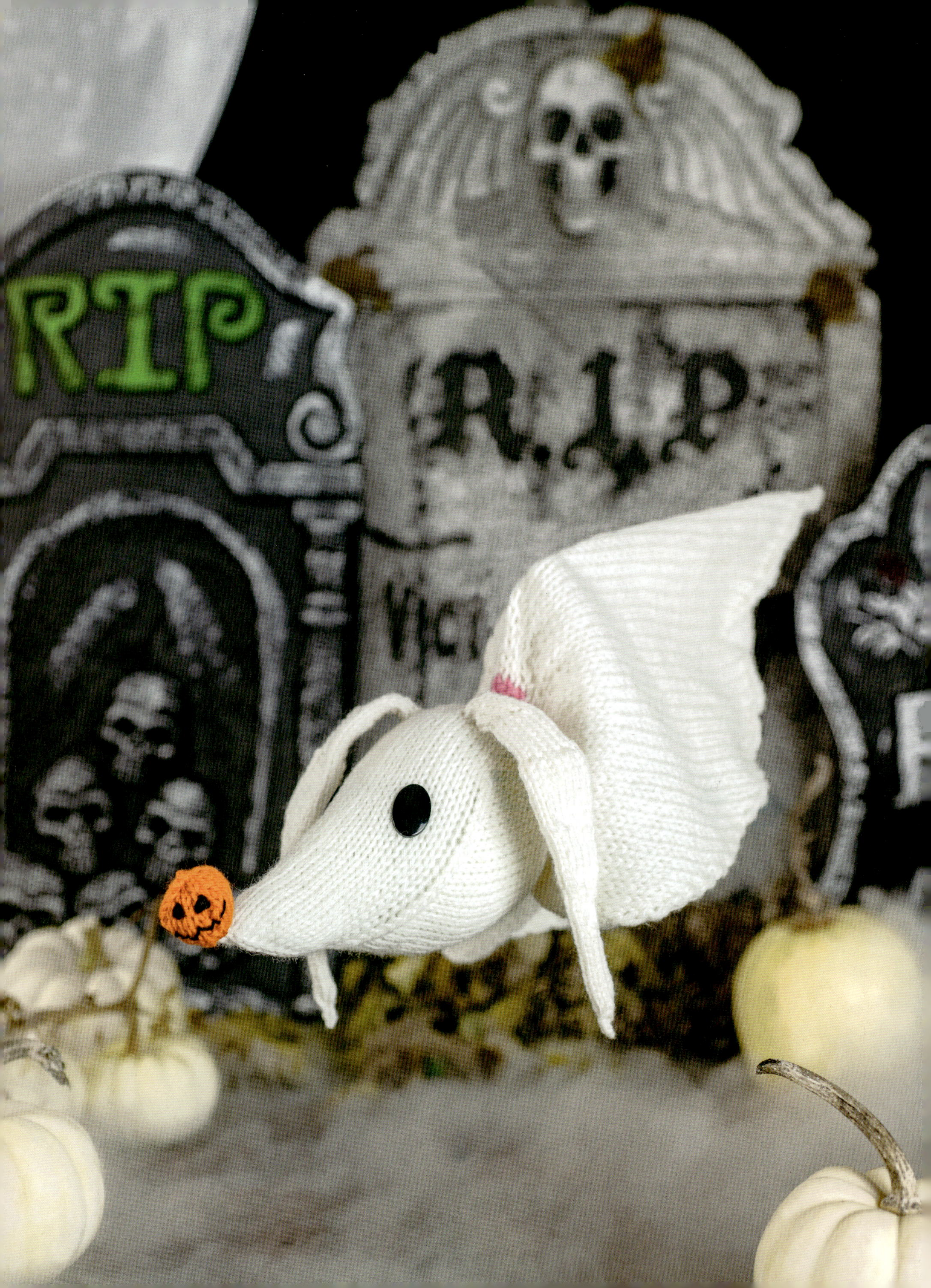
RIP
R.I.P

Zero Toy Figure

Designed by Susan Claudino

"My, what a brilliant nose you have. The better to light my way!"
–Jack Skellington

SKILL LEVEL

With his glowing orange pumpkin nose and fierce loyalty to his master, Zero is the ghost dog companion to Jack Skellington. In tune with Jack's melancholy mood, Zero keeps Jack company whther by playing in the cemetery during walks or by curling up in his basket in the tower for a nap. During that pivotal moment in the film when Sally is desperately trying to ground the sleigh to keep Jack in Halloween Town where he belongs, Zero's dazzling nose earns him his place at the head of the skeleton reindeer pack, guiding the way through the thick fog. To give Zero his wraithlike appearance, sometimes he was double-exposed on film, a technique where two layers of film shot separately are placed on top of one another creating a ghostlike effect, other times he was filmed in front of an additional backdrop using a beam splitter, a device that splits the light of an object into two making a hazy effect. A diffusion filter went between the splitter and the puppet, giving him a ghostly look.

Good boy! Designed to be knit in as few pieces as possible, using the Magic Loop method of knitting in the round, with minimal sewing for effortless finishing, this project is suitable for adventurous beginner knitters. This ghostly pup is worked in one continuous piece and stuffed as you go, with construction beginning at the back end of his body, and finishing with his pumpkin nose. Eye and ear placements are marked with purl stitches, and all shaping is done with simple increase and decrease stitches. The collar is knit in the round, then moves directly into the sheet worked flat. The ears are knit separately in the round and then sewn onto the head, completing this faithful companion.

SIZES
One size

FINISHED MEASUREMENTS
Length (nose to backside): 12 in. / 30.5 cm

Length (collar to end of sheet): 10 in. / 25.5 cm

YARN
Worsted weight yarn, shown in Cascade Yarns *Cascade 220* (100% Peruvian Highland wool; 220 yd. / 201 m per 3½ oz. / 100 g hank) #8505 White, 1 hank

NEEDLES
US 5 / 3.75 mm, 40 in. / 100 cm circular needle or size needed to obtain gauge

US 9 / 5.5 mm, 40 in. / 100 cm circular needle

NOTIONS
Stitch markers (3; 1 unique for BOR, optional)

Polyester stuffing (approx. 8 oz. / 227 g)

¼ oz. / 5 g worsted weight orange scrap yarn (for nose)

¼ oz. / 5 g worsted weight pink scrap yarn (for collar)

1 yd. / 1 m black embroidery floss *OR* fingering weight black scrap yarn

15 by 22 mm oval safety eyes *OR* black felt to cut to the same dimensions

Fabric glue (for felt eyes)

Row counter (optional)

Tapestry needle

GAUGE
24 sts and 30 rows = 4 in. / 10 cm over stockinette stitch worked in the round on smaller needle, without blocking

PATTERN NOTES

- The body, head, and nose are worked in the round, contiguously, for minimal finishing, using the Magic Loop method. Do not break yarn between sections unless specified.
- During the head construction, the fabric is marked with purl stitches to indicate eye and ear placement locations.
- The ears are worked in the round, separate from the body, and are sewn onto the head.
- The collar and sheet are knit as one piece; the collar is worked in the round, and the sheet is worked flat. Wet block the sheet aggressively to achieve maximum drape.
- The beginning of round will be on the underside of the toy, along the center of the body.
- Gauge is not critical for this project; however, a difference in gauge may affect the required yardage and finished size of the toy. The ideal fabric for the body is dense enough to keep the stuffing from showing through.
- The larger needle should be 4 needle sizes larger than the gauge-size needle.
- Written instructions are provided for the entirety of the project.

PATTERN INSTRUCTIONS

CAST ON & BODY

Using the smaller needles, CO 4 sts using the Long Tail Cast On method. Pm for BOR (if desired) and join to work in the rnd, being careful not to twist the sts.

RND 1 (INC): (Kfb) to end of rnd—8 sts.
RND 2 (INC): (K1, kfb) to end of rnd—12 sts.
RND 3: Knit.
RND 4 (INC): (K2, kfb) to end of rnd—16 sts.
RND 5: Knit.
RND 6 (INC): (K3, kfb) to end of rnd—20 sts.
RND 7: Knit.
RND 8 (INC): (K4, kfb) to end of rnd—24 sts.
RND 9: Knit.
RND 10 (INC): (K5, kfb) to end of rnd—28 sts.
RND 11: Knit.
RND 12 (INC): (K6, kfb) to end of rnd—32 sts.
RND 13: Knit.
RND 14 (INC): (K7, kfb) to end of rnd—36 sts.
RND 15: Knit.
RND 16 (INC): (K8, kfb) to end of rnd—40 sts.
RND 17: Knit.
RND 18 (INC): (K9, kfb) to end of rnd—44 sts.
RND 19: Knit.
RND 20 (INC): (K10, kfb) to end of rnd—48 sts.
RNDS 21–38: Knit.
RND 39 (DEC): (K4, k2tog) to end of rnd—40 sts.
RND 40: Knit.
RND 41 (DEC): (K3, k2tog) to end of rnd—32 sts.
RND 42: Knit.
Using polyester, begin stuffing the body. Continue to add stuffing as you finish the body.
RND 43 (DEC): (K2, k2tog) to end of rnd—24 sts.
RND 44: Knit.
RND 45 (DEC): (K1, k2tog) to end of rnd—16 sts.
RNDS 46–48: Knit.

HEAD

RND 49 (INC): (Kfb) to end of rnd—32 sts.
RND 50 (INC): (Kfb) to end of rnd—64 sts.
RNDS 51–54: Knit.
The purl sts in the following rnd will mark the ear placement.
RND 55: K26, p1, k10, p1, k26.
RNDS 56–63: Knit.
The decreases in the remainder of this section begin the head shaping and create the mouth.
For a clean line, work a modified ssk as follows: Slip the first stitch as if to purl, slip the second stitch as if to knit, return sts to the LHN purlwise, and knit together through the back loops.
RND 64 (DEC): K20, k2tog, pm, k20, pm, ssk, knit to end of rnd—62 sts.
RND 65 (DEC): Knit to 2 sts before M, k2tog, sm, k20, sm, ssk, knit to end of rnd—2 sts dec.
RNDS 66–68 (DEC): Rep [Rnd 65] 3 times—54 sts.
The purl sts in the following rnd will mark the eye placement.
RND 69 (DEC): Knit to 2 sts before M, k2tog, sm, k4, p1, k10, p1, k4, sm, ssk, knit to end of rnd—52 sts.
RNDS 70–84 (DEC): Rep [Rnd 65] 15 times—22 sts.
Using polyester, begin stuffing the head. Continue to add stuffing as you finish the head.
If using safety eyes, insert and attach them now, using the purl bumps in Rnd 69 for placement. If using felt eyes, wait until the head is finished before applying fabric glue and felt.
RND 85: Knit, rm as encountered (leave BOR in place).
RNDS 86–89: Knit.
RND 90 (DEC): K1, ssk, knit to last 3 sts, k2tog, k1—2 sts dec.
RNDS 91–98 (DEC): Rep [Rnd 90] 8 times—4 sts.
Break yarn; join orange scrap yarn.

NOSE

RND 99: Knit.
RND 100 (INC): (Kfb) to end of rnd—8 sts.
RND 101 (INC): (Kfb) to end of rnd—16 sts.
RND 102 (INC): K1, kfb, k4, kfb, k2, kfb, k4, kfb, k1—20 sts.
RND 103: (K3, p2) to end of rnd.
RND 104: Knit.
RND 105: (K3, p2) to end of rnd.
RND 106: Knit.
RND 107 (DEC): (K3, p2tog) to end of rnd—16 sts.
RND 108 (DEC): (K2, k2tog) to end of rnd—12 sts.
Using polyester, begin stuffing the nose. Continue to add stuffing as you finish the nose.
RND 109 (DEC): (K1, k2tog) to end of rnd—8 sts.
RND 110 (DEC): (K2tog) to end of rnd—4 sts.
Break yarn. Thread the tapestry needle with the yarn tail and weave tail through rem live sts and cinch closed. Use the yarn tails to anchor the jack-o'-lantern nose to the snout; weave remaining ends to the inside of the toy. Gently squish, smooth, and tug the snout into desired shape.

EARS (MAKE 2 THE SAME)

Using the smaller needles, CO 6 sts using the Long Tail Cast On method. Pm for BOR (if desired) and join to work in the rnd, being careful not to twist the sts.
RNDS 1–3: Knit.
RND 4 (INC): (K1, kfb, k1) 2 times—8 sts.
RNDS 5–9: Knit.
RND 10 (INC): (K1, kfb, kfb, k1) 2 times—12 sts.
RNDS 11–17: Knit.
RND 18 (INC): (K1, kfb, k2, kfb, k1) 2 times—16 sts.
RNDS 19–27: Knit.
RND 28 (DEC): (K1, ssk, k2, k2tog, k1) 2 times—12 sts.
RNDS 29–35: Knit.
RND 36 (DEC): (K1, ssk, k2tog, k1) 2 times—8 sts.
RNDS 37–41: Knit.
RND 42 (DEC): (K1, ssk, k1) 2 times—6 sts.
RNDS 43–53: Knit.
RND 54 (DEC): (S2kp) 2 times—2 sts.
RNDS 55–57: Knit.
Break yarn. Thread the tapestry needle with the yarn tail and weave tail through rem live sts and cinch closed. Secure BO tail to inside of the ear.
Using the CO tail of each ear, and the purl bumps in Rnd 55 of the head for placement, sew on the ears making sure to cover the purl bump completely.

COLLAR AND SHEET

COLLAR (WORKED IN THE ROUND)

Using the larger needles and pink scrap yarn, CO 24 sts using the Long Tail Cast On method. Pm for BOR (if desired) and join to work in the rnd, being careful not to twist the sts.
RNDS 1–3: (K2, p2) to end of rnd.
Break pink scrap yarn; join working yarn.

SHEET (WORKED FLAT)

ROW 1 (RS): Knit to end of rnd, rm (if placed), turn.

ROW 2 (WS): Purl.
ROW 3 (INC): (K1, kfb) to end of row—36 sts.
ROW 4: Purl.
ROW 5 (INC): (K1, kfb) to end of row—54 sts.
ROW 6: Purl.
ROW 7 (INC): (K2, kfb) to end of row—72 sts.
ROW 8: Purl.
ROW 9: Sl1 wyib, knit to end of row.
ROW 10: Sl1 wyif, purl to end of row.
ROWS 11–18: Rep [Rows 9 and 10] 4 times.
ROW 19 (DEC): Sl1 wyib, ssk, knit to last 3 sts, k2tog, k1—2 sts dec.
ROW 20: Sl1 wyif, purl to end of row.
ROWS 21–50 (DEC): Rep [Rows 19 and 20] 15 times—40 sts.
ROW 51 (DEC): BO 3 sts knitwise, knit to end of row—37 sts.
ROW 52 (DEC): BO 3 sts purlwise, purl to end of row—34 sts.
ROWS 53–62 (DEC): Rep [Rows 51 and 52] 5 times—4 sts.
ROW 63 (DEC): BO 1 st knitwise, k2—3 sts.
ROW 64: Sl1 wyif, p2.
ROW 65: Sl1 wyib, k2.
ROW 66: Sl1 wyif, p2.
ROW 67 (DEC): S2kp—1 st.
Break yarn. Pull tail through the rem st to fasten off.

FINISHING

Wet block the collar and sheet, being careful not to stretch the collar. Pin out the sheet, stretching as much as possible; the more you stretch out the sheet, the drapier the fabric will become, providing a more ghostly effect.

Once dry, slip the collar over the body and up to the neck (do not go over the head).

Weave in rem ends, using the CO tails to add a few stitches around the collar to secure it to the body and keep it from sliding around.

Add a mouth and eyes to the jack-o'-lantern nose with black embroidery floss or scrap yarn.

If using the felt eyes, glue the eyes to the face using the purl sts in Rnd 69 of the head to help with placement.

FRIGHTENING FACT

The film was nominated for the Academy Award for Best Visual Effects in 1994 and won Best Music and Best Fantasy Film at the Academy of Science Fiction, Fantasy & Horror Films.

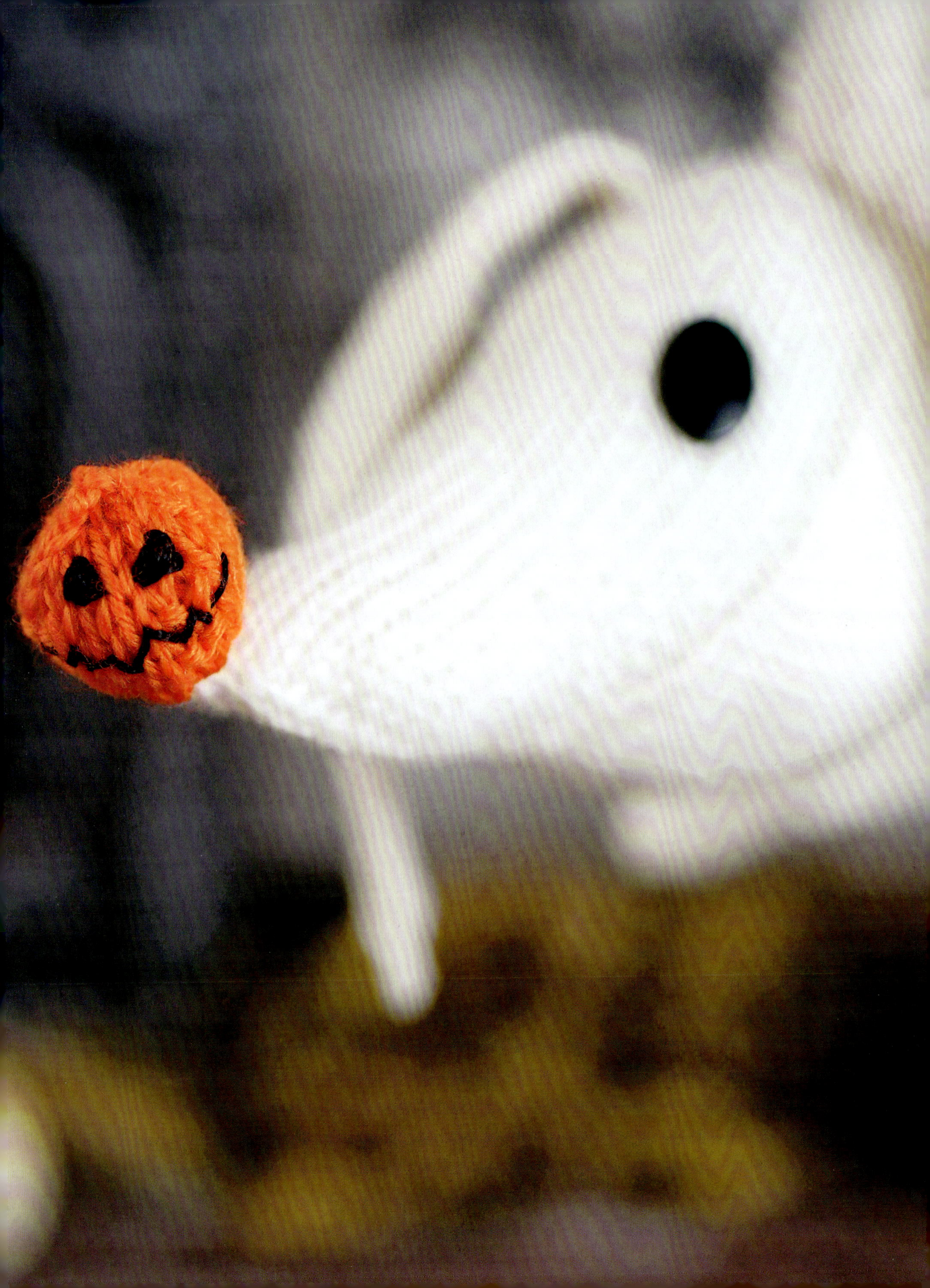

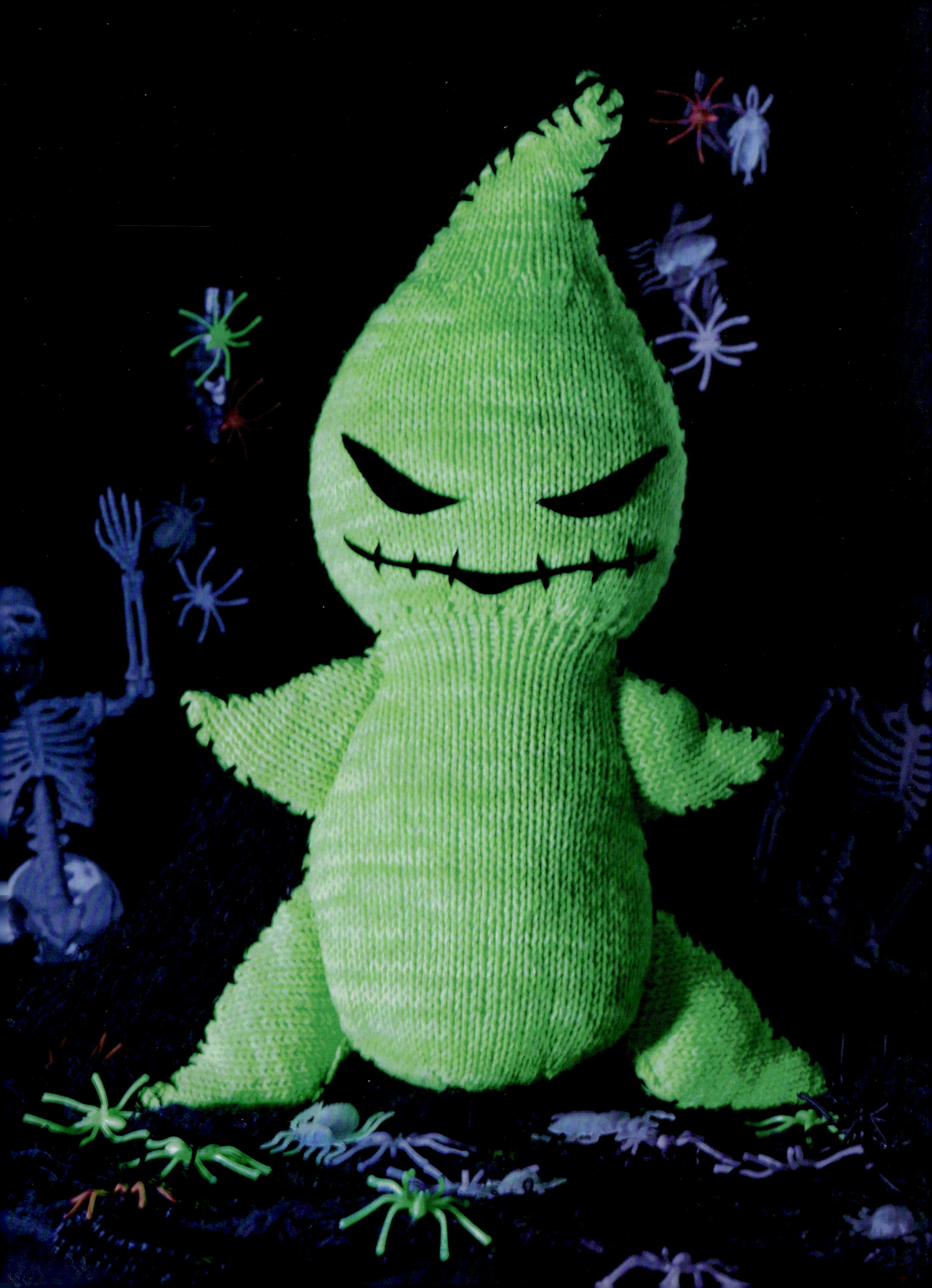

Oogie Boogie Toy Figure

Designed by Susan Claudino

SKILL LEVEL
💀💀💀

"Leave that no-account Oogie Boogie out of this!"
—Jack Skellington

One of the most sinister characters in a town filled with all kinds of nightmares, Oogie Boogie is a particularly ominous villain. This large burlap sack stuffed full of crawling insects, with a snakelike tongue, deep voice, vaudeville-style dance moves, an eerie green glow, and dark angry eyes, was the most difficult puppet to work with, according to the puppet makers. To create the puppets for the film, they were first sculpted in oil-based clay, then molds were poured and made for each character. Handcrafted, unique steel armatures made with ball-and-socket joints and hinges (for posing) were laid into each mold and then injected with foam latex, completely encasing the armature. After being baked and dried, the puppet was brought to fabrication, where paint, hair, fur, and texture were added. Over sixty individual characters were created, all with three to four copies of each spread across multiple sets and scenes, all being shot simultaneously. Oogie Boogie's puppet was the largest, coming in at two feet high, with the others being half that size, on average. Animator Mike Belzer says, "I had to dig in with my feet and physically push the Oogie Boogie puppet. He's so huge and there's so much foam, therefore the armature needs to be very tight; it's literally wrestling with the puppet."

You might split a seam if you don't die laughing first while making this adorably evil Oogie Boogie stuffed toy! Each of his four limbs is knit separately and bound off before the body is worked. The body and head are knit in one continuous piece, stuffing as you go, and once the head is bound off, the limbs are stuffed and attached. Faux stitches running along the sides are added post-knitting along with a bit of felt for eyes and stitched-on grin. Be alone with him in the dark if you dare, and watch him glow under UV light!

SIZES
One size

FINISHED MEASUREMENTS
Height: 15 in. / 38 cm

Width (widest points of arms): 9 in. / 23 cm

YARN
UV Light Reactive: DK weight yarn, shown in The Lemonade Shop *DK Classic* (100% fine superwash merino; 231 yd. / 211 m per 3½ oz. / 100 g per hank) in color The Boogie Man, 1 hank

or

DK weight yarn, shown in A Whimsical Wood Yarn Co. *Dreamy DK Classic* (100% superwash merino; 250 yd. / 229 m per 4 oz. / 115 g hank) in color Eerie Glow, 1 hank

NEEDLES
US 4 / 3.5 mm, 40 in. / 100 cm circular needle or size needed to obtain gauge

NOTIONS
Stitch marker (optional)

Round counter (optional)

Tapestry needle

¼ oz. / 5 g worsted or DK weight black scrap yarn

Black felt

Fabric glue

Polyester stuffing

GAUGE
20 sts and 31 rows = 4 in. / 10 cm over stockinette worked in the round on larger needle, taken without blocking

PATTERN NOTES

- The toy is knit in pieces, each in the round, and joined using mattress stitch or the invisible horizontal seaming method (at the knitter's preference).
- The hands/arms are worked in the round from the outer point toward the widest part, which becomes the seaming edge. The feet/legs are worked similarly, starting with the narrowest point, and worked in the round toward the widest edge, where they are seamed to the body.
- The body and head are made after the limbs are complete and are worked in the round from the bottom up, contiguously, using the Magic Loop method. Stuffing is added to the toy as the body and head are shaped. Do not break yarn between sections unless specified.
- Gauge is not critical for this project; however, a difference in gauge may affect the required yardage and finished size of the toy. The ideal fabric for the body is dense enough to keep the stuffing from showing through.
- The beginning of round will be along one side/edge of the toy.
- Written instructions are provided for the entirety of the project.
- Use dpns to help with the limb placement when sewing onto the body. The dpns can be used like t-pins to hold the limbs in the desired position as they are joined.

PATTERN INSTRUCTIONS

HANDS/ARMS (MAKE 2 THE SAME)

CO 4 sts using the Long Tail Cast On method. Pm for BOR (if desired) and join to work in the rnd, being careful not to twist the sts.

RND 1: Knit.
RND 2 (INC): K1, kfb, kfb, k1—6 sts.
RND 3: Knit.
RND 4 (INC): K2, kfb, kfb, k2—8 sts.
RND 5: Knit.
RND 6 (INC): K3, kfb, kfb, k3—10 sts.
RND 7: Knit.
RND 8 (INC): K4, kfb, kfb, k4—12 sts.
RND 9: Knit.
RND 10 (INC): K5, kfb, kfb, k5—14 sts.
RND 11: Knit.
RND 12 (INC): K6, kfb, kfb, k6—16 sts.
RND 13: Knit.
RND 14 (INC): K7, kfb, kfb, k7—18 sts.
RND 15 (INC): K8, kfb, kfb, k8—20 sts.
RND 16 (INC): K9, kfb, kfb, k9—22 sts.
RND 17 (INC): K10, kfb, kfb, k10—24 sts.
RND 18: Knit.

Using polyester, begin stuffing the limb. Continue to add stuffing as you finish each piece.

RND 19 (INC): K11, kfb, kfb, k11—26 sts.
RND 20: Knit.
RND 21 (INC): K12, kfb, kfb, k12—28 sts.
RND 22: Knit.
RND 23 (INC): K13, kfb, kfb, k13—30 sts.
RND 24: Knit.

BO all sts knitwise. The top (bound off edge) of the limbs will remain open. Once seamed to the body, the stuffing will remain inside the limb.

FEET/LEGS (MAKE 2 THE SAME)

CO 4 sts using the Long Tail Cast On method. Pm for BOR (if desired) and join to work in the rnd, being careful not to twist the sts.

Work Rnds 1–24 of Hands/Arms. Do not break yarn; continue with Rnds 25–32 below.

RND 25 (INC): K14, kfb, kfb, k14—32 sts.
RND 26: Knit.
RND 27: K1, ssk, k12, kfb, kfb, k12, k2tog, k1.
RNDS 28 AND 29: Rep [Rnd 27] 2 times.
RND 30 (DEC): K1, ssk, k26, k2tog, k1—30 sts.
RND 31 (DEC): K1, ssk, k24, k2tog, k1—28 sts.
RND 32 (DEC): K1, ssk, k22, k2tog, k1—26 sts.

BO all sts knitwise.

BODY

CO 6 sts using the Long Tail Cast On method. Pm for BOR (if desired) and join to work in the rnd, being careful not to twist the sts.

RND 1 (INC): (Kfb) to end of rnd—12 sts.
RND 2 (INC): (K1, kfb) to end of rnd—18 sts.
RND 3 (INC): (K2, kfb) to end of rnd—24 sts.
RND 4 (INC): (K3, kfb) to end of rnd—30 sts.
RND 5 (INC): (K4, kfb) to end of rnd—36 sts.
RND 6 (INC): (K5, kfb) to end of rnd—42 sts.
RND 7 (INC): (K6, kfb) to end of rnd—48 sts.
RND 8 (INC): (K7, kfb) to end of rnd—54 sts.
RND 9 (INC): (K8, kfb) to end of rnd—60 sts.
RND 10: Knit.
RND 11 (INC): (Kfb, k29) 2 times—62 sts.
RND 12 (INC): (K30, kfb) 2 times—64 sts.
RND 13: Knit.
RND 14 (INC): (Kfb, k31) 2 times—66 sts.
RND 15 (INC): (K32, kfb) 2 times—68 sts.
RND 16: Knit.
RND 17 (INC): (Kfb, k33) 2 times—70 sts.

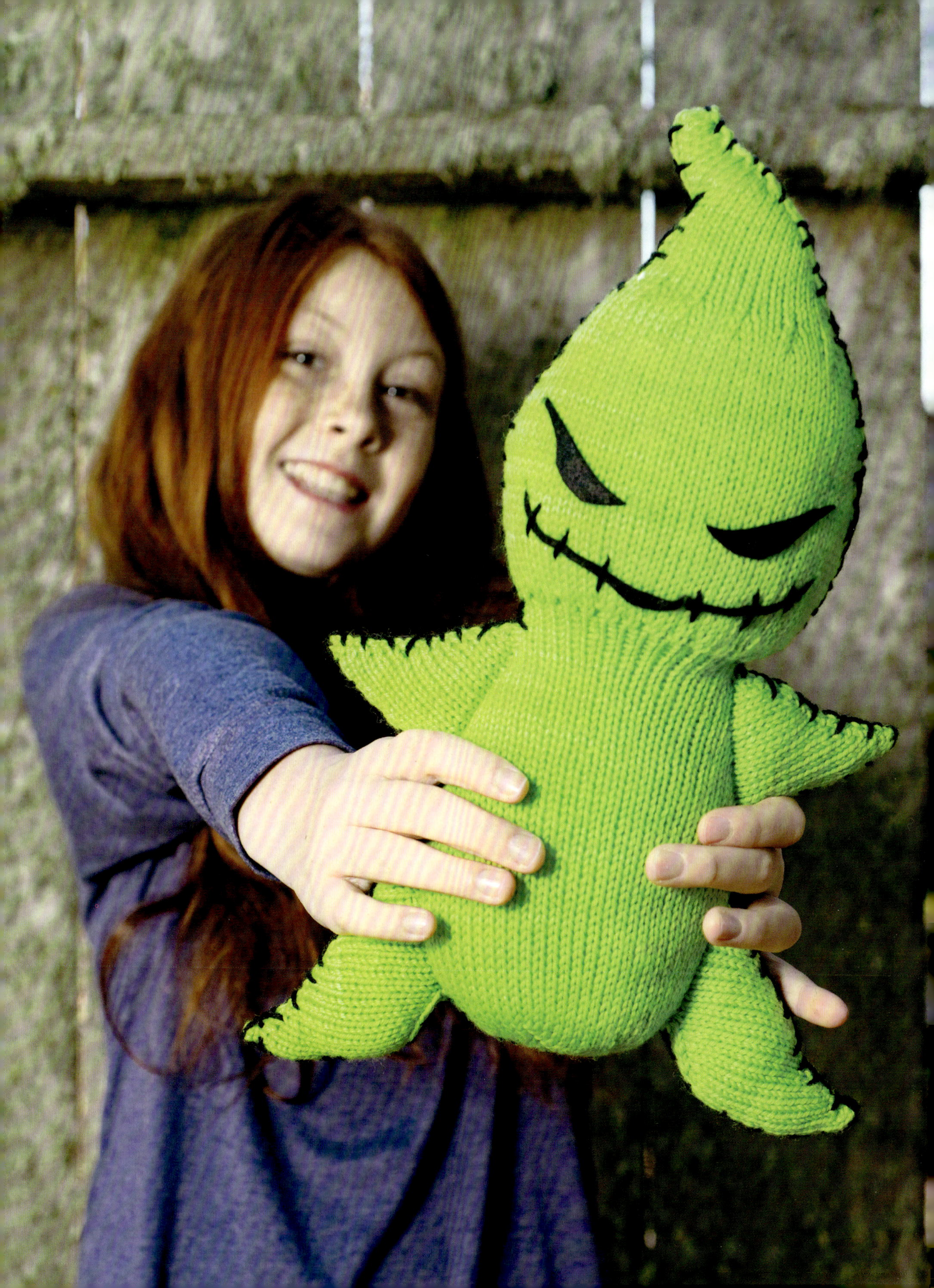

RND 18 (INC): (K34, kfb) 2 times—72 sts.
RNDS 19–28: Knit.
RND 29 (DEC): (Ssk, k34) 2 times—70 sts.
RND 30 (DEC): (K33, k2tog) 2 times—68 sts.
RND 31: Knit.
RND 32 (DEC): (Ssk, k32) 2 times—66 sts.
RND 33 (DEC): (K31, k2tog) 2 times—64 sts.
RND 34: Knit.
RND 35 (DEC): (Ssk, k30) 2 times—62 sts.
RND 36 (DEC): (K29, k2tog) 2 times—60 sts.
RND 37: Knit.
RND 38 (DEC): (Ssk, k28) 2 times—58 sts.
RND 39 (DEC): (K27, k2tog) 2 times—56 sts.
RND 40: Knit.
RND 41 (DEC): (Ssk, k26) 2 times—54 sts.
RND 42 (DEC): (K25, k2tog) 2 times—52 sts.
RND 43: Knit.
RND 44 (DEC): (Ssk, k24) 2 times—50 sts.
RND 45 (DEC): (K23, k2tog) 2 times—48 sts.
RND 46: Knit.
RND 47 (DEC): (Ssk, k22) 2 times—46 sts.
RND 48 (DEC): (K21, k2tog) 2 times—44 sts.
RND 49: Knit.
RND 50 (DEC): (Ssk, k20) 2 times—42 sts.
RND 51 (DEC): (K19, k2tog) 2 times—40 sts.
RND 52: Knit.
RND 53 (DEC): (Ssk, k18) 2 times—38 sts.
RND 54 (DEC): (K17, k2tog) 2 times—36 sts.
RND 55: Knit.
RND 56 (DEC): (Ssk, k16) 2 times—34 sts.
RND 57 (DEC): (K15, k2tog) 2 times—32 sts.
RND 58: Knit.

Using polyester, begin stuffing the body. Continue to add stuffing as you work the head.

HEAD

RND 59 (INC): (Kfb) to end of rnd—64 sts.
RND 60 (INC): (K3, kfb) to end of rnd—80 sts.
RNDS 61–78: Knit.
RND 79 (DEC): (Ssk, k38) 2 times—78 sts.
RND 80 (DEC): (K37, k2tog) 2 times—76 sts.
RND 81: Knit.
RND 82 (DEC): (Ssk, k36) 2 times—74 sts.
RND 83 (DEC): (K35, k2tog) 2 times—72 sts.
RND 84: Knit.
RND 85 (DEC): (Ssk, k34) 2 times—70 sts.

RND 86 (DEC): (K33, k2tog) 2 times—68 sts.
RND 87: Knit.
RND 88 (DEC): (Ssk, k32) 2 times—66 sts.
RND 89 (DEC): (K31, k2tog) 2 times—64 sts.
RND 90: Knit.
RND 91 (DEC): (Ssk, k30) 2 times—62 sts.
RND 92 (DEC): (K29, k2tog) 2 times—60 sts.
RND 93: Knit.
RND 94 (DEC): (K3, k2tog) to end of rnd—48 sts.
RND 95: Knit.
Continue to add stuffing as you finish the head. Be sure all stuffing of the head is complete before working Rnd 120, where the head will be closed.
RND 96 (DEC): (K2, k2tog) to end of rnd—36 sts.
RNDS 97–101: Knit.
RND 102 (DEC): (Ssk, k14, k2tog) 2 times—32 sts.
RND 103: Knit.
RND 104 (DEC): (Ssk, k12, k2tog) 2 times—28 sts.
RND 105: Knit.
RND 106 (DEC): (Ssk, k10, k2tog) 2 times—24 sts.
RND 107: Knit.
RND 108: Ssk, k9, kfb, kfb, k9, k2tog.
RNDS 109–112: Rep [Rnd 108] 4 times.
RND 113 (DEC): S2kp, k8, kfb, kfb, k8, k3tog—22 sts.
RND 114 (DEC): S2kp, k7, kfb, kfb, k7, k3tog—20 sts.
RND 115 (DEC): S2kp, k6, kfb, kfb, k6, k3tog—18 sts.
RND 116 (DEC): S2kp, k5, kfb, kfb, k5, k3tog—16 sts.
RND 117 (DEC): S2kp, k10, k3tog—12 sts.
RND 118 (DEC): S2kp, k6, k3tog—8 sts.
RND 119 (DEC): S2kp, k2, k3tog—4 sts.
RND 120 (DEC): Ssk, k2tog—2 sts.
Break yarn. Thread the tapestry needle with the yarn tail and weave tail through rem live sts and cinch closed. Weave in ends.

FINISHING

Thread the tapestry needle with working yarn. Attach the limbs to the body of the doll using mattress stitch or the invisible horizontal seam, referencing the photos as inspiration for placement. Attach the limbs at the sides of the body. Weave in all seaming ends to the inside of the toy.

Using black scrap yarn, thread the tapestry needle and create a faux seam all around the sides of the body with a decorative running stitch. After the outline "seam" is complete, go around again and add small perpendicular stitches to create a ragged seam. Weave in ends.

Use the Oogie Boogie Face Template to cut out shapes of black felt. Use the fabric glue to secure the felt in place, referencing the photos as inspiration for placement. Using black scrap yarn, thread the tapestry needle and add a few perpendicular stitches to the sides of the mouth. Weave in ends.

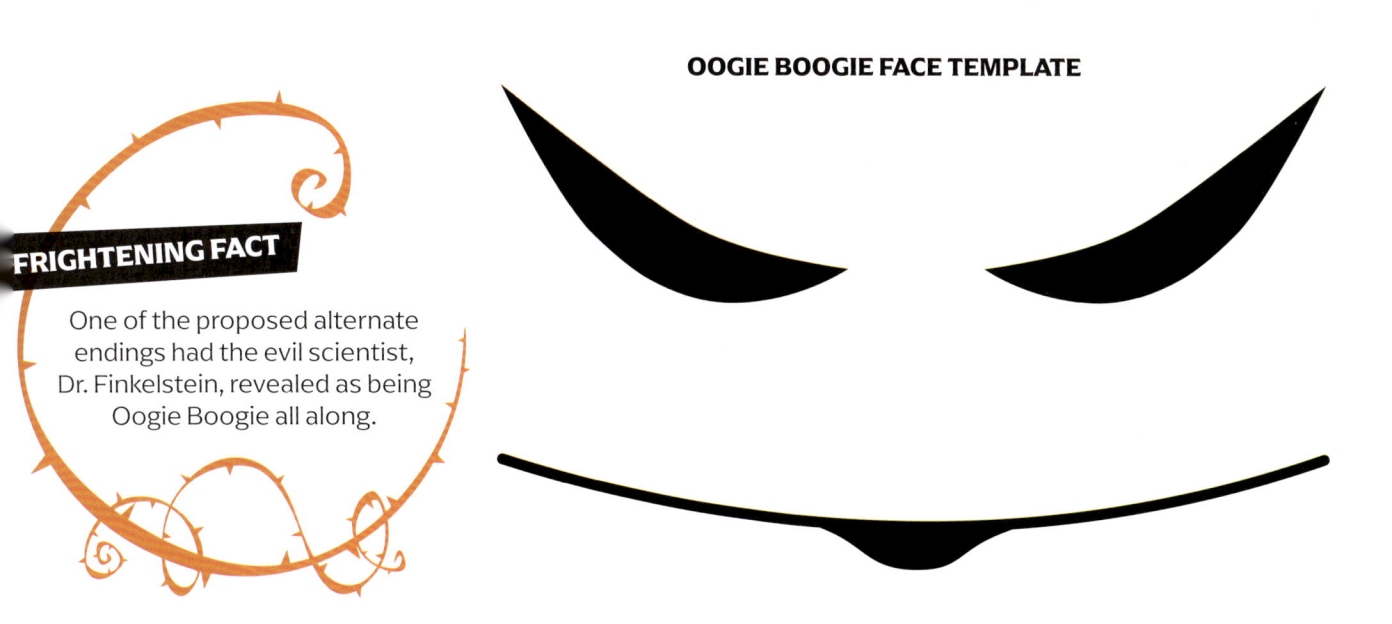

OOGIE BOOGIE FACE TEMPLATE

FRIGHTENING FACT

One of the proposed alternate endings had the evil scientist, Dr. Finkelstein, revealed as being Oogie Boogie all along.

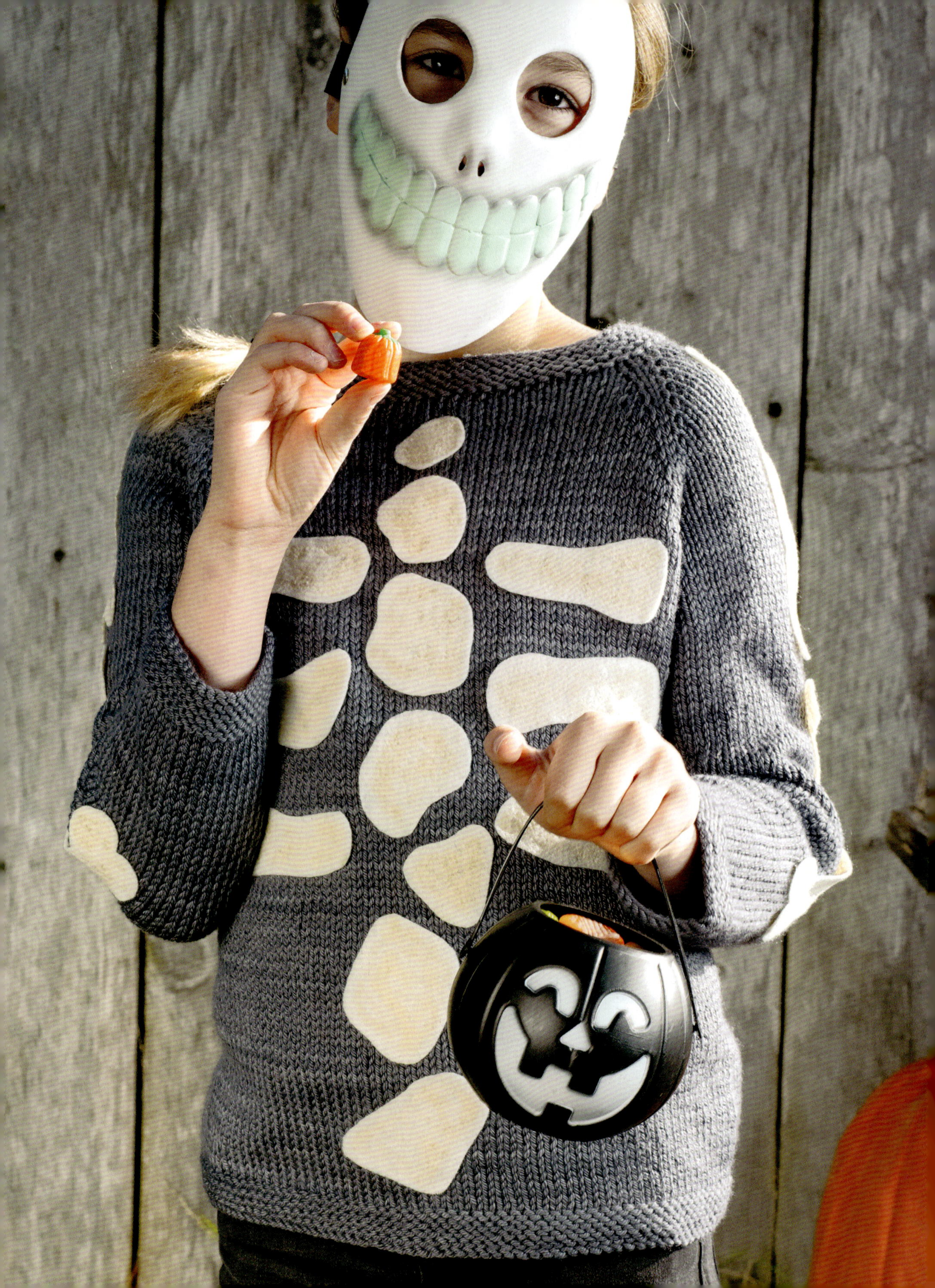

Creepy Costume Replicas

MAYOR

The Mayor's Badge

Designed by Tanis Gray

"Splendid idea, this 'Christmas' sounds fun! I fully endorse it, let's try it at once."
—The Mayor

SKILL LEVEL

With his two-faced demeanor demonstrated by his scary spinning head, the Mayor had even more movement than many of the other characters for the animators to address. Stop-motion animation is older than traditional two-dimensional or celluloid (cel) animation. Movie viewers' experience of movement is directly connected to the speed of the moving film. When cinema first began, film cameras had to be hand-cranked. One crank was the equivalent to one frame of film; therefore, to keep the film moving and to be able to capture an actor's movement seamlessly, the camera operator would simply keep cranking. Human brains can identify individual images at a rate of 10 to 12 frames per second, and the more images that are added, the more our brain will "fill in the gaps" and those images appear to move. Early film was shot at a rate of 16 to 20 frames per second, which is why the first films ever created tend to seem choppy. It was later discovered that a higher frame rate led to more fluid movements. Live-action films today are shot at a rate between 23.976 and 60 frames per second, while stop-motion animation is shot at 24 frames per second.

Become your own elected official with this delightful badge! It's begun with the center medallion worked in the round from the center out on dpns. Each ribbon spoke is worked flat individually off the live circle edge. Hanging ribbons are added to the bottom. A duplicate center medallion is created and adorned with hand-stitched letters and attached. Declare yourself the Mayor of Halloween Town, or personalize the center for added flair! Adhesive craft felt is added to the back of the costume replica badge for stability, and a sticky pin back allows for easy attachment when it's time for town proclamations.

SIZES
One size

FINISHED MEASUREMENTS
Badge Diameter: 4 in. / 10 cm

Total Height (from top spoke to end of longest ribbon): 10 in. / 25.5 cm

Total Width (including spokes): 7 in. / 18 cm

YARN
Sport weight yarn, shown in Cascade Yarns *220 Superwash Sport* (100% superwash merino wool; approx. 136½ yd. / 125 m per 1¾ oz. / 50 g hank)

COLORWAYS:
- Main Color (MC): #326 Harvest Pumpkin, 1 hank
- Contrast Color (CC): #817 Ecru, 1 hank

NEEDLES
US 3 / 3.25 mm set of 4 double-pointed needles

NOTIONS
Stitch marker (optional)

Smooth waste yarn

Tapestry needle

Adhesive back felt fabric (1 sheet)

Adhesive safety pin back (1 pin)

DMC embroidery floss in #310 Black (1 skein)

Sewing needle

GAUGE
A specific gauge is not necessary for this pattern.

To achieve the finished sizes as listed, aim for a finished row gauge of 28 rows = 4 in. / 10 cm in stockinette stitch worked in the round, taken after blocking.

PATTERN NOTES

- The main badge and spokes are worked from the center out, contiguously, to reduce seaming. The center of the main badge is worked in the round; each spoke is worked separately, flat.
- Adhesive back felt fabric is recommended to back the badge to create stability and structure.

PATTERN INSTRUCTIONS

MAIN BADGE (MAKE 1)

Using MC, CO 9 sts using the Circular Cast On method. Distribute the sts evenly over the dpns (3 sts per needle). Pm for BOR (if desired) and join to work in the rnd.
RND 1: Knit.
RND 2 (INC): [Kfb] to end of rnd—18 sts.
RNDS 3 AND 4: Knit.
RND 5 (INC): [Kfb] to end of rnd—36 sts.
RNDS 6–9: Knit.
RND 10 (INC): [Kfb] to end of rnd—72 sts.
RNDS 11–18: Knit.
Without binding off any stitches, create the following 8 spokes around the main badge.

SPOKE 1

From the BOR, knit 9 sts. Place the rem 63 sts on waste yarn. Turn.
**Work garter stitch (knit every row) for 9 more rows (10 total rows worked; 5 garter ridges from start of spoke).
ROW 11 (RS, INC): Kfb, k7, kfb—11 sts.
Work garter stitch for 9 more rows (20 total rows worked; 10 garter ridges from start of spoke).
With RS facing, BO all sts knitwise.******

SPOKE 2

Place the next 9 live stitches of the main badge onto one dpn. Rejoin MC with the RS facing and knit all 9 sts. Turn.
Work from ** to ** of Spoke 1.

SPOKES 3–8

Work as for Spoke 2 six more times; 8 total spokes have been made and all live stitches have been used.
Using the tapestry needle, weave in all ends.

LONG RIBBON (MAKE 1)

Using MC, CO 9 sts using the Long Tail Cast On method. Do not join to work in the rnd.
Work in garter stitch until the ribbon measures 3½ in. / 9 cm from the CO edge.
NEXT ROW (DEC): K2tog, k7—8 sts.
NEXT ROW (DEC): K6, k2tog—7 sts.
NEXT ROW (DEC): K2tog, k5—6 sts.
NEXT ROW (DEC): K4, k2tog—5 sts.
NEXT ROW (DEC): K2tog, k3—4 sts.
NEXT ROW (DEC): K2, k2tog—3 sts.
NEXT ROW (DEC): K2tog, k1—2 sts.
NEXT ROW (DEC): K2tog—1 st.
Break yarn and pull tail through rem st; cinch tight to secure.

SHORT RIBBON (MAKE 1)

Using MC, CO 9 sts using the Long Tail Cast On method. Do not join to work in the rnd.
Work in garter stitch until the ribbon measures 3 in. / 7.5 cm from the CO edge.
Continue as for the Long Ribbon, working all decreases until 1 st rem. Break yarn and pull tail through rem st; cinch tight to secure.
Using the tapestry needle, weave in all ends.
Attach the cast on edges of both ribbons to the bottom edge of the main badge using the whipstitch method. Inner edges of the ribbons should be touching (use the pattern image as a reference), ensuring that the ribbons are sewn on behind the existing spokes.

CENTER OF BADGE (MAKE 1)

Using CC, CO 9 sts using the Circular Cast On method. Distribute the sts evenly over the dpns (3 sts per needle). Pm for BOR (if desired) and join to work in the rnd.
RND 1: Knit.
RND 2 (INC): [Kfb] to end of rnd—18 sts.
RNDS 3 AND 4: Knit.

RND 5 (INC): [Kfb] to end of rnd—36 sts.
RNDS 6–9: Knit.
RND 10 (INC): [Kfb] to end of rnd—72 sts.
RNDS 11–14: Knit.
BO all sts knitwise.
Using the tapestry needle, weave in all ends.

FINISHING

Wet block all pieces well.
Thread sewing needle with black embroidery floss and embroider "MAYOR" onto center of badge (using the pattern image as a reference for layout and scale).
Attach center of badge to main badge by whipstitching the center of badge into place using CC.
Using the tapestry needle, weave in any remaining loose ends.
Lay finished knitting on adhesive back felt fabric and trace around outer edge. Cut out and stick to WS. Attach pin back.

FRIGHTENING FACT

Voice actor Glenn Shadix, who brought the Mayor to life, also worked with Tim Burton in *Beetlejuice,* as Otho.

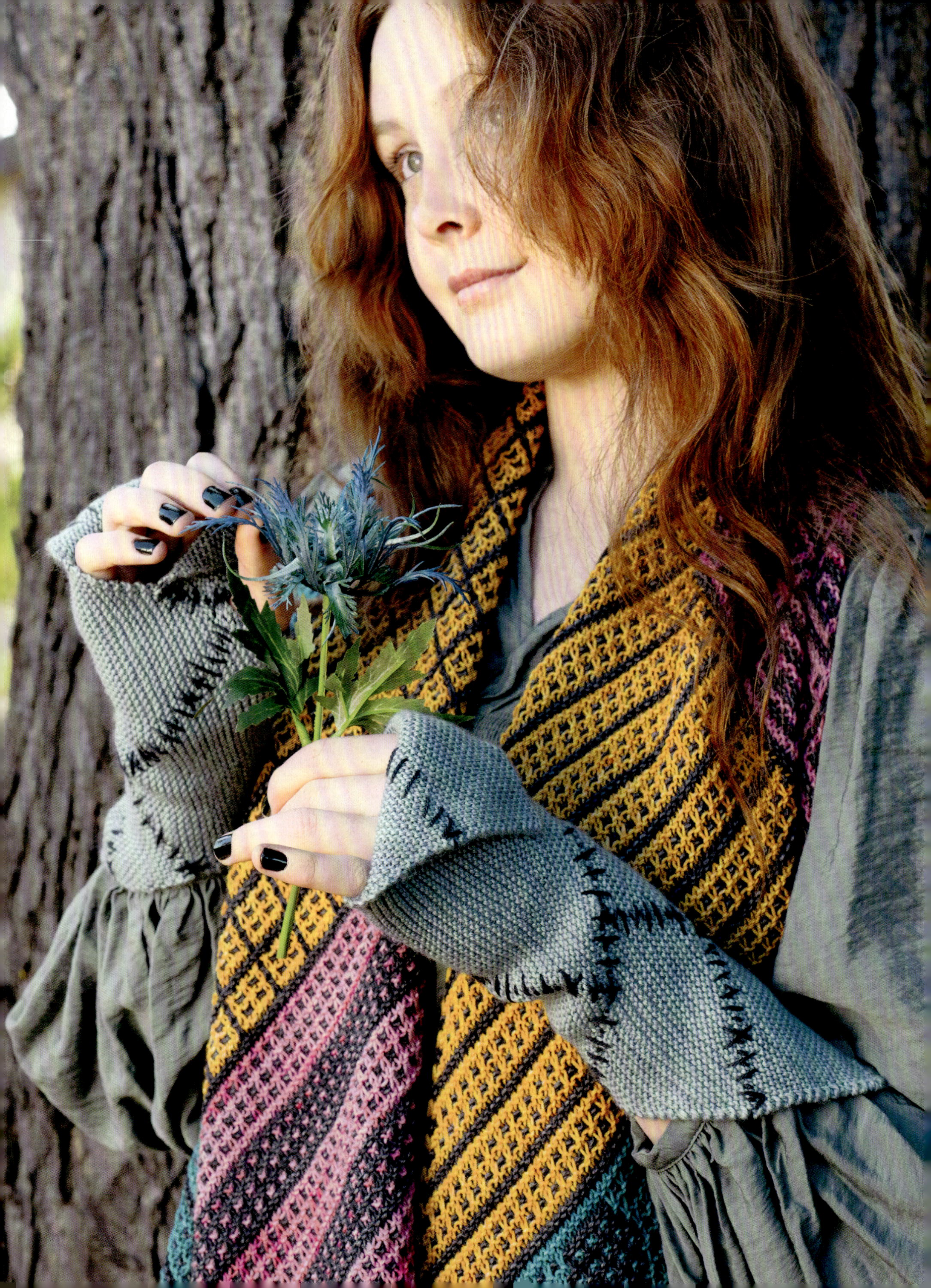

Sally's Fingerless Mitts

Designed by
Jenny Noto

"I, myself, am made entirely of flaws, stitched together with good intentions."
—Sally

SKILL LEVEL
💀💀💀

Out of necessity, Sally is an excellent seamstress. Because her limbs are detachable and have a life of their own (a talent she uses to her advantage multiple times throughout the film, often to escape difficult situations), she keeps a needle tucked behind her ear and thread in her dress to reattach parts and make other repairs. Of course, this would be scary in the real world, but in Halloween Town, Sally fits right in.

There's no need to be as good a seamstress as Sally when making these beginner-friendly fingerless mitts! Knit flat on the bias in garter stitch, the rectangle is then folded into a tube and seamed together with imperfect rag doll-like stitches. An opening is left for the thumb, and the top and bottom edges can be folded back or worn long. Embrace your inner rag doll and make a pair for yourself, or for your favorite friend from Halloween Town.

SIZES
1 (2, 3, 4) [5, 6, 7]

FINISHED MEASUREMENTS
Circumference: 5½ (6, 6½, 7) [7½, 8, 8½] in. / 14 (15, 16.5, 18) [19, 20.5, 21.5] cm

Designed to fit with ¼ to ½ in. / 0.5 to 1.5 cm negative ease.

YARN
Fingering weight yarn, shown in Magpie Fibers *Swanky Sock* (80% superwash merino, 10% cashmere, 10% nylon; 400 yd. / 366 m per 4 oz. / 115 g) in color Magpie, 1 hank

NEEDLES
US 0 / 2 mm, 16 in. / 40 cm long circular needle (or straight needles) or size needed to obtain gauge

NOTIONS
5 yd. / 4½ m black fingering weight scrap yarn

Locking stitch markers

Row counter (optional)

Tapestry needle

GAUGE
32 sts and 72 rows = 4 in. / 10 cm over garter stitch worked flat, taken after blocking

PATTERN NOTES

- These fingerless mitts are worked on the bias, flat, beginning with one stitch and ending with one stitch.
- Instructions are provided for size 1 first, with additional sizes in parentheses and brackets. When only one set of numbers is provided, it applies to all sizes.
- A locking stitch marker can be used to help identify RS from WS since both sides of garter stitch fabric look the same.
- All increases and decreases are done on the RS of the work. Except for the cast on slipknot and the final k2tog, stitch counts are always an even number.
- To seam, use the mattress stitch method to join the edges together. Once seamed, embellish the seams with decorative stitches using the black yarn.
- Written instructions are provided for the entirety of the project. Seaming schematics are provided to ensure the mitts are seamed correctly. Note that if seamed differently than instructed, the finished circumference may vary.

PATTERN INSTRUCTIONS

CAST ON & SETUP

Make a slipknot and place on the LHN.
SETUP ROW 1 (RS, INC): Kfb—2 sts.
SETUP ROW 2 (WS): Knit.
SETUP ROW 3 (INC): Kfb twice—4 sts.
SETUP ROW 4: Knit.

INCREASE SHAPING

ROW 1 (RS, INC): Kfb, knit to last st, kfb—2 sts inc.
ROW 2 (WS): Knit.
Rep [Rows 1 and 2] 19 (21, 23, 25) [27, 29, 31] more times—40 (44, 48, 52) [56, 60, 64] sts inc; 44 (48, 52, 56) [60, 64, 68] sts total.

BIAS SECTION

ROW 1 (RS): Kfb, knit to last 2 sts, k2tog.
ROW 2 (WS): Knit.
Rep Rows 1 and 2 until Long Edge A (see schematic) measures 11 (12, 13, 14) [15, 16, 17] in. / 28 (30.5, 33, 35.5) [38, 40.5, 43] cm, ending with a WS row.

DECREASE SHAPING

ROW 1 (RS, DEC): K2tog, knit to last 2 sts, k2tog—2 sts dec.
ROW 2 (WS): Knit.
Rep Rows 1 and 2 until 2 sts rem, ending with a WS row.
FINAL ROW (RS, DEC): K2tog—1 st rem.
Break yarn, leaving a tail for weaving in, and pull tail through rem st; pull tight to secure.
Repeat all instructions to make the second mitt.

FINISHING

Weave in all ends carefully along the edges so the fabric is reversible. Wet block each mitt flat using the schematic for dimensions.

SEAM MITTS

Use locking stitch markers to help secure the edges together in a spiral before seaming.

TO CREATE THE SPIRAL—RIGHT MITT (SEE RIGHT MITT SEAMING SCHEMATIC):

Step 1: Fold Edge A down at a 45-degree angle along Centerline (the Centerline is the halfway point of Long Edge A).
Step 2: Fold Edge B up at a 45-degree angle along Centerline. Resulting shape is Shape 1 Right.
Step 3: Flip Shape 1 Right over vertically so the meeting of Edges A and B is on the underside. The resulting shape is Shape 2 Right.
Step 4: Fold point B1 down at a 45-degree angle to point B2 at the midpoint of Edge C.
Step 5: Fold point A1 up at a 45-degree angle to point A2 at the midpoint of Edge D. The resulting shape is Shape 3 Right.

TO SEAM THE SPIRAL—RIGHT MITT:

Beginning at point B1/2, and using the mattress stitch method, seam toward Edge E for approx. 1 in. / 2.5 cm. Break yarn. Leave a gap in the seaming edge large enough to accommodate your thumb. Beginning on the back (along the Centerline, where Edges A and B meet), seam all the way down to Edge F, and continue seaming to point A1/2.

TO CREATE THE SPIRAL—LEFT MITT (SEE LEFT MITT SEAMING SCHEMATIC):

Step 1: Fold Edge A up at a 45-degree angle along Centerline (the Centerline is the halfway point of Long Edge A).
Step 2: Fold Edge B down at a 45-degree angle along Centerline. Resulting shape is Shape 1 Left.
Step 3: Flip Shape 1 Left over vertically so the meeting of Edges A and B is on the underside. The resulting shape is Shape 2 Left.

Step 4: Fold point A1 down at a 45-degree angle to point A2 at the midpoint of Edge C.

Step 5: Fold point B1 up at a 45-degree angle to point B2 at the midpoint of Edge D. The resulting shape is Shape 3 Left.

TO SEAM THE SPIRAL—LEFT MITT:
Beginning at point A1/2, and using the mattress stitch method, seam toward Edge E for approx. 1 in. / 2.5 cm. Break yarn. Leave a gap in the seaming edge large enough to accommodate your thumb. Beginning on the back (along the Centerline, where Edges A and B meet), seam all the way down to Edge F, and continue seaming to point B1/2.

BOTH MITTS: Embellish the seamed edges with the black yarn. Weave in any remaining ends.

Sally's Fingerless Mitts Dimensions Schematic

Last stitch

Direction of knitting

Bias width before seaming:
5½ (6, 6½, 7) [7½, 8, 8½] in.
14 (15, 16.5, 18) [19, 20.5, 21.5] cm

Long Edge A:
11 (12, 13, 14) [15, 16, 17] in.
28 (30.5, 33, 35.5) [38, 40.5, 43] cm

Cast on

FRIGHTENING FACT

Animators acted out every scene in character before animating the puppets to get realistic and lifelike movements, breaking them down into tiny increments to replicate in the puppets.

Sally's Fingerless Mitts Seaming Schematic - Right Mitt

Steps 1 & 2

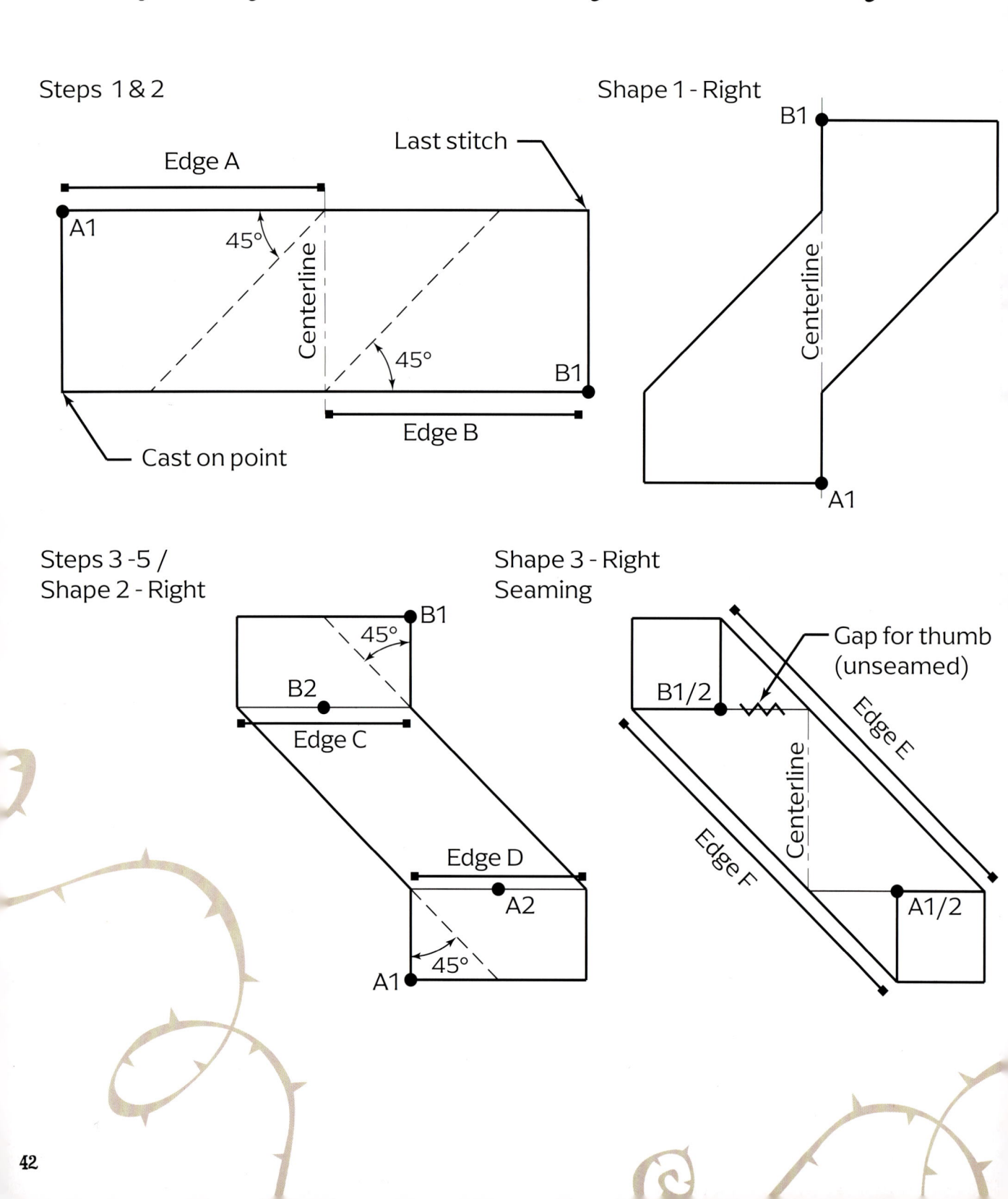

- Edge A
- A1
- 45°
- Centerline
- Last stitch
- 45°
- B1
- Edge B
- Cast on point

Shape 1 - Right

- B1
- Centerline
- A1

Steps 3-5 / Shape 2 - Right

- B1
- 45°
- B2
- Edge C
- Edge D
- A2
- A1
- 45°

Shape 3 - Right Seaming

- B1/2
- Gap for thumb (unseamed)
- Edge E
- Centerline
- Edge F
- A1/2

Sally's Fingerless Mitts Seaming Schematic - Left Mitt

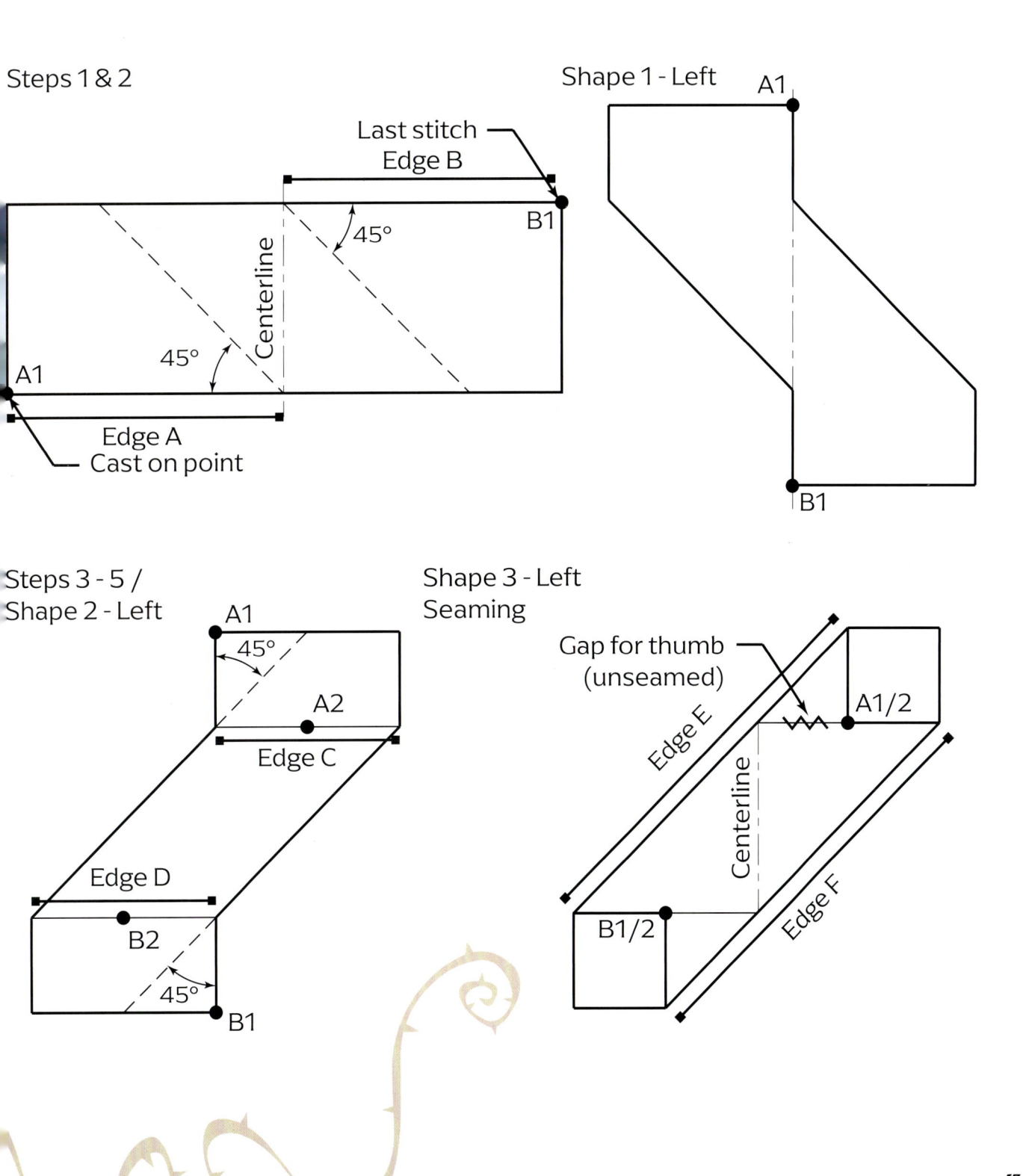

Steps 1 & 2

- Last stitch
- Edge B
- B1
- 45°
- Centerline
- 45°
- A1
- Edge A
- Cast on point

Shape 1 - Left

- A1
- B1

Steps 3 - 5 / Shape 2 - Left

- A1
- 45°
- A2
- Edge C
- Edge D
- B2
- 45°
- B1

Shape 3 - Left Seaming

- Gap for thumb (unseamed)
- A1/2
- Edge E
- Centerline
- Edge F
- B1/2

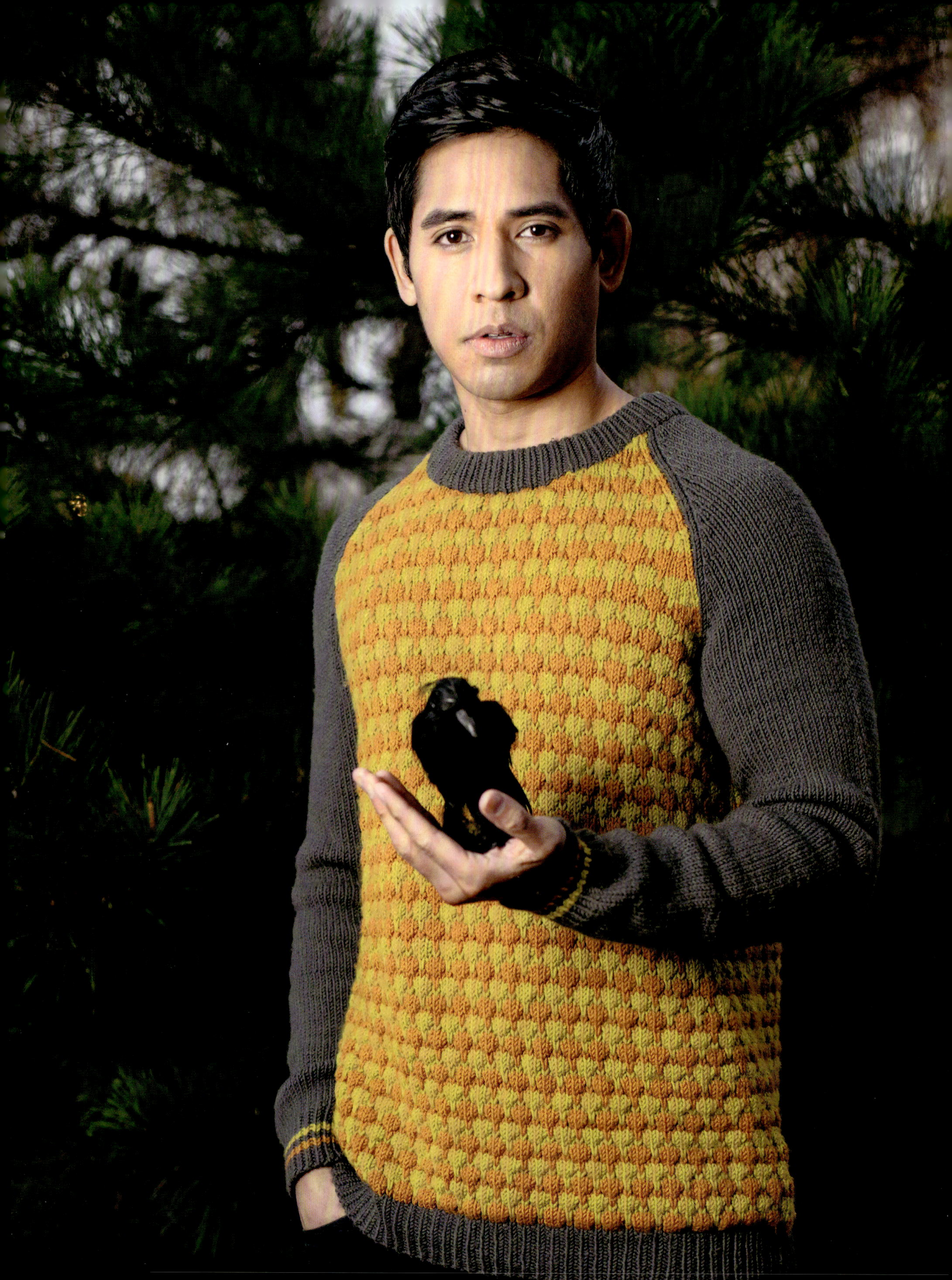

Harlequin Pullover

Designed by
Paul Haesemeyer

"Did anyone think to dredge the lake?"
—The Mayor

SKILL LEVEL
💀 💀 💀

The green, orange, and tentacled Harlequin Demon is covered in feathers and has a set of very sharp teeth. When screened for children in Hollywood before the film was released to mass audiences, Walt Disney Studios determined it was too scary for a G rating. With creepy characters, dark and scary sets, and a storyline that might frighten younger kids, it was decided that the film would be released under the sister studio Touchstone Films with a PG rating. The title changed from *The Nightmare Before Christmas* to *Tim Burton's The Nightmare Before Christmas* to attract an older audience who was familiar with his style and storytelling.

After premiering at the New York Film Festival on October 9, 1993, the film was released to theaters, where it was branded a "sleeper hit." American film critic Roger Ebert wrote in his review, "[Selick's] achievement is enormous. . . . First, go for the story. Then go back just to look in the corners of the screen and appreciate the little visual surprises and inspirations that are tucked into every nook and cranny." Despite its quiet beginnings, with its home video and DVD rentals and sales, followed by multiple rereleases in theaters over the years, and a rebranding under the Disney banner, the film has grossed close to $100 million as of 2020, becoming a cult favorite across the globe.

The Harlequin Demon captures hearts like no other with his creepy smile and his hat-making talents. This bottom-up pullover is worked flat and utilizes a bubble stitch in the body reminiscent of feathers. Contrast raglan sleeves reflect the Harlequin Demon's sporty nature with varsity stripes at the cuff, and seams stabilize the garment. Sleeves knit on a larger needle provide a natural curve along the seamlines facilitating an excellent fit, and a double tall, folded over collar ensures Halloween coziness.

SIZES
1 (2, 3, 4, 5) [6, 7, 8, 9, 10]

FINISHED MEASUREMENTS
Chest Circumference: 36 (40, 44, 48, 52) [56, 60, 64, 68, 72] in. / 91.5 (101.5, 112, 122, 132) [142, 152.5, 162.5, 172.5, 183] cm

Garment designed to be worn with 2 to 4 in. / 5 to 10 cm positive ease.

YARN
Worsted weight yarn, shown in O-Wool *O-Wash Worsted* (100% machine washable certified organic merino; 179 yd. / 163 m per 3½ oz. / 100 g hank)

COLORWAYS:
- Main Color (MC): Slate, 3 (3, 3, 3, 4) [4, 4, 4, 4, 4] hanks
- Contrast Color 1 (CC1): Feldspar, 3 (3, 3, 4, 4) [4, 5, 5, 5, 6] hanks
- Contrast Color 2 (CC2): Partridge Pea, 3 (3, 3, 4, 4) [4, 5, 5, 5, 5] hanks

NEEDLES
US 7 / 4.5 mm, 16 and 32 in. / 40 and 80 cm long circular needle

US 8 / 5 mm, 24 in. / 60 cm long circular needle

NOTIONS
Stitch marker

Smooth waste yarn or stitch holder

Row counter (optional)

Tapestry needle

GAUGE
Note: Two fabrics are used to create this garment. Be sure to use the needle size you need for each fabric.

CONTINUED ON THE NEXT PAGE

Bubble Stitch: 17 sts and 42 rows = 4 in. / 10 cm over 2-color bubble st worked flat on smaller needle, taken after blocking

Stockinette Stitch: 20 sts and 27 rows = 4 in. / 10 cm over stockinette st worked flat on larger needle, taken after blocking

Make sure to check your gauge.

PATTERN NOTES

- The body of the sweater is worked in pieces from the bottom up, flat, beginning with the smaller needle for the ribbing, continuing with the smaller needle for the bubble stitch pattern.
- The sleeves are worked flat from the bottom up, using the smaller needle for the ribbing, and the larger needle for the remainder of the sleeve. The adjustment in needle size allows the different fabrics to match in drape and provides a natural curve to the raglan seaming edge.
- Written instructions are provided for the entirety of the sweater.
- The collar is picked up and knit outward from the body in the round. It is knit double length, then folded and whipstitched into place.
- Do not break yarn between rows unless otherwise noted; carry the unused yarn loosely up the edge to save on yardage and ends to weave in. Color changes occur on the wrong side in the bubble stitch pattern.

PATTERN STITCHES

Two-Color Bubble Stitch
(worked over a multiple of 4 + 3)

Setup Row (RS, CC1): Knit.

Using CC1:

Row 1 (WS): Purl.

Row 2 (RS): Knit.

Rows 3–6: Rep [Rows 1 and 2] 2 times.

CC2:

Row 7 (WS): Purl.

Row 8 (RS): K3, *k6below, k3; rep from * to end of row.

Row 9: Purl.

Row 10: Knit.

Rows 11–14: Rep [Rows 9 and 10] 2 times.

CC1:

Row 15 (WS): Purl.

Row 16 (RS): K5, *k6below, k3; rep from * to last 2 sts, k2.

Rep Rows 1–16 for patt.

PATTERN INSTRUCTIONS

BACK CAST ON & HEM

Using the smaller needle and MC, CO 77 (85, 95, 105, 111) [121, 129, 137, 147, 155] sts using the Alternating Cable Cast On method. Do not join to work in the rnd.

ROW 1 (RS): K2, *p1, k1; rep from * to last st, k1.

ROW 2 (WS): P2, *k1, p1; rep from * to last st, p1.

Rep Rows 1 and 2 until the hem measures 2 in. / 5 cm from the CO edge, ending with a WS row. Break MC.

BACK BODY

Join CC1.
SETUP ROW (RS): Knit.

SIZES 1 (2, -, 4, -) [6, 7, 8, -, -] ONLY

Using CC1:
ROW 1 (WS): Purl.
ROW 2 (RS): Knit.
ROWS 3–6: Rep [Rows 1 and 2] 2 times.
CC2:
ROW 7 (WS): Purl.
ROW 8 (RS): K4, *k6below, k3; rep from * to last st, k1.
ROW 9: Purl.
ROW 10: Knit.
ROWS 11–14: Rep [Rows 9 and 10] 2 times.
CC1:
ROW 15 (WS): Purl.
ROW 16 (RS): K6, *k6below, k3; rep from * to last 3 sts, k3.

SIZES - (-, 3, -, 5) [-, -, -, 9, 10] ONLY

Using CC1:
ROW 1 (WS): Purl.
ROW 2 (RS): Knit.
ROWS 3–6: Rep [Rows 1 and 2] 2 times.
CC2:
ROW 7 (WS): Purl.
ROW 8 (RS): K3, *k6below, k3; rep from * to end of row.
ROW 9: Purl.
ROW 10: Knit.
ROWS 11–14: Rep [Rows 9 and 10] 2 times.

CC1:
ROW 15 (WS): Purl.
ROW 16 (RS): K5, *k6below, k3; rep from * to last 2 sts, k2.

ALL SIZES
Rep Rows 1–16 for your size until the body measures 18 in. / 45 cm from the CO edge, ending after Row 3 or 11.

BACK ARMHOLE SHAPING—SECTION 1
ROW 1 (RS): BO 3 (4, 5, 6, 6) [7, 7, 7, 8, 10] sts knitwise, work est patt to end of row.
ROW 2 (WS): BO 3 (4, 5, 6, 6) [7, 7, 7, 8, 10] sts purlwise, work est patt to end of row.
6 (8, 10, 12, 12) [14, 14, 14, 16, 20] sts BO; 71 (77, 85, 93, 99) [107, 115, 123, 131, 135] sts rem.
SIZE 1 ONLY: Proceed to Armhole Shaping—Section 3.
SIZE 2 ONLY: Proceed to Armhole Shaping—Section 2.

SIZES 3-10 ONLY
ROW 3 (RS, DEC): K2, k2tog, work est patt to last 4 sts, ssk, k2—2 sts dec.
ROW 4 (WS, DEC): P2, ssp, work est patt to last 4 sts, p2tog, p2—2 sts dec.
Rep [Rows 3 and 4] - (-, -, 1, 2, 3) [4, 4, 5, 6, 6] more time(s).
- (-, 8, 12, 16) [20, 20, 24, 28, 28] sts dec; - (-, 77, 81, 83) [87, 95, 99, 103, 107] sts rem.

BACK ARMHOLE SHAPING—SECTION 2

SIZES 2-10 ONLY
ROW 1 (RS, DEC): K2, k2tog, work est patt to last 4 sts, ssk, k2—2 sts dec.
ROW 2 (WS): Work est patt to end of row.
Rep [Rows 1 and 2] - (1, 0, 1, 0) [2, 6, 8, 7, 9] more time(s).
- (4, 2, 4, 2) [6, 14, 18, 16, 20] sts dec; - (73, 75, 77, 81) [81, 81, 81, 87, 87] sts rem.

BACK ARMHOLE SHAPING—SECTION 3

ALL SIZES
ROW 1 (RS, DEC): K2, k2tog, work est patt to last 4 sts, ssk, k2—2 sts dec.
ROWS 2–4: Work est patt to end of row.
Rep [Rows 1–4] 16 (16, 16, 16, 16) [15, 14, 13, 14, 14] more times, then work Row 1 once more.
36 (36, 36, 36, 36) [34, 32, 30, 32, 32] sts dec; 35 (37, 39, 41, 45) [47, 49, 51, 55, 55] sts rem.
With WS facing, bind off all sts purlwise.

FRONT
Work as for the Back through the end of Back Armhole Shaping—Section 2.
71 (73, 75, 77, 81) [81, 81, 81, 87, 87] sts rem.

FRONT ARMHOLE SHAPING—SECTION 3
ROW 1 (RS, DEC): K2, k2tog, work est patt to last 4 sts, ssk, k2—2 sts dec.
ROWS 2–4: Work est patt to end of row.
Rep [Rows 1–4] 12 (12, 12, 11, 11) [10, 8, 8, 8, 8] more times.
26 (26, 26, 24, 24) [22, 18, 18, 18, 18] sts dec; 45 (47, 49, 53, 57) [59, 63, 63, 69, 69] sts rem.

SIZES - (-, -, 4, 5) [-, 7, -, -, -] ONLY
NEXT ROW (RS, DEC): K2, k2tog, work est patt to last 4 sts, ssk, k2— - (-, -, 51, 55) [-, 61, -, -, -] sts rem.
NEXT ROW (WS): Work est patt to end of row.

NECKLINE BIND OFF

SIZES 1 (2, 3, -, -) [6, -, 8, 9, 10] ONLY
NECKLINE BIND OFF ROW (RS, DEC): K2, k2tog, work 14 (15, 15, -, -) [19, -, 20, 23, 23] sts in est patt, place the 17 (18, 18, -, -) [22, -, 23, 26, 26] just worked sts onto waste yarn or stitch holder for the Left Front Shoulder, BO 9 (9, 11, -, -) [13, -, 15, 15, 15] sts knitwise, work est patt to last 4 sts, k2tog, k2.

SIZES - (-, -, 4, 5) [-, 7, -, -, -] ONLY
NECKLINE BIND OFF ROW (RS): Work - (-, -, 20, 21) [-, 24, -, -, -] sts in est patt, place the - (-, -, 20, 21) [-, 24, -, -, -] just worked sts onto waste yarn or stitch holder for the Left Front Shoulder, BO - (-, -, 11, 13) [-, 13, -, -, -] sts knitwise, work est patt to end of row.

ALL SIZES
17 (18, 18, 20, 21) [22, 24, 23, 26, 26] sts rem for each front. Cont with Right Front Shoulder only. Break unused CC.

RIGHT FRONT SHOULDER
Rejoin CC as necessary to cont in est patt.

SIZE 1 ONLY
ROW 1 (WS, DEC): Work est patt to last 2 sts, ssp—16 sts rem.
ROW 2 (RS, DEC): Ssk, work est patt to end of row—15 sts rem.
ROW 3 (DEC): Work est patt to last 2 sts, ssp—14 sts rem.
ROW 4 (DEC): Ssk, work est patt to last 4 sts, k2tog, k2—12 sts rem.
ROW 5 (DEC): Work est patt to last 2 sts, ssp—11 sts rem.
ROW 6 (DEC): Ssk, work est patt to end of row—10 sts rem.
ROW 7: Work est patt to end of row.
ROW 8 (DEC): Ssk, work est patt to last 4 sts, k2tog, k2—2 sts dec.
ROW 9: Work est patt to end of row.
ROW 10 (DEC): Ssk, work est patt to end of row—1 st dec.
ROW 11: Work est patt to end of row.

ROWS 12–15: Rep [Rows 8–11] 1 time—4 sts rem.
ROW 16 (DEC): Ssk, work est patt to last 4 sts, k2tog, k2—2 sts rem.

SIZES 2 AND 3 ONLY
ROW 1 (WS, DEC): Work est patt to last 2 sts, ssp—1 st dec.
ROW 2 (RS, DEC): Ssk, work est patt to end of row—1 st dec.
ROW 3 (DEC): Work est patt to last 2 sts, ssp—1 st dec.
ROW 4 (DEC): Ssk, work est patt to last 4 sts, k2tog, k2—2 sts dec.
ROWS 5–8: Rep [Rows 1–4] 1 time—8 sts rem.
ROW 9: Work est patt to end of row.
ROW 10 (DEC): Ssk, work est patt to end of row—1 st dec.
ROW 11: Work est patt to end of row.
ROW 12 (DEC): Ssk, work est patt to last 4 sts, k2tog, k2—2 sts dec.
ROWS 13–16: Rep [Rows 9–12] 1 time—2 sts rem.

SIZE 4 ONLY
ROW 1 (WS, DEC): Work est patt to last 2 sts, ssp—19 sts rem.
ROW 2 (RS, DEC): Ssk, work est patt to last 4 sts, k2tog, k2—17 sts rem.
ROW 3 (DEC): Work est patt to last 2 sts, ssp—16 sts rem.
ROW 4 (DEC): Ssk, work est patt to end of row—15 sts rem.
ROW 5 (DEC): Work est patt to last 2 sts, ssp—14 sts rem.
ROW 6 (DEC): Ssk, work est patt to last 4 sts, k2tog, k2—12 sts rem.
ROW 7 (DEC): Work est patt to last 2 sts, ssp—11 sts rem.
ROW 8 (DEC): Ssk, work est patt to end of row—10 sts rem.
ROW 9: Work est patt to end of row.
ROW 10 (DEC): Ssk, work est patt to last 4 sts, k2tog, k2—8 sts rem.
ROW 11: Work est patt to end of row.
ROW 12 (DEC): Ssk, work est patt to end of row—1 st dec.
ROW 13: Work est patt to end of row.
ROW 14 (DEC): Ssk, work est patt to last 4 sts, k2tog, k2—2 sts dec.
ROWS 15–18: Rep [Rows 11–14] 1 time—2 sts rem.

SIZE 5 ONLY
ROW 1 (WS, DEC): Work est patt to last 2 sts, ssp—20 sts rem.
ROW 2 (RS, DEC): Ssk, work est patt to last 4 sts, k2tog, k2—18 sts rem.
ROW 3 (DEC): Work est patt to last 2 sts, ssp—1 st dec.
ROW 4 (DEC): Ssk, work est patt to end of row—1 st dec.
ROW 5 (DEC): Work est patt to last 2 sts, ssp—1 st dec.
ROW 6 (DEC): Ssk, work est patt to last 4 sts, k2tog, k2—2 sts dec.
ROWS 7–10: Rep [Rows 3–6] 1 time—8 sts rem.
ROW 11: Work est patt to end of row.
ROW 12 (DEC): Ssk, work est patt to end of row—1 st dec.
ROW 13: Work est patt to end of row.
ROW 14 (DEC): Ssk, work est patt to last 4 sts, k2tog, k2—2 sts dec.
ROWS 15–18: Rep [Rows 11–14] 1 time—2 sts rem.

SIZE 6 ONLY
ROW 1 (WS, DEC): Work est patt to last 2 sts, ssp—1 st dec.
ROW 2 (RS, DEC): Ssk, work est patt to end of row—1 st dec.
ROW 3 (DEC): Work est patt to last 2 sts, ssp—1 st dec.
ROW 4 (DEC): Ssk, work est patt to last 4 sts, k2tog, k2—2 sts dec.
ROWS 5–8: Rep [Rows 1–4] 1 time—12 sts rem.
ROW 9 (DEC): Work est patt to last 2 sts, ssp—11 sts rem.
ROW 10 (DEC): Ssk, work est patt to end of row—10 sts rem.
ROW 11: Work est patt to end of row.
ROW 12 (DEC): Ssk, work est patt to last 4 sts, k2tog, k2—8 sts rem.
ROW 13: Work est patt to end of row.
ROW 14 (DEC): Ssk, work est patt to end of row—1 st dec.
ROW 15: Work est patt to end of row.
ROW 16 (DEC): Ssk, work est patt to last 4 sts, k2tog, k2—2 sts dec.
ROWS 17–20: Rep [Rows 13–16] 1 time—2 sts rem.

SIZE 7 ONLY
ROW 1 (WS, DEC): Work est patt to last 2 sts, ssp—23 sts rem.
ROW 2 (RS, DEC): Ssk, work est patt to last 4 sts, k2tog, k2—21 sts rem.
ROW 3 (DEC): Work est patt to last 2 sts, ssp—1 st dec.
ROW 4 (DEC): Ssk, work est patt to end of row—1 st dec.
ROW 5 (DEC): Work est patt to last 2 sts, ssp—1 st dec.
ROW 6 (DEC): Ssk, work est patt to last 4 sts, k2tog, k2—2 sts dec.
ROWS 7–10: Rep [Rows 3–6] 1 time—11 sts rem.
ROW 11: Work est patt to end of row.
ROW 12 (DEC): Ssk, work est patt to end of row—1 st dec.
ROW 13: Work est patt to end of row.
ROW 14 (DEC): Ssk, work est patt to last 4 sts, k2tog, k2—2 sts dec.
ROWS 15–22: Rep [Rows 11–14] 2 times—2 sts rem.

SIZE 8 ONLY
ROW 1 (WS, DEC): Work est patt to last 2 sts, ssp—1 st dec.
ROW 2 (RS, DEC): Ssk, work est patt to end of row—1 st dec.
ROW 3 (DEC): Work est patt to last 2 sts, ssp—1 st dec.
ROW 4 (DEC): Ssk, work est patt to last 4 sts, k2tog, k2—2 sts dec.
ROWS 5–12: Rep [Rows 1–4] 2 times—8 sts rem.
ROW 13: Work est patt to end of row.
ROW 14 (DEC): Ssk, work est patt to end of row—1 st dec.
ROW 15: Work est patt to end of row.
ROW 16 (DEC): Ssk, work est patt to last 4 sts, k2tog, k2—2 sts dec.
ROWS 17–20: Rep [Rows 13–16] 1 time—2 sts rem.

SIZES 9 AND 10 ONLY
ROW 1 (WS, DEC): Work est patt to last 2 sts, ssp—1 st dec.
ROW 2 (RS, DEC): Ssk, work est patt to end of row—1 st dec.
ROW 3 (DEC): Work est patt to last 2 sts, ssp—1 st dec.
ROW 4 (DEC): Ssk, work est patt to last 4 sts, k2tog, k2—2 sts dec.
ROWS 5–12: Rep [Rows 1–4] 2 times—11 sts rem.
ROW 13: Work est patt to end of row.
ROW 14 (DEC): Ssk, work est patt to end of row—1 st dec.

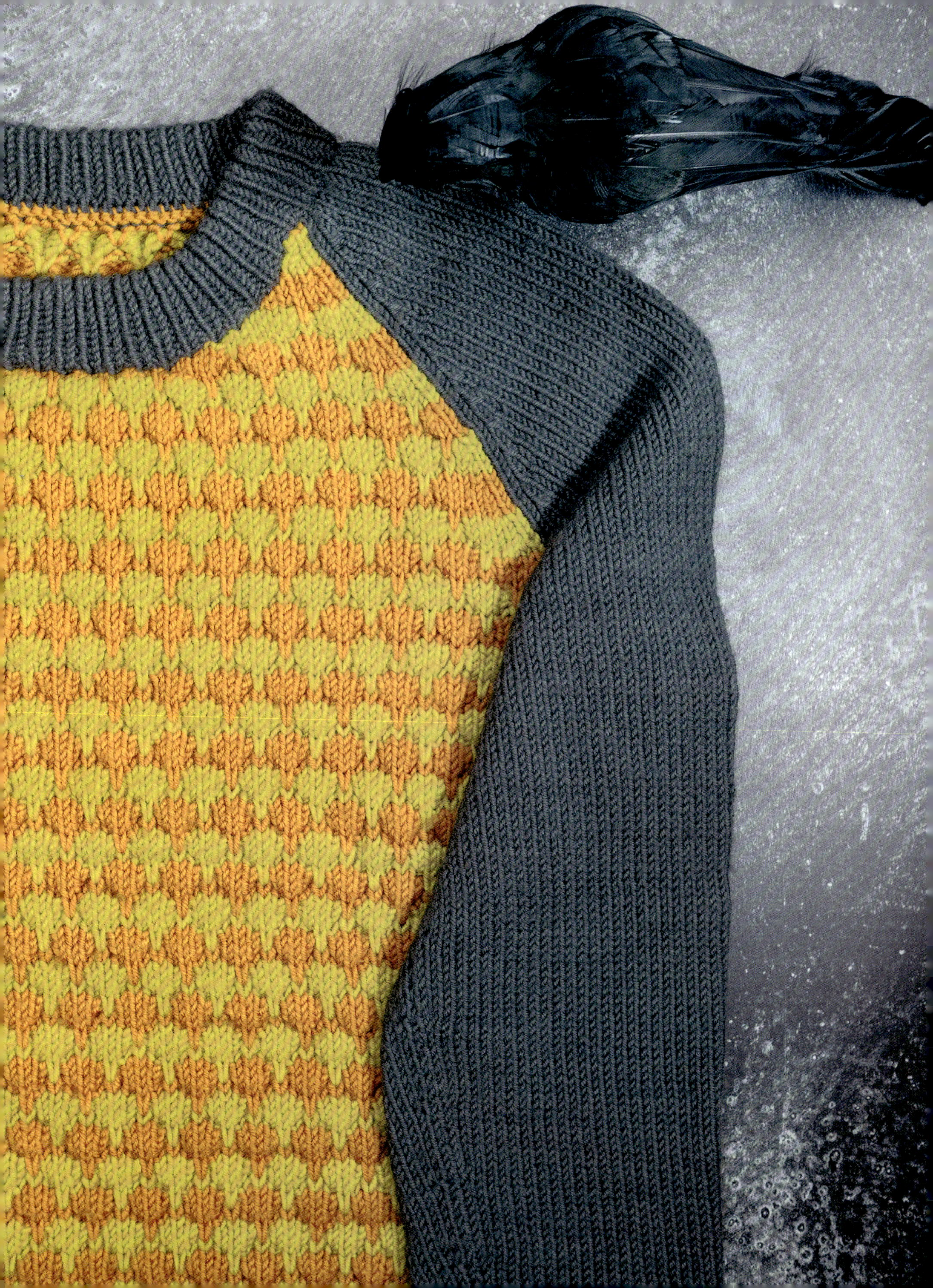

ROW 15: Work est patt to end of row.
ROW 16 (DEC): Ssk, work est patt to last 4 sts, k2tog, k2—2 sts dec.
ROWS 17–24: Rep [Rows 13–16] 2 times—2 sts rem.

ALL SIZES

NEXT ROW (WS, DEC): P2tog—1 st rem.
Break both CC yarns leaving a tail for weaving in. Pull tail through rem st and cinch closed to secure.

LEFT FRONT SHOULDER

Place the 17 (18, 18, 20, 21) [22, 24, 23, 26, 26] sts for the Left Front Shoulder back onto the smaller needle. Rejoin CCs with the WS facing to cont in est patt.

SIZE 1 ONLY

ROW 1 (WS, DEC): P2tog, work est patt to end of row—16 sts rem.
ROW 2 (RS, DEC): Work est patt to last 2 sts, k2tog—15 sts rem.
ROW 3 (DEC): P2tog, work est patt to end of row—14 sts rem.
ROW 4 (DEC): K2, ssk, work est patt to last 2 sts, k2tog—12 sts rem.
ROW 5 (DEC): P2tog, work est patt to end of row—11 sts rem.
ROW 6 (DEC): Work est patt to last 2 sts, k2tog—10 sts rem.
ROW 7: Work est patt to end of row.
ROW 8 (DEC): K2, ssk, work est patt to last 2 sts, k2tog—2 sts dec.
ROW 9: Work est patt to end of row.
ROW 10 (DEC): Work est patt to last 2 sts, k2tog—1 st dec.
ROW 11: Work est patt to end of row.
ROWS 12–15: Rep [Rows 8–11] 1 time—4 sts rem.
ROW 16 (DEC): K2, ssk, work est patt to last 2 sts, Ssk, k2tog—2 sts rem.

SIZES 2 AND 3 ONLY

ROW 1 (WS, DEC): P2tog, work est patt to end of row—1 st dec.
ROW 2 (RS, DEC): Work est patt to last 2 sts, k2tog—1 st dec.
ROW 3 (DEC): P2tog, work est patt to end of row—1 st dec.
ROW 4 (DEC): K2, ssk, work est patt to last 2 sts, k2tog—2 sts dec.
ROWS 5–8: Rep [Rows 1–4] 1 time—8 sts rem.
ROW 9: Work est patt to end of row.
ROW 10 (DEC): Work est patt to last 2 sts, k2tog—1 st dec.
ROW 11: Work est patt to end of row.
ROW 12 (DEC): K2, ssk, work est patt to last 2 sts, k2tog—2 sts dec.
ROWS 13–16: Rep [Rows 9–12] 1 time—2 sts rem.

SIZE 4 ONLY

ROW 1 (WS, DEC): P2tog, work est patt to end of row—19 sts rem.
ROW 2 (RS, DEC): K2, ssk, work est patt to last 2 sts, k2tog—17 sts rem.
ROW 3 (DEC): P2tog, work est patt to end of row—16 sts rem.
ROW 4 (DEC): Work est patt to last 2 sts, k2tog—15 sts rem.
ROW 5 (DEC): P2tog, work est patt to end of row—14 sts rem.
ROW 6 (DEC): K2, ssk, work est patt to last 2 sts, k2tog—12 sts rem.
ROW 7 (DEC): P2tog, work est patt to end of row—11 sts rem.
ROW 8 (DEC): Work est patt to last 2 sts, k2tog—10 sts rem.
ROW 9: Work est patt to end of row.
ROW 10 (DEC): K2, ssk, work est patt to last 2 sts, k2tog—8 sts rem.
ROW 11: Work est patt to end of row.

ROW 12 (DEC): Work est patt to last 2 sts, k2tog—1 st dec.
ROW 13: Work est patt to end of row.
ROW 14 (DEC): K2, ssk, work est patt to last 2 sts, k2tog—2 sts dec.
ROWS 15–18: Rep [Rows 11–14] 1 time—2 sts rem.

SIZE 5 ONLY
ROW 1 (WS, DEC): P2tog, work est patt to end of row—20 sts rem.
ROW 2 (RS, DEC): K2, ssk, work est patt to last 2 sts, k2tog—18 sts rem.
ROW 3 (DEC): P2tog, work est patt to end of row—1 st dec.
ROW 4 (DEC): Work est patt to last 2 sts, k2tog—1 st dec.
ROW 5 (DEC): P2tog, work est patt to end of row—1 st dec.
ROW 6 (DEC): K2, ssk, work est patt to last 2 sts, k2tog—2 sts dec.
ROWS 7–10: Rep [Rows 3–6] 1 time—8 sts rem.
ROW 11: Work est patt to end of row.
ROW 12 (DEC): Work est patt to last 2 sts, k2tog—1 st dec.
ROW 13: Work est patt to end of row.
ROW 14 (DEC): K2, ssk, work est patt to last 2 sts, k2tog—2 sts dec.
ROWS 15–18: Rep [Rows 11–14] 1 time—2 sts rem.

SIZE 6 ONLY
ROW 1 (WS, DEC): P2tog, work est patt to end of row—1 st dec.
ROW 2 (RS, DEC): Work est patt to last 2 sts, k2tog—1 st dec.
ROW 3 (DEC): P2tog, work est patt to end of row—1 st dec.
ROW 4 (DEC): K2, ssk, work est patt to last 2 sts, k2tog—2 sts dec.
ROWS 5–8: Rep [Rows 1–4] 1 time—12 sts rem.
ROW 9 (DEC): P2tog, work est patt to end of row—11 sts rem.
ROW 10 (DEC): Work est patt to last 2 sts, k2tog—10 sts rem.
ROW 11: Work est patt to end of row.
ROW 12 (DEC): K2, ssk, work est patt to last 2 sts, k2tog—8 sts rem.
ROW 13: Work est patt to end of row.

ROW 14 (DEC): Work est patt to last 2 sts, k2tog—1 st dec.
ROW 15: Work est patt to end of row.
ROW 16 (DEC): K2, ssk, work est patt to last 2 sts, k2tog—2 sts dec.
ROWS 17–20: Rep [Rows 13–16] 1 time—2 sts rem.

SIZE 7 ONLY
ROW 1 (WS, DEC): P2tog, work est patt to end of row—23 sts rem.
ROW 2 (RS, DEC): K2, ssk, work est patt to last 2 sts, k2tog—21 sts rem.
ROW 3 (DEC): P2tog, work est patt to end of row—1 st dec.
ROW 4 (DEC): Work est patt to last 2 sts, k2tog—1 st dec.
ROW 5 (DEC): P2tog, work est patt to end of row—1 st dec.
ROW 6 (DEC): K2, ssk, work est patt to last 2 sts, k2tog—2 sts dec.
ROWS 7–10: Rep [Rows 3–6] 1 time—11 sts rem.
ROW 11: Work est patt to end of row.
ROW 12 (DEC): Work est patt to last 2 sts, k2tog—1 st dec.
ROW 13: Work est patt to end of row.
ROW 14 (DEC): K2, ssk, work est patt to last 2 sts, k2tog—2 sts dec.
ROWS 15–22: Rep [Rows 11–14] 2 times—2 sts rem.

SIZE 8 ONLY
ROW 1 (WS, DEC): P2tog, work est patt to end of row—1 st dec.
ROW 2 (RS, DEC): Work est patt to last 2 sts, k2tog—1 st dec.
ROW 3 (DEC): P2tog, work est patt to end of row—1 st dec.
ROW 4 (DEC): K2, ssk, work est patt to last 2 sts, k2tog—2 sts dec.
ROWS 5–12: Rep [Rows 1–4] 2 times—8 sts rem.
ROW 13: Work est patt to end of row.
ROW 14 (DEC): Work est patt to last 2 sts, k2tog—1 st dec.
ROW 15: Work est patt to end of row.
ROW 16 (DEC): K2, ssk, work est patt to last 2 sts, k2tog—2 sts dec.
ROWS 17–20: Rep [Rows 13–16] 1 time—2 sts rem.

SIZES 9 AND 10 ONLY
ROW 1 (WS, DEC): P2tog, work est patt to end of row—1 st dec.
ROW 2 (RS, DEC): Work est patt to last 2 sts, k2tog—1 st dec.
ROW 3 (DEC): P2tog, work est patt to end of row—1 st dec.
ROW 4 (DEC): K2, ssk, work est patt to last 2 sts, k2tog—2 sts dec.
ROWS 5–12: Rep [Rows 1–4] 2 times—11 sts rem.
ROW 13: Work est patt to end of row.
ROW 14 (DEC): Work est patt to last 2 sts, k2tog—1 st dec.
ROW 15: Work est patt to end of row.
ROW 16 (DEC): K2, ssk, work est patt to last 2 sts, k2tog—2 sts dec.
ROWS 17–24: Rep [Rows 13–16] 2 times—2 sts rem.

ALL SIZES
NEXT ROW (WS, DEC): P2tog—1 st rem.
Break both CC yarns leaving a tail for weaving in. Pull tail through rem st and cinch closed to secure.

SLEEVES (MAKE 2 THE SAME)

CAST ON & CUFF
Using the smaller needle and MC, CO 43 (45, 47, 49, 51) [53, 55, 55, 57, 57] sts using the Alternating Cable Cast On method. Do not join to work in the rnd.
ROW 1 (RS): K2, *p1, k1; rep from * to last st, k1.
ROW 2 (WS): P2, *k1, p1; rep from * to last st, p1.
Work [Rows 1 and 2] 8 times total.
AT THE SAME TIME, work the following color sequence while repeating Rows 1 and 2:
Work 4 rows MC; do not break MC.
Join CC1, work 2 rows with CC1; break CC1.
Work 2 rows with MC; do not break MC.
Join CC2, work 2 rows with CC2; break CC2.
Work 6 rows with MC; do not break MC.

BODY OF SLEEVE

Switch to larger needle. The remainder of the sleeve will be worked with MC only.

Work in St st (knit on RS, purl on WS) until the sleeve measures 19 in. / 48.5 cm (or desired total length) from the CO edge, ending with a WS row.

AT THE SAME TIME, beginning on Row 11, work the Inc Row, below, every 10 (10, 10, 8, 8) [6, 6, 6, 6, 4] rows 10 (6, 2, 9, 3) [18, 16, 10, 6, 27] times, then every 8 (8, 8, 6, 6) [0, 4, 4, 4, 0] rows 1 (6, 11, 6, 14) [0, 3, 12, 18, 0] time(s) *(the Inc Row will always be a RS row)*.

INC ROW (RS): K2, M1L, knit to last 2 sts, M1R, k2—2 sts inc.

22 (24, 26, 30, 34) [36, 38, 44, 48, 54] sts inc; 65 (69, 73, 79, 85) [89, 93, 99, 105, 111] total sts.

SLEEVE CAP—SECTION 1

ROW 1 (RS): BO 3 (4, 5, 6, 6) [7, 7, 7, 8, 10] sts knitwise, knit to end of row.

ROW 2 (WS): BO 3 (4, 5, 6, 6) [7, 7, 7, 8, 10] sts purlwise, purl to end of row.

6 (8, 10, 12, 12) [14, 14, 14, 16, 20] sts BO; 59 (61, 63, 67, 73) [75, 79, 85, 89, 91] sts rem.

SIZE 1 ONLY:
Proceed to Sleeve Cap—Section 3.

SIZE 2 ONLY:
Proceed to Sleeve Cap—Section 2.

SIZES 3-10 ONLY:
ROW 3 (RS, DEC): K2, k2tog, knit to last 4 sts, ssk, k2—2 sts dec.

ROW 4 (WS, DEC): P2, ssp, purl to last 4 sts, p2tog, p2—2 sts dec.

Rep [Rows 3 and 4] - (-, 1, 2, 3) [4, 4, 5, 6, 6] more time(s).

- (-, 8, 12, 16) [20, 20, 24, 28, 28] sts dec; - (-, 55, 55, 57) [55, 59, 61, 61, 63] sts rem.

SLEEVE CAP—SECTION 2

SIZES 2-10 ONLY:
ROW 1 (RS, DEC): K2, k2tog, knit to last 4 sts, ssk, k2—2 sts dec.

ROW 2 (WS): Purl.

Rep [Rows 1 and 2] - (1, 0, 1, 0) [2, 6, 8, 7, 9] more time(s).

- (4, 2, 4, 2) [6, 14, 18, 16, 20] sts dec; - (57, 53, 51, 55) [49, 45, 43, 45, 43] sts rem.

SLEEVE CAP—SECTION 3

ALL SIZES:
ROW 1 (RS, DEC): K2, k2tog, knit to last 4 sts, ssk, k2—2 sts dec.

ROWS 2–4: Work in St st.

Rep [Rows 1–4] 16 (16, 16, 16, 16) [15, 14, 13, 14, 14] more times, then work Row 1 once more.

36 (36, 36, 36, 36) [34, 32, 30, 32, 32] sts dec; 23 (21, 17, 15, 19) [15, 13, 13, 13, 11] sts rem.

FRIGHTENING FACT

In 2018, Disney released a sing-along edition of the DVD to celebrate the twenty-fifth anniversary of the film.

With WS facing, bind off all sts purlwise.

SEAMING

Seam sleeve caps to body at armholes using mattress stitch and MC yarn. Seam the underside of the sleeves with MC yarn, and the sides of the body using CC1 or CC2, both using mattress stitch. Ease side seams as necessary to match dimensions provided in schematic; side seams may want to hang longer due to the lack of k6below worked at the seam.

COLLAR

Using the smaller 16 in. / 40 cm circular needle and MC, beginning at the back right shoulder seam, pick up and knit 33 (35, 37, 39, 43) [45, 47, 49, 53, 53] back neck sts, 21 (19, 15, 13, 17) [13, 11, 11, 11, 9] sts across the left shoulder, 15 (16, 16, 17, 18) [19, 20, 20, 22, 22] sts down the left front of the neckline edge, 9 (9, 11, 11, 13) [13, 13, 15, 15, 15] neckline bind off sts, 15 (16, 16, 17, 18) [19, 20, 20, 22, 22] sts up the right front of the neckline edge, and 21 (19, 15, 13, 17) [13, 11, 11, 11, 9] sts across the right shoulder. Pm for BOR and join to work in the rnd—114 (114, 110, 110, 126) [122, 122, 126, 134, 130] sts.

Rib Rnd: *K1, p1; rep from * to end of rnd.

Rep Rib Rnd until the collar measures 3 in. / 7.5 cm from the picked-up edge.

Without binding off any sts, break the yarn leaving a tail approx. 3 times the length of the collar circumference. Fold the collar in half inward, WS together. Thread the tapestry needle with the long tail and secure the live sts to the picked-up edge using whipstitch.

FINISHING

Weave in all ends. Wet block the garment per the schematic. Trim all ends.

Harlequin Pullover Schematic

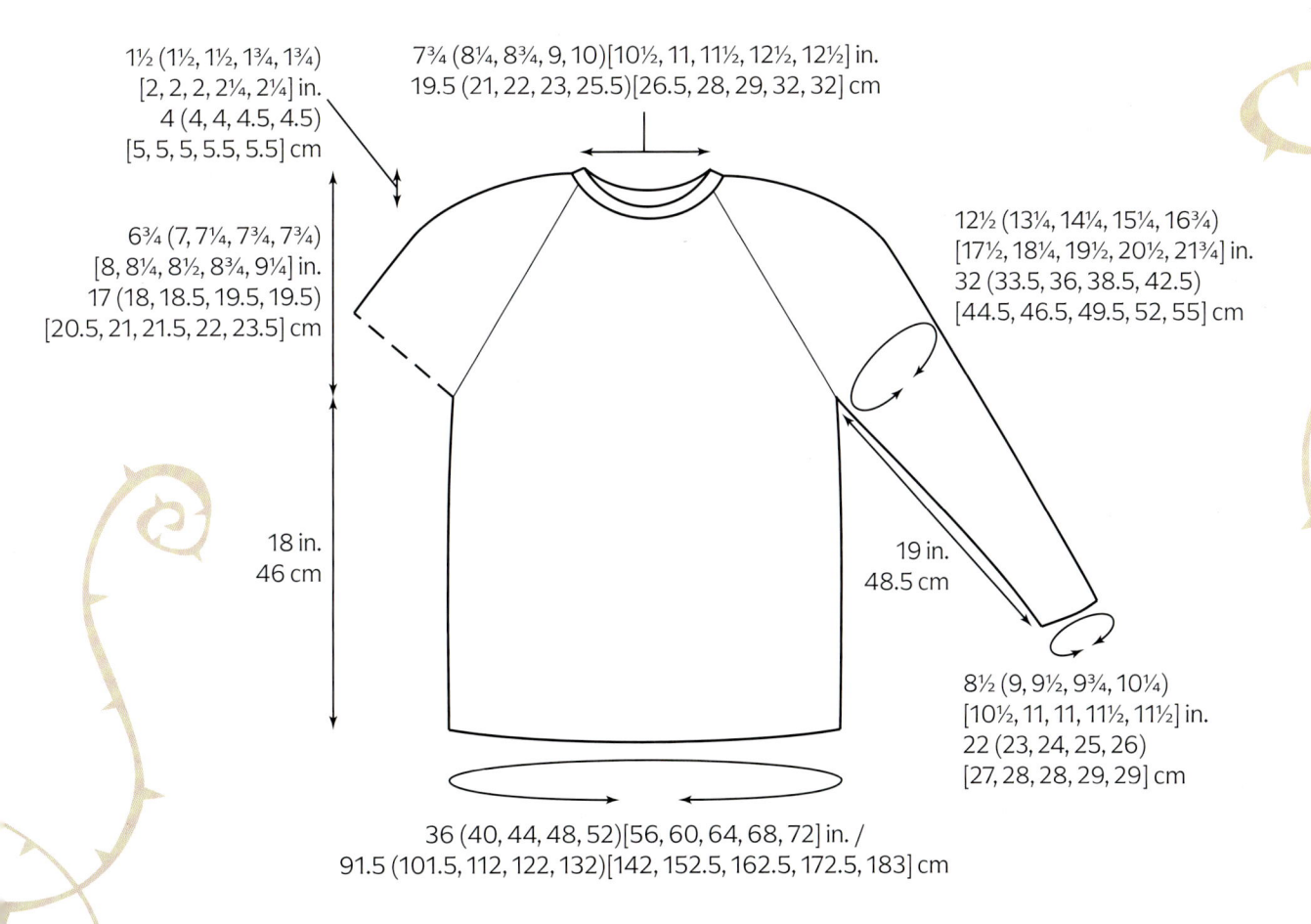

1½ (1½, 1½, 1¾, 1¾) [2, 2, 2, 2¼, 2¼] in.
4 (4, 4, 4.5, 4.5) [5, 5, 5, 5.5, 5.5] cm

7¾ (8¼, 8¾, 9, 10)[10½, 11, 11½, 12½, 12½] in.
19.5 (21, 22, 23, 25.5)[26.5, 28, 29, 32, 32] cm

12½ (13¼, 14¼, 15¼, 16¾) [17½, 18¼, 19½, 20½, 21¾] in.
32 (33.5, 36, 38.5, 42.5) [44.5, 46.5, 49.5, 52, 55] cm

6¾ (7, 7¼, 7¾, 7¾) [8, 8¼, 8½, 8¾, 9¼] in.
17 (18, 18.5, 19.5, 19.5) [20.5, 21, 21.5, 22, 23.5] cm

18 in.
46 cm

19 in.
48.5 cm

8½ (9, 9½, 9¾, 10¼) [10½, 11, 11, 11½, 11½] in.
22 (23, 24, 25, 26) [27, 28, 28, 29, 29] cm

36 (40, 44, 48, 52)[56, 60, 64, 68, 72] in. / 91.5 (101.5, 112, 122, 132)[142, 152.5, 162.5, 172.5, 183] cm

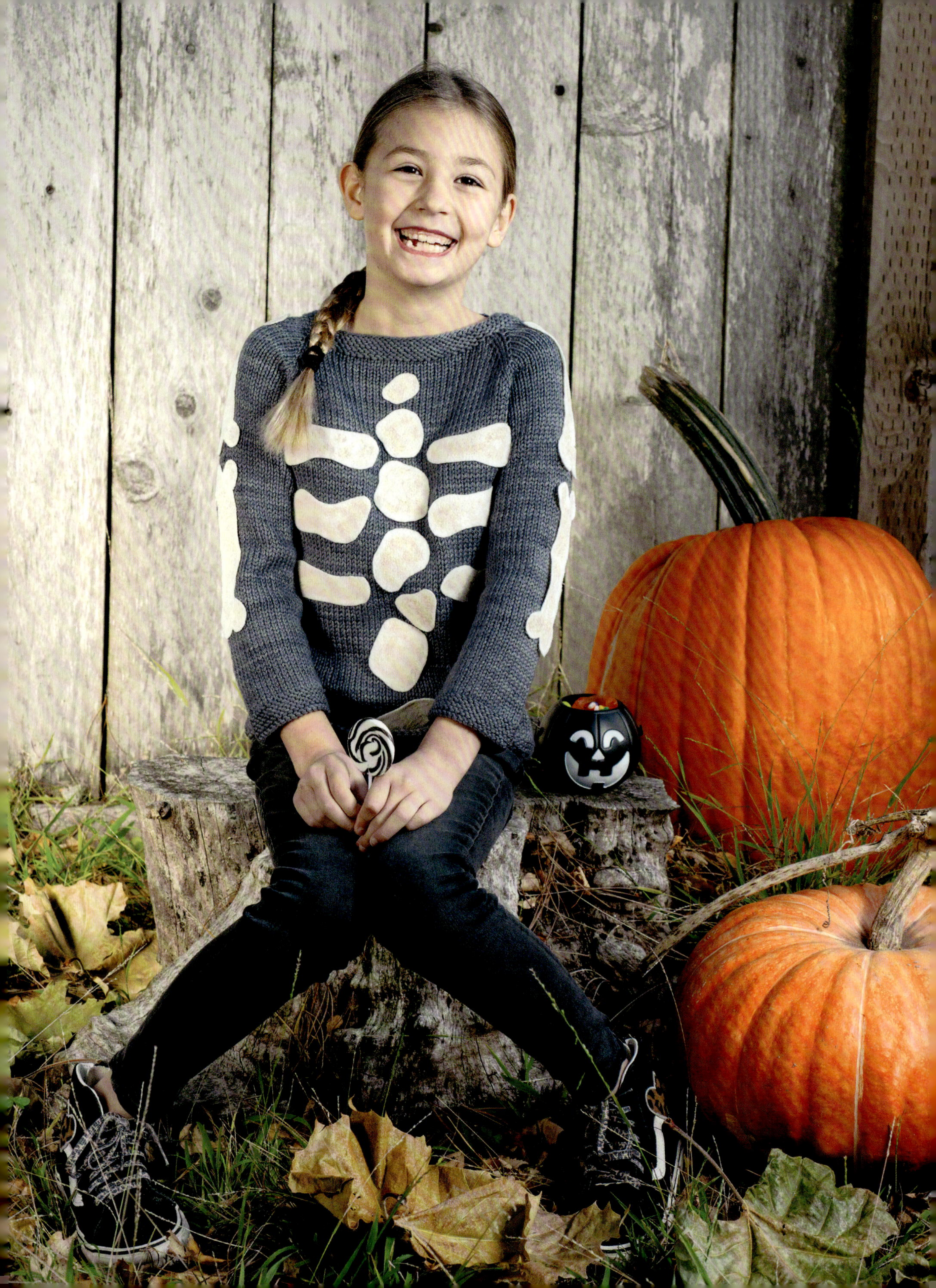

Barrel's Pullover

Designed by
Tanis Gray

"Jack sent for us specifically, by name. Lock! Shock! Barrel!"

Jack: *"Ah, Halloween's finest Trick-or-Treaters. The job I have for you is top secret. It requires craft, cunning, mischief . . ."*

SKILL LEVEL

Lock, Shock, and Barrel are a trio of young trick-or-treaters who live in a creepy, topsy-turvy tree house above Oogie Boogie's lair. Put in charge of kidnapping Sandy Claws by Jack, they serve Oogie Boogie out of fear, as well as the delight in making mischief and harassing the residents of Halloween Town. Traveling by enchanted bathtub, the trio mistakenly kidnaps the Easter Bunny, but eventually makes it right by kidnapping Santa and pushing him down a metal tube into the hands of Oogie Boogie, going expressly against Jack's instructions. The trio all wear masks that eerily resemble their actual faces.

Perfect for a first sweater project, this top-down costume replica raglan is knit in the round with garter edgings—a surprisingly mischief-free knit! Easy German short rows raise up the back neck for a better fit, and top-down construction means adding torso or sleeve length for your ever-growing henchman is an easier task than kidnapping Sandy Claws. Bone motifs are cut from washable craft felt and attached with either needle and thread or waterproof craft glue.

SIZES
1 (2, 3, 4, 5)

FINISHED MEASUREMENTS
Chest: 22¼ (24, 26½, 28¼, 31) in. / 56.5 (61, 67.5, 72.5, 79) cm

Garment designed to be worn with 2 to 4 in. / 5 to 10 cm positive ease. Sample modeled is size modeled with 2 1/4 in. / 5.5 cm positive ease.

YARN
Worsted weight yarn, shown in SweetGeorgia Yarns *Superwash Worsted* (100% superwash merino wool; 200 yd. / 182 m per 4 oz. / 115 g hank): 2 (3, 3, 3, 4) hanks in color Slate

NEEDLES
US 6 / 4 mm, 16 to 32 in. / 40 to 80 cm long circular needle and set of double-pointed needles

US 8 / 5 mm, 16 to 32 in. / 40 to 80 cm long circular needle and set of double-pointed needles or size needed to obtain gauge

NOTIONS
Stitch markers

Waste yarn

Row counter (optional)

Tapestry needle

Washable craft felt in antique white

Waterproof craft glue or sewing needle and thread to match the felt

GAUGE
18 sts and 25 rnds = 4 in. / 10 cm over St st in the round on larger needle, taken after blocking

Make sure to check your gauge.

PATTERN NOTES

- This pullover is a top-down raglan-style sweater, knit seamlessly in the round.
- Short row shaping is added to raise up the back neck for a better fit.
- The felt bones are applied post-blocking with waterproof craft glue or sewn on with thread.
- *Note:* If using the waterproof craft glue, be sure to place a piece of cardboard inside the garment while the pieces are being applied to avoid gluing the front and back of the sweater together.

PATTERN INSTRUCTIONS

CAST ON & COLLAR

With smaller dpns or 16 in. / 40 cm circular needle, CO 68 (72, 72, 72, 76) sts using the Long Tail Cast On method. Pm for BOR and join to work in the rnd, being careful not to twist the sts.

The BOR M will be at the center back of the sweater until the short rows are complete.

RND 1: Purl.
RND 2: Knit.
Rep Rnds 1 and 2 until the collar measures approx. 1 in. / 2.5 cm from the CO edge, ending with Rnd 1.

YOKE

Switch to larger needles.

WORK SHORT ROWS

SHORT ROW 1 (RS): K20 (21, 21, 21, 23), turn.
SHORT ROW 2 (WS): DS, purl to BOR M, sm, p20 (21, 21, 21, 23), turn.
SHORT ROW 3: DS, knit to 10 (11, 11, 11, 12) sts before previous DS, turn.
SHORT ROW 4: DS, purl to 10 (11, 11, 11, 12) sts before previous DS, turn.
SHORT ROW 5: DS, knit to BOR M.

YOKE SHAPING

On the following rnd, process all DS as encountered. As the yoke circumference increases, change to longer needles as needed for comfort.

Setup Rnd: Remove BOR M, k11 (12, 13, 13, 14), pm (new BOR), k12 (12, 10, 10, 10) [right sleeve], pm, k22 (24, 26, 26, 28) [front sts], pm, k12 (12, 10, 10, 10) [left sleeve], knit to new BOR M [back sts]. *The BOR M is now located at the back of the right sleeve.*

RND 1 (INC): *K1, M1L, knit to 1 st before M, M1R, k1; rep from * to end of rnd—8 sts inc.
RND 2: Knit, slipping M as encountered.
Rep [Rnds 1 and 2] 12 (13, 14, 16, 17) more times.
104 (112, 120, 136, 144) sts inc; 172 (184, 192, 208, 220) sts total:
48 (52, 56, 60, 64) sts for each front and back
38 (40, 40, 44, 46) sts for each sleeve

SEPARATE BODY AND SLEEVES

Remove BOR M, place the next 38 (40, 40, 44, 46) sts onto waste yarn for right sleeve, rm, CO 1 (1, 2, 2, 3) st(s) using the Backward Loop method for the underarm, pm (new BOR), CO 1 (1, 2, 2, 3) more st(s), knit to next M, rm, place the next 38 (40, 40, 44, 46) sts onto waste yarn for left sleeve, rm, CO 2 (2, 4, 4, 6) sts using the Backward Loop method for the underarm, knit to the new BOR M—100 (108, 120, 128, 140) total sts.

BODY

Cont in St st until body measures approx. 8 (8½, 9½, 10½, 12½) in. / 20.5 (21.5, 24, 26.5, 32) cm from underarm (or 1 in. / 2.5 cm less than total desired body length).

HEM

Switch to smaller needles.
RND 1: Purl.
RND 2: Knit.
Rep Rnds 1 and 2 until the hem measures approx. 1 in. / 2.5 cm ending with Rnd 1. Bind off all sts loosely knitwise using the larger needle.

SLEEVES (MAKE 2 THE SAME)

Place the 38 (40, 40, 44, 46) sts of one sleeve onto the set of larger dpns and distribute evenly. Rejoin the yarn at the center of the underarm sts and pick up and knit 1 (1, 2, 2, 3) st(s), pick up and knit 1 additional stitch to close the gap, knit across the live sleeve sts, pick

Barrel's Pullover Schematic

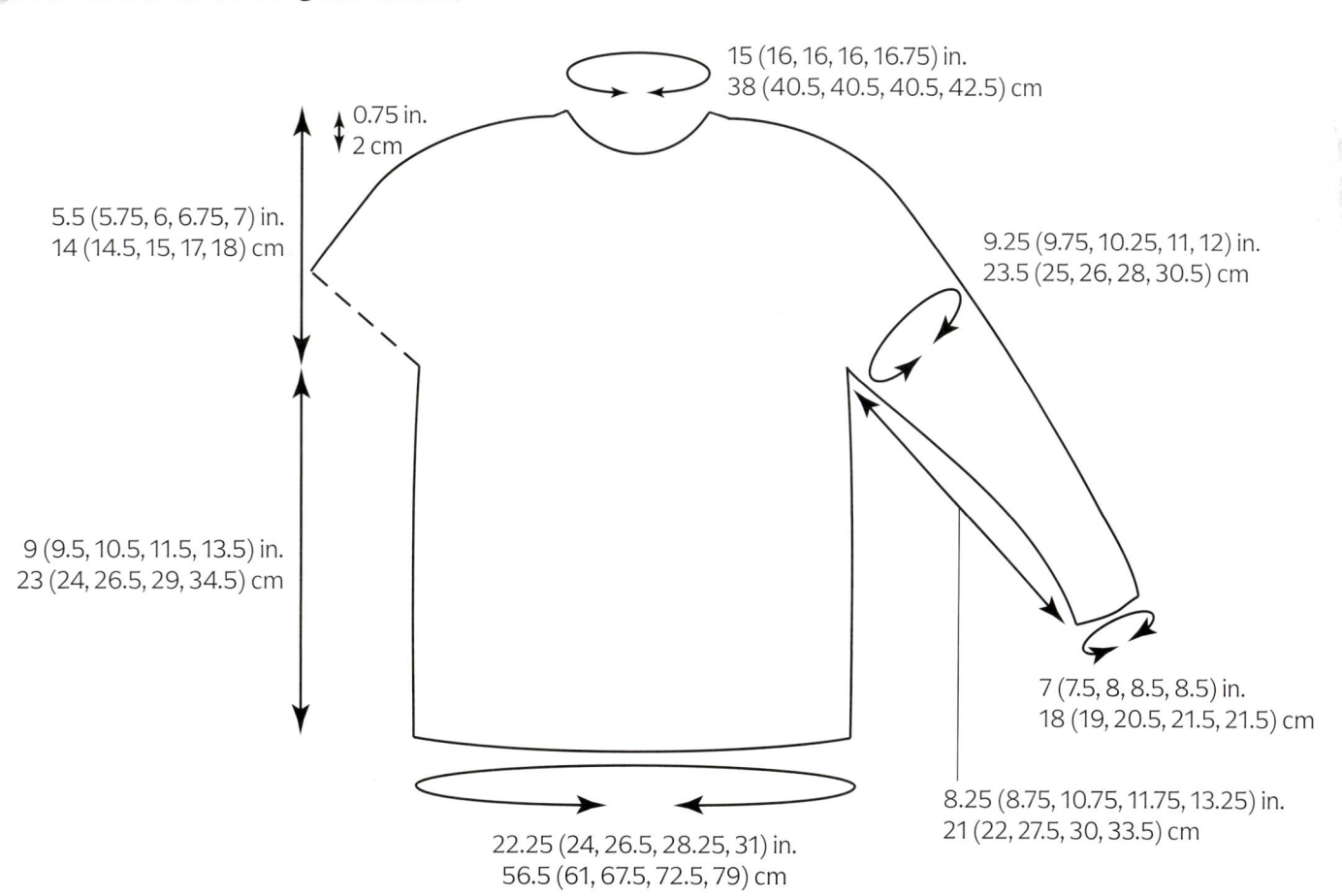

15 (16, 16, 16, 16.75) in.
38 (40.5, 40.5, 40.5, 42.5) cm

0.75 in.
2 cm

5.5 (5.75, 6, 6.75, 7) in.
14 (14.5, 15, 17, 18) cm

9.25 (9.75, 10.25, 11, 12) in.
23.5 (25, 26, 28, 30.5) cm

9 (9.5, 10.5, 11.5, 13.5) in.
23 (24, 26.5, 29, 34.5) cm

7 (7.5, 8, 8.5, 8.5) in.
18 (19, 20.5, 21.5, 21.5) cm

8.25 (8.75, 10.75, 11.75, 13.25) in.
21 (22, 27.5, 30, 33.5) cm

22.25 (24, 26.5, 28.25, 31) in.
56.5 (61, 67.5, 72.5, 79) cm

up and knit 1 st to close the gap, pick up and knit 1 (1, 2, 2, 3) more st(s). Pm for BOR and join to work in the rnd—42 (44, 46, 50, 54) total sts.

Knit 1 rnd.

DEC RND: K1, k2tog, knit to last 3 sts, ssk, k1—2 sts dec.

Cont in St st until the sleeve measures 7¼ (7¾, 9¾, 10¾, 12¼) in. / 18.5 (19.5, 25, 27.5, 31) cm from the underarm (or 1 in. / 2.5 cm less than total desired sleeve length).

AT THE SAME TIME, repeat the Dec Rnd every 1½ (1½, 2, 2, 1½) in. / 4 (4, 5, 5, 4) cm 4 (4, 4, 5, 7) more times.

10 (10, 10, 12, 16) sts dec; 32 (34, 36, 38, 38) total sts.

CUFF

Switch to smaller set of dpns.

RND 1: Purl.
RND 2: Knit.

Rep Rnds 1 and 2 until the cuff measures approx. 1 in. / 2.5 cm ending with Rnd 1. Bind off all sts loosely knitwise using the larger needle.

FINISHING

Weave in all ends and wet block to dimensions provided in the schematic. Once dry, trim all ends.

Using the Bone Templates on pages 60 and 61, make 1 tracing of each of the 17 pieces.

Scale the tracings by −25% (−20%, −10%, 0%, +10%).

After scaling the tracings, cut the tracings out of washable craft felt into 7 spinal column pieces (S1–S7), 6 rib pieces (1–3L and 1–3R), and 4 arm bone pieces (A1/2R and A1/2L), making sure to label each piece for assembly.

With needle and thread OR waterproof craft glue, attach pieces as shown in the Bone Placement Schematic. *Note: The arm bones should be placed over the fold of the top of the sleeve; the placement in the schematic is approximated for easy reading.*

FRIGHTENING FACT

The trio's names are in reference to "lock, stock, and barrel," a phrase referring to a complete set of something since the three are always seen as a group.

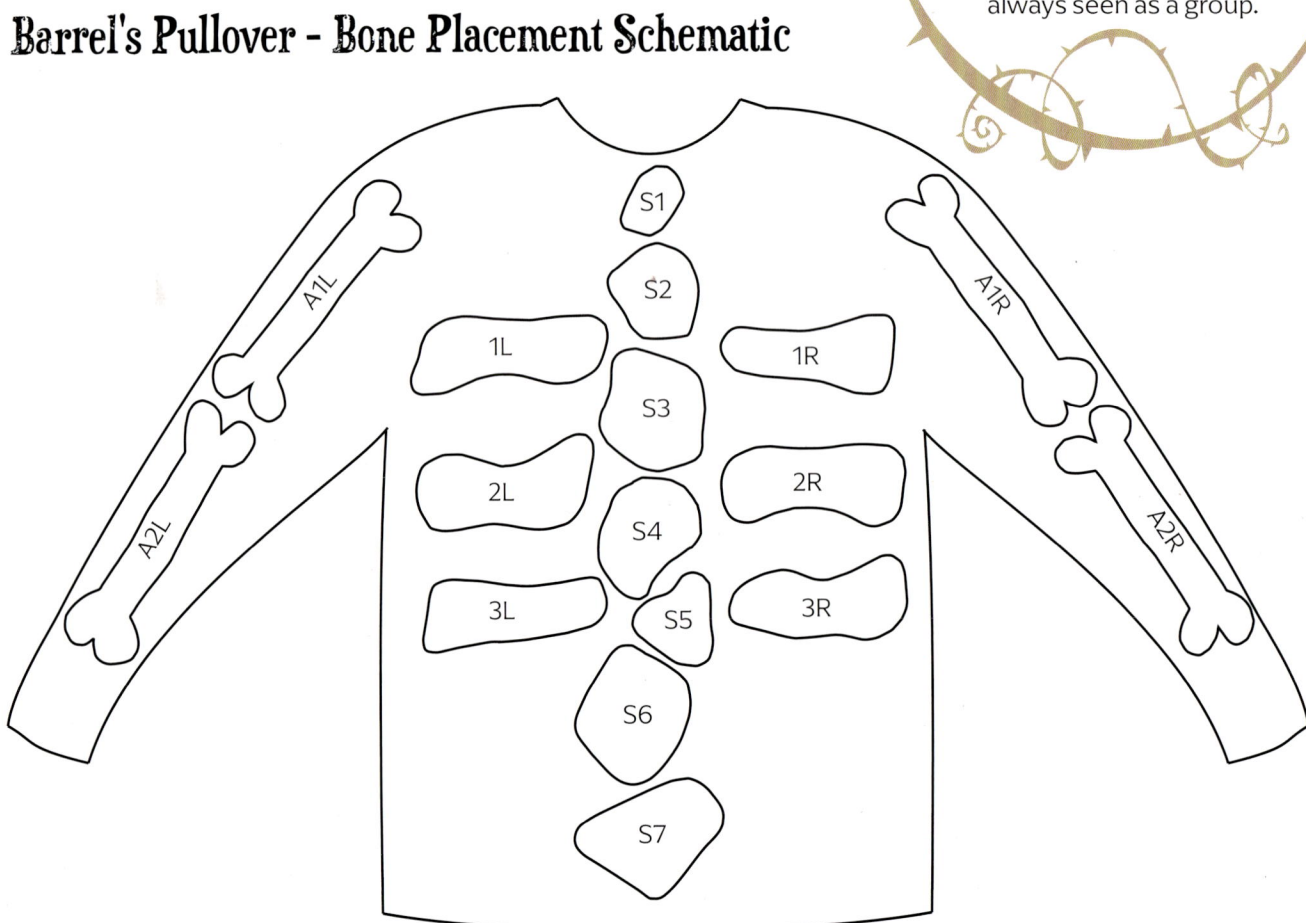

Barrel's Pullover - Bone Placement Schematic

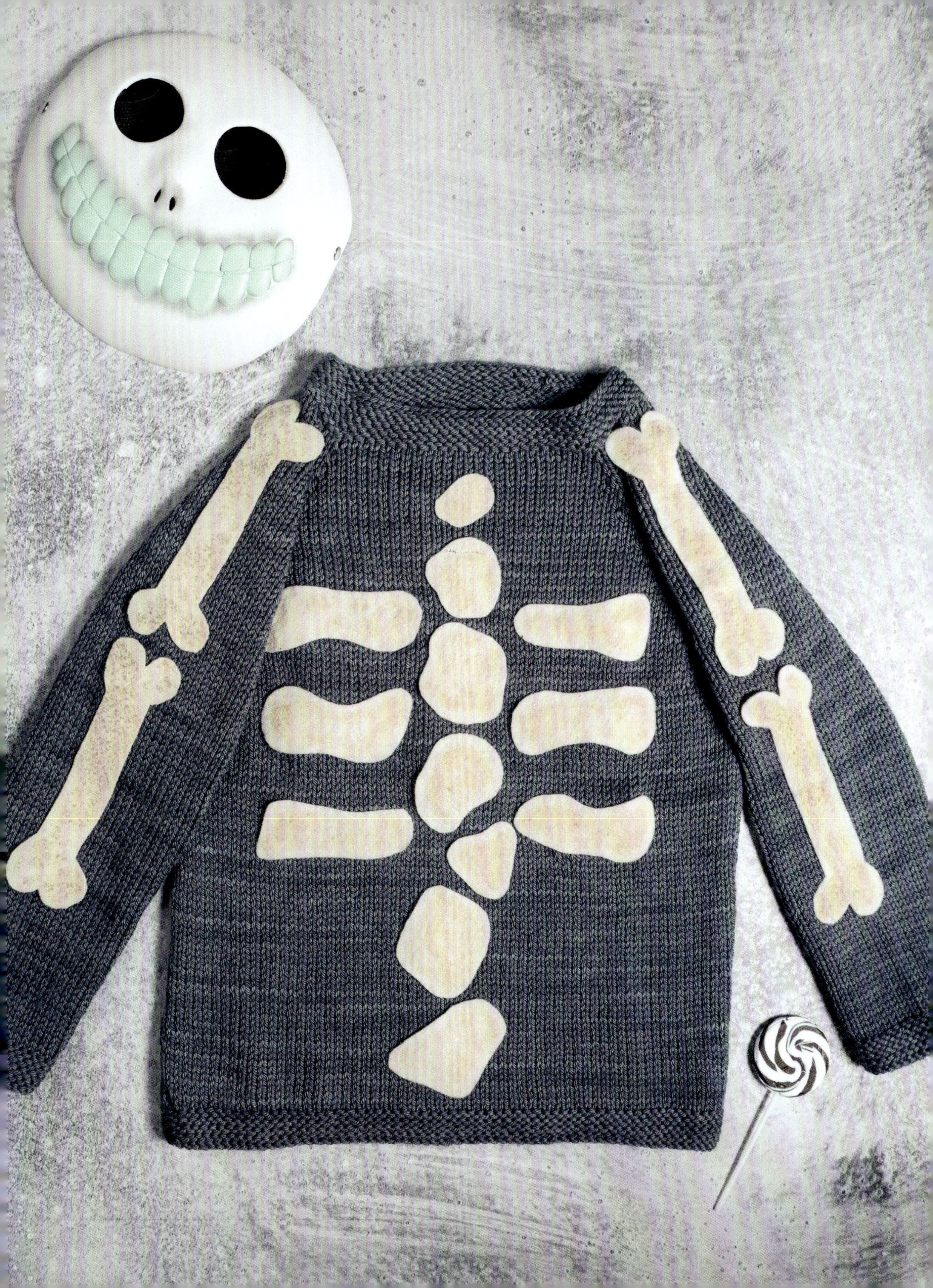

Barrel's Pullover - Bone Templates

A1R

A2R

A1L

A2L

S1

S2

S3

Barrel's Pullover - Bone Templates

1L

1R

2L

2R

3L

3R

S4

S5

S6

S7

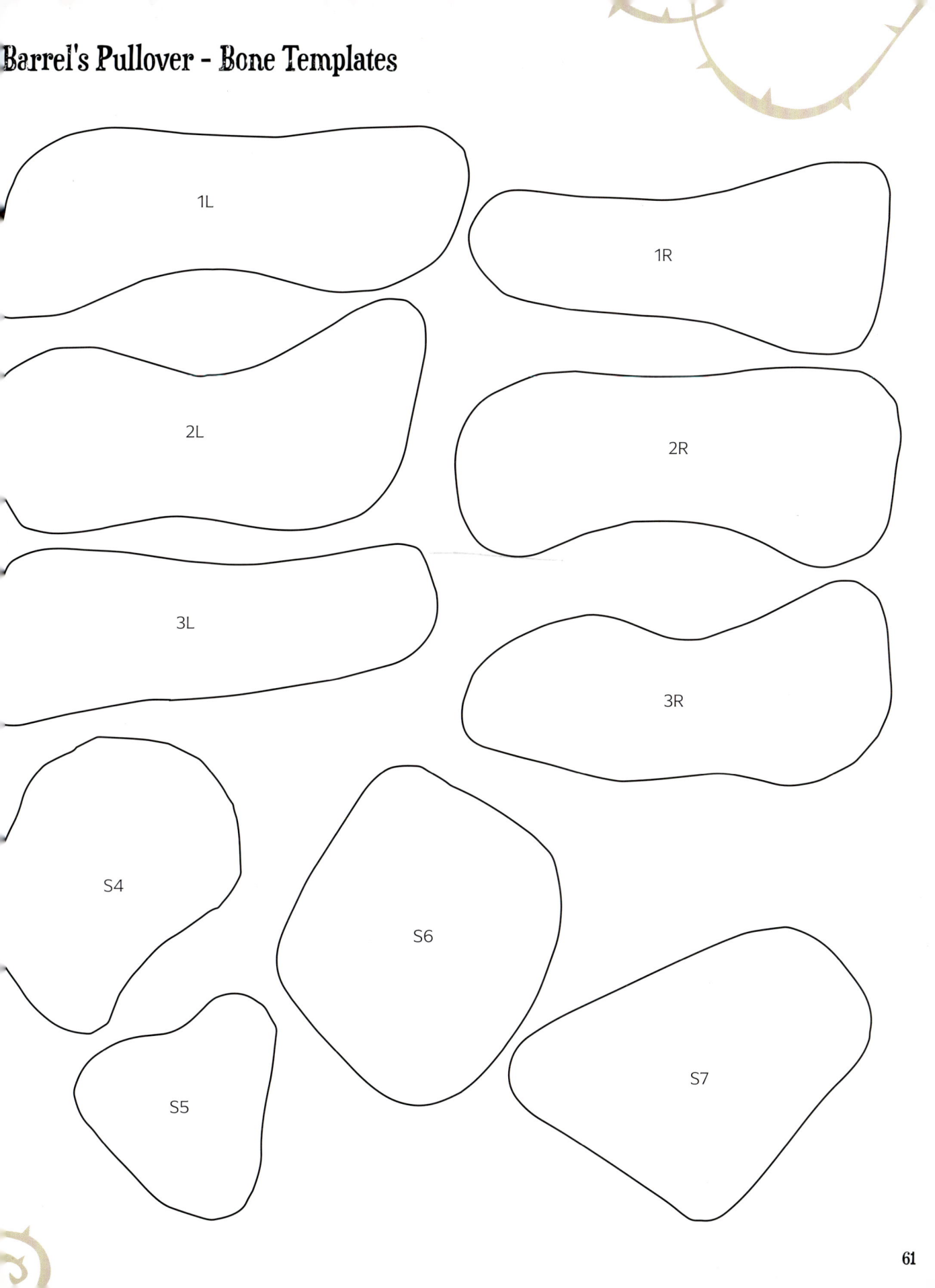

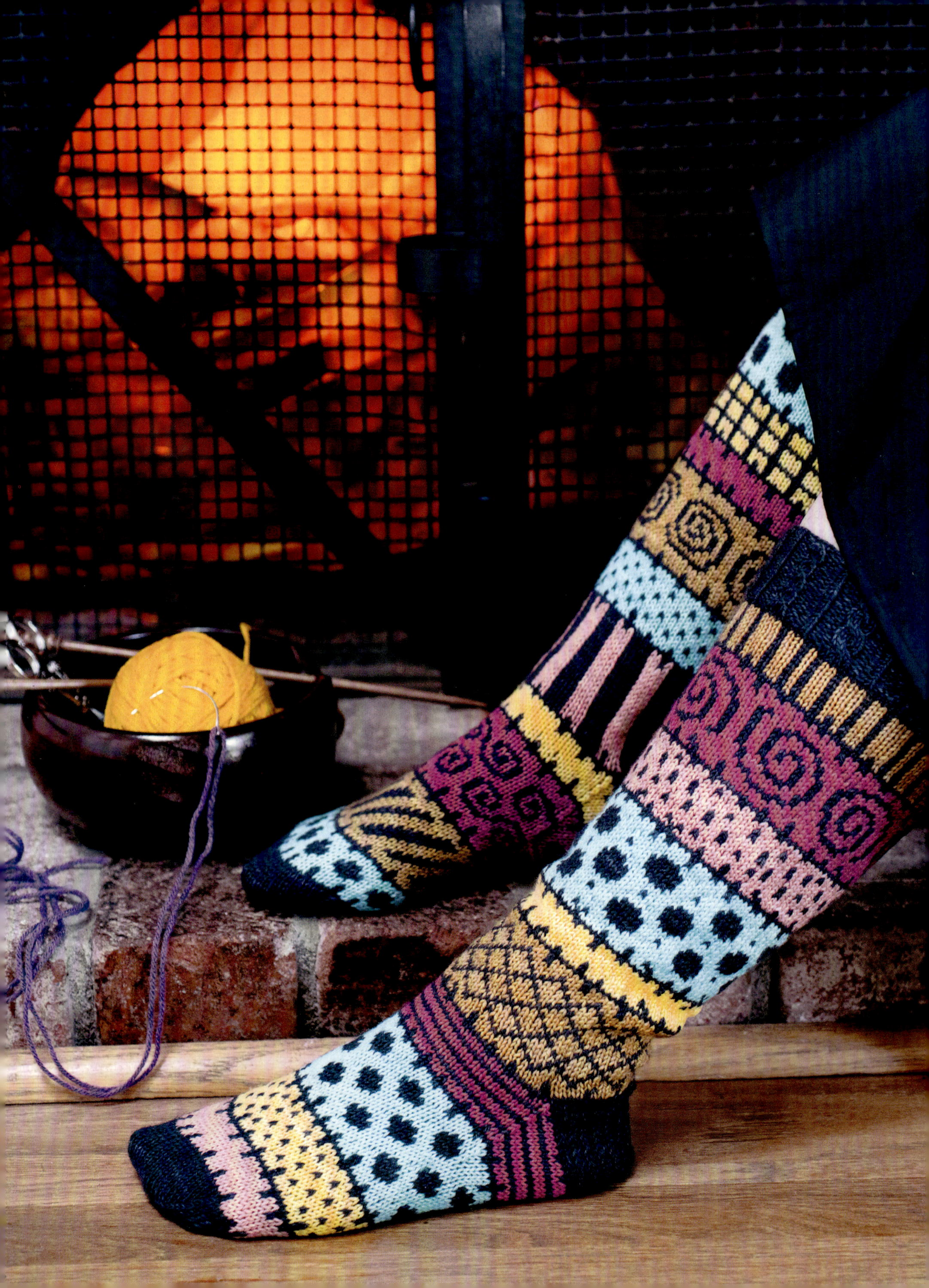

Inspired Apparel

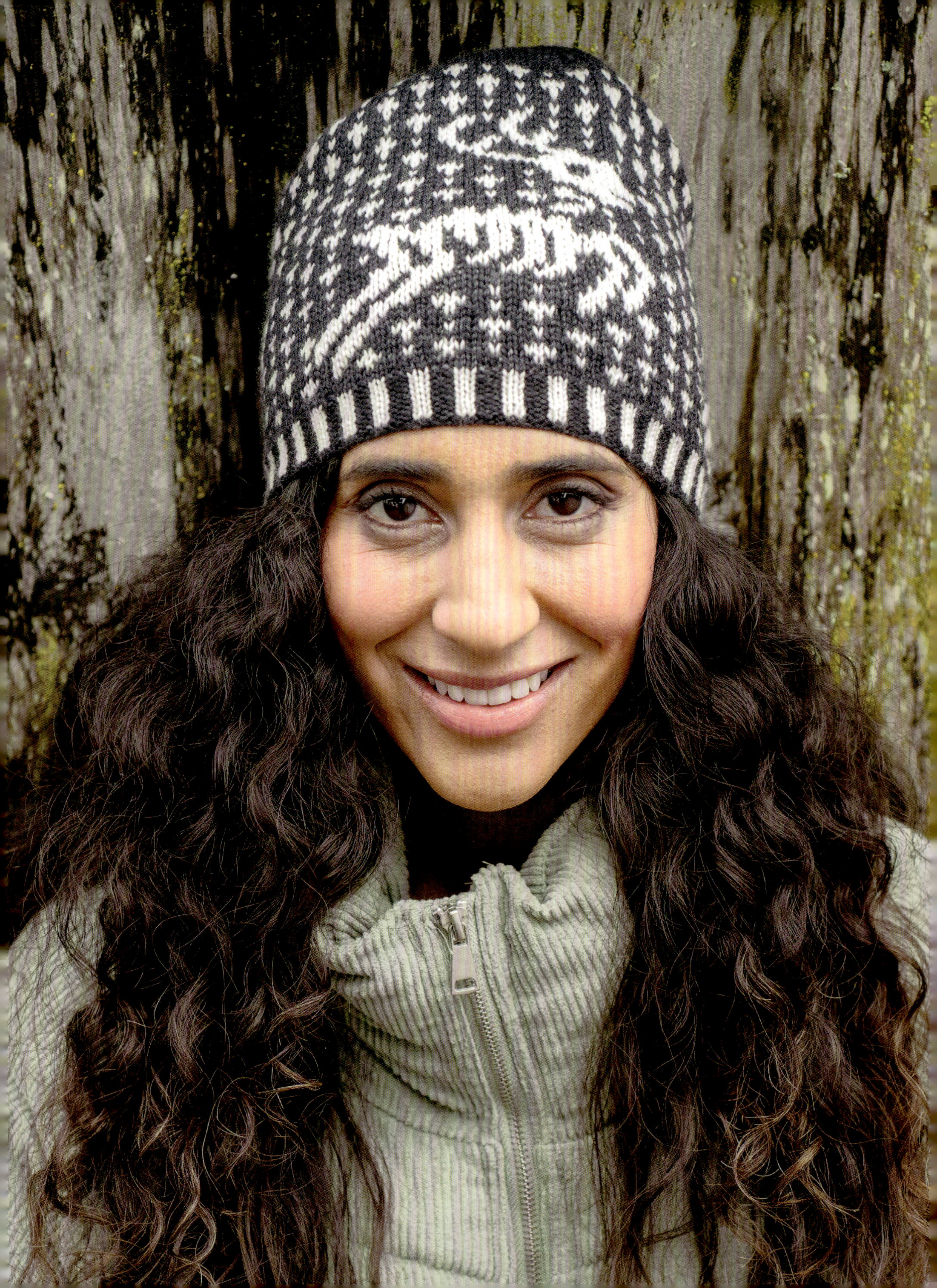

Skeletal Reindeer Hat

Designed by
Alina Appasova

"Hmm... Their construction should be exceedingly simple. I think."
–Dr. Finkelstein

SKILL LEVEL

Fellow knitters may appreciate the hands-on artistry that went into bringing the beloved skeletal reindeer to life. Once all the stop-motion animation was complete and the film was edited, the final touch of atmospheric animation was added by hand as a top layer: effects like snow, ghosts, smoke, shadows, fire, and the electricity that brings the skeletal reindeer to life in Dr. Finkelstein's laboratory. Using a technique from the 1890s called rotoscoping, an animator would draw on top of the existing stop-motion footage one frame at a time, adding the desired effect into the scene. While traditional rotoscoping was done with a projected image and traced onto glass, today it is done on the computer, still one frame at a time. The footage and rotoscoping are composited together, creating a seamless special effect.

You don't have to be an evil genius like Dr. Finkelstein to have a herd of experimental reindeer—you can knit your own! Beginning with a high-contrast corrugated rib brim, this beanie is worked in the round from the bottom up. Flying skeletal reindeer circle around set against a backdrop of falling snow worked in stranded colorwork. Coming in three sizes, this hat is perfect for all the mad scientists in your life!

SIZES
Small (Medium, Large)

FINISHED MEASUREMENTS
Circumference: 15½ (18½, 21½) in. / 39.5 (47, 54.5) cm

Height: 8¼ (9, 9¾) in. / 21 (23, 24.5) cm

The hat is designed to be worn with 1–3" / 2.5–7.5 cm negative ease.

YARN
Fingering weight yarn, shown in LolaBean Yarn Co. *Turtle Bean* (80% merino, 10% cashmere, 10% nylon; 435 yd. / 398 m per 3½ oz. / 100 g hank)

COLORWAYS:
- Color A: Darkness Falls, 1 hank
- Color B: Au Naturel, 1 hank

NEEDLES
US 3 / 3.25 mm, 16 in. / 40 cm long circular needle and set of 4 or 5 double-pointed needles or size needed to obtain gauge

NOTIONS
Stitch markers (8; 1 unique for BOR)

Tapestry needle

GAUGE
31 sts and 35 rounds = 4 in. / 10 cm in stranded colorwork pattern, taken after blocking

Make sure to check your gauge.

PATTERN NOTES

- The hat is worked in the round from the bottom up. It may be helpful to place a marker between pattern repeats in the colorwork portion of the hat.
- Instructions are provided for size Small first, with larger sizes in parentheses. When only one set of numbers is provided, it applies to all sizes.
- When working the stranded colorwork chart, catch floats longer than 5 stitches.
- When working the corrugated rib, be sure to move the Color A yarn to the back between the needles after completing the second purl stitch so all floats are on the WS of the hat.
- When the circumference of the hat becomes too small for the circular needle during the Crown Shaping, change to dpns to finish the hat.

PATTERN STITCHES

Corrugated Rib (worked over a multiple of 4 sts)

All Rnds: *K2 with Color B, p2 with Color A; rep from * to end of rnd.

PATTERN INSTRUCTIONS

CAST ON & BRIM

With circular needle and Color A, CO 112 (136, 160) sts using the Twisted German Cast On method. Pm for BOR and join to work in the rnd, being careful not to twist the sts.
Join Color B.
Work in Corrugated Rib for 8 rnds.
Do not break Color B; carry it loosely up the inside of the hat until it is used again.

BODY

SETUP RND 1: With Color A, *k2, p2; rep from * to end of rnd.
SETUP RND 2 (INC): With Color A, *k13 (16, 19), kfb; rep from * to end of rnd—120 (144, 168) sts.
Begin Skeletal Reindeer chart, reading all rows from right to left as for working in the rnd. Work Rnds 1–48 (51, 54) once (the chart for each size is worked three times across each rnd). On the final rnd, remove all markers as encountered except the BOR M. Once complete, break Color B. The remainder of the hat will be worked with Color A only.

CROWN SHAPING
ADJUSTMENT RND:

SIZE SMALL ONLY (DEC):
*K2tog, k13, pm; rep from * to end of rnd—112 sts rem.

SIZE MEDIUM ONLY:
*K18, pm; rep from * to end of rnd—144 sts.

SIZE LARGE ONLY (DEC):
*K2tog, k19, pm; rep from * to end of rnd—160 sts rem.

ALL SIZES:
Next Rnd: Knit.
RND 1 (DEC): *K2tog, knit to 2 sts before M, ssk, sm; rep from * to end of rnd—16 sts dec.
RND 2: Knit.
Rep [Rnds 1 and 2] 4 (6, 7) more times—32 sts rem.
Next Rnd (dec): *K2tog, ssk, rm; rep from * to end of rnd—16 sts rem. *Leave the BOR M in place.*
Next Rnd: Knit.
Next Rnd (dec): *K2tog; rep from * to end of rnd—8 sts rem.
Break yarn, pull tail through remaining live sts, and cinch closed. Secure tail to WS.

FINISHING

Weave in all ends and wet block to measurements. Allow to dry completely. Trim all ends.

Skeletal Reindeer Chart

Key

☐ Knit
■ Color A
☐ Color B
▭ Pattern repeat - Size Small Only (40 sts)
▭ Pattern repeat - Size Medium Only (48 sts)
▭ Pattern repeat - Size Large Only (56 sts)

FRIGHTENING FACT

Jack's sleigh is shaped like a coffin.

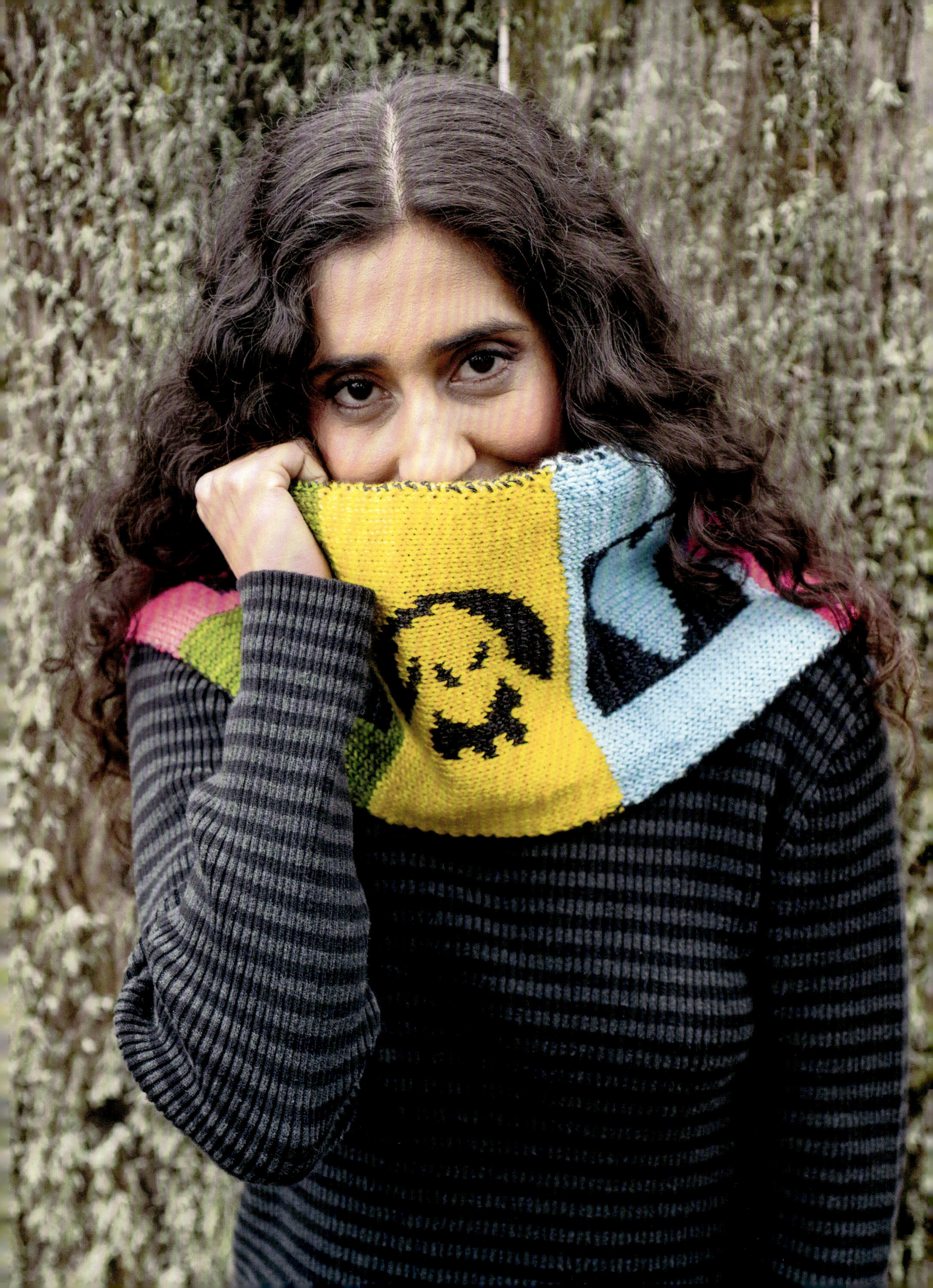

Oogie Boogie Roulette Cowl

Designed by Jessica Goddard

"What's that you were sayin' about luck, rag doll?"
— Oogie Boogie

SKILL LEVEL

Wanting a dual look for Oogie Boogie's underground lair, designers created a jagged, heavy space with lots of torture devices when the regular set lights were on, and a more primitive, ghoulish look with ultraviolet paint under black lights. Oogie Boogie's central table goes from a stone slab to a sinister roulette wheel with the flick of a switch—the perfect backdrop for the audience's introduction to a scary, green Oogie Boogie and his terrifying casino-style chamber. Complete with evil slot machine robots, playing card soldiers, and snakes in the dice, Oogie Boogie is not above cheating to get what he wants and enjoys gambling with the lives of others.

Place your bets! Inspired by Oogie Boogie's neon-colored lair and roulette wheel, and adorned with skulls, Oogie Boogie, hearts, diamonds, clubs, and spades, this double-knit cowl is more cozy than menacing. Beginning with a provisional or temporary cast on, the cowl is worked flat back and forth in rows sideways. The cast on is removed and live stitches are grafted together to create a seamless loop with inverted colors on either side. Hope for a winning spin and cast on!

SIZES
One size

FINISHED MEASUREMENTS
Height: 7½ in. / 19 cm
Circumference: 37 in. / 94 cm

YARN
DK weight yarn, shown in Biscotte Yarns *DK Pure* (90% merino wool superwash, 10% silk; 284 yd. / 260 m per 4 oz. / 115 g hank)

COLORWAYS:
- Main Color (MC): Charbon, 1 hank
- Contrast Color 1 (CC1): Poudreuse, 1 hank
- Contrast Color 2 (CC2): Rose Neon, 1 hank
- Contrast Color 3 (CC3): Vert Biscotte, 1 hank
- Contrast Color 4 (CC4): Soleil, 1 hank

NEEDLES
US 6 / 4 mm straight knitting needles and set of 3 dpns or size needed to obtain gauge

NOTIONS
Locking stitch marker

G-6 / 4 mm crochet hook

Smooth waste yarn in 2 contrasting colors

Tapestry needle

GAUGE
23 sts and 29½ rows = 4 in. / 10 cm in 2-color double knitting, taken before blocking

Make sure to check your gauge.

PATTERN NOTES

- The cowl is worked flat, from end to end, using the Double Knitting method. Charts are provided (pages 72 and 73) for the entirety of the double-knitting work.
- A provisional cast on is used to allow a seamless joining of the work in the round using Kitchener stitch.
- Double knitting is a technique that produces a double thickness of fabric that looks like right-side stockinette stitch on both sides. The two sides of the knitting are inverse colors; the two sides mirror one another.
- The stitch count does not change for the entire project.
- All odd-numbered rows are RS rows and should be read from right to left; all even-numbered rows are WS rows and should be read from left to right.
- Orange lines in the chart indicate where it is recommended to swap colors.
- Edge stitches are worked at each end of the chart rows to keep the edges neat; these stitches are not represented on the chart.

PATTERN INSTRUCTIONS

CAST ON & SETUP

*Using 1 color of waste yarn and the crochet hook, CO 43 sts using the Crochet Provisional Cast On method onto 1 dpn.

Rep from * using a second color of waste yarn.

43 sts on each of 2 dpns (86 sts total). Clip a locking marker into the edge stitch of the back dpn. This marker will be used during grafting; do not remove this marker until directed.

Holding the dpns parallel, work a slip stitch row (no stitches are knit) as follows: **Slip 1 st purlwise from front dpn to straight needle, slip 1 st purlwise from back dpn to same straight needle; rep from ** until all 86 sts are on one straight needle (sts are alternating in color).

BODY OF COWL

Work Rows 1–271 of Chart A (pages 72 and 73) once, reading RS rows from right to left and WS rows from left to right, joining/breaking CCs as required, as follows:

RS Rows: Holding MC and CC yarns together, k2tog. Work across the 41 sts of the charted RS row using the Double Knitting method. Holding MC and CC yarns together, k2tog.

WS Rows: Holding MC and CC yarns together, p2tog. Work across the 41 sts of the charted WS row using the Double Knitting method. Holding MC and CC yarns together, p2tog.

When finished, break MC and CC4 leaving a tail of each yarn approx. 4 times the width of the scarf.

GRAFTING

Hold the working needle in your left hand; hold 2 dpns in your right hand, parallel, one in front of the other.

Work a slip stitch row (no stitches are knit) as follows: *Slip 1 CC4 st purlwise from LHN to front dpn, slip 1 MC st purlwise from LHN to back dpn; rep from * until the front dpn holds 43 CC4 sts and the back dpn holds 43 MC sts.

Carefully remove the provisional CO waste yarn from cast on row with the locking marker and place the live sts onto a third dpn. The locking marker can be removed.

Fold the scarf into a loop so the live sts from the provisional CO are parallel to the dpn holding the CC4 sts. Graft these two sets of live sts using the CC4 tail and Kitchener stitch.

Carefully remove the remaining provisional CO waste yarn and place the live sts onto a dpn.

Holding the two remaining dpns parallel, graft these two sets of live sts using the MC tail and Kitchener stitch.

FINISHING

Weave in the ends carefully by inserting a tail into the tapestry needle and weaving the tail into the hollow of the double knitting. The original sample was not blocked, but if you would like to smooth out your stitches, you may wish to do a gentle steam block.

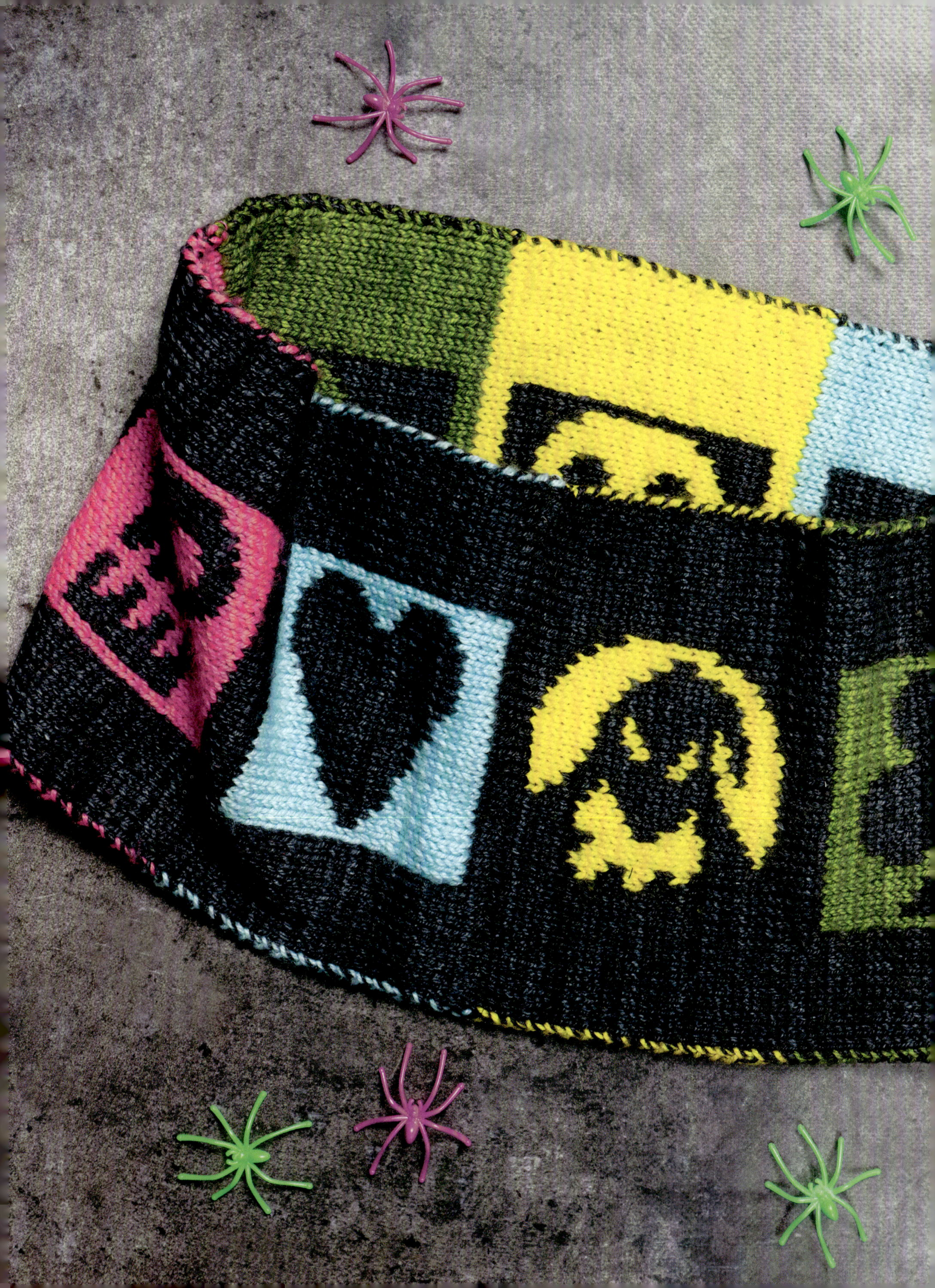

Chart A

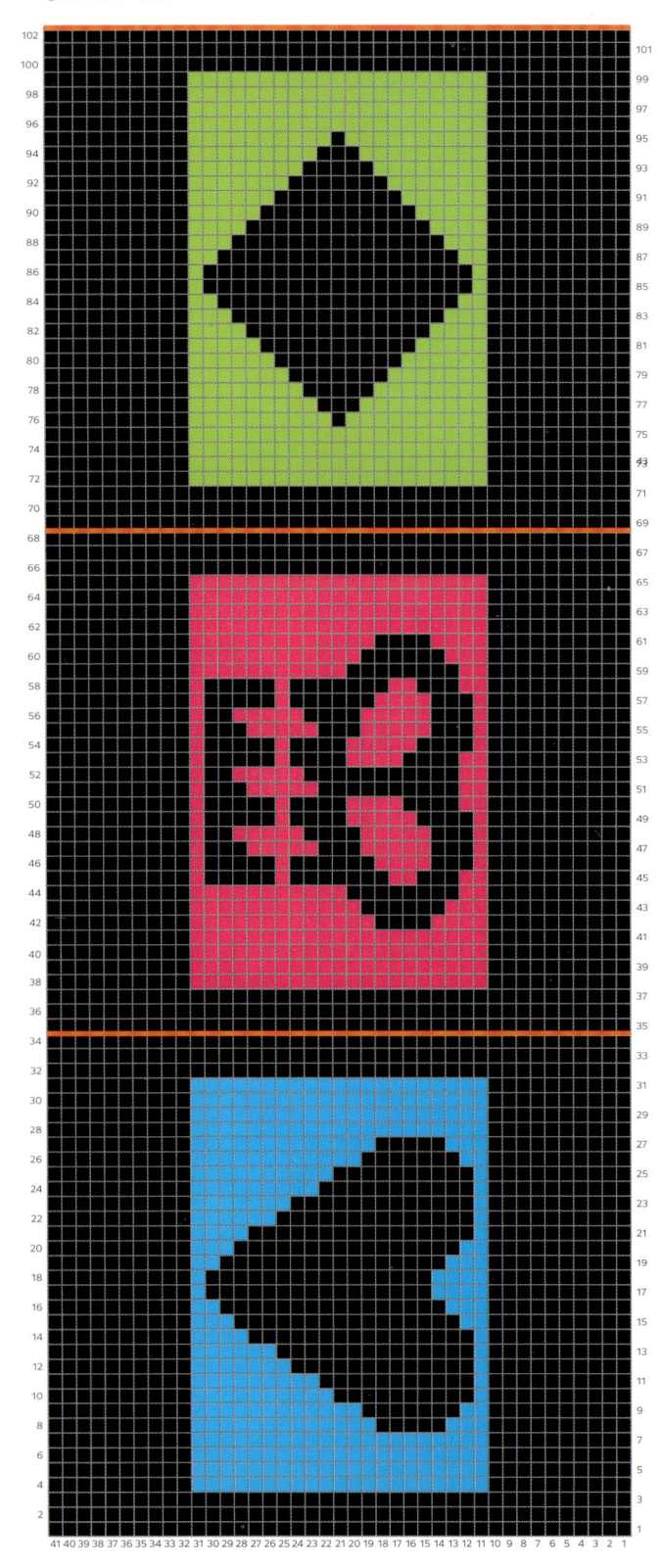

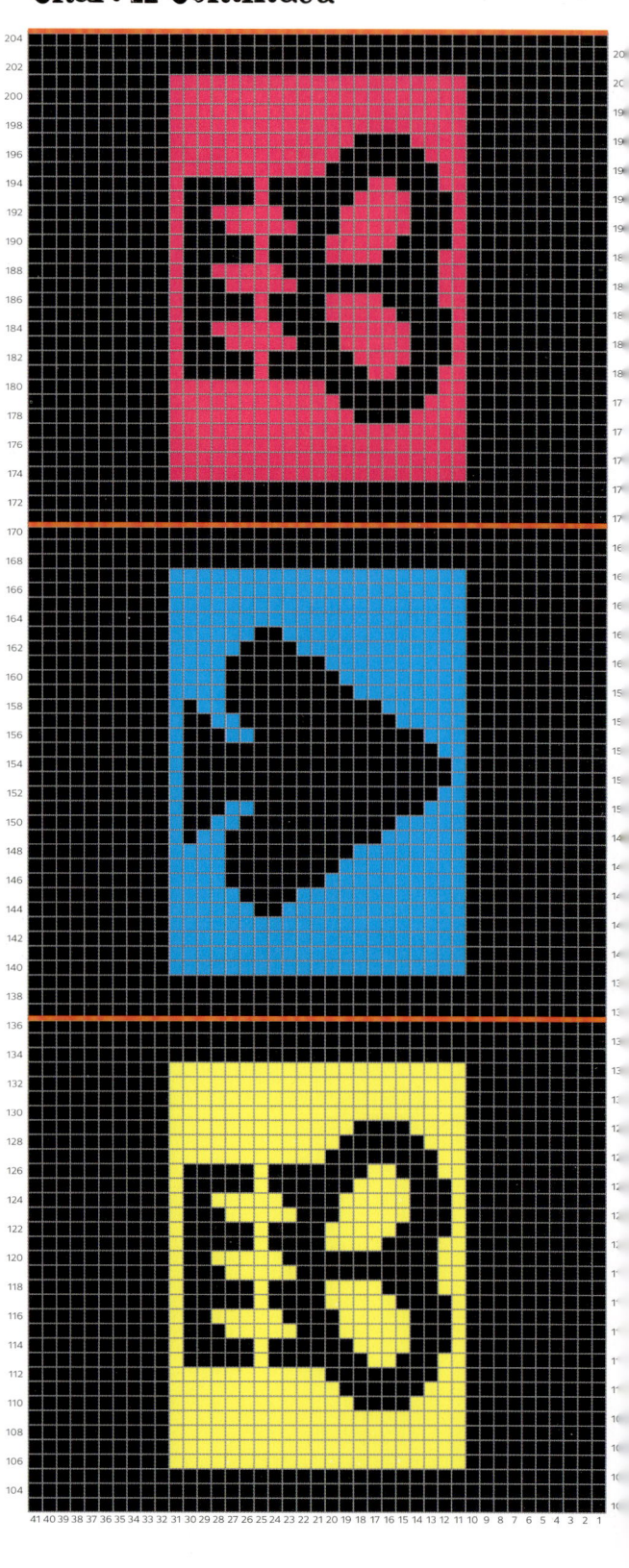

Chart A Continued

72

Chart A Continued

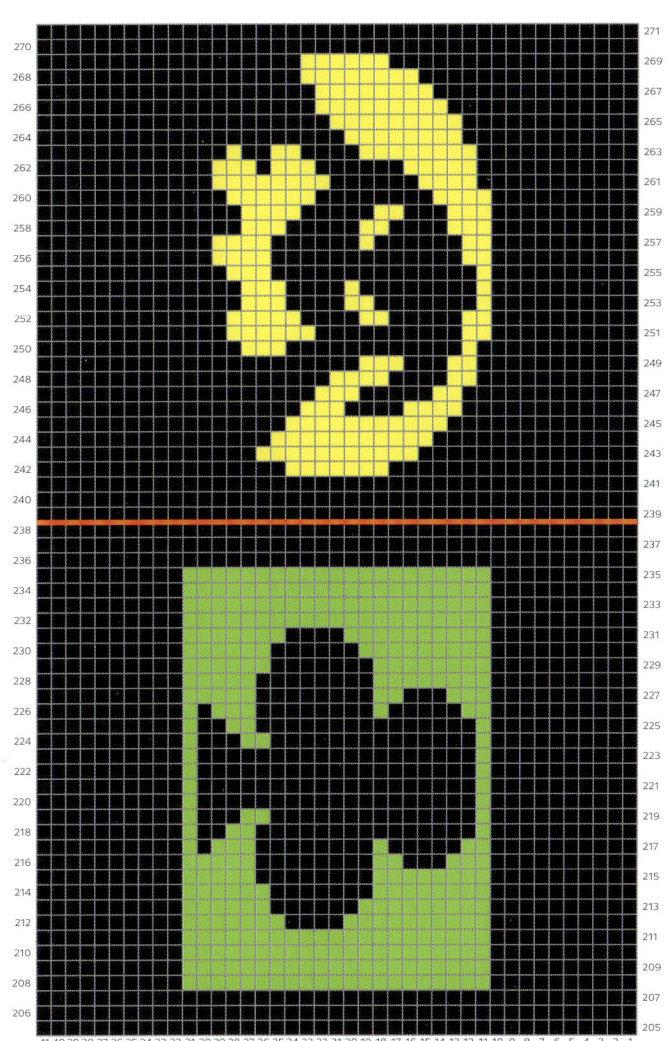

Key

- ☐ Knit
- ■ MC
- ■ CC1
- ■ CC2
- ■ CC3
- ■ CC4
- — Location of color change

FRIGHTENING FACT

The scene when Oogie Boogie's seam comes undone and it's revealed that he's filled with bugs took animators four months to film.

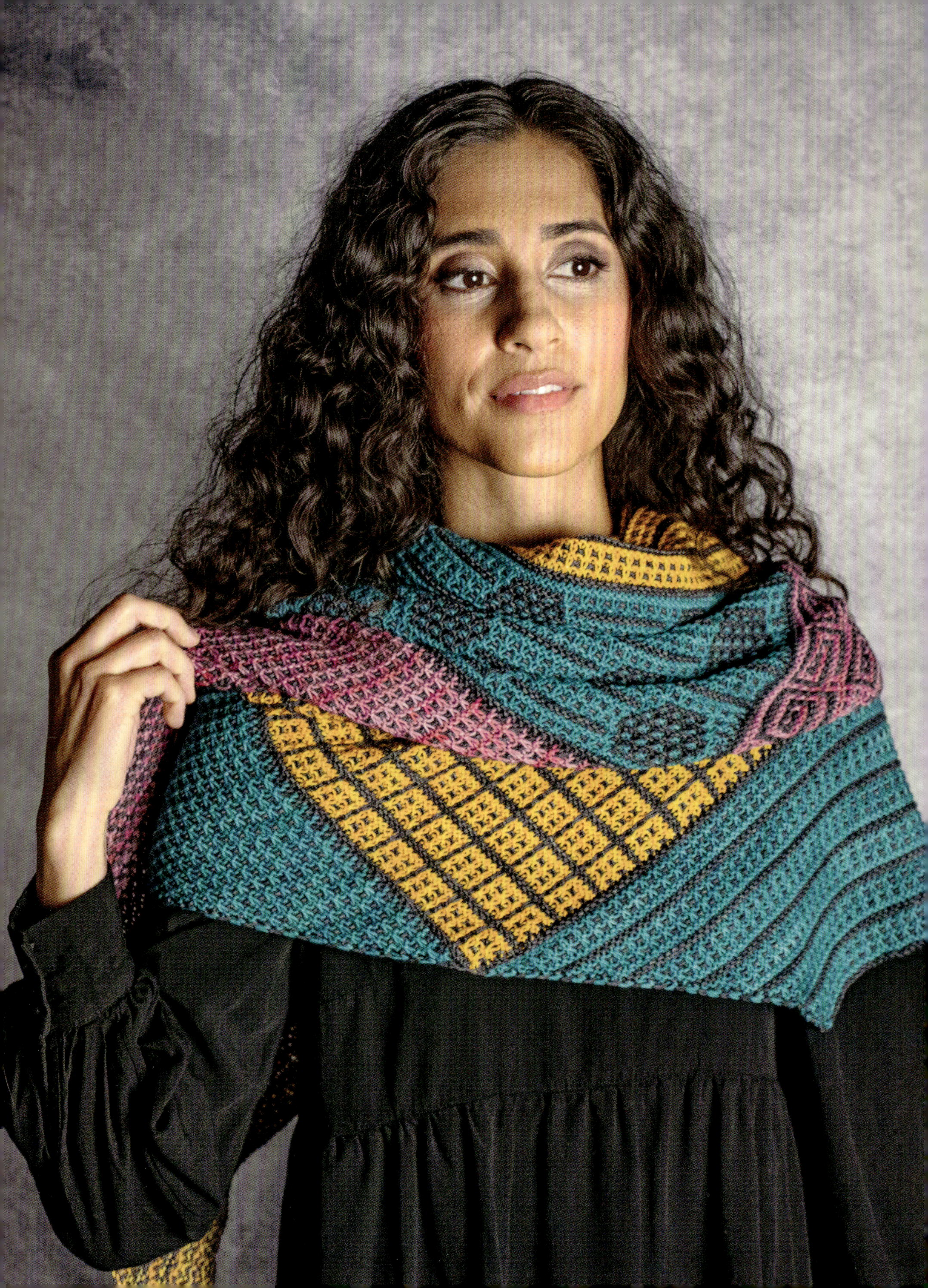

Sally's Dress Wrap

Designed by
Alina Appasova

Jack: "Sally, I need your help more than anyone."

Sally: "You certainly do, Jack. I had the most terrible vision."

Jack: "That's splendid!"

SKILL LEVEL

Sewn together by Dr. Finkelstein, Sally was created as a caretaker and companion for the mad scientist. Scraps of blue fabric for skin, bits of random cloth for a dress, and dry leaves for stuffing, as well as her visible stitching and jerky movements, give her the appearance of a full-size rag doll. Mold-making supervisor John Reed states, "She's basically a Frankenstein-like puppet. She looks like she's sewn together from a bunch of scraps." Although she depends on Dr. Finkelstein for her basic needs like shelter and food, Sally feels little connection to Dr. Finkelstein. Instead, she finds a kindred spirit in Jack, whom she watches from afar. While she may not agree with Jack's intentions regarding Christmas, she does what she can to assist him in his quest to bring Christmas to Halloween Town.

Writer Caroline Thompson describes the self-reliant and clever Sally as "Jack's truest friend, resourceful and brave. Only she understands what Jack is going through because she, too, dreams of something else from life. They are very much alike, but there is one crucial difference: While Jack's dilemma gives *Nightmare Before Christmas* its plot, Sally gives it its heart."

Inspired by Sally's iconic patchwork dress, this modular parallelogram wrap is made entirely out of triangles. Worked flat back and forth in garter slip-stitch colorwork, or mosaic knitting, the wrap has no stranding along the back. A triangle is completed, then the subsequent triangle is made by picking stitches up along the edge and working off the previous one. There's no need to patchwork pieces together like Sally does! A slip-stitch edging is worked on all sides to create a stretchy and tidy edge.

SIZES
One size

FINISHED MEASUREMENTS
Length: 88 in. / 223.5 cm

Width: 14 in. / 35.5 cm

YARN
Fingering weight yarn, shown in Keenan Hand Dyed Yarn *Sock Yarn* (75% superwash merino, 25% nylon; 463 yd. / 423 m per 3½ oz. / 100 g hank)

COLORWAYS:
- Color A: Melancholy Oyster Boy, 2 hanks
- Color B: Zero's Way, 1 hank
- Color C: Burton's Bunny, 1 hank
- Color D: You Poisoned Me for the Last Time, 1 hank

NEEDLES
US 4 / 3.5 mm, 24 in. / 60 cm long circular needle or size needed to obtain gauge

NOTIONS
Tapestry needle

Stitch markers

Locking stitch markers (2; in different colors)

GAUGE
24 sts and 48 rows = 4 in. / 10 cm worked flat in 2-color mosaic st, taken after blocking

Make sure to check your gauge.

PATTERN NOTES

- The shawl is a parallelogram made from triangles. You will start with one triangle, then pick up stitches along one edge to create the next triangle, and so on.

- Written instructions are provided for the entirety of the pattern. Optional charts are provided. Read carefully through all written instructions before working from the charts to ensure no instructions get missed. When working from the charts, colors are used to indicate which yarn (Color A, B, C, or D) to use. However, in some cases, charts will be used in multiple sections, and therefore, the stitches are shown in white. Follow the written instructions to determine what color will be used for those charts / rows of the chart.

- Carry unused yarns up the edge rather than cutting between each row used. Color changes always occur at the beginning of the right-side rows. To change colors, pick up new yarn from the back without twisting.

- To work from the charts, read all RS (odd-numbered) rows from right to left. The WS rows are not charted except for the final row of the charts to ensure that the pattern is ended with a WS row; read this WS row from left to right.

- To work the WS rows from the charts:
  - For Left Triangles and Parallelogram (Sections 1, 3, and 5): With yarn used on previous RS row, sl1 knitwise wyib, knit the knit sts and slip the slipped sts purlwise wyif to last 2 sts, sl2 wyif.
  - For Right Triangles (Sections 2 and 4): With yarn used on previous RS row, sl1 wyif, knit the knit sts and slip the slipped sts purlwise wyif to last st, sl1 wyif (sm as encountered).

PATTERN STITCHES

Garter Ridge Left (worked over any number of sts)

Row 1 (RS, dec): K2tog tbl, knit to last st, p1—1 st dec.

Row 2 (WS): Sl1 knitwise wyib, knit to last 2 sts, sl2 wyif.

Rep Rows 1 and 2 for patt.

Garter Ridge Right (worked over any number of sts)

Row 1 (RS, dec): K1 tbl, knit to last 2 sts, k2tog—1 st dec.

Row 2 (WS): Sl1 wyif, knit to last st, sl1 wyif.

Rep Rows 1 and 2 for patt.

PATTERN INSTRUCTIONS

CAST ON & SETUP

With Color A, CO 124 sts using the Twisted German Cast On method. Do not join to work in the rnd.

NEXT ROW (WS): Sl1 knitwise wyib, clip locking M-A to slipped st, knit to last 2 sts, sl2 wyif.

SECTION 1: LEFT TRIANGLE

Join Color B.
With Color B, work Garter Ridge Left 1 time—123 sts rem.

PART 1-A

Follow written instructions below or work from Chart A (page 82).

ROW 1 (RS, DEC): With A, k2tog tbl, k1, (k1, sl1 wyib) 3 times, *k3, sl1 wyib, (k1, sl1 wyib) 2 times; rep from * to last 2 sts, k1, p1—1 st dec.

ROW 2 (WS, AND ALL WS ROWS): With yarn used on previous RS row, sl1 knitwise wyib, knit the knit sts and slip the slipped sts purlwise wyif to last 2 sts, sl2 wyif.

ROW 3 (DEC): With B, k2tog tbl, k6, *sl1 wyib, k1, sl1 wyib, k5; rep from * to last 2 sts, k1, p1—1 st dec.

ROW 5 (DEC): With A, k2tog tbl, k1, (k1, sl1 wyib) 2 times, *k3, sl1 wyib, (k1, sl1 wyib) 2 times; rep from * to last 2 sts, k1, p1—1 st dec.

ROW 7 (DEC): With B, k2tog tbl, knit to last st, p1—1 st dec.

ROW 9 (DEC): With A, k2tog tbl, k1, (k1, sl1 wyib) 3 times, *k3, sl1 wyib, (k1, sl1 wyib) 2 times; rep from * to last 6 sts, k3, sl1 wyib, k1, p1—1 st dec.

ROW 11 (DEC): With B, k2tog tbl, k6, *sl1 wyib, k1, sl1 wyib, k5; rep from * to last 6 sts, (k1, sl1 wyib) 2 times, k1, p1—1 st dec.

ROW 13 (DEC): With A, k2tog tbl, k1, (k1, sl1 wyib) 2 times, *k3, sl1 wyib, (k1, sl1 wyib) 2 times; rep from * to last 6 sts, k3, sl1 wyib, k1, p1—1 st dec.

ROW 15 (DEC): With B, k2tog tbl, knit to last st, p1—1 st dec.

ROW 16: With B, sl1 knitwise wyib, knit to last 2 sts, sl2 wyif.
Rep [Rows 1–16] 5 more times. 48 sts dec; 75 sts rem.
Break Color B.

PART 1-B

With Color A, work Garter Ridge Left 1 time—74 sts rem.
Join Color C.
With C, work Garter Ridge Left 1 time—73 sts rem.

Follow the written instructions below or work from Chart B (page 82) using Color A for the black charted rows and Color C for the white charted rows:

ROW 1 (RS, DEC): With A, k2tog tbl, k2, *sl1 wyib, k1; rep from * to last st, p1—1 st dec.

ROW 2 (WS): With yarn used on previous RS row, sl1 knitwise wyib, knit the knit sts and slip the slipped sts purlwise wyif to last 2 sts, sl2 wyif.

ROW 3 (DEC): With C, k2tog tbl, knit to last st, p1—1 st dec.

ROW 4: With C, sl1 knitwise wyib, knit to last 2 sts, sl2 wyif.

Rep [Rows 1–4] 33 more times. 68 sts dec; 5 sts rem.
Break Color C. Continue with Color A only.

ROW 137 (RS, DEC): K2tog tbl, k2, p1—4 sts rem.

ROW 138 (WS): Sl1 knitwise wyib, k1, sl2 wyif.

ROW 139 (DEC): K2tog tbl, k1, p1—3 sts rem.

ROW 140 (DEC): Sl1 knitwise wyib, k2tog—2 sts rem.

ROW 141: Sl1 wyif, clip locking M-B to slipped st, k1.

SECTION 2: RIGHT TRIANGLE

Rotate the work 90 degrees clockwise (2 sts on RHN). With Color A still attached and RS facing, pick up and knit 121 sts along the adjacent edge of the piece (under both legs of the slipped sts). *Note: The first stitch should be picked up from the stitch below the leftmost st on the RHN. Knit into the st marked by M-A, rm-A—124 sts total.*
Do not remove M-B.

SETUP ROW (WS): Sl1 wyif, knit to last st, sl1 wyif.
Join Color D.
With D, work Garter Ridge Right 1 time—123 sts rem.

PART 2-A

Follow written instructions below or work from Chart C (page 82).

ROW 1 (RS, DEC): With A, k1 tbl, (k1, sl1 wyib) 2 times, k7, sl1 wyib, k1, pm, *(sl1 wyib, k1) 7 times, sl1 wyib, k7, sl1 wyib, k1, pm; rep from * to last 13 sts, (sl1 wyib, k1) 4 times, sl1 wyib, k2, k2tog—1 st dec.

ROW 2 (WS, AND ALL WS ROWS): With yarn used on previous RS row, sl1 wyif, knit the knit sts and slip the slipped sts purlwise wyif to last st, sl1 wyif (sm as encountered).

ROW 3 (DEC): With D, k1 tbl, k4, (sl1 wyib, k1) 3 times, sl1 wyib, k2, *sm, k15, (sl1 wyib, k1) 3 times, sl1 wyib, k2; rep from * to last M, sm, k10, k2tog—1 st dec.

ROW 5 (DEC): With A, k1 tbl, k2, sl1 wyib, k9, sl1 wyib, *sm, k13, sl1 wyib, k9, sl1 wyib; rep from * to last M, sm, k9, k2tog—1 st dec.

ROW 7 (DEC): With D, k1 tbl, k3, (sl1 wyib, k1) 5 times, *sm, k14, (sl1 wyib, k1) 5 times; rep from * to last M, sm, k8, k2tog—1 st dec.

ROW 9 (DEC): With A, k1 tbl, k1, sl1 wyib, k11, *sm, (sl1 wyib, k1) 6 times, sl1 wyib, k11; rep from * to last M, sm, (sl1 wyib, k1) 3 times, k1, k2tog—1 st dec.

ROW 11 (DEC): With D, k1 tbl, k2, (sl1 wyib, k1) 5 times, sl1 wyib, *sm, k13, (sl1 wyib, k1) 5 times, sl1 wyib; rep from * to last M, sm, k6, k2tog—1 st dec.

ROW 13 (DEC): With A, k1 tbl, k1, sl1 wyib, k11, *sm, (sl1 wyib, k1) 6 times, sl1 wyib, k11; rep from * to last M, sm, (sl1 wyib, k1) 2 times, k1, k2tog—1 st dec.

ROW 15 (DEC): With D, k1 tbl, k3, (sl1 wyib, k1) 5 times, *sm, k14, (sl1 wyib, k1) 5 times; rep from * to last M, sm, k4, k2tog—1 st dec.

ROW 17 (DEC): With A, k1 tbl, k2, sl1 wyib, k9, sl1 wyib, *sm, k13, sl1 wyib, k9, sl1 wyib; rep from * to last M, sm, k3, k2tog—1 st dec.

ROW 19 (DEC): With D, k1 tbl, k4, (sl1 wyib, k1) 3 times, sl1 wyib, k2, *sm, k15, (sl1 wyib, k1) 3 times, sl1 wyib, k2; rep from * to last M, sm, k2, k2tog—1 st dec.

ROW 21 (DEC): With A, k1 tbl, (k1, sl1 wyib) 2 times, k7, sl1 wyib, k1, *sm, (sl1 wyib, k1) 7 times, sl1 wyib, k7, sl1 wyib, k1; rep from * to last M, sm, k1, k2tog—1 st dec.

ROW 23 (DEC): With D, k1 tbl, knit to last 2 sts, rm as encountered, k2tog—1 st dec.

ROW 25 (DEC): With A, k1 tbl, k1, pm, *(sl1 wyib, k1) 7 times, sl1 wyib, k7, sl1 wyib, k1, pm; rep from * to last 13 sts, (sl1 wyib, k1) 5 times, k1, k2tog—1 st dec.

ROW 27 (DEC): With D, k1 tbl, k1, *sm, k15, (sl1 wyib, k1) 3 times, sl1 wyib, k2; rep from * to last M, sm, k10, k2tog—1 st dec.

ROW 29 (DEC): With A, k1 tbl, k1, *sm, k13, sl1 wyib, k9, sl1 wyib; rep from * to last M, sm, k9, k2tog—1 st dec.

ROW 31 (DEC): With D, k1 tbl, k1, *sm, k14, (sl1 wyib, k1) 5 times; rep from * to last M, sm, k8, k2tog—1 st dec.

ROW 33 (DEC): With A, k1 tbl, k1, *sm, (sl1 wyib, k1) 6 times, sl1 wyib, k11; rep from * to last M, sm, (sl1 wyib, k1) 3 times, k1, k2tog—1 st dec.

ROW 35 (DEC): With D, k1 tbl, k1, *sm, k13, (sl1 wyib, k1) 5 times, sl1 wyib; rep from * to last M, sm, k6, k2tog—1 st dec.

ROW 37 (DEC): With A, k1 tbl, k1, *sm, (sl1 wyib, k1) 6 times, sl1 wyib, k11; rep from * to last M, sm, (sl1 wyib, k1) 2 times, k1, k2tog—1 st dec.

ROW 39 (DEC): With D, k1 tbl, k1, *sm, k14, (sl1 wyib, k1) 5 times; rep from * to last M, sm, k4, k2tog—1 st dec.

ROW 41 (DEC): With A, k1 tbl, k1, *sm, k13, sl1 wyib, k9, sl1 wyib; rep from * to last M, sm, k3, k2tog—1 st dec.

ROW 43 (DEC): With D, k1 tbl, k1, *sm, k15, (sl1 wyib, k1) 3 times, sl1 wyib, k2; rep from * to last M, sm, k2, k2tog—1 st dec.

ROW 45 (DEC): With A, k1 tbl, k1, *sm, (sl1 wyib, k1) 7 times, sl1 wyib, k7, sl1 wyib, k1; rep from * to last M, sm, k1, k2tog—1 st dec.
ROW 47 (DEC): With D, k1 tbl, knit to last 2 sts, rm as encountered, k2tog—1 st dec.
ROW 48: With D, sl1 wyif, knit to last st, sl1 wyif.
Rep [Rows 1–48] 1 more time.
48 sts dec; 75 sts rem.
Break Color D.

PART 2-B
Join Color B.
Follow written instructions below or work from Chart D (page 83).
ROW 1 (RS, DEC): With A, k1 tbl, knit to last 2 sts, k2tog—1 st dec.
ROW 2 (WS, AND ALL WS ROWS): With yarn used on previous RS row, sl1 wyif, knit the knit sts and slip the slipped sts purlwise wyif to last st, sl1 wyif.
ROWS 3 AND 4: With B, rep [Rows 1 and 2] 1 time—1 st dec.
ROW 5 (DEC): With A, k1 tbl, *k1, sl1 wyib; rep from * to last 4 sts, k2, k2tog—1 st dec.
ROW 7 (DEC): With B, k1 tbl, knit to last 2 sts, k2tog—1 st dec.
ROW 8: With B, sl1 wyif, knit to last st, sl1 wyif.
ROWS 9–12: Rep [Rows 5–8] 1 time—2 sts dec.
Rep [Rows 1–12] 10 more times, then rep [Rows 1–8] 1 more time. 70 sts dec; 5 sts rem.
Break Color B. Continue with Color A only.
ROW 141 (RS, DEC): K1 tbl, k2, k2tog—4 sts rem.
ROW 142 (WS): Sl1 wyif, k2, p1.
ROW 143 (DEC): Sl1 wyib, k1, k2tog—3 sts rem.
ROW 144: Sl1 wyif, k1, p1.
ROW 145 (DEC): Sl1 wyib, k2tog—2 sts rem.
ROW 146: Sl1 wyif, p1.
Using a locking M-A, place 2 rem sts on hold.
Break Color A.

SECTION 3: LEFT TRIANGLE
Rotate the work 90 degrees counterclockwise. With RS facing, join Color A and k1 tbl into st marked by M-B (placed at the end of Section 1), rm-B, pick up and knit 121 sts along the edge (under both legs of the slipped sts), transfer 2 live sts from M-A to LHN and knit these 2 sts—124 sts total. Clip locking M-A to last st knit.
SETUP ROW (WS): Sl1 knitwise wyib, knit to last 2 sts, sl2 wyif.
Join Color C.
With C, work Garter Ridge Left 1 time—123 sts rem.

PART 3-A
Follow written instructions below or work from Chart E (page 83).
ROW 1 (RS, DEC): With A, k2tog tbl, k2, (sl1 wyib, k1) 3 times, sl1 wyib, *k9, sl1 wyib; rep from * to last 2 sts, k1, p1—1 st dec.
ROW 2 (WS, AND ALL WS ROWS): With yarn used on previous RS row, sl1 knitwise wyib, knit the knit sts and slip the slipped sts purlwise wyif to last 2 sts, sl2 wyif.
ROW 3 (DEC): With C, k2tog tbl, k8, *sl1 wyib, k7, sl1 wyib, k1; rep from * to last 2 sts, k1, p1—1 st dec.
ROW 5 (DEC): With A, k2tog tbl, k2, (sl1 wyib, k1) 2 times, sl1 wyib, *k1, sl1 wyib, k5, sl1 wyib, k1, sl1 wyib; rep from * to last 2 sts, k1, p1—1 st dec.
ROW 7 (DEC): With C, k2tog tbl, k6, *sl1 wyib, k1; rep from * to last 2 sts, k1, p1—1 st dec.
ROW 9 (DEC): With A, k2tog tbl, k2, sl1 wyib, k1, sl1 wyib, *k1, sl1 wyib, k3, (sl1 wyib, k1) 2 times, sl1 wyib; rep from * to last 2 sts, k1, p1—1 st dec.
ROW 11 (DEC): With C, k2tog tbl, k4, *sl1 wyib, k5, (sl1 wyib, k1) 2 times; rep from * to last 2 sts, k1, p1—1 st dec.
ROW 13 (DEC): With A, k2tog tbl, k2, sl1 wyib, *k7, sl1 wyib, k1, sl1 wyib; rep from * to last 2 sts, k1, p1—1 st dec.
ROW 15 (DEC): With C, k2tog tbl, k2, *k8, sl1 wyib, k1; rep from * to last 2 sts, k1, p1—1 st dec.
ROW 17 (DEC): With A, k2tog tbl, k1, *k1, sl1 wyib, k7, sl1 wyib; rep from * to last 2 sts, k1, p1—1 st dec.
ROW 19 (DEC): With C, k2tog tbl, knit to last st, p1—1 st dec.
ROW 20: With C, sl1 knitwise wyib, knit to last 2 sts, sl2 wyif.
Rep [Rows 1–20] 4 more times.
50 sts dec; 73 sts rem.
Break Color C.
With A, work Garter Ridge Left 1 time—72 sts rem.
Join Color D.
With D, work Garter Ridge Left 1 time—71 sts rem.

PART 3-B
Follow the written instructions below or work from Chart B (page 82) using Color A for the black charted rows and Color D for the white charted rows:
ROW 1 (RS, DEC): With A, k2tog tbl, k2, *sl1 wyib, k1; rep from * to last st, p1—1 st dec.
ROW 2 (WS): With yarn used on previous RS row, sl1 knitwise wyib, knit the knit sts and slip the slipped sts purlwise wyif to last 2 sts, sl2 wyif.
ROW 3 (DEC): With D, k2tog tbl, knit to last st, p1—1 st dec.
ROW 4: With D, sl1 knitwise wyib, knit to last 2 sts, sl2 wyif.
Rep [Rows 1–4] 32 more times.
66 sts dec; 5 sts rem.
Break Color D. Continue with Color A only.
ROW 133 (RS, DEC): K2tog tbl, k2, p1—4 sts rem.
ROW 134 (WS): Sl1 knitwise wyib, k1, sl2 wyif.
ROW 135 (DEC): K2tog tbl, k1, p1—3 sts rem.
ROW 136 (DEC): Sl1 knitwise wyib, k2tog—2 sts rem.
ROW 137: Sl1 wyif, clip locking M-B to slipped st, k1.

SECTION 4: RIGHT TRIANGLE

Rotate the work 90 degrees clockwise (2 sts on RHN). With Color A still attached and RS facing, pick up and knit 121 sts along the adjacent edge of the piece (under both legs of the slipped sts). *Note: The first stitch should be picked up from the stitch below the leftmost st on the RHN.* Knit into the st marked by M-A, rm-A—124 sts total.
Do not remove M-B.
SETUP ROW (WS): Sl1 wyif, knit to last st, sl1 wyif.
Join Color B.

PART 4-A
Follow written instructions below or work from Chart F (page 83).
ROW 1 (RS, DEC): With B, k1 tbl, k4, sl1 wyib, *k5, sl1 wyib; rep from * to last 10 sts, k8, k2tog—1 st dec.
ROW 2 (WS, AND ALL WS ROWS): With yarn used on previous RS row, sl1 wyif, knit the knit sts and slip the slipped sts purlwise wyif to last st, sl1 wyif.
ROW 3 (DEC): With A, k1 tbl, *k1, sl1 wyib; rep from * to last 4 sts, k2, k2tog—1 st dec.
ROW 5 (DEC): With B, k1 tbl, k4, sl1 wyib, *k5, sl1 wyib; rep from * to last 8 sts, k6, k2tog—1 st dec.
ROW 7 (DEC): With A, k1 tbl, *k1, sl1 wyib; rep from * to last 2 sts, k2tog—1 st dec.
ROW 9 (DEC): With B, k1 tbl, k4, sl1 wyib, *k5, sl1 wyib; rep from * to last 6 sts, k4, k2tog—1 st dec.
ROW 11 (DEC): With A, k1 tbl, knit to last 2 sts, k2tog—1 st dec.
ROW 12: With A, sl1 wyif, knit to last st, sl1 wyif.
Rep [Rows 1–12] 7 more times.
48 sts dec; 76 sts rem.
Break Color B.

PART 4-B
Join Color C.
Follow written instructions below or work from Chart G (page 83).
ROW 1 (RS, DEC): With C, k1 tbl, knit to last 2 sts, k2tog—1 st dec.
ROW 2 (WS): With C, sl1 wyif, knit to last st, sl1 wyif.
ROW 3 (DEC): With A, k1 tbl, *k1, sl1 wyib; rep from * to last 4 sts, k2, k2tog—2 sts dec.
ROW 4: With A, sl1 wyif, knit the knit sts and slip the slipped sts purlwise wyif to last st, sl1 wyif.
ROWS 5–12: Rep [Rows 1–4] 2 times—4 sts dec.
ROW 13 (DEC): With C, k1 tbl, knit to last 2 sts, k2tog—1 st dec.
ROW 14: With C, sl1 wyif, knit to last st, sl1 wyif.
ROW 15 (DEC): With A, k1 tbl, knit to last 2 sts, k2tog—1 st dec.
ROW 16: With A, sl1 wyif, knit to last st, sl1 wyif.

ROW 17 (DEC): With C, k1 tbl, *k1, sl1 wyib; rep from * to last 5 sts, k3, k2tog—67 sts.

ROW 18: With C, sl1 wyif, knit the knit sts and slip the slipped sts purlwise wyif to last st, sl1 wyif.

ROWS 19–26: Rep [Rows 15–18] 2 times—4 sts dec.

ROW 27 (DEC): With A, k1 tbl, knit to last 2 sts, k2tog—1 st dec.

ROW 28: With A, sl1 wyif, knit to last st, sl1 wyif.

Rep [Rows 1–28] 4 more times. 70 sts dec; 6 sts rem.

With C, work Garter Ridge Right 1 time—5 sts rem.

Break Color C. Continue with Color A only.

ROW 143 (RS, DEC): K1 tbl, k2, k2tog—4 sts rem.

ROW 144 (WS): Sl1 wyif, k2, p1.

ROW 145 (DEC): Sl1 wyib, k1, k2tog—3 sts rem.

ROW 146: Sl1 wyif, k1, p1.

ROW 147 (DEC): Sl1 wyib, k2tog—2 sts rem.

ROW 148: Sl1 wyif, p1.

Using a locking M-A, place 2 rem sts on hold.

Break Color A.

SECTION 5: LEFT PARALLELOGRAM

Rotate the work 90 degrees counterclockwise. With RS facing, join Color A and k1 tbl into st marked by M-B (placed at the end of Section 3), rm-B, pick up and knit 121 sts along the edge (under both legs of the slipped sts), transfer 2 live sts from M-A to LHN and knit these 2 sts—124 sts total.

Note: The stitch count will remain at 124 sts throughout this final section.

SETUP ROW (WS): Sl1 knitwise wyib, knit to last 2 sts, sl2 wyif.

Join Color D.

Follow written instructions below or work from Chart H (page 83).

ROW 1 (RS): With D, k2tog tbl, knit to last 2 sts, kfb, p1.

ROW 2 (WS, AND ALL WS ROWS): With yarn used on previous RS row, sl1 knitwise wyib, knit the knit sts and slip the slipped sts purlwise wyif to last 2 sts, sl2 wyif.

ROW 3: With A, k2tog tbl, k2, *sl1 wyib, k1; rep from * to last 2 sts, kfb, p1.

ROW 5: With D, k2tog tbl, knit to last 2 sts, kfb, p1.

ROW 7: With A, k2tog tbl, k2, *sl1 wyib, k1; rep from * to last 2 sts, kfb, p1.

ROW 9: With D, k2tog tbl, knit to last 2 sts, kfb, p1.

ROW 11: With A, k2tog tbl, knit to last 2 sts, kfb, p1.

ROW 12: With A, sl1 knitwise wyib, knit to last 2 sts, sl2 wyif.

Rep [Rows 1–12] 5 more times, then rep [Rows 11 and 12] 1 more time.

Break Color D. Continue with Color A only.

ROW 75 (RS): K2tog tbl, knit to last 2 sts, kfb, p1.

With WS facing, bind off all the stitches using the Modified Icelandic Bind Off method. Break yarn.

FINISHING

Weave in all ends and wet block to measurements. Allow to dry completely. Trim all ends.

FRIGHTENING FACT

Sally is voiced by Canadian-American actress Catherine O'Hara, who has been in several of Burton's films, such as *Beetlejuice* and *Frankenweenie*.

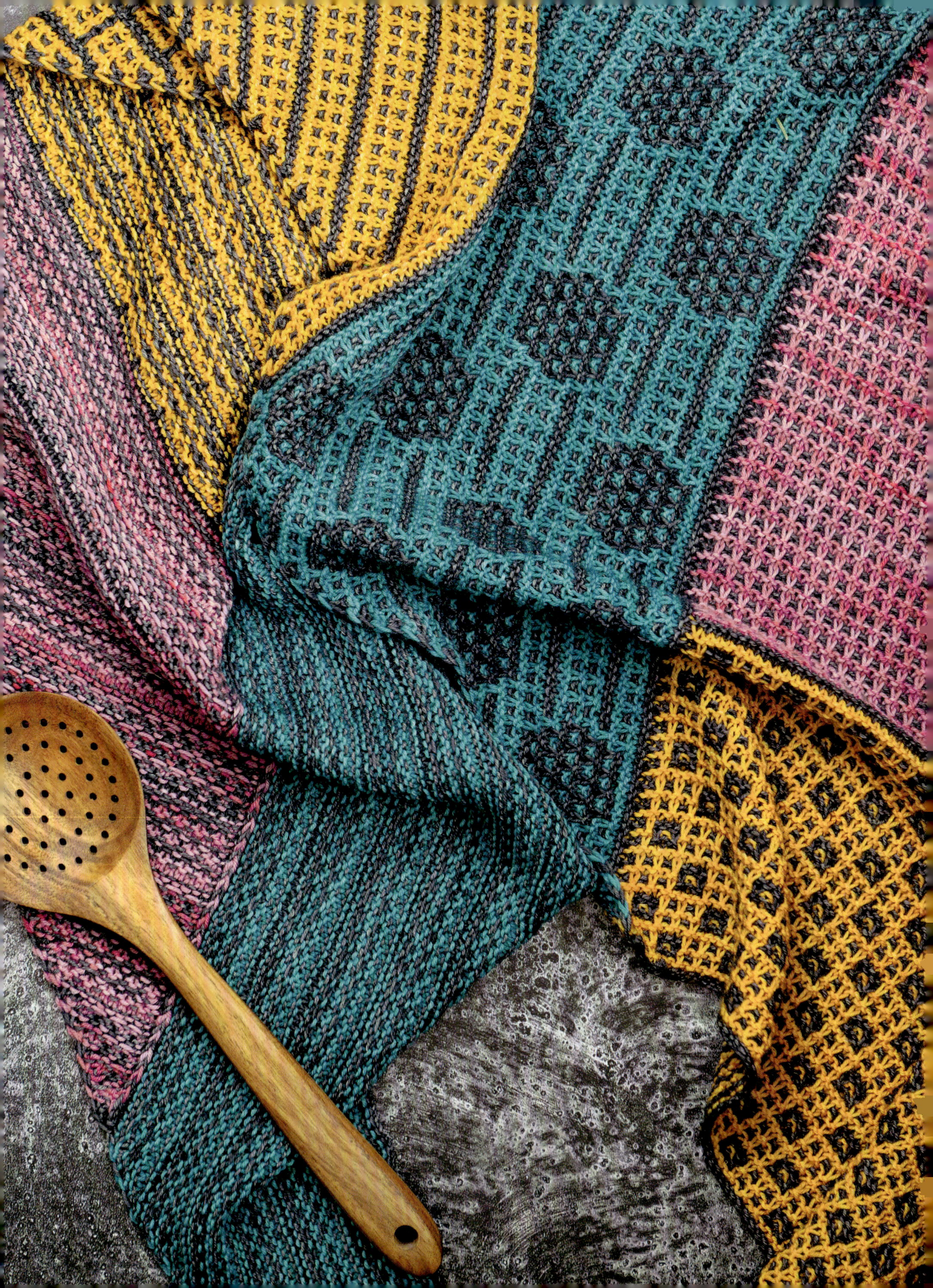

Key

- ☐ Knit on RS, purl on WS
- – Purl on RS, knit on WS
- V Slip st purlwise: wyib on RS, wyif on WS
- V Slip st knitwise wyib
- ∕ K2tog
- ℛ K2tog tbl
- Q K tbl on RS, p tbl on WS
- ⌄ Kfb
- ■ Color A
- ▦ Color B
- ▦ Color C
- ▦ Color D
- ▭ Stitch pattern repeat

Garter Ridge Left Chart

Garter Ridge Right Chart

Chart A

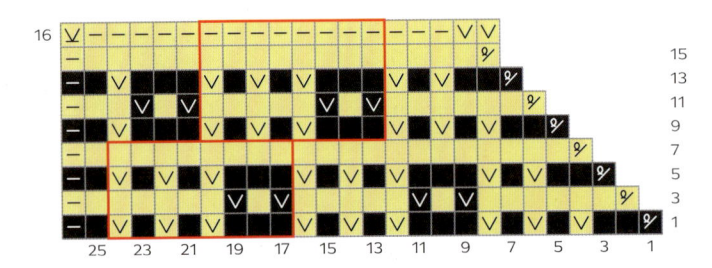

Chart B

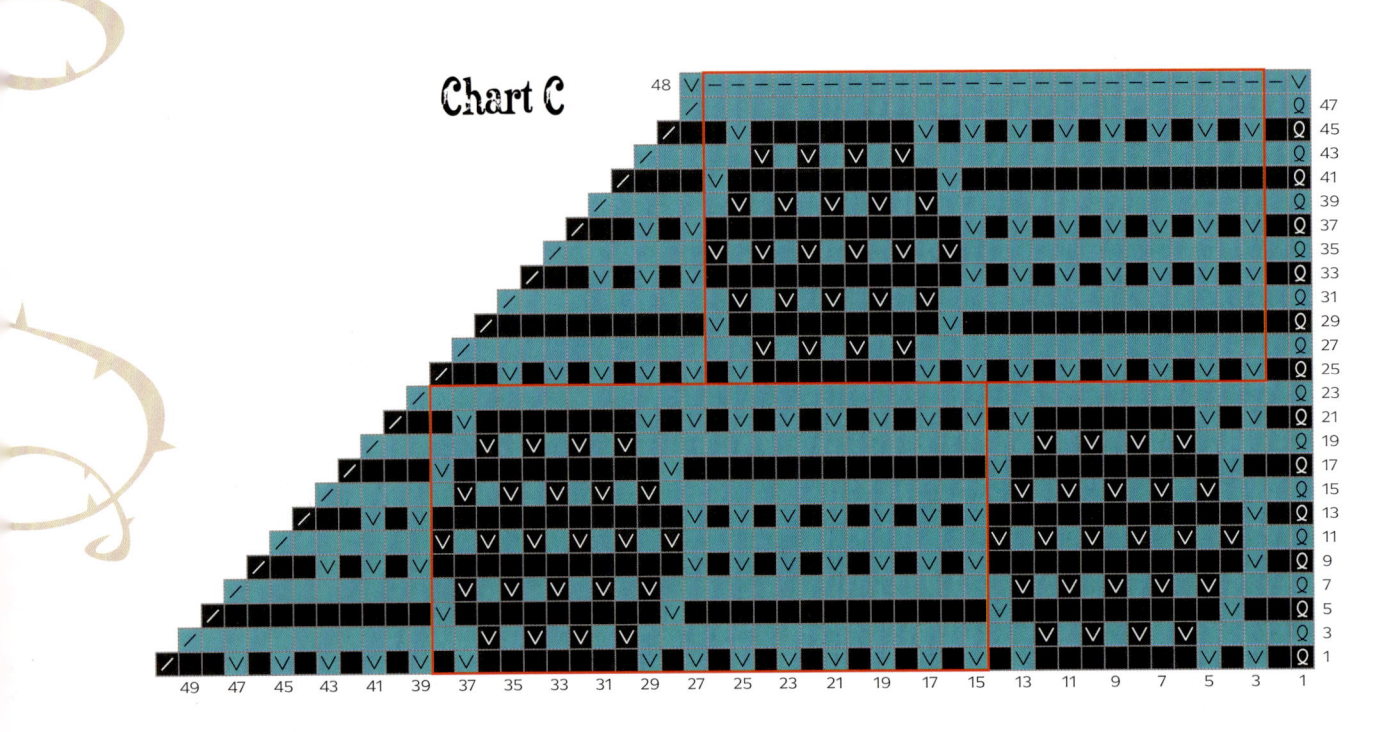

Chart C

82

Chart D

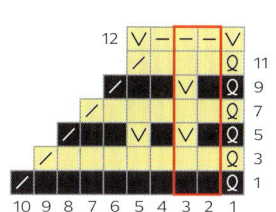

Chart E

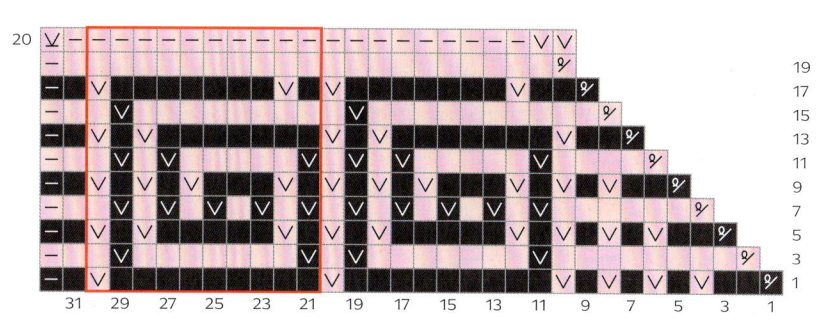

Chart F

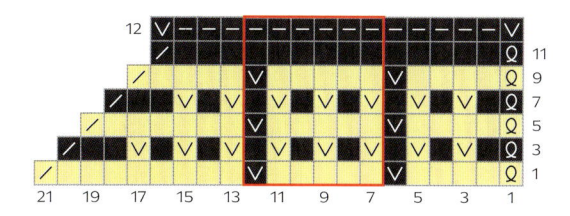

Chart G

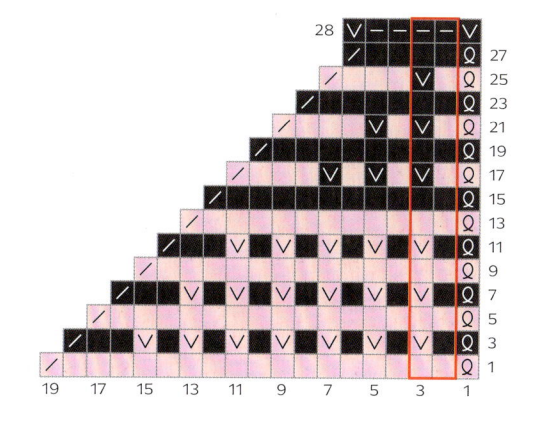

Chart H

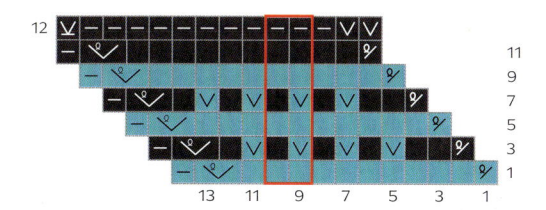

Sally's Dress Wrap Schematic

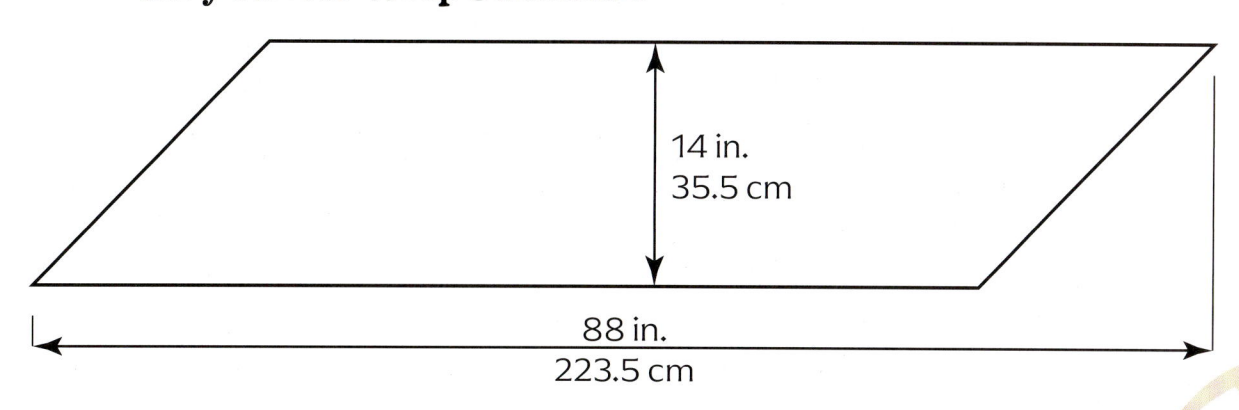

14 in.
35.5 cm

88 in.
223.5 cm

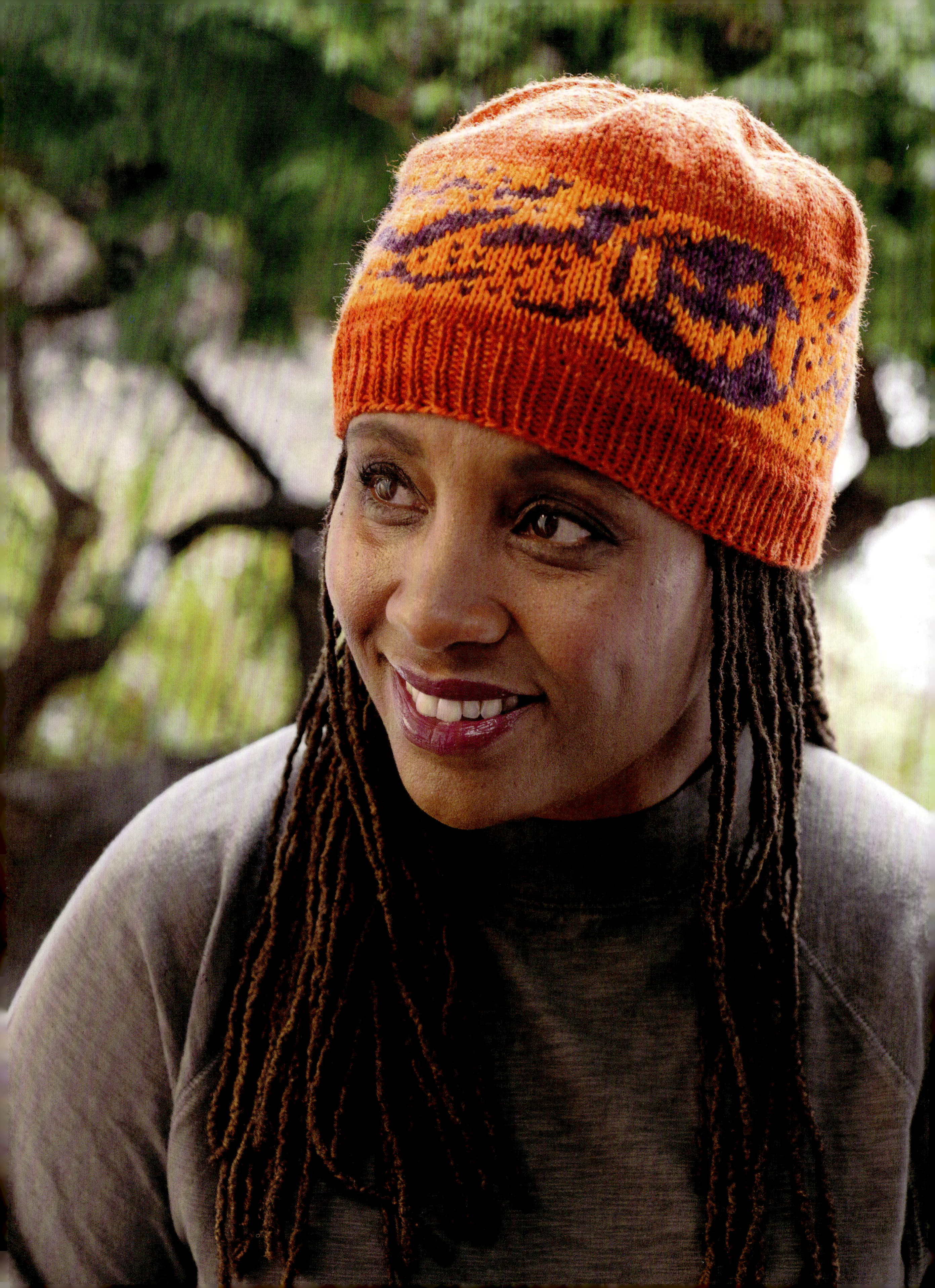

Full Moon Oogie Boogie Hat

Designed by Jacquline Rivera

"Are you a gambling man, Sandy? Let's play!"
—Oogie Boogie

SKILL LEVEL

In the quintessential "This Is Halloween" song that introduces the audience to the spooky world of Halloween Town and its inhabitants, we see Oogie Boogie's shadow across the moon. Although all the other residents of Halloween Town are harmless monsters who were born into a supernatural world and love a an innocent scare, Oogie Boogie is intent on actual harm and maliciousness. However, creator Tim Burton doesn't view him as evil, saying, "*The Nightmare Before Christmas* is a happy story with no truly bad characters. Everyone is trying to do something good and just gets a little mixed up along the way." Despite being the film's main antagonist and having only ten minutes of screen time, Oogie Boogie is a fan favorite.

In this town of Halloween, fill your knitting to the brim with fright! This beanie is worked in the round from the bottom up, beginning with an easy 1x1 ribbed brim. A band of stranded colorwork featuring flapping bats surrounding Oogie Boogie's menacing shadow on the moon wreathes the wearer, topped off with simple decreases to close up the crown. Beware!

SIZES

1 (2, 3, 4)

FINISHED MEASUREMENTS

Circumference: 18½ (20, 21½, 23) in. / 47 (51, 54.5, 58.5) cm

Height: 7½ (8, 8½, 9) in. / 19 (20.5, 21.5, 23) cm

Designed to fit with little to no ease; choose a size closest to your head circumference for the best fit.

YARN

Sport weight yarn, shown in Lattes & Llamas *Geek-A-Long* (3-ply; 80% superwash merino, 20% nylon; 328 yd. / 300 m per 3½ oz. / 100 g hank)

COLORWAYS:

- Main Color (MC): Hep Alien, 1 hank
- Contrast Color 1 (CC1): Plastic Pumpkins, 1 hank
- Contrast Color 2 (CC2): Jessica Jones, 1 hank

NEEDLES

US 3 / 3.25 mm, 16 in. / 40 cm long circular needles and set of double-pointed needles or size needed to obtain gauge

US 4 / 3.5 mm, 16 in. / 40 cm long circular needle

NOTIONS

Stitch markers (5; 1 unique for BOR)

Row counter (optional)

Tapestry needle

GAUGE

26 sts and 34 rnds = 4 in. / 10 cm over St st in the round on smaller needle, taken after blocking

Make sure to check your gauge.

PATTERN NOTES

- This hat is worked in the round from the brim up, using the smaller needle for the brim, body, and crown of the hat; the larger needle is used for the Colorwork Band of the hat only.
- When working the Colorwork Band, catch floats longer than 5 stitches.
- When the circumference of the hat becomes too small for the circular needle during the Crown Shaping, change to dpns to finish the hat.
- The pattern is written for size 1 first with additional sizes in parentheses. When only one number is provided, it applies to all sizes.

PATTERN INSTRUCTIONS

CAST ON & BRIM

With smaller circular needle and MC, CO 110 (120, 130, 140) sts using the Long Tail Cast On method. Place unique M for BOR and join to work in the rnd, being careful not to twist the sts.

RNDS 1–12: *K1, p1; rep from * to end of rnd.

SIZES 1 (-, 3, -) ONLY:
RND 13 (INC): *Kfb, work in est rib patt over next 11 (-, 13, -) sts, kfb, work in est rib patt over next 9 (-, 11, -) sts; rep from * to end of rnd—10 sts inc; 120 (-, 140, -) sts total.

SIZES - (2, -, 4) ONLY:
RND 13 (INC): *Kfb, work in est rib patt over next - (11, -, 13) sts; rep from * to end of rnd—10 sts inc; - (130, -, 150) sts total.

ALL SIZES:
RNDS 14–16: Knit.
Break MC.

COLORWORK BAND

Join CC1.
SETUP RND: K50, pm-A, k60 (60, 80, 80), pm-B, knit to end of rnd.
Switch to larger needle. Join CC2.
Begin working from Charts A, B, and C, reading all rows from right to left as for working in the rnd, as follows:
RNDS 1–19: Work Chart A 1 time to M-A, sm, work Chart B 3 (3, 4, 4) times to M-B, sm, work Chart C 1 (2, 1, 2) time(s) to end of rnd.
Break CC2.
Change to smaller circular needle.
RND 20: With CC1, knit to end of rnd, rm as encountered except BOR M.
Break CC1.

FINISH BODY OF HAT

Join MC.
Knit 9 (11, 13, 15) rnds, or until the hat measures approx. 5½ (5¾ 6, 6¼) in. / 14 (14.5, 15, 16) cm from the CO edge.

CROWN SHAPING

SETUP RND: *K24 (26, 28, 30), pm; rep from * to end of rnd.
Note: The BOR M will take the place of the final marker; 5 total markers will be in place.
RND 1 (DEC): *K1, ssk, knit to 3 sts before M, k2tog, k1, sm; rep from * to end of rnd—10 sts dec.
RND 2: Knit, sm as encountered.
Rep [Rnds 1 and 2] 5 (6, 7, 8) more times—60 sts rem.
Then rep Rnd 1 only 4 more times—20 sts rem.
FINAL RND (DEC): *Ssk, k2tog, rm; rep from * to end of rnd—10 sts rem.
Break yarn, pull tail through remaining live sts, and cinch closed. Secure tail to WS.

FINISHING

Weave in all ends and wet block lightly. Allow to dry completely. Trim all ends.

FRIGHTENING FACT

Oogie Boogie voice actor Ken Page looked to Bert Lahr, who played the Cowardly Lion from *The Wizard of Oz*, and Mercedes McCambridge, who voiced the demon from *The Exorcist*, for inspiration when he was getting ready to play this ominous role.

Chart A

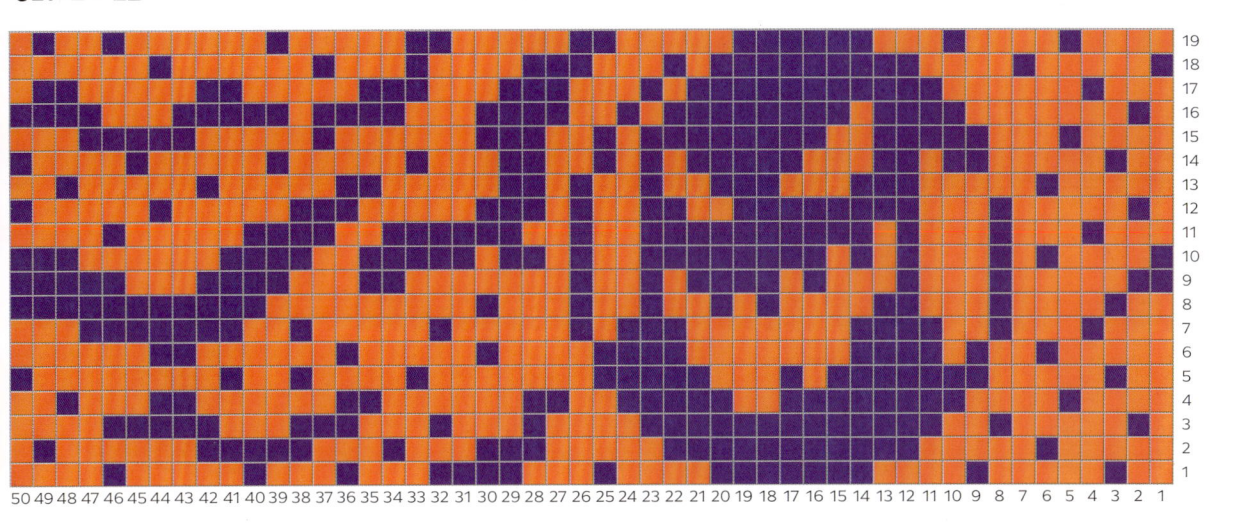

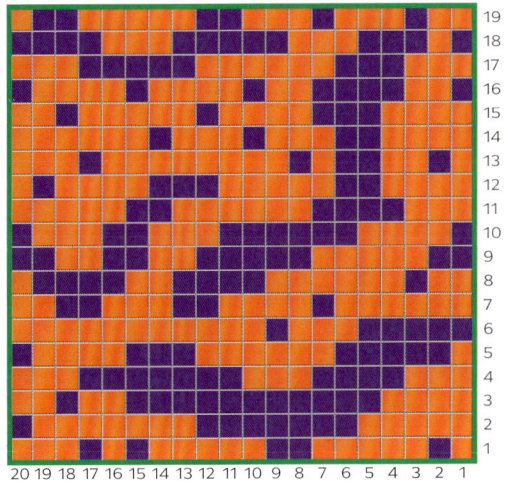

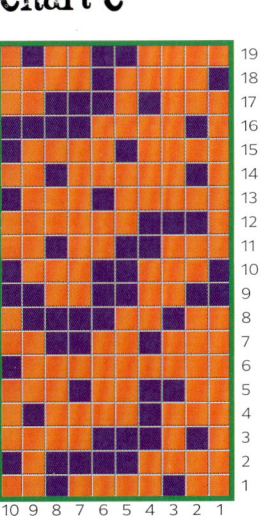

Chart B

Chart C

Key

- ☐ Knit
- 🟧 CC1
- 🟪 CC2
- ▭ Pattern repeat

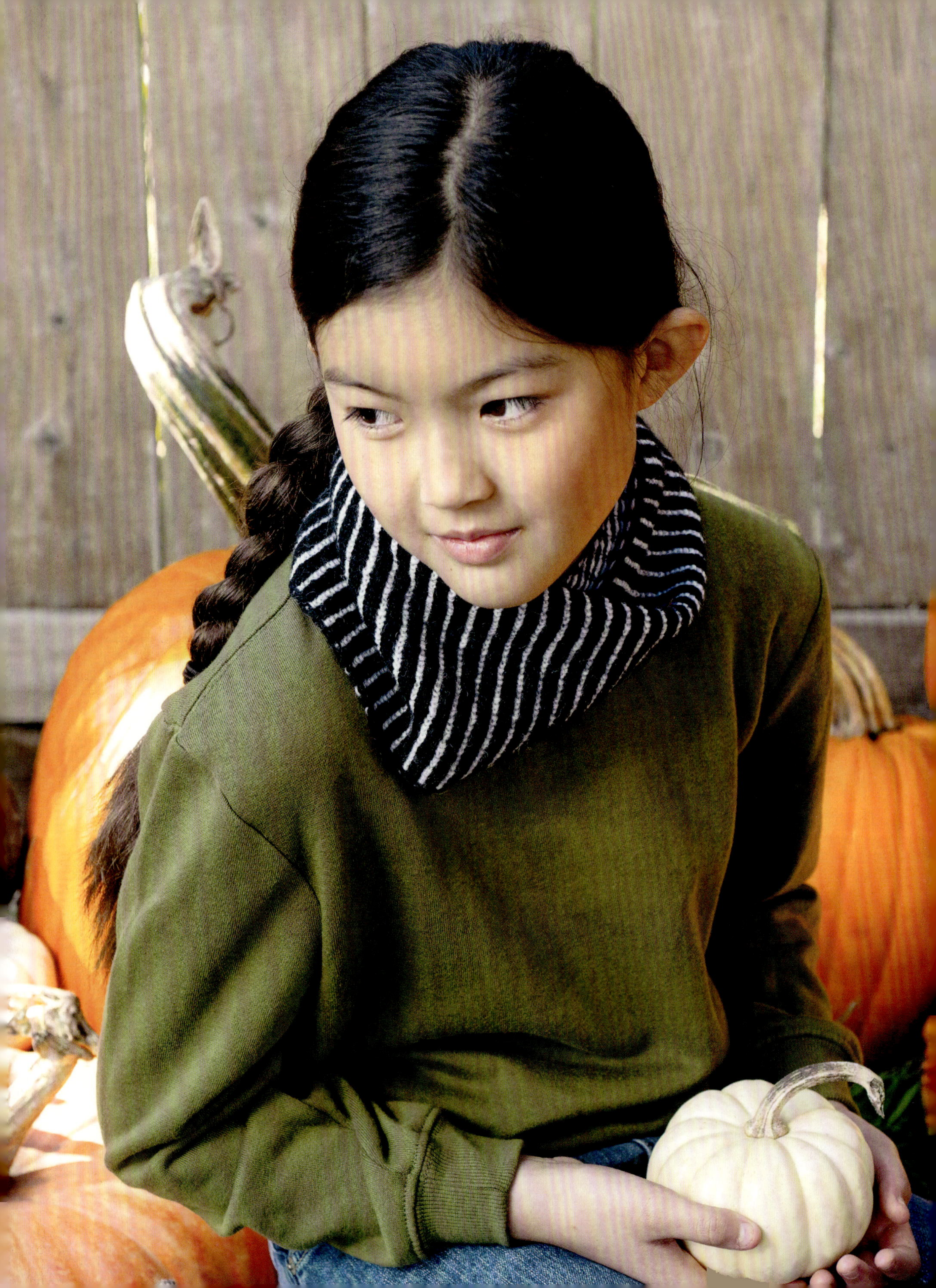

Jack's Pinstripe Cowl

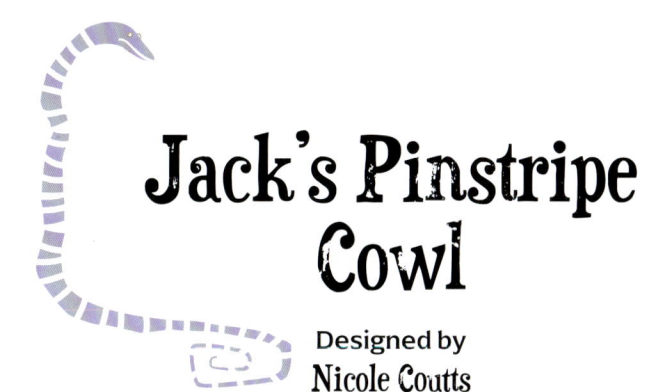

Designed by Nicole Coutts

"Great Halloween, everybody. I believe it was our most horrible yet. Thank you, everyone."
–Jack Skellington

SKILL LEVEL

Beginning at quarter-scale size, stop-motion animation sets are designed not only to create the setting and overall mood for the film, but also to figure out how animators can work in that environment, as well as how to hide tear-away sections for transport and trapdoors for cameras. Once the final sketches and mock-ups are approved, they go to the paint and model shops for full-scale fabrication and detailing. Inspired by pen and ink illustrators Edward Gory and Ronald Searle, *Tim Burton's The Nightmare Before Christmas*'s set designers utilized crosshatching—a technique used by artists to create texture and shade with intersecting mesh-like lines. For this film, sets were covered in soft clay and manipulated to add texture to look like an illustration come to life. Visual consultant Rick Heinrichs states, "You're free to design whatever you want without the limitations imposed by full size and live action."

Significantly easier than "making Christmas," this cowl is an ideal project for beginners. Just two colors and a three-stitch repeat are all it takes! Worked in the round seamlessly from the bottom up, the cowl consists of corrugated ribbing in highly contrasting colors inspired by Jack Skellington's pinstripe suit worked throughout. It's simple to adjust the height by knitting until the yarn runs out, or the desired height is reached.

SIZES
One size

FINISHED MEASUREMENTS
Circumference: 20½ in. / 52 cm
Height: 7¾ in. / 19.5 cm

YARN
Fingering weight yarn, shown in Jamieson's of Shetland *Shetland Spindrift* (2-ply; 100% pure Shetland wool; 115 yd. / 105 m per ¾ oz. / 25 g ball)

COLORWAYS:
- Main Color (MC): #999 Black, 2 balls
- Contrast Color (CC): #304 White, 1 ball

NEEDLES
US 3 / 3.25 mm, 16 in. / 40 cm long circular needle or size needed to obtain gauge

NOTIONS
Stitch marker

Row counter (optional)

Tapestry needle

GAUGE
30½ sts and 37 rnds = 4 in. / 10 cm in 2-color corrugated rib pattern in the round, taken after blocking

Make sure to check your gauge.

PATTERN NOTES
- The cowl is worked in the round, from bottom to top, using stranded colorwork.
- Written instructions are provided for the construction of the cowl; a chart for the 2-color corrugated rib pattern is provided. Read chart row from right to left as for working in the round.

PATTERN INSTRUCTIONS

CAST ON

Using MC, CO 156 sts using the Long Tail Cast On method. Pm for BOR and join to work in the rnd, being careful not to twist the sts.

BODY OF COWL

Begin working from Chart A, reading the chart row from right to left for every rnd, joining CC as required (chart is worked 52 times across the rnd). Work [Row 1] 70 times total.

When the chart is complete, break CC. Using MC, bind off all sts loosely in patt.

FINISHING

Weave in all ends to the WS.
Wet block the cowl to dimensions and allow to dry completely. Trim all ends.

Key

■ Knit with MC
– Purl with CC
☐ Pattern repeat

Chart A

FRIGHTENING FACT

Because the original poem by Tim Burton focuses on only three characters—Jack, Zero, and Santa Claus—more creatures and characters like Sally, the Mayor, Lock, Shock, and Barrel, and Oogie Boogie were added to the film to expand the story and give it more depth.

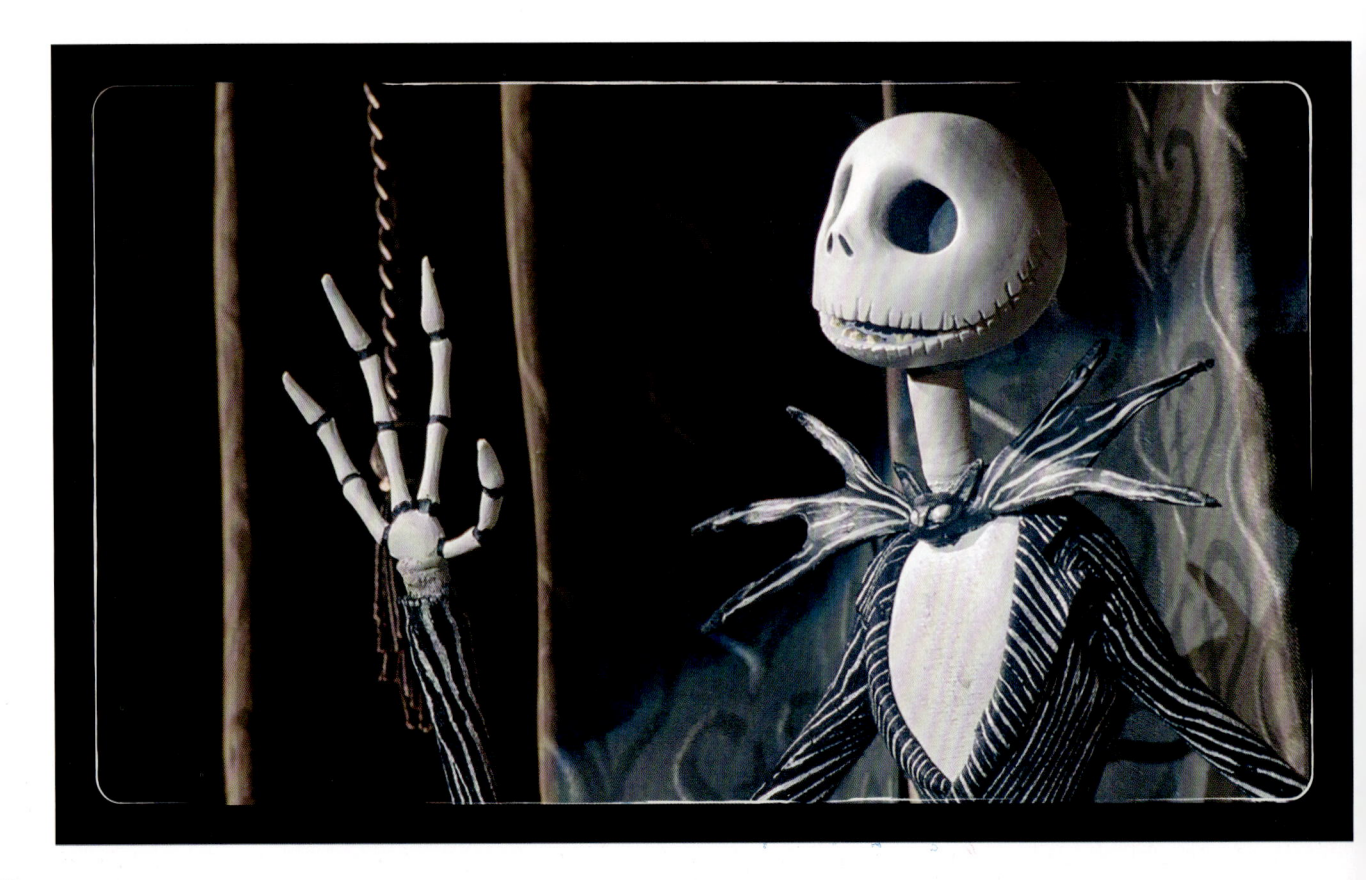

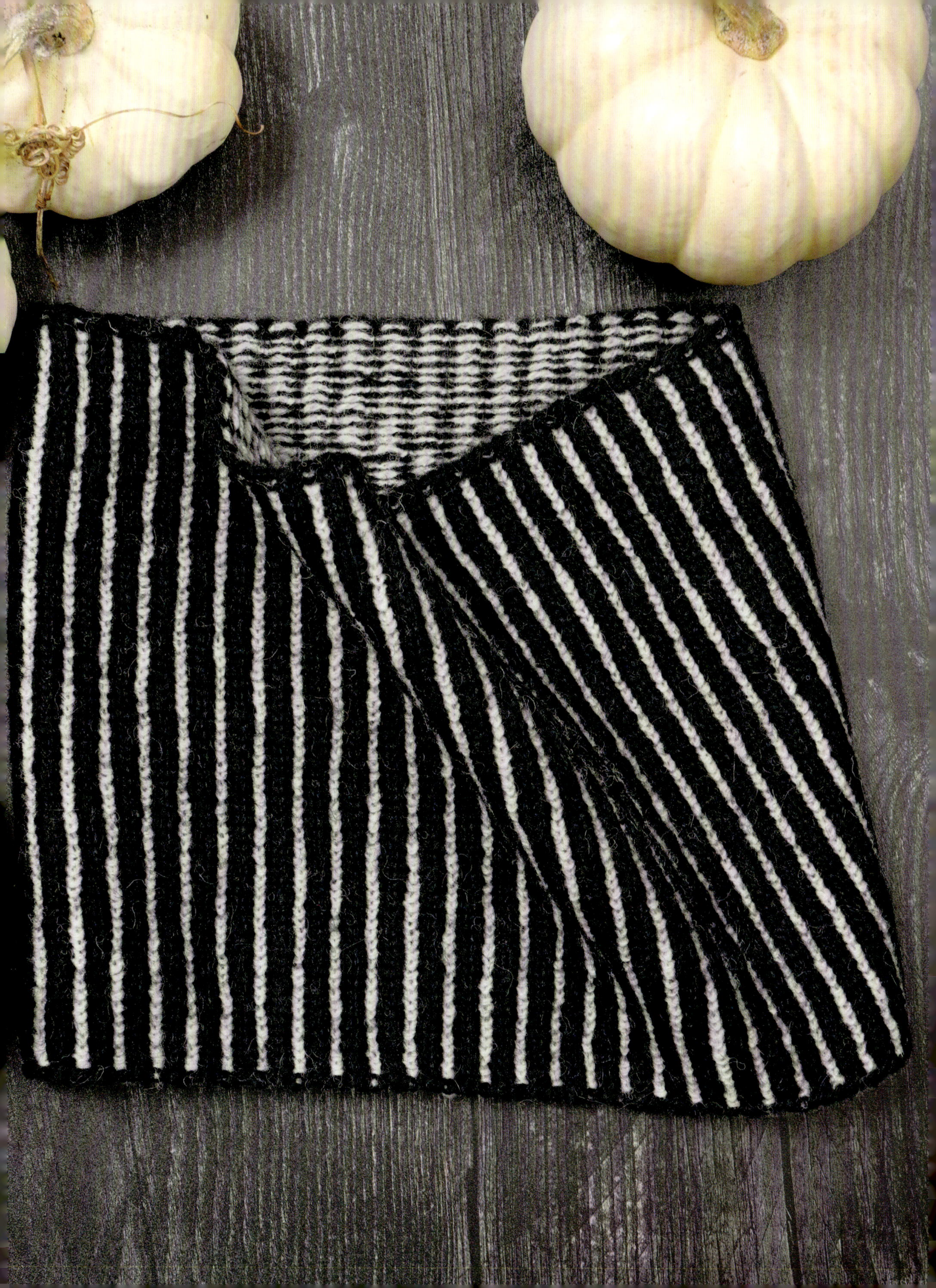

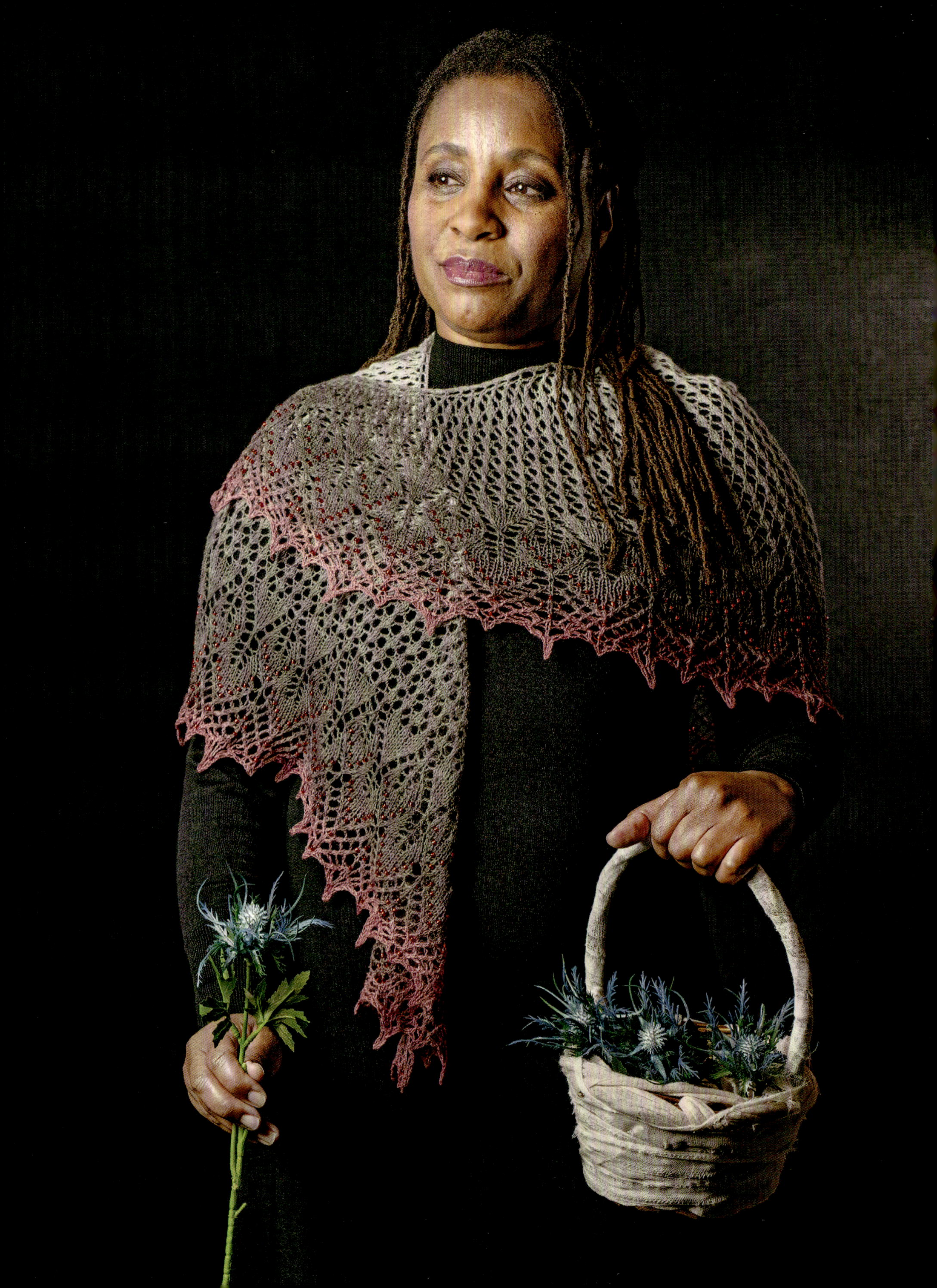

Sally's Shawl

Designed by Susanna IC

"He wants to change his life, and I want to change mine, too."
—Sally

SKILL LEVEL
💀 💀 💀

Stop-motion animators try to avoid fabrics and hair that tend to move on their own and cause choppy movements on film, ruining the illusion. Because Sally has waist-length red hair, it was decided early on that her hair wouldn't move naturally, except for a few moments in the film. This created a conundrum for the puppet makers who needed to provide dozens of different heads with a plethora of facial expressions and mouth shapes. Unlike Jack, who has no hair and a head that could easily be popped on and off during filming (allowing him to speak and sing realistically), Sally presented a problem: It would have been almost impossible to create so many heads with Sally's hair staying consistent. The team came up with a solution: Make Sally's face like a mask, removing only the front part of the face rather than the whole head to avoid disturbing her hair. Tiny eyelids could be placed into the mask to allow her to blink. Replacement parts for all the characters were also important. Puppet maker Bonita DeCarlo states, "We keep a ready supply of hands, shoes, even extra castings of arms, which can quickly be replaced for damaged or broken pieces. One person spends a lot of time making sure we never run low."

The impeccable combination of chic and classic (like Sally herself), worked from the center top down, the shawl incorporates Halloween Town's ever-present spiderwebs in its main body, created with a simple two-row lace pattern. A blinged-up beaded lace border of leaf motifs reflects Sally's patchwork and stitched body stuffed with leaves. With the beads added with a small crochet hook as you knit, there's no pre-stringing required. An elegant abstract bat-shaped border completes this Sally-inspired shawl.

SIZES
One size

FINISHED MEASUREMENTS
Wingspan: 64 in. / 162.5 cm
Center Depth: 24 in. / 61 cm

YARN
Lace weight yarn, shown in Freia Fine Handpaint Yarns *Ombré Merino Lace* (2-ply; 100% cruelty-free US merino wool; 712 yd. / 651 m per 2⅔ oz. / 75 g ball), 1 ball: in color Vintage

NEEDLES
US 7 / 4.5 mm, 32 in. / 80 cm long circular needle or size needed to obtain gauge

US 8 / 5 mm double-pointed needle or spare circular needle (any length)

NOTIONS
Approx. 700 beads, size 6/0 / 4 mm (optional)

US 10 / 0.75 mm crochet hook (or smaller as needed to fit through holes of beads, optional)

Stitch markers (optional)

Tapestry needle

Blocking pins

GAUGE
17 sts and 22 rows = 4 in. / 10 cm in stockinette stitch worked flat on smaller needle, taken after blocking

Make sure to check your gauge.

PATTERN NOTES

- The shawl is worked, in one piece, from the center top down to the elaborate border. The body of the shawl is worked in a two-row lace pattern using only basic lace stitches on the right side; the wrong-side rows are purled.
- Optional beads are added throughout the border.
- Optional stitch markers may be placed to separate the charted stitch pattern repeats in the border charts.
- The shawl is finished by wet blocking, which opens up the lace fully.

PATTERN INSTRUCTIONS

CAST ON & SETUP

With smaller needles, cast on 7 sts using the Long Tail Cast On method. Do not join to work in the rnd.

Knit 3 rows.

ROW 1 (RS, INC): K2, yo, k3, yo, k2—9 sts.

ROW 2 (WS): K2, purl to last 2 sts, k2.

ROW 3 (INC): K2, yo, (k1, yo) 5 times, k2—15 sts.

ROW 4: K2, purl to last 2 sts, k2.

ROW 5 (INC): K2, (yo, k1) 2 times, yo, k2tog, yo, k3, yo, ssk, (yo, k1) 2 times, yo, k2—21 sts.

ROW 6: K2, purl to last 2 sts, k2.

BODY OF SHAWL

ROW 1 (RS, INC): K2, (yo, k1) 2 times, yo, k2tog, yo, *k3, yo, s2kp, yo; rep from * to last 9 sts, k3, yo, ssk, (yo, k1) 2 times, yo, k2—6 sts inc.

ROW 2 (WS): K2, purl to last 2 sts, k2. Rep [Rows 1 and 2] 46 more times. 282 sts inc; 303 sts total.

BORDER & BIND OFF

Begin working from charts (pages 96 and 97), reading all RS (odd-numbered) rows from right to left and all WS (even-numbered) rows from left to right. Work Rows 1–34 one time as follows:

RS ROWS: Work Right Edge chart once, work Center chart 23 times, work Left Edge chart once.

WS ROWS: K2, purl to last 2 sts, k2. 405 sts total when chart is complete.

ROW 35 (RS, INC): K1, (k1, yo) 3 times, AB and (k1, yo, k1) into st bead is placed onto, *(k2tog, yo) 2 times, k1, (yo, k1, yo) into 1 stitch, k1, (yo, ssk) 2 times, AB and (k1, yo, k1) into st bead is placed onto; rep from * to last 4 sts, (yo, k1) 3 times, k1—138 sts inc; 543 sts total.

With WS facing and larger needle, bind off as follows:

*K2tog, k1, sl 2 sts back to LHN; rep from * to last 2 sts, k2tog. Break yarn and pull tail through rem st to secure.

FINISHING

Weave in all loose ends but do not trim. Wet block the shawl to measurements, using blocking pins to pin out the points of the shawl border. When completely dry, remove blocking pins and trim all yarn tails.

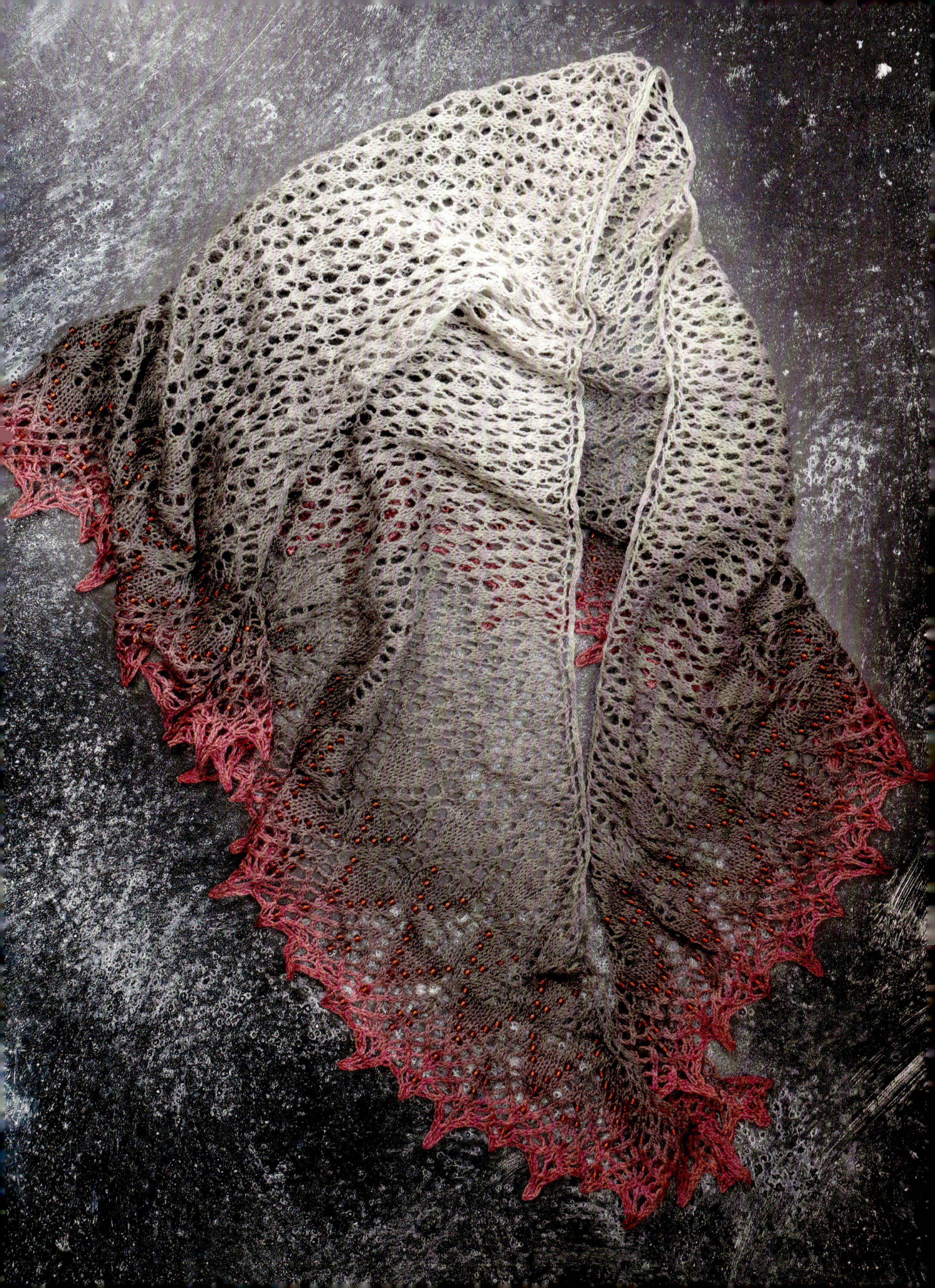

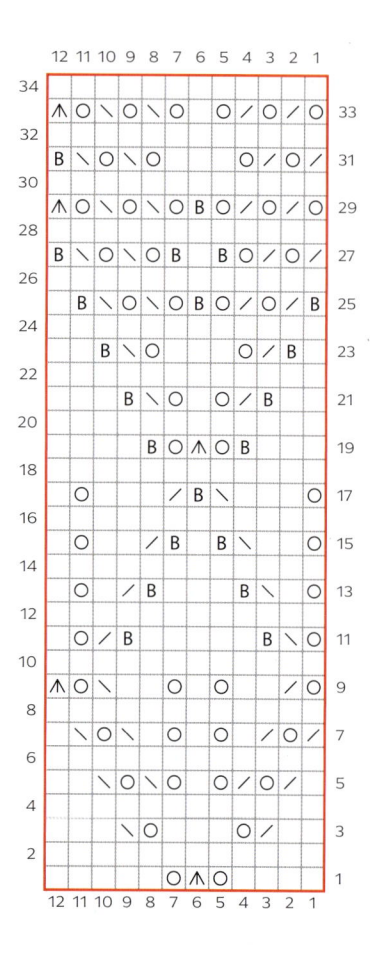

Left Edge Chart

Center Chart

Key

- ☐ k on RS, p on WS
- − p on RS, k on WS
- O yo
- ／ k2tog
- ＼ ssk
- ⋀ s2kp
- B Apply bead
- ▭ Pattern repeat

Right Edge Chart

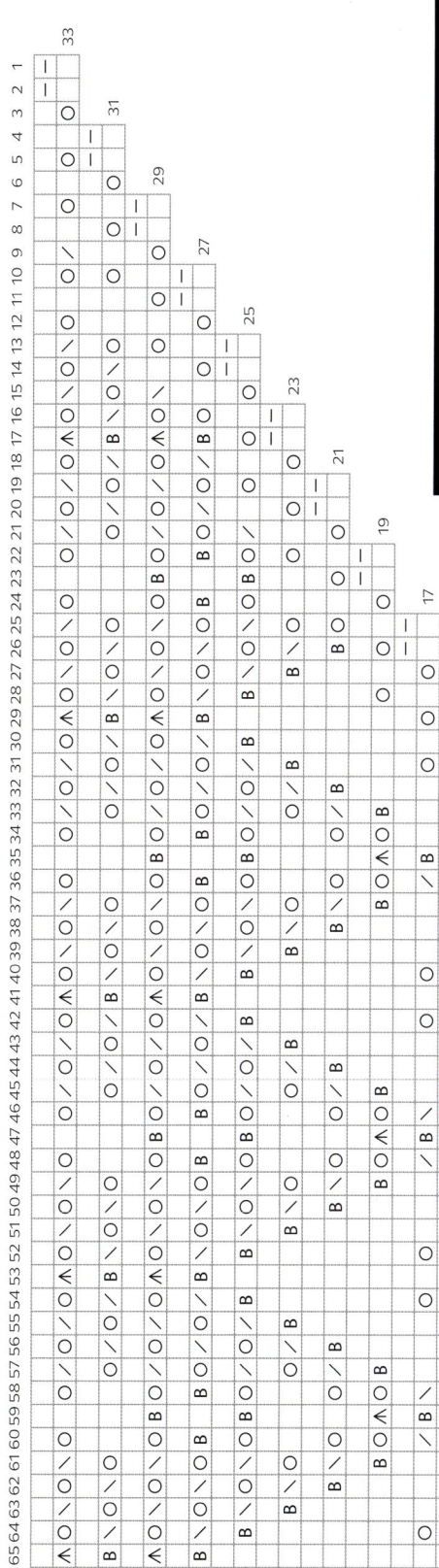

FRIGHTENING FACT

Sometimes the script would change on the fly while filming because of the way director Henry Selick felt the scene needed to go, causing dialogue to have to be rerecorded later.

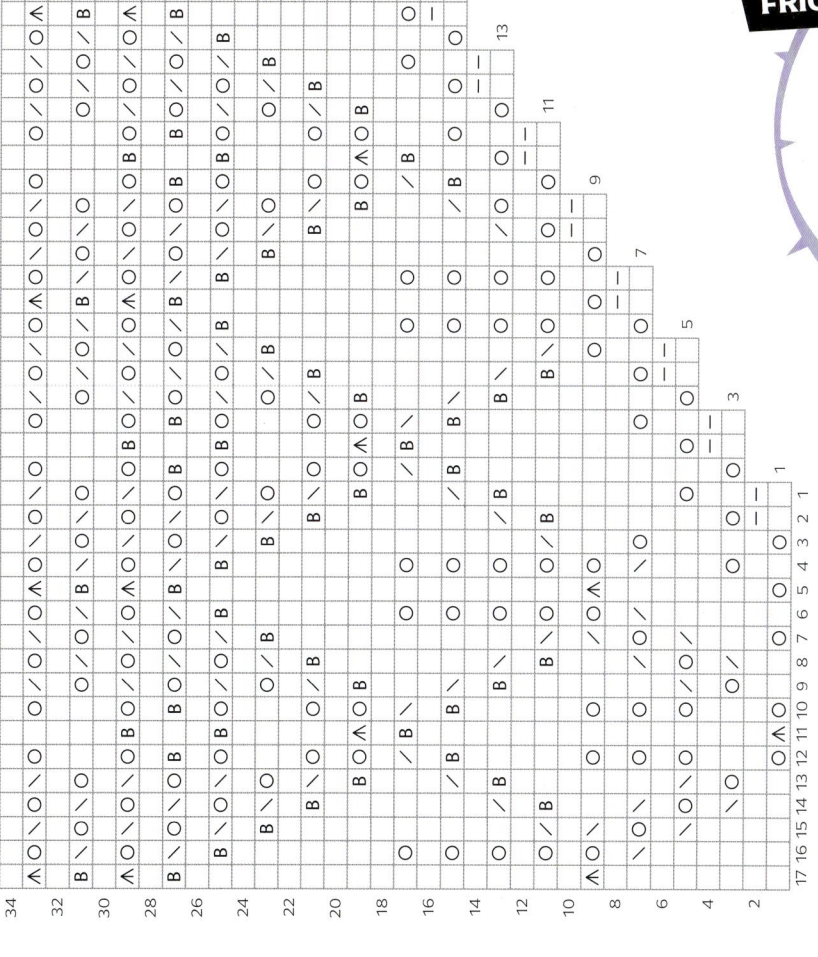

97

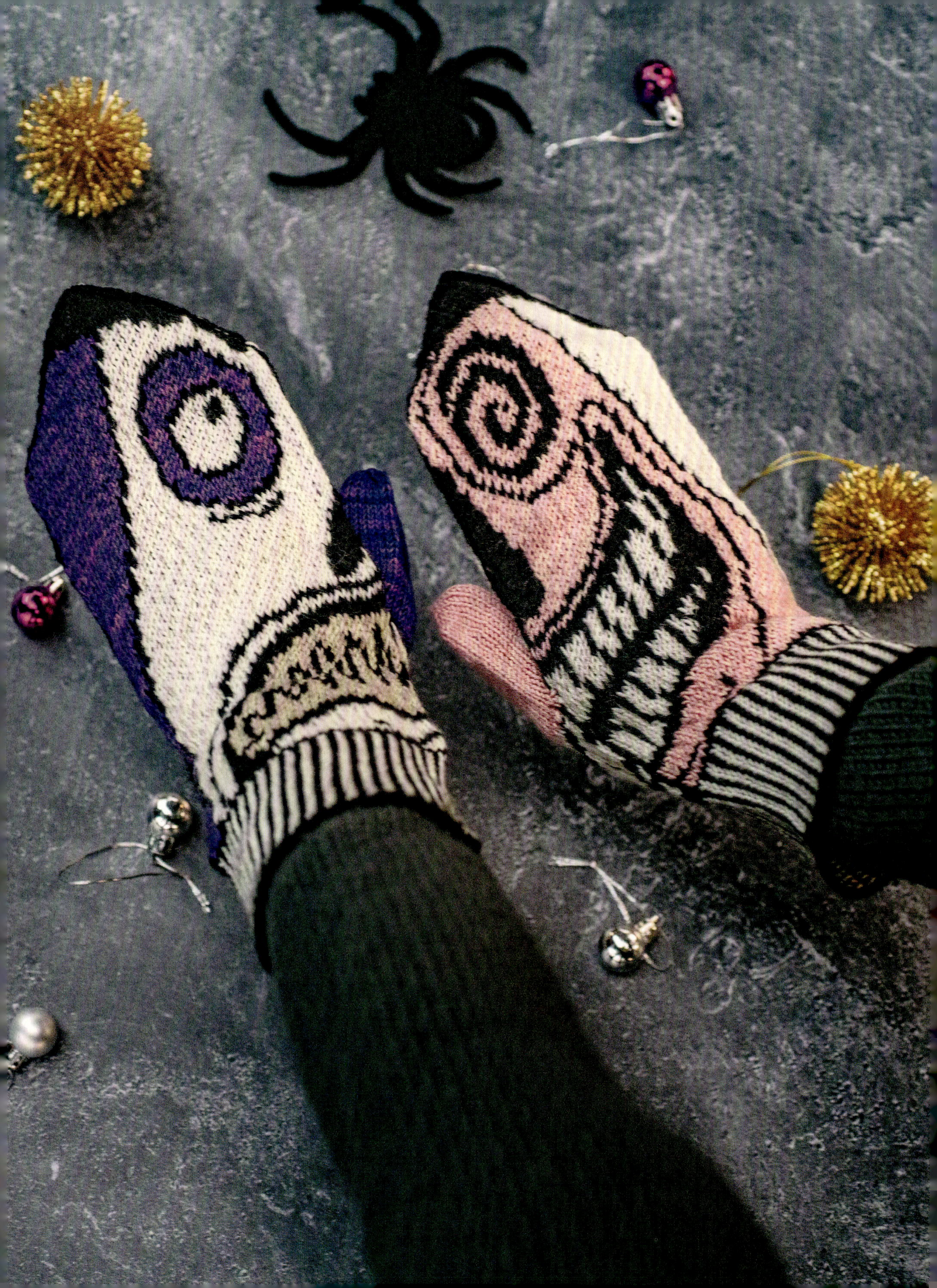

The Mayor Two-Face Mittens

Designed by
Therese Sharp

"I'm only an elected official here. I can't make decisions by myself."
—The Mayor

SKILL LEVEL

A satire of modern-day politicians, the mayor of Halloween Town is the skittish and indecisive official with two faces and a candy corn-shaped body. When confident and happy, he wears a huge smile on his face, but when stressed or sad, his face rotates to reveal a distressed frown. Sporting a top hat, a black widow spider bow tie that had been hiding in his megaphone, and a jaunty mayor badge, the quirky mayor has very little true authority in running Halloween Town. He looks to Jack for any decision-making, even pestering him about next Halloween the day after, and he publicly supports Jack's Christmas plan, despite his own misgivings.

Vote "yea" or "nay" with a simple wave of your hand! The mittens are knit in the round from the bottom up starting with corrugated ribbing, with the two faces of the mayor worked on opposite mitts in stranded colorwork. A desperately unsure mayor on one hand, with a maniacally confident mayor on the other, by holding the two mittens together, both reactions can be seen at once! Swirl motifs dance along the palm sides with afterthought thumbs placed while knitting, then added on at the end.

SIZES

Small (Medium, Large, Extra Large)

FINISHED MEASUREMENTS

Hand Circumference: 8¼ (8¾, 9½, 10½) in. / 21 (22, 24, 26.5) cm

Total Length: 10½ (11¼, 12, 12¾) in. / 26.5 (28.5, 30.5, 32.5) cm

Designed to fit with 0 to ¾ in. / 0 to 2 cm positive ease.

YARN

Fingering weight yarn, shown in The Plucky Knitter *Feet Fingering* (worsted spun; 90% superwash merino, 10% recycled nylon; 425 yd. / 389 m per 4 oz. / 115 g hank)

COLORWAYS:

- Main Color (MC): Bare, 1 hank
- Contrast Color 1 (CC1): Morticia, 1 hank
- Contrast Color 2 (CC2): Sugar Coated, 1 hank
- Contrast Color 3 (CC3): Big Horn, 1 hank
- Contrast Color 4 (CC4): Pinkies Out, 1 hank

NEEDLES

US 1.5 / 2.5 mm, 32 in. / 80 cm circular needle or set of 5 double-pointed needles

US 4 / 3.5 mm, 32 in. / 80 cm circular needle or set of 5 double-pointed needles or size needed to obtain gauge

NOTIONS

Stitch markers (2)

Waste yarn

Tapestry needle

GAUGE

Small: 42 sts and 38 rows = 4 in. / 10 cm in stranded knitting pattern worked in the rnd, taken after blocking

CONTINUED ON THE NEXT PAGE

- Medium: 39 sts and 35 rows = 4 in. / 10 cm in stranded knitting pattern worked in the rnd, taken after blocking
- Large: 36 sts and 32½ rows = 4 in. / 10 cm in stranded knitting pattern worked in the rnd, taken after blocking
- Extra Large: 33 sts and 30 rows = 4 in. / 10 cm in stranded knitting pattern worked in the rnd, taken after blocking

Make sure to check your gauge.

PATTERN NOTES

- To honor the original design of the mittens and ensure a wider range of available fit, rather than compromise on the stitch pattern, these mittens have been graded using different gauges for each size. To achieve the gauge for your finished size of mittens, adjust your needle size as needed.
- These mittens are worked in the round from the bottom up, using stranded knitting to create the colorwork motifs. When working the stranded colorwork, catch floats longer than 5 stitches.
- The 2-color corrugated rib cuff is worked on the smaller needle, and the body of the mitten is worked using the larger needle. The afterthought thumb is worked on the smaller needle.
- When working the corrugated rib, be sure to move the CC1 yarn to the back between the needles after completing the purl stitch so all floats are on the WS of the mitten.
- Written instructions are provided for the construction of the mittens; colorwork charts are provided for the body of the mitten.
- The construction is the same for each mitten; make 2 to complete a pair. Substitute in the appropriate chart and thumb placement instructions for the left and right mittens where appropriate.
- Waste yarn will be used to hold the stitches for the afterthought thumb while the body of the mitten is completed. A smooth waste yarn in fingering weight is recommended to make transferring the stitches back to the working needle easier.
- Instructions are provided for size Small first, with larger sizes in parentheses. When only one set of numbers is provided, it applies to all sizes.

PATTERN STITCHES

Corrugated Rib (worked over a multiple of 2 sts)

All Rnds: *K1 with MC, p1 with CC1; rep from * to end of rnd.

PATTERN INSTRUCTIONS

CAST ON & CUFF

Using the smaller needle and CC1, CO 82 sts using the Long Tail Cast On method. Pm for BOR and join to work in the rnd, being careful not to twist the sts.
Join MC.
Work in Corrugated Rib until the cuff measures approx. 2¼ in. / 5.5 cm from the CO edge.
NEXT RND (INC): Using CC1, *k18, kfb; rep from * 3 more times; knit to end of rnd—86 sts.

BODY OF MITTEN

Change to larger needle.
Begin Mitten chart (pages 102 and 104) for the appropriate hand (left or right), reading all rows from right to left as for working in the round and joining CCs as required. Work Rnds 1–22 once; Rnd 23, where there is a mark for Thumb Placement, will be worked in tandem with written instructions that differ for each mitten.

THUMB PLACEMENT AND BODY OF MITTEN CONTINUED

FOR LEFT HAND MITTEN

Work across all sts in patt (per Row 23) to the last 15 sts. Slip the last 15 sts of the rnd onto waste yarn. Using MC and CC1, cast on 15 new stitches in the colorwork pattern shown in the green Thumb Placement box of the chart using the Backward Loop method.

FOR RIGHT HAND MITTEN

Work across the first 44 sts in patt (per Row 23). Slip the next 15 sts to waste yarn. Using MC and CC1, cast on 15 new stitches in the colorwork pattern shown in the green Thumb Placement box of the chart using the Backward Loop method. Cont to the end of rnd in patt (per Row 23).

BOTH MITTENS

Work Rnds 24–79 of the chart. 6 sts rem at chart completion. Break all yarn except CC1. If not already the case, transfer the rem 6 sts to 2 needles (3 sts per needle).
Break CC1 leaving an 8 in. / 20.5 cm tail. Graft the live sts from the 2 needles held parallel using Kitchener stitch.

AFTERTHOUGHT THUMB

Place the live 15 sts from the Thumb Placement onto the smaller needle.
Join CC2 (for Left Mitten) or CC4 (for Right Mitten) to the left edge of the live sts when the palm of the mitten is facing you.
Pick up and knit 1 st into the gap between the live sts and the cast on sts, pm (SSM), pick up and knit 15 sts along the cast on edge of the back of the thumb, pick up and knit 1 more stitch to close the gap at the right edge of the thumbhole. Pm for BOR and join to work in the rnd—32 sts total.
SETUP RND (DEC): *K14, k2tog, sm; rep from * once more—30 sts rem.
Work in St st (knit every rnd) for 25 rnds, or until the thumb is approx. ¾ in. / 2 cm short of the desired total length.

THUMB DECREASE RND (DEC): *Ssk, knit to 2 sts before M, k2tog, sm; rep from * once more—4 sts dec.
Rep Thumb Decrease Rnd 5 more times.
24 sts dec; 6 sts rem.
Break CC, leaving an 8 in. / 20.5 cm tail. If not already the case, transfer the rem 6 sts to 2 needles (3 sts per needle). Graft the live sts from the 2 needles held parallel using Kitchener stitch.

FINISHING

Weave in all ends and wet block to measurements. Allow to dry completely. Trim all ends.

FRIGHTENING FACT

While the Mayor of Halloween Town is giving his speech before Jack leaves for the Real World to deliver toys for Christmas, he's holding a long paper with his actual speech written out on it in its entirety by the prop department.

Key

- ☐ Knit
- ▓ No stitch
- ☐ MC
- ■ CC1
- ■ CC2
- ▨ CC3
- ▨ CC4
- ╱ k2tog
- ╲ ssk
- ▢ Thumb placement

Mitten Chart - Left Hand

103

Key

- ☐ Knit
- ▨ No stitch
- ☐ MC
- ■ CC1
- ■ CC2
- ■ CC3
- ■ CC4
- ◹ k2tog
- ◺ ssk
- ▭ Thumb placement

Mitten Chart - Right Hand

105

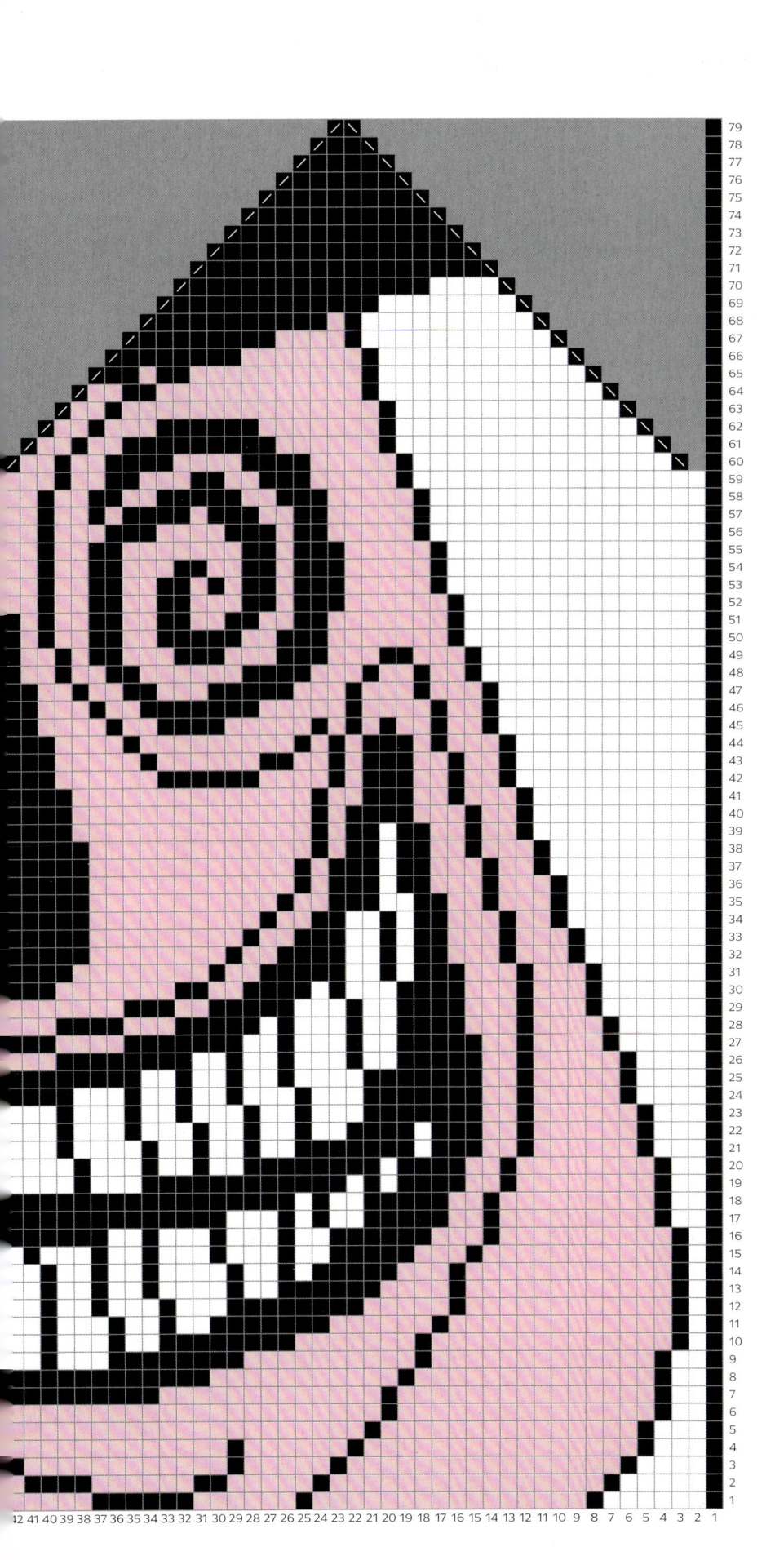

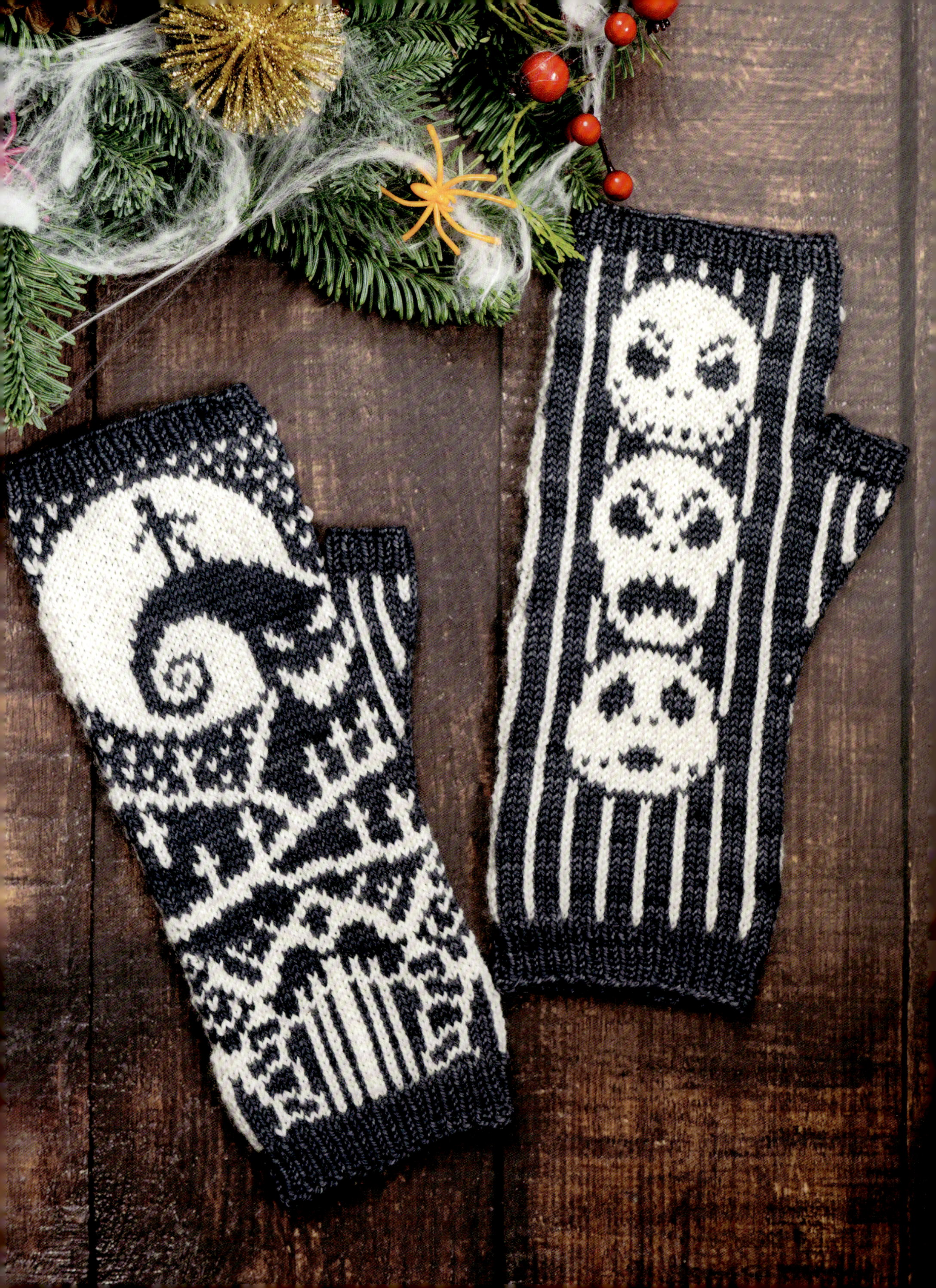

Jack's Lament Fingerless Mitts

Designed by
Jacqueline Rivera

"Jack, I know how you feel."
—Sally

SKILL LEVEL

Knitters create something one stitch at a time—a perfect parallel to *Tim Burton's The Nightmare Before Christmas*'s songwriting method. Before there was even a finished script, Danny Elfman was tapped to write the songs for this musical in an unconventional way. Elfman and Tim Burton would meet, and Burton would tell *The Nightmare Before Christmas* story to him bit by bit, in chronological order. Elfman would take a few days to reflect, write a song, then bring it back for approval, and hear the next part of the story. Elfman says, "It's kind of backwards, but we know what the story is. Let's see how much of it we can tell in the songs. . . . This is the way musicals were done in the thirties and forties." Script writer Caroline Thompson says, "Danny's songs are so thorough in telling Jack's story. . . . There's very little left to do in terms of a script . . ." Once the script and songs were finalized, animators could begin to work their magic on set.

Do you have the urge to walk through graveyards, sing at the full moon, and wonder about the empty place in your bones? Then perhaps it's time to knit yourself a pair of mitts that would do Mister Unlucky, that Pumpkin King with the skeleton grin, proud! Worked in the round from the bottom up with 1x1 ribbed edgings, the mitts feature stranded colorwork that recreates the iconic "Jack's Lament" scene from the film. Increases establish the pinstripe thumb to be put on waste yarn and finished later. Each mitt is worked using a different chart to display more of Jack's expressive faces on the palm side, and showcase Spiral Hill with Jack backlit by the moon and Oogie Boogie's shadow growing on the hand side.

SIZES
1 (2, 3, 4)

FINISHED MEASUREMENTS
Circumference: 7½ (8, 8½, 9) in. / 19 (20.5, 21.5, 23) cm

Length: 9¾ (10¼, 10¾, 11½) in. / 25 (26, 27.5, 29) cm

Designed to fit with 0 in. / 0 cm of ease; choose the size closest to your hand circumference for the best fit.

YARN
Fingering weight yarn, shown in Urban Girl Yarns *Virginia* (2-ply; 90% superwash merino, 10% nylon; 480 yd. / 439 m per 4½ oz. / 125 g hank)

COLORWAYS:
- Main Color (MC): Black Beauty, 1 hank
- Contrast Color (CC): Au Naturel, 1 hank

NEEDLES
US 2 / 2.75 mm, set of 5 double-pointed needles or size needed to obtain gauge

NOTIONS
Stitch marker

Row counter (optional)

Waste yarn

Tapestry needle

GAUGE
Size 1: 34 sts and 40 rnds = 4 in. / 10 cm over stranded colorwork in the round, taken after blocking

Size 2: 32 sts and 38 rnds = 4 in. / 10 cm over stranded colorwork in the round, taken after blocking

Size 3: 30 sts and 36 rnds = 4 in. / 10 cm over stranded colorwork in the round, taken after blocking

Size 4: 28½ sts and 34 rnds = 4 in. / 10 cm over stranded colorwork in the round, taken after blocking

Make sure to check your gauge.

PATTERN NOTES

- To honor the original design of these fingerless mitts and ensure a wider range of available fit, rather than compromise on the stitch pattern, these mitts have been graded using different gauges for each size. To achieve the gauge for your finished size of mitts, adjust your needle size as needed.
- The mitts are worked in the round from the bottom up using stranded knitting. All colorwork portions of the pattern are charted; written instructions are not provided for colorwork or thumb shaping.
- Increases indicated on the chart create shaping for the thumb. Thumb stitches are then placed on waste yarn to be picked up and finished later.
- When knitting the colorwork, catch floats longer than 5 stitches.

PATTERN INSTRUCTIONS

CAST ON & RIBBED EDGE

With MC, CO 64 sts using the Long Tail Cast On method. Distribute sts evenly across 4 needles—16 sts per needle. Pm for BOR and join to work in the rnd, being careful not to twist the sts.

RNDS 1–9: *K1, p1; rep from * to end of rnd.

FIRST MITT

Join CC.
Begin Left Mitt chart (page 110), reading all rows from right to left as for working in the rnd.
Work Rows 1–61 once—82 sts at completion.
Work 32 sts in patt as per Row 62 of chart, place the next 18 thumb sts onto waste yarn, work the remaining 32 sts of Row 62 of the chart to end of rnd—64 sts rem.
Work Rows 63–84 once.
Break CC yarn.
Proceed to Finish Mitt.

SECOND MITT

Work as for the First Mitt, substituting in the Right Mitt chart (page 111).

FINISH MITT—BOTH MITTS

SETUP RND: Knit.
RNDS 1–4: *K1, p1; rep from * to end of rnd.
Bind off all sts loosely in patt.

THUMB—BOTH MITTS

Carefully remove waste yarn and place 18 live sts on dpns, distributing sts for comfort.
Rejoin MC yarn to the right edge of the live sts with the RS facing.
SETUP ROW (RS): K18, pick up and knit 4 sts to close the gap. Pm for BOR and join to work in the rnd—22 sts total.
RND 1: Knit.
RNDS 2–5: *K1, p1; rep from * to end of rnd.
Bind off all sts loosely in patt.

FINISHING

Weave in all ends and wet block. Allow to dry completely. Trim all ends.

FRIGHTENING FACT

In the film while singing "Jack's Lament," Jack removes his head as a reference to Shakespeare's *Hamlet*, during the "To be, or not to be" soliloquy where the actor holds a skull.

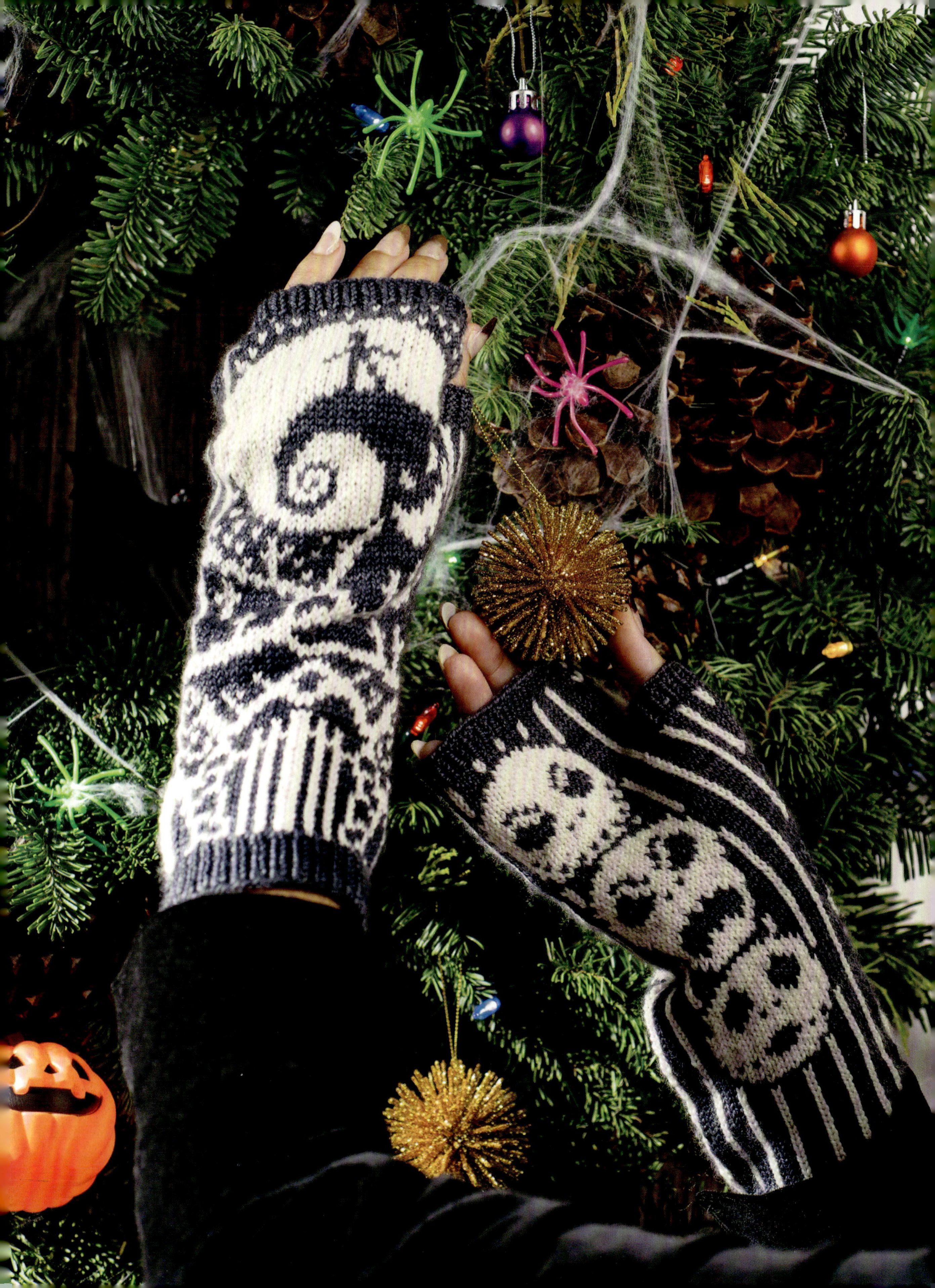

Left Mitt Chart

Key

- ☐ Knit
- ▨ No stitch
- ■ MC
- ☐ CC
- ⌐ M1L
- — Place sts below on waste yarn

Right Mitt Chart

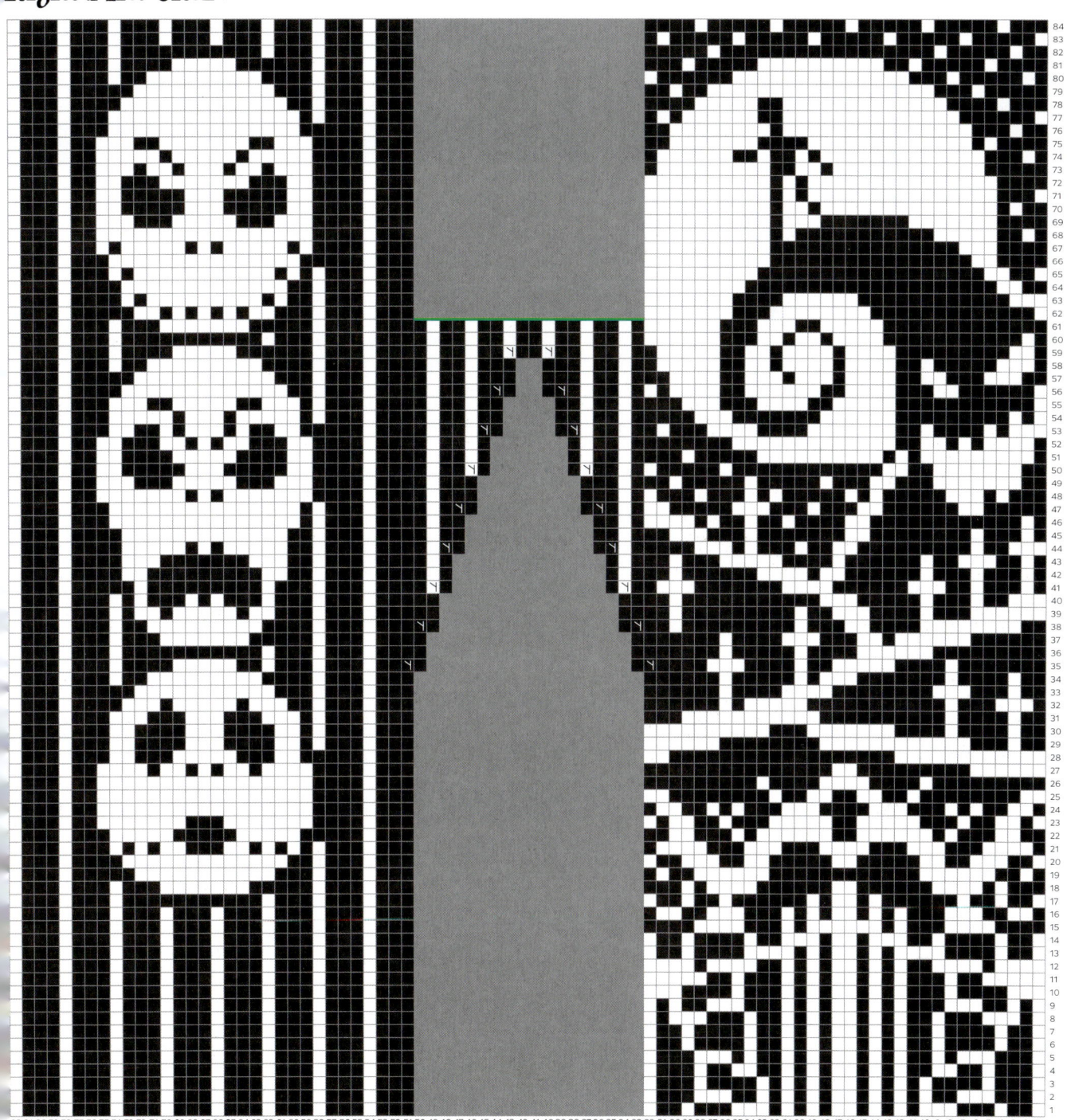

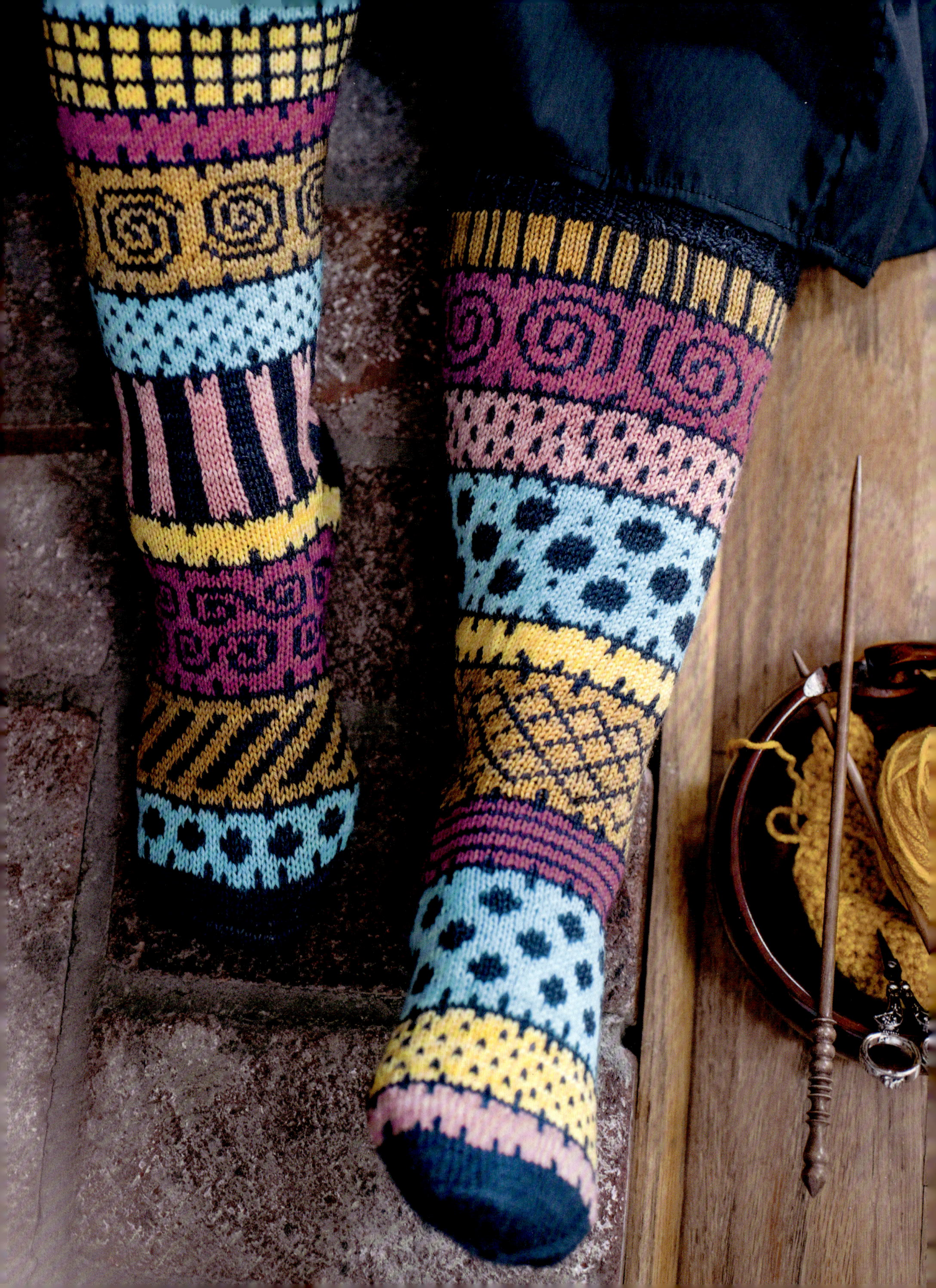

Sally's Socks

Designed by
Heini Perälä

"You can make other creations. I'm restless. I can't help it."
—Sally

SKILL LEVEL
💀💀💀

With her hand-stitched dress and visible seams, there's no doubt that Sally is one of Dr. Finkelstein's creations. Gathered scraps of fabric are sewn together like a patchwork quilt to create her iconic dress. Consistency is necessary in most films, but in *Tim Burton's The Nightmare Before Christmas*, it was key for the film's overall look. Art director Deane Taylor says, "Technical considerations are major. You have to think about getting lights where you need them to be, about access for the animator. It's easy to draw a beautifully lit character, but if you can't get into the set to put the light there, you've lost your look." Eight different camera crews worked on various parts of the film at the same time, with all the track, boom, and pan actions preprogrammed via computer in the camera ahead of time. On average, it took three days of prep before an animator could get on the set with the puppets and begin.

Stop-motion animation requires 24 frames per second, with *Tim Burton's The Nightmare Before Christmas* racking up over 113,000 frames total. Animators had the goal of shooting one second of film per week per camera, requiring over three years to complete the film. Creator Tim Burton says about stop-motion animators, "It requires, in my opinion, quite an artist and technician, and that's a hard combination to find." Although the sets were smaller in scale than a live-action production, they were similarly lit, often requiring between 20 and 30 lights to create dramatic effects. Further delays and reshoots could happen if a light was knocked over accidentally, or if a puppet fell while filming; mistakes often were not noticed until the footage was reviewed.

Be a clever fashionista like Sally with these stunning mismatched knee socks! Inspired by Sally's patchwork dress, these top-down socks have varying stranded colorwork motifs climbing their way up the leg in Sally's colors. Each sock is topped with a different cabled cuff and finished with a wide wedge toe, with the heel worked as a reinforced heel flap and gusset. To ensure a proper fit, be mindful not to knit the colorwork too tightly, or you might get yelled at by Dr. Finkelstein!

SIZES
Extra Small (Small, Medium, Large)

FINISHED MEASUREMENTS
Minimum Foot Length: 8¼ (8½, 9¼, 9½) in. / 21 (21.5, 23.5, 24) cm

Adjustable foot length.

Foot Circumference: 7½ (8, 8½, 9) in. / 19 (20.5, 21.5, 23) cm

Upper Calf Circumference: 11¾ (12½, 13½, 14¼) in. / 30 (32, 34.5, 36) cm

Leg Length: 10½ (11, 11½, 12¼) in. / 26.5 (28, 29, 21) cm

YARN
Fingering weight yarn, shown in Queen City Yarn *NoDa Sock* (75% superwash merino, 25% nylon; 463 yd. / 423 m per 3½ oz. / 100 g hank)

COLORWAYS:
- Main Color (MC): He Only Wears Black, 1 hank
- Contrast Color 1 (CC1): Unicorns of the Sea, 1 hank
- Contrast Color 2 (CC2): Ryan Yeyow, 1 hank
- Contrast Color 3 (CC3): Berry Stomp, 1 hank
- Contrast Color 4 (CC4): Blonde Roast, 1 hank
- Contrast Color 5 (CC5): Rose Gold, 1 hank

NEEDLES
US 1.5 / 2.5 mm, set of 5 double-pointed needles or size needed to obtain gauge

NOTIONS
Stitch marker (optional)

Cable needle

Tapestry needle

CONTINUED ON THE NEXT PAGE

GAUGE

Extra Small: 34 sts and 43 rnds = 4 in. / 10 cm in stranded knitting pattern worked in the rnd, taken after steam blocking

Small: 32 sts and 41 rnds = 4 in. / 10 cm in stranded knitting pattern worked in the rnd, taken after steam blocking

Medium: 30 sts and 39 rnds = 4 in. / 10 cm in stranded knitting pattern worked in the rnd, taken after steam blocking

Large: 28½ sts and 37 rnds = 4 in. / 10 cm in stranded knitting pattern worked in the rnd, taken after steam blocking

Make sure to check your gauge.

PATTERN NOTES

- To honor the original design of the socks and ensure a wider range of available fit, rather than compromise on the stitch pattern, these socks have been graded using different gauges for each size. To achieve the gauge for your finished size of socks, adjust your needle size as needed.
- These socks are worked in the round from the top down starting with the cable ribbing; the socks are not identical and have different cable patterning on the cuff and different colorwork patterns down each leg and foot.
- Socks include the reinforced heel flap and the wide wedge toe.
- When knitting the stranded colorwork, make sure you don't knit too tightly. When considering color dominance, use the Main Color (MC) as the dominant color throughout so that the black pattern stands out against the multicolored backgrounds.
- The colorwork sections of this pattern (leg, gusset, and foot) are charted. The charts are visually broken into four sections representing the stitches held on each of the dpns used to work the sock.
- Written instructions are provided for the non-charted portions of the socks.
- Break the CC yarn at the end of each color-block section; you will only ever have 1 or 2 yarns being used at the same time throughout the pattern.
- Try periodically stretching out the stitches you've just worked on your needle to keep the tension of your knitting and your floats even.
- A lot of time and effort go into knitting long socks like these. As such, they deserve a careful finishing. The designer recommends that you use a steam block method to finish the socks; most residential clothes irons have a steam setting. Steaming softens the fibers and smooths out any inconsistencies in the fabric. When steaming, do not press heavily on the surface of the sock; instead move the iron lightly over the surface with a tea towel between the sock and the iron.

PATTERN INSTRUCTIONS

CAST ON—RIGHT SOCK

Using MC, CO 96 sts using the Long Tail Cast On method. Distribute the sts so you have 24 sts on each needle. Pm for BOR and join to work in the rnd, being careful not to twist the sts.

LEG

Begin Leg chart (page 118 and 119) for the appropriate sock (left or right), reading all rows from right to left as for working in the rnd and joining CCs as required. Work Rnds 1–113 once (chart is worked once across each rnd), catching floats as needed (approx. every 4th st). At the completion of the chart, 71 sts will remain. If not already the case, redistribute the sts so that there are 17 sts on each of Needles 1 and 4, 18 sts on Needle 2, and 19 sts on Needle 3. Cut all CCs.

REINFORCED HEEL FLAP

The heel flap and heel shaping are worked using MC only.

Start the heel flap by knitting across the 17 sts of Needle 1 with Needle 4; 34 heel sts are now on Needle 4. Set Needle 1 aside; leave the sts of Needles 2 and 3 on hold. Turn the work. We will now work the heel flap flat (on the RS and WS) on Needle 4 only.

SETUP ROW (WS, DEC): Sl1 wyif, p2tog, purl to last 3 sts, p2tog, p1—32 sts rem.

ROW 1 (RS): *Sl1 wyib, k1; rep from * to end of row.

ROW 2 (WS): Sl1 wyif, purl to end of row.

Rep [Rows 1 and 2] 15 more times.

REINFORCED HEEL SHAPING

Short rows are worked to shape the bottom of the heel.

ROW 1 (RS, DEC): (Sl1 wyib, k1) 10 times, sl1 wyib, skp, turn—31 sts rem.

ROW 2 (WS, DEC): Sl1 wyif, p10, p2tog, turn—30 sts rem.
ROW 3 (DEC): (Sl1 wyib, k1) 5 times, sl1 wyib, skp, turn—1 st dec.
ROW 4 (DEC): Sl1 wyif, p10, p2tog, turn—1 st dec.

Rep Rows 3 and 4 until only the 12 center sts rem.

To prepare to knit in the rnd once again, k6 with MC. These 6 sts will remain on Needle 4, and this will be the new BOR.

Sl rem 6 sts purlwise to Needle 1. You will now have a total of 49 sts: 6 sts each on Needles 1 and 4, 18 sts on Needle 2, and 19 sts on Needle 3. Resume knitting in the rnd.

GUSSET

The first row of the Gusset chart (page 116–117 and 120–121) and picking up sts occur in tandem. Read carefully through these instructions before beginning.

Begin Gusset chart for the appropriate sock (left or right), reading all rows from right to left as for working in the rnd, joining CCs as required. Work Rows 1–17 once (chart is worked once across each rnd), catching floats as needed (approx. every 4th st).

AT THE SAME TIME, AS YOU WORK ROW 1 OF THE CHART:

Needle 1: K6. Pick up and knit 17 sts along the heel flap edge using the Twisted Heel Flap method; pick up and knit 1 st in the corner between the top of the heel flap and Needle 2—24 sts.

Needles 2 and 3: K18 and k19 in colorwork pattern.

Needle 4: Pick up and knit 1 st in the corner between the top of the heel flap and Needle 3, then pick up and knit 17 sts along the heel flap edge using the Twisted Heel Flap method, k6—24 sts.

Once Rnd 1 is complete, you should have 85 sts. At the completion of the chart, you should have 67 sts. If not already the case, redistribute the sts so that there are 16 sts on each of Needles 1 and 4, 17 sts on Needle 2, and 18 sts on Needle 3. Do not cut the current CC.

FOOT

Begin Foot chart (page 116–117 and 120–121) for the appropriate sock (left or right), reading all rows from right to left as for working in the rnd, joining CCs as required. Work Rows 1–37 once (chart is worked once across each rnd), catching floats as needed (approx. every 4th st). At the completion of the chart, you should have 64 sts. If not already the case, redistribute the sts so that there are 16 sts on each of the 4 needles. Cut all CCs. The remainder of the sock is worked with MC only.

Using MC, work in St st (knit every rnd) until the foot is approx. 1¼ (1¼, 1½, 1½) in. / 3 (3, 4, 4) cm short of the desired total length, when measured from the back of the heel.

WIDE WEDGE TOE

RND 1 (DEC): *Knit to last 3 sts of Needle 1, k2tog, k1, k1, ssk, knit to end of Needle 2; rep from * across Needles 3 and 4—4 sts dec.
RND 2: Knit.

Rep [Rnds 1 and 2] 2 more times—52 sts rem (13 sts on each needle).

Then rep Rnd 1 only 10 more times—12 sts rem (3 sts on each needle).

Cut MC yarn, leaving an 8 in. / 20.5 cm tail. Thread tapestry needle and pull tail through live sts; pull to cinch closed and secure the tail on the inside of the sock.

FINISHING

Weave in all ends. Make the left sock.

CAST ON—LEFT SOCK

Using MC, CO 99 sts using the Long Tail Cast On method. Distribute the sts so you have 25 sts on Needle 1, 24 sts on Needles 2 and 3, and 26 sts on Needle 4. Pm for BOR and join to work in the rnd, being careful not to twist the sts.

Work the Leg, Reinforced Heel Flap, Reinforced Heel Shaping, Gusset, Foot, and Wide Wedge Toe sections, using the charts for the left sock where necessary.

FINISHING

Weave in all ends. Gently steam block your socks.

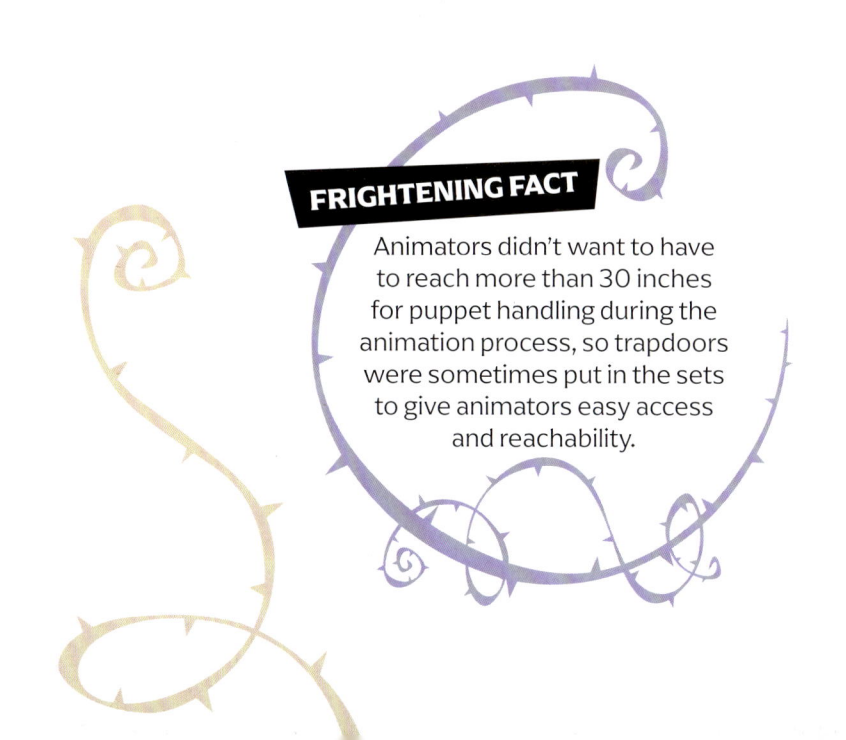

FRIGHTENING FACT

Animators didn't want to have to reach more than 30 inches for puppet handling during the animation process, so trapdoors were sometimes put in the sets to give animators easy access and reachability.

Key

- ☐ Knit
- − Purl
- Q K tbl
- M1R
- ╱ k2tog
- ╲ ssk
- sl3kyok
- 2/2 LC
- 2/2 RC
- ■ MC
- ■ CC1
- ■ CC2
- ■ CC3
- ■ CC4
- ■ CC5
- │ Needle divider

Sally's Socks - Right Gusset

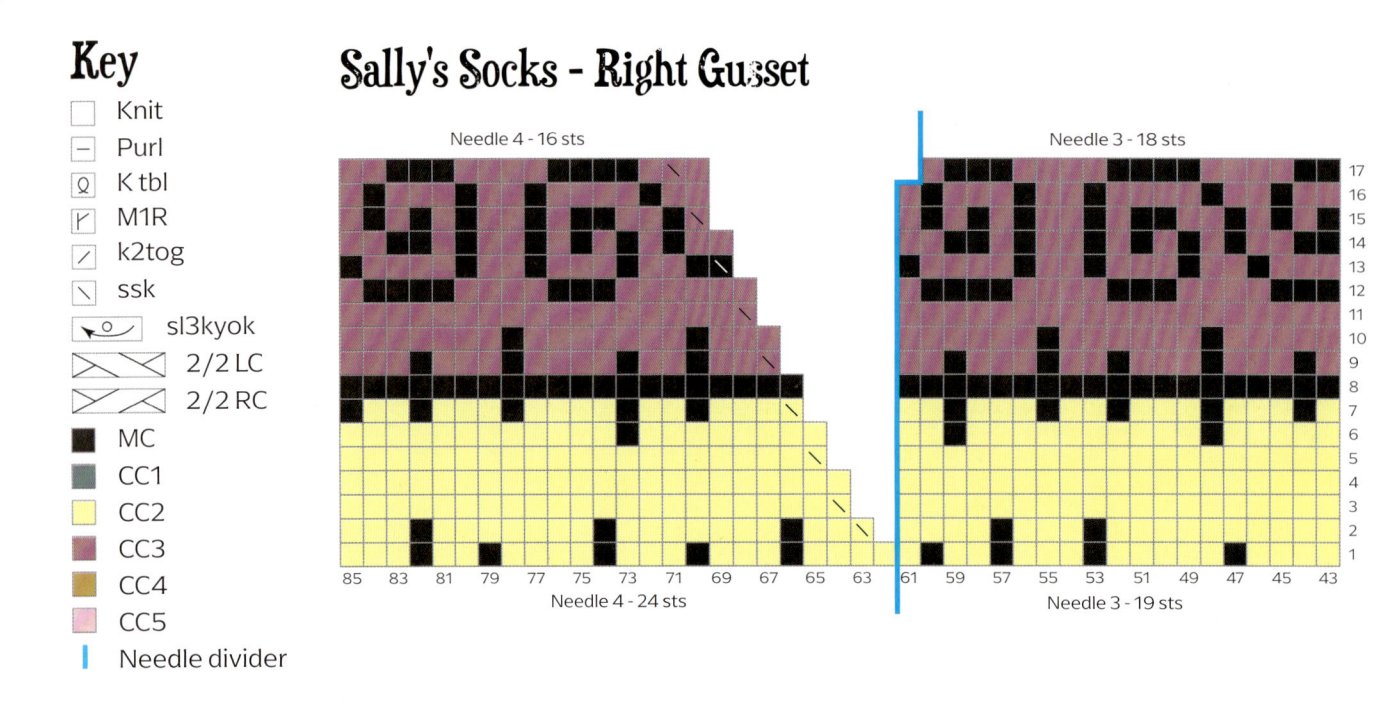

Sally's Socks - Right Foot

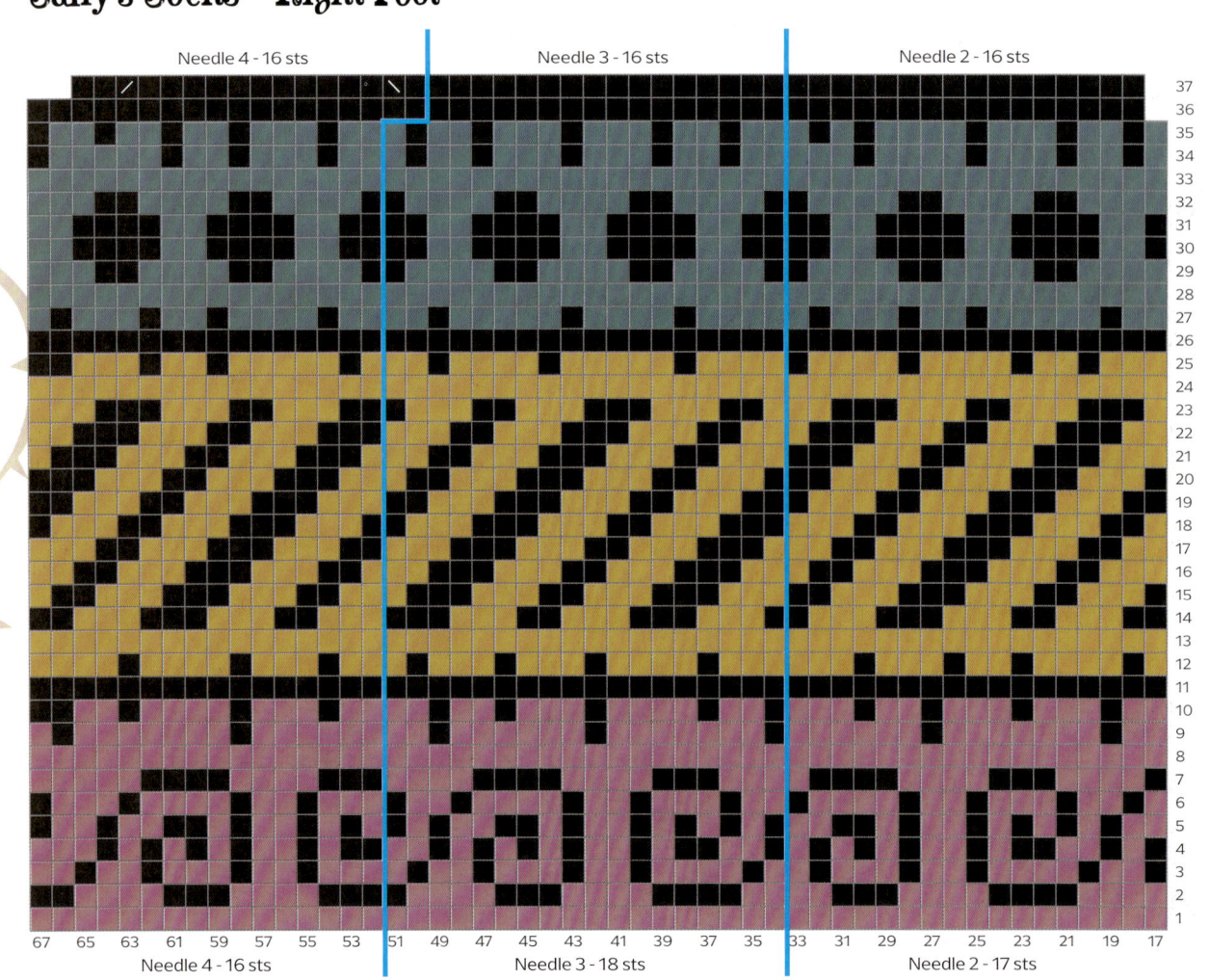

Sally's Socks - Right Gusset

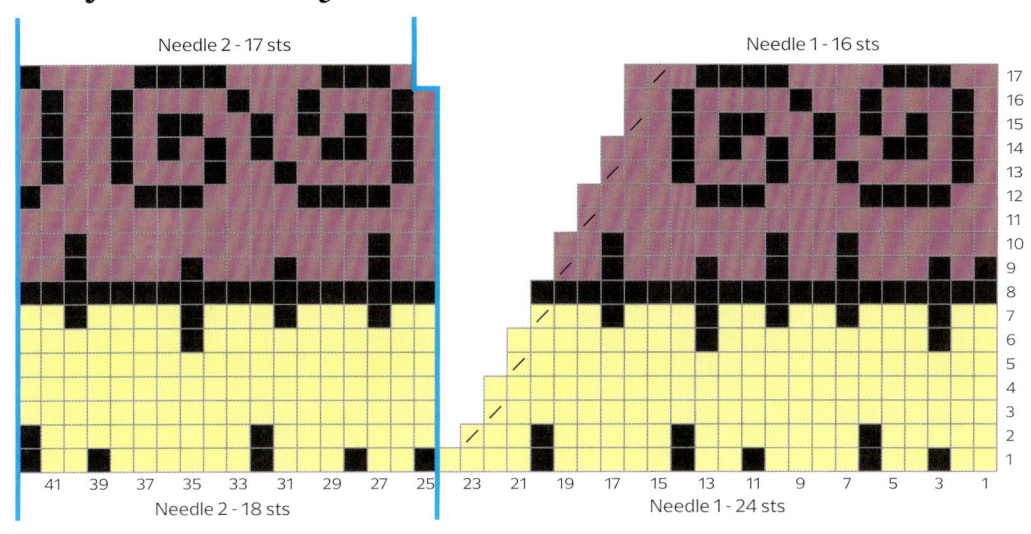

Needle 2 - 17 sts
Needle 2 - 18 sts

Needle 1 - 16 sts
Needle 1 - 24 sts

Sally's Socks - Right Foot

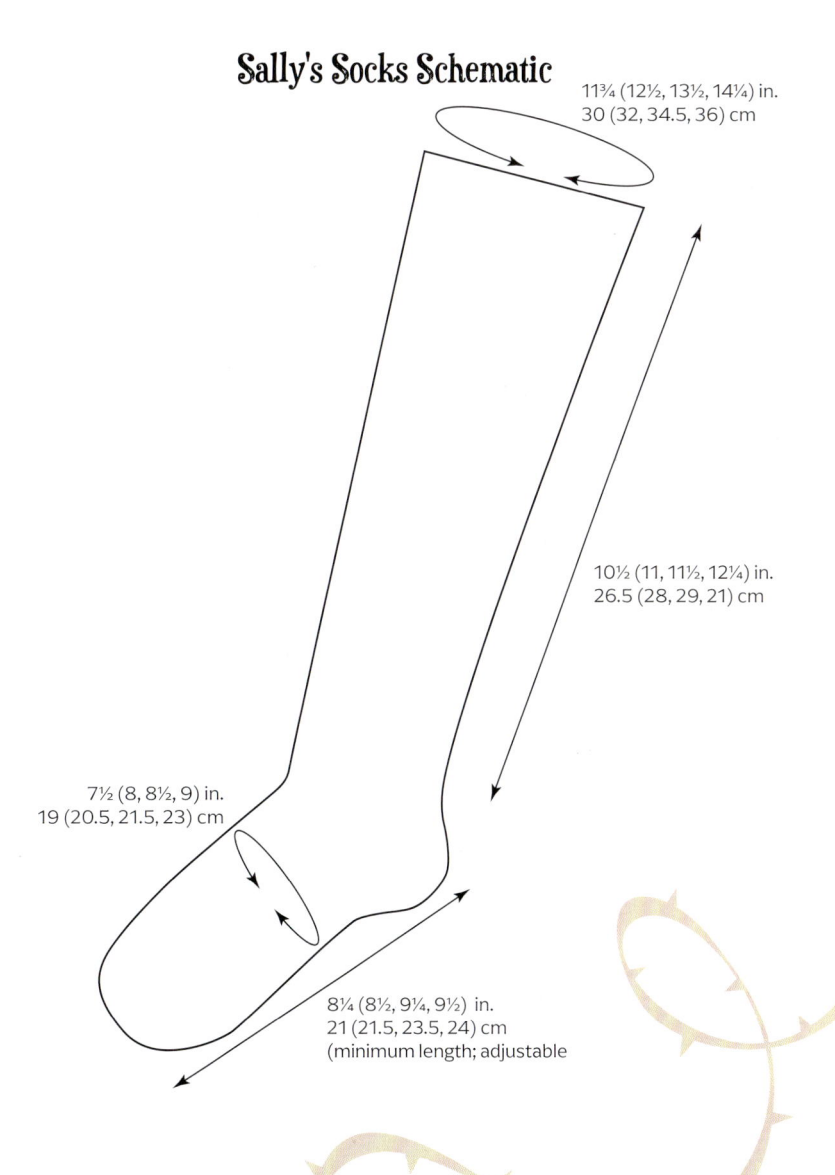

Needle 1 - 16 sts

Sally's Socks Schematic

11¾ (12½, 13½, 14¼) in.
30 (32, 34.5, 36) cm

10½ (11, 11½, 12¼) in.
26.5 (28, 29, 21) cm

7½ (8, 8½, 9) in.
19 (20.5, 21.5, 23) cm

8¼ (8½, 9¼, 9½) in.
21 (21.5, 23.5, 24) cm
(minimum length; adjustable)

Sally's Socks - Right Leg Chart

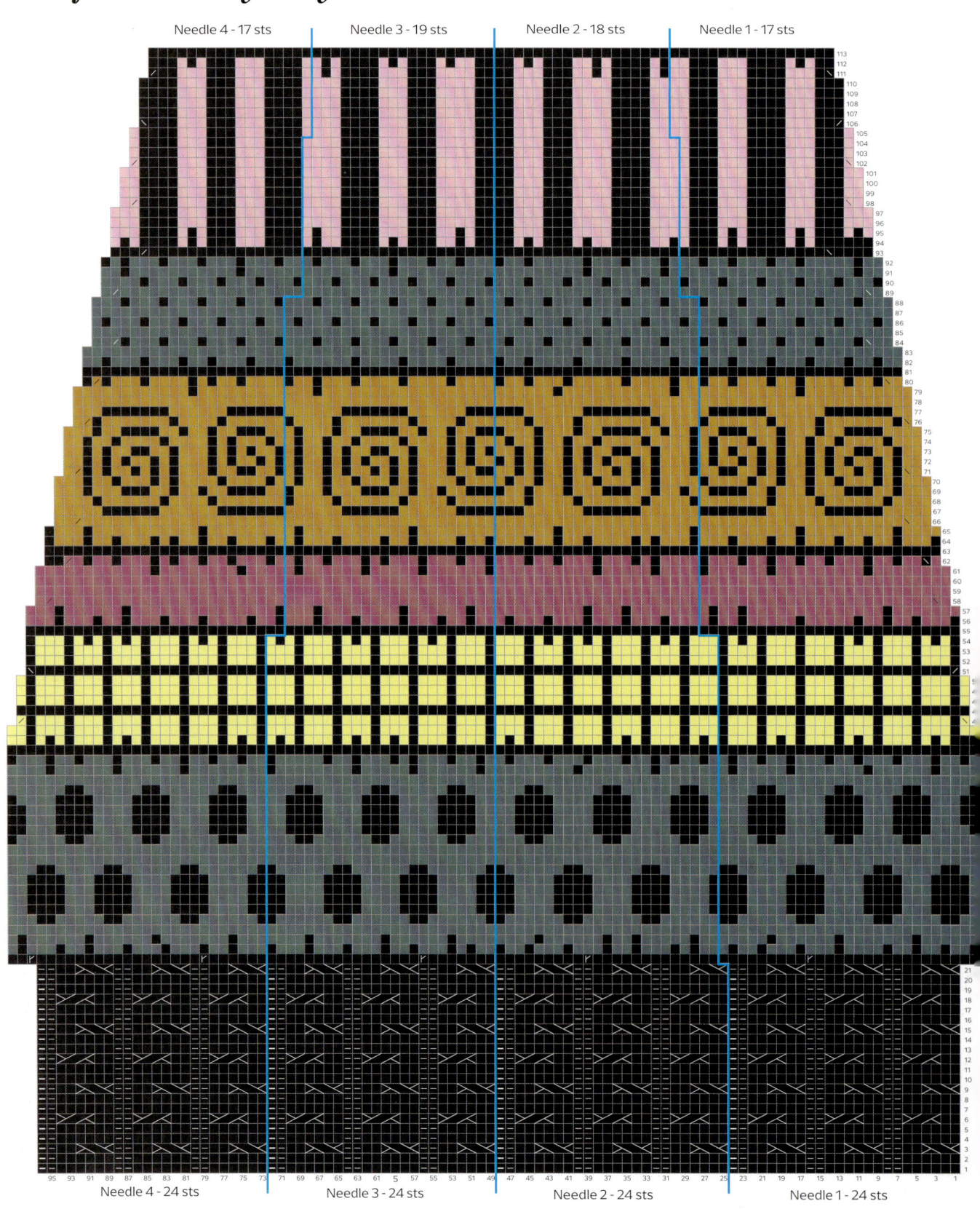

Sally's Socks - Left Leg Chart

Needle 4 - 17 sts • Needle 3 - 19 sts • Needle 2 - 18 sts • Needle 1 - 17 sts

Needle 4 - 26 sts • Needle 3 - 24 sts • Needle 2 - 24 sts • Needle 1 - 25 sts

Key

- ☐ Knit
- − Purl
- Q K tbl
- M1R
- ∕ k2tog
- ∖ ssk
- sl3kyok
- 2/2 LC
- 2/2 RC
- ■ MC
- CC1
- CC2
- CC3
- CC4
- CC5
- | Needle divider

Sally's Socks - Left Gusset

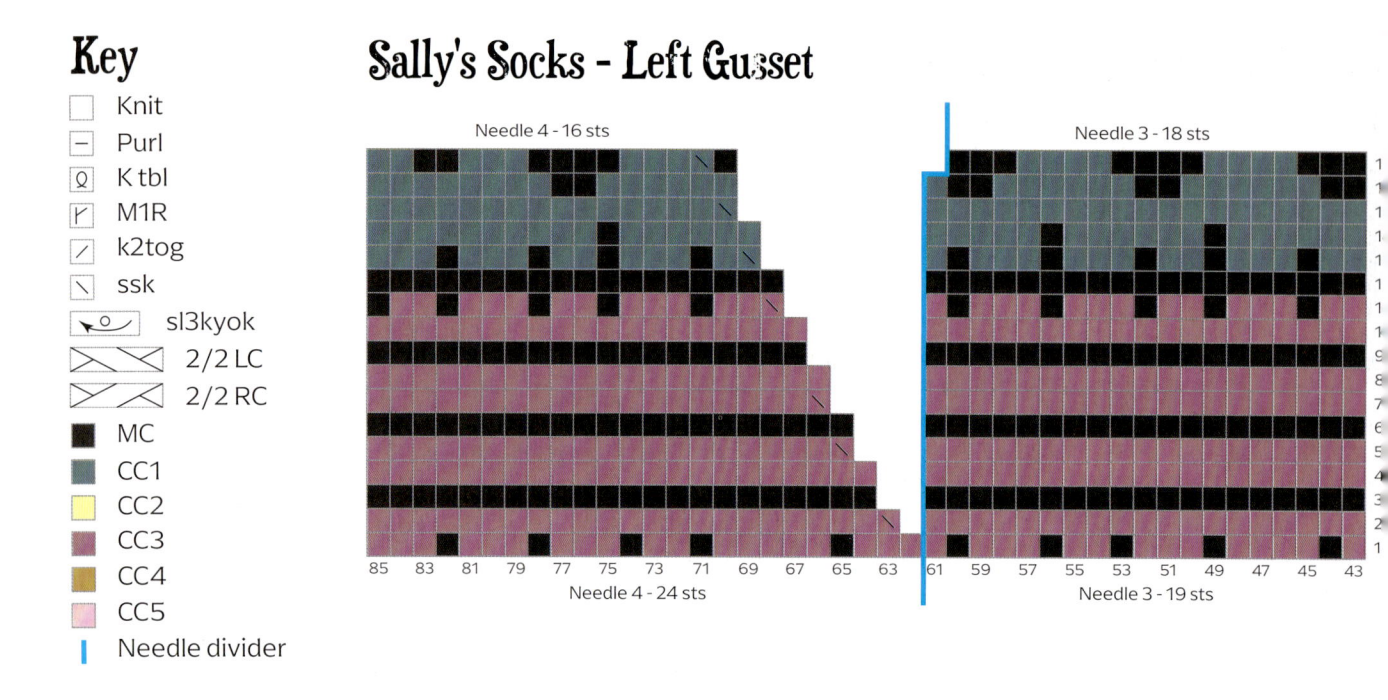

Needle 4 - 16 sts | Needle 3 - 18 sts
Needle 4 - 24 sts | Needle 3 - 19 sts

Sally's Socks - Left Foot

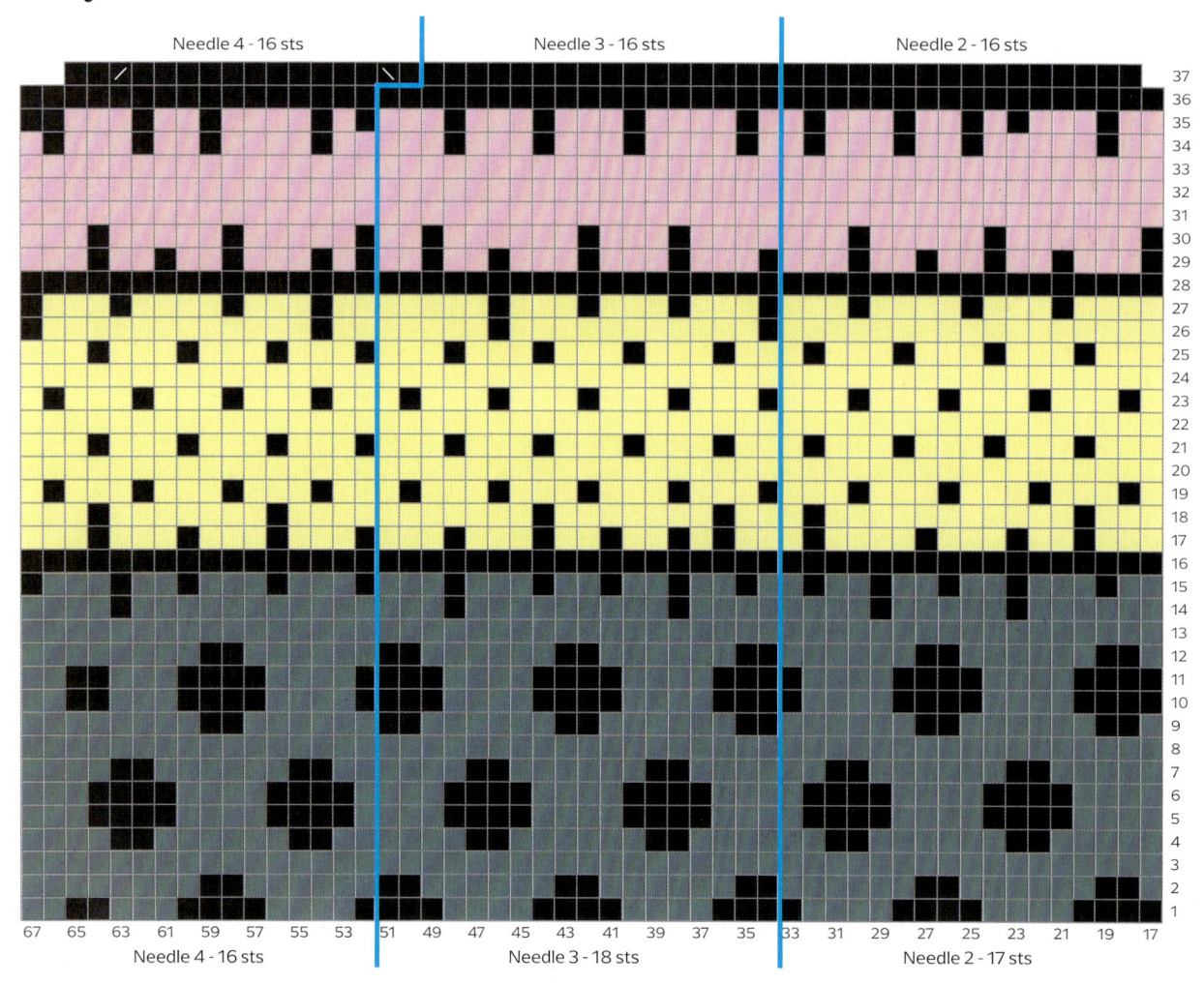

Needle 4 - 16 sts | Needle 3 - 16 sts | Needle 2 - 16 sts
Needle 4 - 16 sts | Needle 3 - 18 sts | Needle 2 - 17 sts

Sally's Socks - Left Gusset

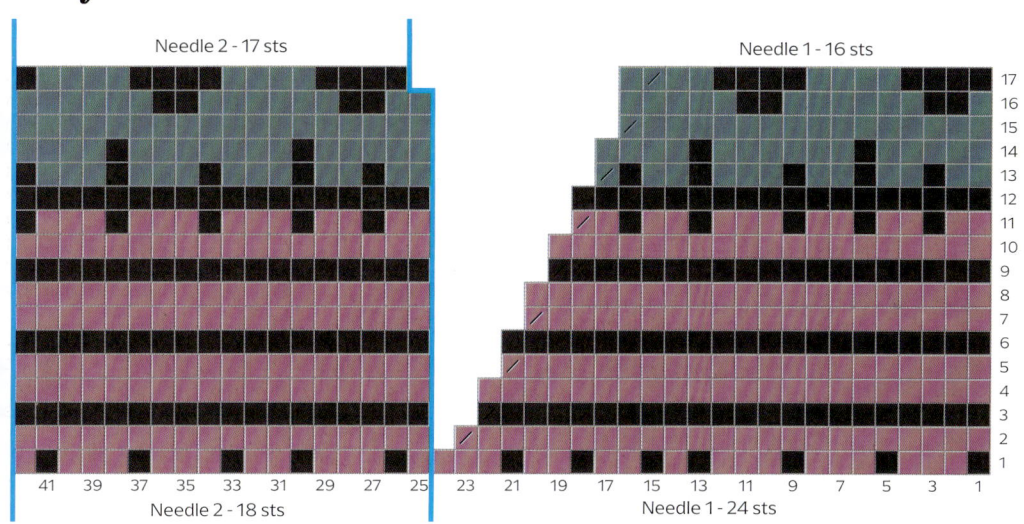

Needle 2 - 17 sts

Needle 2 - 18 sts

Needle 1 - 16 sts

Needle 1 - 24 sts

Sally's Socks - Left Foot

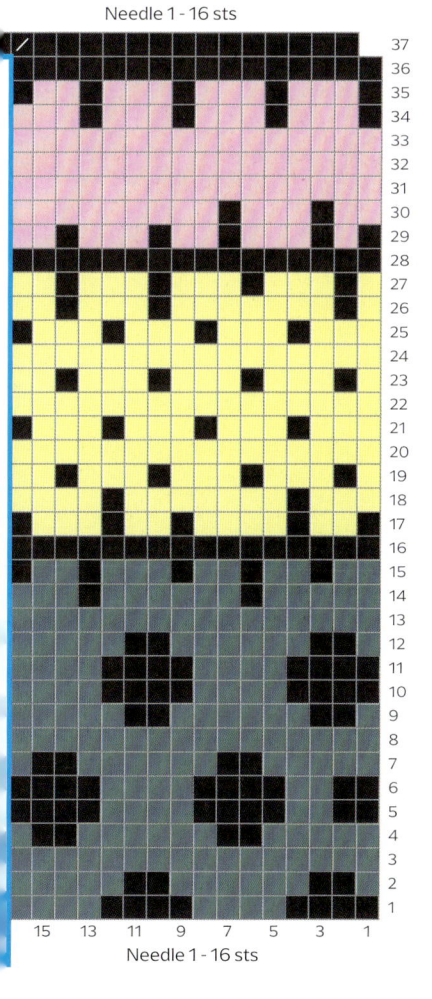

Needle 1 - 16 sts

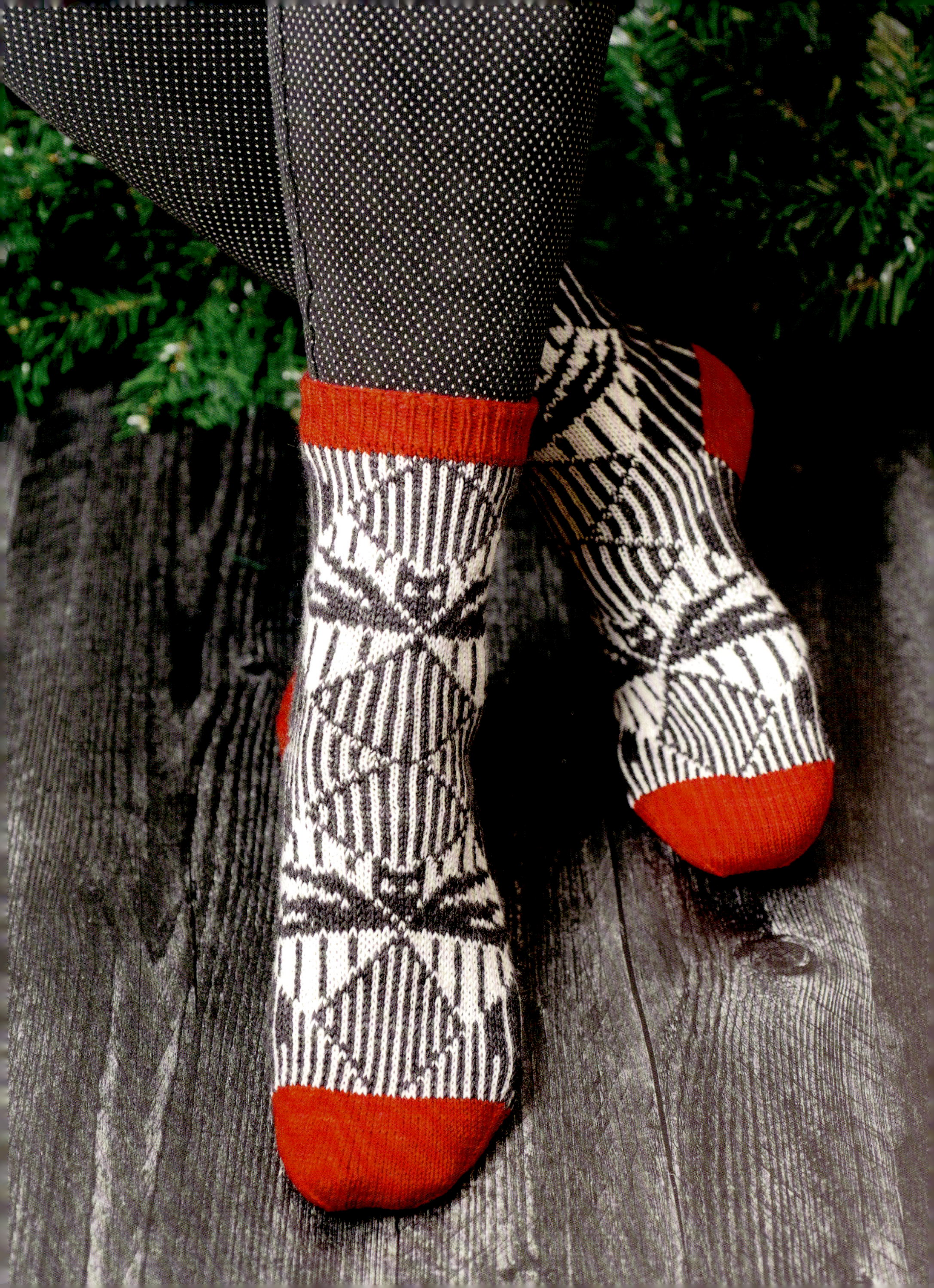

Wickedly Cute Pinstripe Socks

Designed by
Megan-Anne of Lattes & Llamas

"What is this?"
—Jack Skellington

SKILL LEVEL

During initial photography tests, Jack's iconic suit was not pinstripe but solid black. Due to the limited palette of Halloween Town of black, white, and orange, director Henry Selick added thin pinstripes to Jack's suit to make him stand out more against dark backgrounds. The regular, even stripes also help him stand out against the slanted angles of the set. The sets in a stop-motion film play a large part in setting the tone and sometimes require more work than in a live-action film. Some sets measure up to 40 by 20 feet, while others are a square foot. From concept to construction to figuring out every detail, the film's art department was encouraged to push the envelope and come up with a way to make everything slightly off-kilter. Designers began drawing with their nondominant hands, which did the trick according to artist Kelly Asbury, who said, "It made everything just a little unsound." Art director Deane Taylor was also told that "a right angle is a wrong angle" and that Halloween Town should be very jagged and sharp. Heavily influenced by German Expressionism and old monster movies, the overall look is one of whimsy, light and shadows, an anxious atmosphere, and distorted perspective.

Treat your toes to the elegant pinstripes they deserve! Worked in the round from the cuff down, these dapper socks feature stranded colorwork bats flying through a modern argyle motif. As a bold contrast to the classic Jack-inspired black-and-white palette, the 1x1 ribbed cuff, flat short row-shaped heel, and toe are knit in red as a festive alternate to the film's orange accents. Choose the size closest to your actual foot measurement, with little to no ease.

SIZES
1 (2, 3, 4)

FINISHED MEASUREMENTS
Foot Circumference: 7¾ (8½, 9½, 10¼) in. / 19.5 (21.5, 24, 26) cm

Choose the size closest to your foot measurement for the best fit (if between sizes, go down to wear the socks with negative ease).

YARN
Fingering weight yarn, shown in Leading Men Fiber Arts *Show Stopper* (75% superwash merino, 25% nylon; 463 yd. / 423 m per 3½ oz. / 100 g hank)

COLORWAYS:
- Color A: Bare Necessities, 1 hank
- Color B: Darkest Hour, 1 hank

Fingering weight yarn, shown in Leading Men Fiber Arts *Show Stopper Intermission* (75% superwash merino, 25% nylon; 231 yd. / 211 m per 1¾ oz. / 50 g hank)

COLORWAY:
- Color C: Poison Apple, 1 hank

NEEDLES
US 1.5 / 2.5 mm, 32 in. / 80 cm circular needle

US 2 / 2.75 mm, 32 in. / 80 cm circular needle or size needed to obtain gauge

NOTIONS
Stitch markers (2)

Tapestry needle

Waste yarn or stitch holder

CONTINUED ON THE NEXT PAGE

GAUGE

37 sts and 37 rnds = 4 in. / 10 cm over stranded colorwork, worked in the round on larger needle, taken after blocking

Make sure to check your gauge.

PATTERN NOTES

- These socks are worked in the round from the cuff down using the Magic Loop method. The socks can be worked on two 12 in. / 30 cm circular needles or double-pointed needles if preferred.
- These socks are identical; knit two the same to complete a pair. The socks feature a contrast color cuff, heel, and toe; the stranded colorwork continues throughout the leg and foot. The heel is worked flat using Wrap and Turn short rows.
- Waste yarn is used for placing live stitches on hold while the short row heel is constructed. A smooth waste yarn in fingering weight is recommended to make transferring the live stitches back to the working needle easier.
- The colorwork sections of this pattern (leg and foot) are charted. The colorwork pattern is worked off-center on the back of the leg. After completing the heel, the design will continue to be worked off-center down the foot.
- Instructions for size 1 are provided first with additional sizes in parentheses. When only one set of numbers is provided, it applies to all sizes.

PATTERN INSTRUCTIONS

CUFF

Using the smaller needle and Color C, CO 72 (80, 88, 96) sts using the Twisted German Cast On method. Distribute sts evenly across needles. Pm for BOR and join to work in the rnd, being careful not to twist the sts.

RNDS 1–12: [K1, p1] to end of rnd.
Change to larger needle.
RND 13: K12 (20, 28, 36), pm-A, knit to end of rnd.
Break Color C.

LEG

Join Colors A and B.
Begin working from Charts A and B, reading all rows from right to left as for working in the rnd, as follows:
RNDS 1–47: Work Chart A 3 (5, 7, 9) times to M-A, sm, work Chart B once to end of rnd.
Note: If you prefer to work a shorter leg on your sock, begin Chart B on Row 39 and work only Rnds 39–47 before proceeding to Rnd 48.
RND 48: Work Chart A 3 (5, 7, 9) times to M-A, rm, work Chart B to 12 (10, 8, 6) sts before the end of rnd.
Break Colors A and B.

HEEL—SECTION ONE

Place the last 36 (40, 44, 48) sts worked onto waste yarn or stitch holder; the remaining 36 (40, 44, 48) live sts on your needle will make up the heel.
Change to smaller needle.
Beginning 12 (10, 8, 6) sts before the BOR, join Color C. As you work Short Row 1, remove BOR M as encountered.
SHORT ROW 1 (RS): Knit to last st, W&T.
SHORT ROW 2 (WS): Purl to last st, W&T.
SHORT ROW 3: Knit to 1 st before wrapped st, W&T.
SHORT ROW 4: Purl to 1 st before wrapped st, W&T.
Rep [Short Rows 3 and 4] 11 (12, 13, 14) more times; there will be a total of 13 (14, 15, 16) wrapped sts on each side of the heel.

HEEL—SECTION TWO

SHORT ROW 1 (RS): Knit to the first wrapped st, lift the wrap onto the LHN next to the st it was wrapped around, knit the st and wrap together, W&T.
SHORT ROW 2 (WS): Purl to the first wrapped st, lift the wrap onto the LHN next to the st it was wrapped around, purl the st and wrap together, W&T.
SHORT ROW 3: Knit to the next wrapped st, lift both wraps onto the LHN next to the st they were wrapped around, knit the st and wraps together, W&T.
SHORT ROW 4: Purl to the next wrapped st, lift both wraps onto the LHN next to the st they were wrapped around, purl the st and wraps together, W&T.
Rep Short Rows 3 and 4 until one wrapped st rem at each edge.
NEXT ROW (RS): Knit to the last wrapped st, lift both wraps onto the LHN next to the st they were wrapped around, knit the st and wraps together. Turn.
NEXT ROW (WS): Purl to the last wrapped st, lift both wraps onto the LHN next to the st they were wrapped around, purl the st and wraps together. Turn.
NEXT ROW (RS): Sl1 wyib, k11 (9, 7, 5). Pm for BOR. The BOR M is now back in its original position.
Break Color C.

FOOT

Change to larger needle. Place the live sts from the waste yarn or stitch holder back onto the working needle; resume working in the rnd.
Join Colors A and B.

SETUP RND: Work Chart A 3 (5, 7, 9) times, pm-A, work next row of est patt from Chart B once to end of rnd.

Beginning with Row 2 of Chart B, work Charts A and B until the foot is 2¼ (2½, 2¾, 3) in. / 5.5 (6.5, 7, 7.5) cm short of the desired total length, reading all rows from right to left as for working in the rnd, as follows:

ALL FOOT RNDS: Work Chart A 3 (5, 7, 9) times to M-A, sm, work Chart B once to end of rnd.
Break Colors A and B.

TOE

Change to smaller needle.
Join Color C.
SETUP RND: Knit to M-A, rm, knit to 12 (10, 8, 6) sts before the end of rnd, pm (SSM), knit to BOR M, rm, k24 (30, 36, 42), pm (new BOR).
RND 1: Knit to SSM, sm, knit to end of rnd.
RND 2 (DEC): K1, ssk, knit to 3 sts before SSM, k2tog, k1, sm, k1, ssk, knit to 3 sts before BOR M, k2tog, k1—4 sts dec.
Rep [Rnds 1 and 2] 7 (8, 9, 10) more times—40 (44, 48, 52) sts rem.
Then rep Rnd 2 only 5 more times—20 (24, 28, 32) sts rem.

Break Color C, leaving a 12 in. / 30.5 cm tail. Thread the tapestry needle and graft the remaining live sts together using Kitchener stitch.

FINISHING

Weave in all ends and wet block. Allow to dry completely. Trim all ends.

Key

☐ Knit
☐ Color A
■ Color B
▭ Pattern repeat

Chart A

Chart B

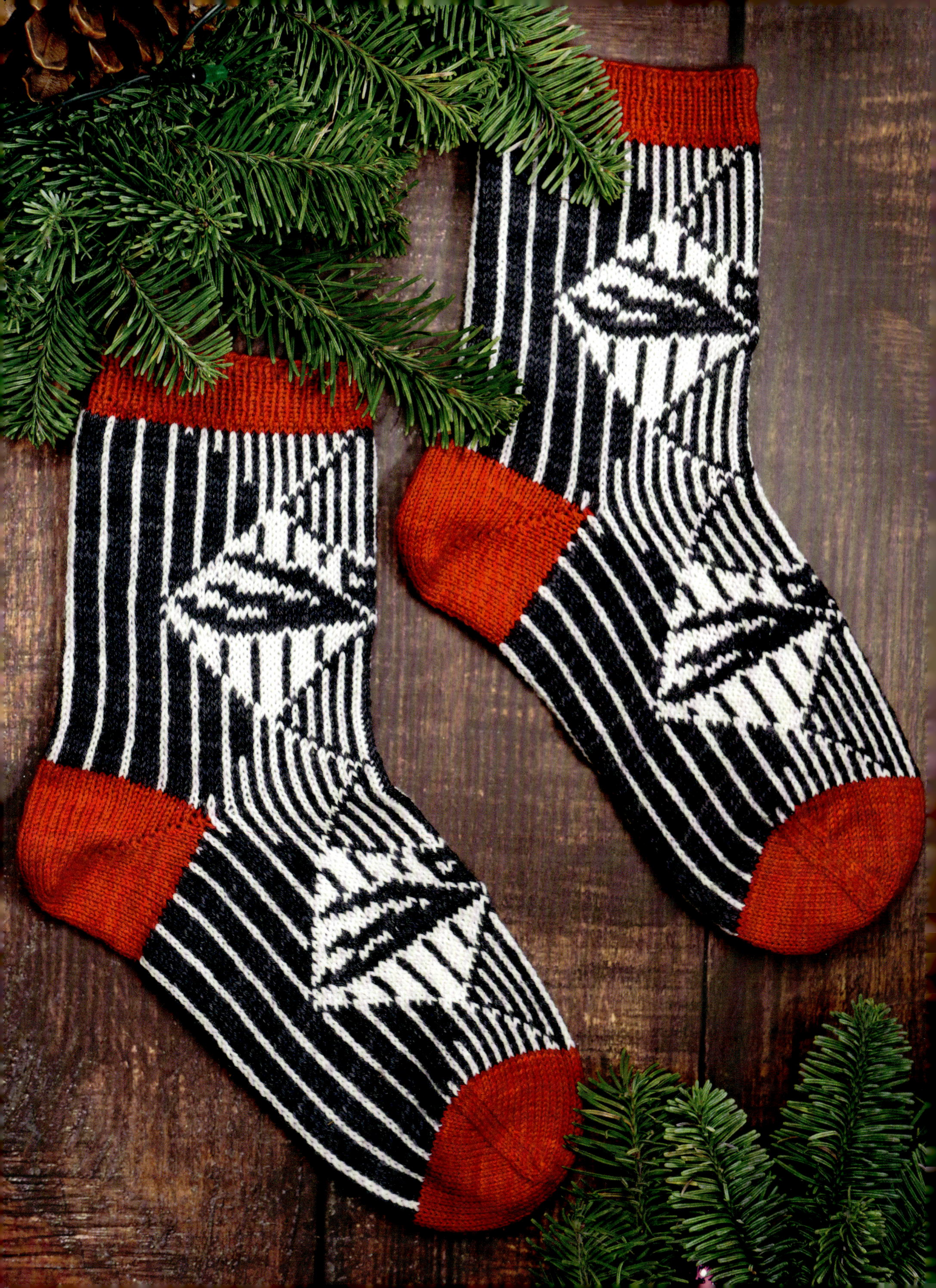

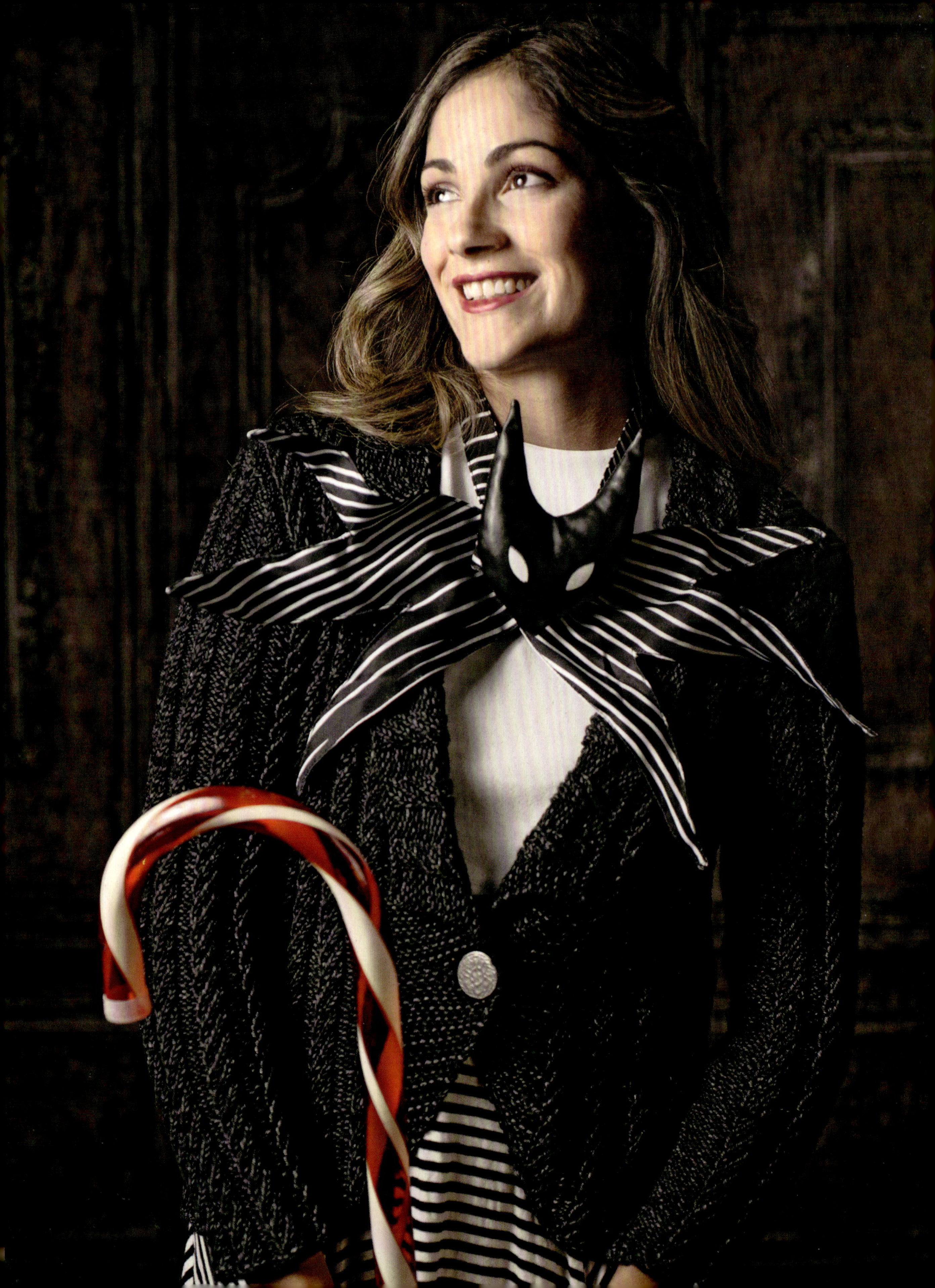

Jack's Tailcoat Cardigan

Designed by Nicole Winona Reeves

Vampire: "You're such a scream, Jack!"

Witch 1: "You're a witch's fondest dream."

Witch 2: "You made walls fall, Jack."

Witch 3: "Walls fall? You made the very mountains crack, Jack."

SKILL LEVEL

💀 💀 💀

Composer Danny Elfman had never written a musical before. However, when asked about the finished songs in *Tim Burton's The Nightmare Before Christmas*, he says, "It was the simplest writing I'd ever done." After coming to a crossroads in his personal life and toying with the idea of leaving his successful band Oingo Boingo (due to hearing loss and performance fatigue), Danny recognized a striking parallel between himself and Jack. Elfman states, "I was really attached to singing Jack's parts. Jack was an extension of what I was feeling at the time. A lead singer in a band is like a king of their own little world, but I was at the point where I didn't want to be in a band anymore. I was writing from my own heart. He's got all these fans and people love him, but he's not happy." Actor Chris Sarandon was brought on as Jack's speaking voice but was not a singer. Since Elfman had recorded himself in the temporary track, had singing experience from his band, and was a good fit for the character, he rerecorded the songs himself for the final cut.

Inspired by Jack's dashing tail coat jacket, this cardigan is worked flat in pieces from the bottom up. Mock cables take the place of pinstripes, and the low, wide neckline brings elegance and a flattering fit. After the pieces are seamed together, stitches are picked up and knit around the neckline to create the fold-over lapel.

SIZES

1 (2, 3, 4, 5, 6) [7, 8, 9, 10, 11]

FINISHED MEASUREMENTS

Chest Circumference (buttoned): 30¾ (34, 39½, 41½, 46¾, 49) [55½, 58, 62¾, 67½, 71½] in./78 (86.5, 100.5, 105.5, 118.5, 124.5) [141, 147.5, 159.5, 171.5, 181.5] cm

Garment is designed to be worn with 2 to 3 in. / 5 to 7.5 cm positive ease.

YARN

Worsted weight yarn, shown in Seven Sisters Arts *Zodiac* (80% superwash merino, 10% cashmere, 10% nylon; 210 yd. / 192 m per 4 oz. / 113 g hank), 7 (7, 7, 8, 9, 9) [10, 11, 11, 12, 12] hanks in color Tungsten

NEEDLES

US 7 / 4.5 mm, 24 to 40 in. / 60 to 100 cm long circular needle or size needed to obtain gauge

NOTIONS

Stitch markers (2)

Locking stitch markers (3)

Tapestry needle

One 1 in. / 2.5 cm diameter button

GAUGE

21 sts and 24 rows = 4 in. / 10 cm in Mock Cables pattern worked flat, taken after blocking

Make sure to check your gauge.

PATTERN NOTES

- The pieces of this sweater are worked flat, from the bottom up, then seamed. The collar is worked by picking up stitches along the neckline and back neck edges and is worked flat, outward from the body. The collar is designed so that the right side of the pattern is facing when folded down.
- The first and last stitch of each row (unless otherwise noted) are selvedge stitches; knit these stitches on the wrong side and purl on the right side to create a reverse stockinette stitch selvedge.
- A chart is provided for the Mock Cables pattern in addition to the Pattern Stitches written option. Rows 1 and 3 are wrong-side rows and should be read from left to right; Rows 2 and 4 are right-side rows and should be read from right to left.
- When decreases interrupt the Mock Cables stitch pattern, continue working remaining stitches in pattern whenever possible. If a full cable cannot be completed, knit the available stitches.
- Instructions are provided for size 1 first, with additional sizes in parentheses and brackets. If only one set of instructions is provided, it applies to all sizes.

PATTERN STITCHES

Mock Cables (worked over a multiple of 7 sts)

Row 1 (WS): *P4, k3; rep from * to end.
Row 2 (RS): *P3, (RT) 2 times; rep from * to end.
Row 3: *P4, k3; rep from * to end.
Row 4: *P3, k1, RT, k1; rep from * to end.
Rep Rows 1–4 for patt.

PATTERN INSTRUCTIONS

BACK

CO 82 (89, 103, 110, 124, 131) [145, 152, 166, 180, 187] sts using the Long Tail Cast On method. Do not join to work in the rnd.
SETUP ROW (RS): Purl.
ROW 1 (WS): K4, *p4, k3; rep from * to last st, k1.
ROW 2 (RS): P1, *p3, (RT) 2 times; rep from * to last 4 sts, p4.
ROW 3: K4, *p4, k3; rep from * to last st, k1.
ROW 4: P1, *p3, k1, RT, k1; rep from * to last 4 sts, p4.
Rep [Rows 1–4] until the back measures 16 in. / 40.5 cm from the CO edge, ending with a WS row. *Make a note of how many total rows were worked to reach this length; this number will be needed to match the front armhole position.*

BACK ARMHOLE SHAPING

ROW 1 (RS): BO 3 (1, 3, 3, 5, 4) [5, 5, 5, 5, 5] st(s) knitwise, work est patt to end of row.
ROW 2 (WS): BO 3 (1, 3, 3, 5, 4) [5, 5, 5, 5, 5] st(s) purlwise, work est patt to end of row.
Rep [Rows 1 and 2] 0 (4, 0, 1, 0, 2) [2, 2, 2, 4, 4] more time(s).
6 (10, 6, 12, 10, 24) [30, 30, 30, 50, 50] sts dec; 76 (79, 97, 98, 114, 107) [115, 122, 136, 130, 137] sts rem.

SIZES 1 AND 2 ONLY:
Proceed to All Sizes.

SIZES 3-11 ONLY:
NEXT RS ROW A: BO - (-, 2, 2, 4, 3) [4, 4, 4, 4, 4] sts knitwise, work est patt to end of row.
NEXT WS ROW A: BO - (-, 2, 2, 4, 3) [4, 4, 4, 4, 4] sts purlwise, work est patt to end of row.
Rep [Next RS and WS Row A] - (-, 1, 0, 0, 0) [0, 0, 2, 1, 2] more time(s).
- (-, 8, 4, 8, 6) [8, 8, 24, 16, 24] sts dec; - (-, 89, 94, 106, 101) [107, 114, 112, 114, 113] sts rem.

NEXT RS ROW B: BO - (-, 1, 1, 3, 2) [3, 3, 3, 3, 3] st(s) knitwise, work est patt to end of row.
Next WS ROW B: BO - (-, 1, 1, 3, 2) [3, 3, 3, 3, 3] st(s) purlwise, work est patt to end of row.
Rep [Next RS and WS Row B] - (-, 1, 1, 0, 0) [0, 0, 0, 0, 0] more time(s).
- (-, 4, 4, 2, 2) [2, 2, 2, 2, 2] sts dec; - (-, 85, 90, 100, 97) [101, 108, 106, 108, 107] sts rem.

SIZES 3 AND 4 ONLY:
Proceed to All Sizes.

SIZES 5-11 ONLY:
NEXT RS ROW C: BO - (-, -, -, 2, 1) [2, 2, 2, 2, 2] st(s) knitwise, work est patt to end of row.
NEXT WS ROW C: BO - (-, -, -, 2, 1) [2, 2, 2, 2, 2] st(s) purlwise, work est patt to end of row.
- (-, -, -, 4, 2) [4, 4, 4, 4, 4] sts dec; - (-, -, -, 96, 95) [97, 104, 102, 104, 103] sts rem.

SIZE 6 ONLY:
Proceed to All Sizes.

SIZES 5 AND 7-11 ONLY:
NEXT RS ROW D: BO 1 st knitwise, work est patt to end of row.
NEXT WS ROW D: BO 1 st purlwise, work est patt to end of row.
Rep [Next RS and WS Row D] - (-, -, -, 1, -) [0, 1, 0, 0, 0] more time(s).
- (-, -, -, 4, -) [2, 4, 2, 2, 2] sts dec; - (-, -, -, 92, -) [95, 100, 100, 102, 101] sts rem.

ALL SIZES:
On the next RS row, reestablish selvedge sts and cont in est patt until the back armhole measures 6½ (7, 7½, 8, 8½, 9) [9½, 10, 10½, 11, 11½] in. / 16.5 (18, 19, 20.5, 21.5, 23) [24, 25.5, 26.5, 28, 29] cm from the first bind off row, ending with a WS row.
With RS facing, BO all sts knitwise.

LEFT FRONT

Note: The first 6 front edge increases are incorporated into the Mock Cables pattern; the rem 14 front edge increases are worked in garter stitch. The front edge selvedge will be worked in garter stitch (knit on RS and WS) following Row 8; the armhole selvedge will be worked in St st as per the Back.

CO 25 (30, 37, 39, 46, 48) [58, 61, 67, 72, 79] sts using the Long Tail Cast On method. Do not join to work in the rnd.

SETUP ROW (RS): Purl.

ROW 1 (WS): K1, *p4, k3; rep from * to last 3 (1, 1, 3, 3, 5) [1, 4, 3, 1, 1] st(s), knit to end.

ROW 2 (RS, INC): P3 (1, 1, 3, 3, 5) [1, 4, 3, 1, 1], *p3, (RT) 2 times; rep from * to last st, M1LPx2, p1—27 (32, 39, 41, 48, 50) [60, 63, 69, 74, 81] total sts.

ROW 3: K3, *p4, k3; rep from * to last 3 (1, 1, 3, 3, 5) [1, 4, 3, 1, 1] st(s), knit to end.

ROW 4 (INC): P3 (1, 1, 3, 3, 5) [1, 4, 3, 1, 1], *p3, k1, RT, k1; rep from * to last 3 sts, p2, (M1LP, M1L) on same running thread, k1—29 (34, 41, 43, 50, 52) [62, 65, 71, 76, 83] total sts.

ROW 5: P2, k3, *p4, k3; rep from * to last 3 (1, 1, 3, 3, 5) [1, 4, 3, 1, 1] st(s), knit to end.

ROW 6 (INC): P3 (1, 1, 3, 3, 5) [1, 4, 3, 1, 1], *p3, (RT) 2 times; rep from * to last 5 sts, p3, k1, M1L, k1—30 (35, 42, 44, 51, 53) [63, 66, 72, 77, 84] total sts.

ROW 7: P3, k3, *p4, k3; rep from * to last 3 (1, 1, 3, 3, 5) [1, 4, 3, 1, 1] st(s), knit to end.

ROW 8 (INC): P3 (1, 1, 3, 3, 5) [1, 4, 3, 1, 1], *p3, k1, RT, k1; rep from * to last 6 sts, p3, k2, M1L, k1—31 (36, 43, 45, 52, 54) [64, 67, 73, 78, 85] total sts.

ROW 9: K1, p3, k3, *p4, k3; rep from * to last 3 (1, 1, 3, 3, 5) [1, 4, 3, 1, 1] st(s), knit to end.

ROW 10 (INC): P3 (1, 1, 3, 3, 5) [1, 4, 3, 1, 1], *p3, (RT) 2 times; rep from * to last 7 sts, p3, RT, k1, M1L, pm, k1—32 (37, 44, 46, 53, 55) [65, 68, 74, 79, 80] total sts.

ROW 11: K1, sm, *p4, k3; rep from * to last 3 (1, 1, 3, 3, 5) [1, 4, 3, 1, 1] st(s), knit to end.

ROW 12 (INC): P3 (1, 1, 3, 3, 5) [1, 4, 3, 1, 1], *p3, k1, RT, k1; rep from * to M, sm, M1L, k1—33 (38, 45, 47, 54, 56) [66, 69, 75, 80, 81] total sts.

ROW 13: Knit to M, sm, *p4, k3; rep from * to last 3 (1, 1, 3, 3, 5) [1, 4, 3, 1, 1] st(s), knit to end.

ROW 14 (INC): P3 (1, 1, 3, 3, 5) [1, 4, 3, 1, 1], *p3, (RT) 2 times; rep from * to M, sm, knit to last st, M1L, k1—1 st inc.

ROW 15: Knit to M, sm, *p4, k3; rep from * to last 3 (1, 1, 3, 3, 5) [1, 4, 3, 1, 1] st(s), knit to end.

ROW 16 (INC): P3 (1, 1, 3, 3, 5) [1, 4, 3, 1, 1], *p3, k1, RT, k1; rep from * to M, sm, knit to last st, M1L, k1—1 st inc.

Rows 17–24: Rep [Rows 13–16] 2 times—39 (44, 51, 53, 60, 62) [72, 75, 81, 86, 93] total sts.

ROW 25 (WS): Knit to M, sm, *p4, k3; rep from * to last 3 (1, 1, 3, 3, 5) [1, 4, 3, 1, 1] st(s), knit to end.

ROW 26 (RS, INC): P3 (1, 1, 3, 3, 5) [1, 4, 3, 1, 1], *p3, (RT) 2 times; rep from * to M, sm, knit to last st, M1L, k1—1 st inc.

ROW 27: Knit to M, sm, *p4, k3; rep from * to last 3 (1, 1, 3, 3, 5) [1, 4, 3, 1, 1] st(s), knit to end.

ROW 28: P3 (1, 1, 3, 3, 5) [1, 4, 3, 1, 1], *p3, k1, RT, k1; rep from * to M, sm, knit to end of row.

ROWS 29–48: Rep [Rows 25–28] 5 times—45 (50, 57, 59, 66, 68) [78, 81, 87, 92, 99] total sts.

ROW 49 (WS): Knit to M, sm, *p4, k3; rep from * to last 3 (1, 1, 3, 3, 5) [1, 4, 3, 1, 1] st(s), knit to end.

ROW 50 (RS): P3 (1, 1, 3, 3, 5) [1, 4, 3, 1, 1], *p3, (RT) 2 times; rep from * to M, sm, knit to end of row. Clip a locking marker into the last stitch of this row once worked; do not remove until instructed.

ROW 51: Knit to M, sm, *p4, k3; rep from * to last 3 (1, 1, 3, 3, 5) [1, 4, 3, 1, 1] st(s), knit to end.

ROW 52: P3 (1, 1, 3, 3, 5) [1, 4, 3, 1, 1], *p3, k1, RT, k1; rep from * to M, rm, knit to end of row.

LEFT FRONT NECKLINE DECREASES

Read carefully through the following instructions as multiple steps occur at the same time.

WS BIND OFF ROW: BO 1 st at front edge knitwise, work est patt to end of row.

Cont in est patt, rep WS Bind Off Row every 2 (2, 4, 4, 4, 4) [4, 4, 4, 6, 4] rows 7 (1, 21, 21, 19, 21) [19, 13, 6, 14, 4] more time(s), then every 4 (4, 6, 6, 6, 0) [6, 6, 6, 8, 6] rows 16 (20, 0, 0, 2, 0) [3, 7, 13, 2, 15] times.

AT THE SAME TIME, when the left front measures 16 in. / 40.5 cm from the CO edge, ending with a WS row (the same number of rows worked for the Back before the Back Armhole Shaping), work the Left Front Armhole Shaping, below. *The neckline shaping always occurs on WS rows, and the armhole shaping always occurs on RS rows.*

LEFT FRONT ARMHOLE SHAPING

ROW 1 (RS): BO 3 (1, 3, 3, 5, 4) [5, 5, 5, 5, 5] st(s) knitwise, work est patt to end of row.

ROW 2 (WS): Work est patt to end of row.

Rep [Rows 1 and 2] 0 (4, 0, 1, 0, 2) [2, 2, 2, 4, 4] more time(s).

3 (5, 3, 6, 5, 12) [15, 15, 15, 25, 25] sts dec.

SIZES 1 AND 2 ONLY:
Proceed to All Sizes.

SIZES 3-11 ONLY:
NEXT RS ROW A: BO - (-, 2, 2, 4, 3) [4, 4, 4, 4, 4] sts knitwise, work est patt to end of row.

NEXT WS ROW A: Work est patt to end of row.

Rep [Next RS and WS Row A] - (-, 1, 0, 0, 0) [0, 0, 2, 1, 2] more time(s).

- (-, 4, 2, 4, 3) [4, 4, 12, 8, 12] sts dec.

NEXT RS ROW B: BO - (-, 1, 1, 3, 2) [3, 3, 3, 3, 3] st(s) knitwise, work est patt to end of row.

NEXT WS ROW B: Work est patt to end of row.

Rep [Next RS and WS Row B] - (-, 1, 1, 0, 0) [0, 0, 0, 0, 0] more time(s).

- (-, 2, 2, 1, 1) [1, 1, 1, 1, 1] st(s) dec.

SIZES 3 AND 4 ONLY:
Proceed to All Sizes.

SIZES 5-11 ONLY:
NEXT RS ROW C: BO - (-, -, -, 2, 1) [2, 2, 2, 2, 2] st(s) knitwise, work est patt to end of row.

NEXT WS ROW C: Work est patt to end of row.

- (-, -, -, 2, 1) [2, 2, 2, 2, 2] st(s) dec.

SIZE 6 ONLY:
Proceed to All Sizes.

SIZES 5 AND 7-11 ONLY:
NEXT RS ROW D: BO 1 st knitwise, work est patt to end of row.

NEXT WS ROW D: Work est patt to end of row.

Rep [Next RS and WS Row D] - (-, -, -, 1, -) [0, 1, 0, 0, 0] more time(s).

- (-, -, -, 2, -) [1, 2, 1, 1, 1] st(s) dec.

ALL SIZES:
On the next RS row, reestablish selvedge sts and cont in est patt until the front armhole measures 6½ (7, 7½, 8, 8½, 9) [9½, 10, 10½, 11, 11½] in. / 16½ (18, 19, 20.5, 21.5, 23) [24, 25.5, 26.5, 28, 29] cm from the first bind off row, ending with a WS row. When all neckline and armhole shaping is complete, 18 (23, 26, 27, 28, 28) [30, 34, 34, 36, 36] sts rem.

With RS facing, BO all sts knitwise.

RIGHT FRONT

The shaping mirrors the Left Front edge.

CO 25 (30, 37, 39, 46, 48) [58, 61, 67, 72, 79] sts using the Long Tail Cast On method. Do not join to work in the rnd.

SETUP ROW (RS): Purl.

ROW 1 (WS): K3 (1, 1, 3, 3, 5) [1, 4, 3, 1, 1], *p4, k3; rep from * to last st, k1.

ROW 2 (RS, INC): P1, M1RPx2, *(RT) 2 times, p3; rep from * to last 3 (1, 1, 3, 3, 5) [1, 4, 3, 1, 1] st(s), purl to end—27 (32, 39, 41, 48, 50) [60, 63, 69, 74, 81] total sts.

ROW 3: K3 (1, 1, 3, 3, 5) [1, 4, 3, 1, 1], *k3, p4; rep from * to last 3 sts, k3.

ROW 4 (INC): K1, M1R, M1RP, p2, *k1, RT, k1, p3; rep from * to last 3 (1, 1, 3, 3, 5) [1, 4, 3, 1, 1] st(s), purl to end—29 (34, 41, 43, 50, 52) [62, 65, 71, 76, 83] total sts.

ROW 5: K3 (1, 1, 3, 3, 5) [1, 4, 3, 1, 1], *k3, p4; rep from * to last 5 sts, k3, p2.

ROW 6 (INC): K1, M1R, k1, p3, *(RT) 2 times, p3; rep from * to last 3 (1, 1, 3, 3, 5) [1, 4, 3, 1, 1] st(s), purl to end—30 (35, 42, 44, 51, 53) [63, 66, 72, 77, 84] total sts.

ROW 7: K3 (1, 1, 3, 3, 5) [1, 4, 3, 1, 1], *k3, p4; rep from * to last 6 sts, k3, p3.

ROW 8 (INC): K1, M1R, k2, p3, *k1, RT, k1, p3; rep from * to last 3 (1, 1, 3, 3, 5) [1, 4, 3, 1, 1] st(s), purl to end—31 (36, 43, 45, 52, 54) [64, 67, 73, 78, 85] total sts.

ROW 9: K3 (1, 1, 3, 3, 5) [1, 4, 3, 1, 1], *k3, p4; rep from * to last 7 sts, k3, p3, k1.

ROW 10 (INC): K1, pm, M1R, k1, RT, p3, *(RT) 2 times, p3; rep from * to last 3 (1, 1, 3, 3, 5) [1, 4, 3, 1, 1] st(s), purl to end—32 (37, 44, 46, 53, 55) [65, 68, 74, 79, 80] total sts.

ROW 11: K3 (1, 1, 3, 3, 5) [1, 4, 3, 1, 1], *k3, p4; rep from * to M, sm, k1.

ROW 12 (INC): K1, M1R, sm, *k1, RT, k1, p3; rep from * to last 3 (1, 1, 3, 3, 5) [1, 4, 3, 1, 1] st(s), purl to end—33 (38, 45, 47, 54, 56) [66, 69, 75, 80, 81] total sts.

ROW 13: K3 (1, 1, 3, 3, 5) [1, 4, 3, 1, 1], *k3, p4; rep from * to M, sm, knit to end.

ROW 14 (INC): K1, M1R, knit to M, sm, *(RT) 2 times, p3; rep from * to last 3 (1, 1, 3, 3, 5) [1, 4, 3, 1, 1] st(s), purl to end—1 st inc.

ROW 15: K3 (1, 1, 3, 3, 5) [1, 4, 3, 1, 1], *k3, p4; rep from * to M, sm, knit to end.

ROW 16 (INC): K1, M1R, knit to M, sm, *k1, RT, k1, p3; rep from * to last 3 (1, 1, 3, 3, 5) [1, 4, 3, 1, 1] st(s), purl to end—1 st inc.

ROWS 17–24: Rep [Rows 13–16] 2 times—39 (44, 51, 53, 60, 62) [72, 75, 81, 86, 93] total sts.

ROW 25 (WS): K3 (1, 1, 3, 3, 5) [1, 4, 3, 1, 1], *k3, p4; rep from * to M, sm, knit to end.

ROW 26 (RS, INC): K1, M1R, knit to M, sm, *(RT) 2 times, p3; rep from * to last 3 (1, 1, 3, 3, 5) [1, 4, 3, 1, 1] st(s), purl to end—1 st inc.

ROW 27: K3 (1, 1, 3, 3, 5) [1, 4, 3, 1, 1], *k3, p4; rep from * to M, sm, knit to end.

ROW 28: Knit to M, sm, *k1, RT, k1, p3; rep from * to last 3 (1, 1, 3, 3, 5) [1, 4, 3, 1, 1] st(s), purl to end.

ROWS 29–47: Rep [Rows 25–28] 4 times, then Rows 25–27 once more—45 (50, 57, 59, 66, 68) [78, 81, 87, 92, 99] total sts.

ROW 48 (RS): K3, make 4-stitch One Row Buttonhole, knit to M, sm, *k1, RT, k1, p3; rep from * to last 3 (1, 1, 3, 3, 5) [1, 4, 3, 1, 1] st(s), purl to end.

ROW 49 (WS): K3 (1, 1, 3, 3, 5) [1, 4, 3, 1, 1], *k3, p4; rep from * to M, sm, knit to end.

ROW 50 (RS): Knit to M (clip a locking marker into the first stitch of this row once worked; do not remove until instructed), sm, *(RT) 2 times, p3; rep from * to last 3 (1, 1, 3, 3, 5) [1, 4, 3, 1, 1] st(s), purl to end.

ROW 51: K3 (1, 1, 3, 3, 5) [1, 4, 3, 1, 1], *k3, p4; rep from * to M, rm, knit to end.

RIGHT FRONT NECKLINE DECREASES

Read carefully through the following instructions as multiple steps occur at the same time. Note that the neckline and armhole decreases are reversed; the right front neckline shaping begins 1 row before the left front neckline shaping.

RS BIND OFF ROW: BO 1 st at front edge knitwise, work est patt to end of row.

Cont in est patt, rep RS Bind Off Row every 2 (2, 4, 4, 4) [4, 4, 4, 6, 4] rows 7 (1, 21, 21, 19, 21) [19, 13, 6, 14, 4] more time(s), then every 4 (4, 6, 6, 6, 0) [6, 6, 6, 8, 6] rows 16 (20, 0, 0, 2, 0) [3, 7, 13, 2, 15] times.

AT THE SAME TIME, when the right front measures 16 in. / 40.5 cm from the CO edge, ending with a WS row (the same number of rows worked for the Back before the Back Armhole Shaping), work the Right Front Armhole Shaping, below. *The neckline shaping always occurs on RS rows, and the armhole shaping always occurs on WS rows.*

RIGHT FRONT ARMHOLE SHAPING

ROW 1 (RS): Work est patt to end of row.

ROW 2 (WS): BO 3 (1, 3, 3, 5, 4) [5, 5, 5, 5, 5] st(s) purlwise, work est patt to end of row.

Rep [Rows 1 and 2] 0 (4, 0, 1, 0, 2) [2, 2, 2, 4, 4] more time(s).

3 (5, 3, 6, 5, 12) [15, 15, 15, 25, 25] sts dec.

SIZES 1 AND 2 ONLY:
Proceed to All Sizes.

SIZES 3–11 ONLY:
NEXT RS ROW A: Work est patt to end of row.

NEXT WS ROW A: BO - (-, 2, 2, 4, 3) [4, 4, 4, 4, 4] sts purlwise, work est patt to end of row.

Rep [Next RS and WS Row A] - (-, 1, 0, 0, 0) [0, 0, 2, 1, 2] more time(s).

- (-, 4, 2, 4, 3) [4, 4, 12, 8, 12] sts dec.

NEXT RS ROW B: Work est patt to end of row.

NEXT WS ROW B: BO - (-, 1, 1, 3, 2) [3, 3, 3, 3, 3] st(s) purlwise, work est patt to end of row.

Rep [Next RS and WS Row B] - (-, 1, 1, 0, 0) [0, 0, 0, 0, 0] more time(s).

- (-, 2, 2, 1, 1) [1, 1, 1, 1, 1] st(s) dec.

SIZES 3 AND 4 ONLY:
Proceed to All Sizes.

SIZES 5–11 ONLY:
NEXT RS ROW C: Work est patt to end of row.

NEXT WS ROW C: BO - (-, -, -, 2, 1) [2, 2, 2, 2, 2] st(s) purlwise, work est patt to end of row.

- (-, -, -, 2, 1) [2, 2, 2, 2, 2] sts dec.

SIZE 6 ONLY:
PROCEED TO ALL SIZES.

SIZES 5 AND 7–11 ONLY:
NEXT RS ROW D: Work est patt to end of row.

NEXT WS ROW D: BO 1 st purlwise, work est patt to end of row.

Rep [Next RS and WS Row D] - (-, -, -, 1, -) [0, 1, 0, 0, 0] more time(s).

- (-, -, -, 2, -) [1, 2, 1, 1, 1] st(s) dec.

ALL SIZES:
On the next RS row, reestablish selvedge sts and cont in est patt until the front armhole measures 6½ (7, 7½, 8, 8½, 9) [9½, 10, 10½, 11, 11½] in. / 16.5 (18, 19, 20.5, 21.5, 23) [24, 25.5, 26.5, 28, 29] cm from the first bind off row, ending with a WS row. When all neckline and armhole shaping is complete, 18 (23, 26, 27, 28, 28) [30, 34, 34, 36, 36] sts rem.

With RS facing, BO all sts knitwise.

SLEEVES (MAKE 2 THE SAME)

CO 47 (47, 54, 54, 54, 61) [61, 68, 68, 75, 75] sts using the Long Tail Cast On method. Do not join to work in the rnd.

SETUP ROW 1 (RS): P1, pm, purl to last 4 sts, pm, p4.

SETUP ROW 2 (WS): Knit to M, sm, *p4, k3; rep from * to M, sm, p1.

Note: All sleeve increases are worked purlwise to maintain the reverse St st fabric at the underside of the sleeve. Read carefully through the following instructions as multiple steps occur at the same time.

INC ROW 1 (RS): P1, M1RP, sm, *p3, (RT) 2 times; rep from * to M, sm, M1LP, p1—49 (49, 56, 56, 56, 63) [63, 70, 70, 77, 77] total sts.

Beginning with Row 3 of the Mock Cables stitch pattern, rep Rows 1–4 until the sleeve measures 18 in. / 45.5 cm from the CO edge (or desired total sleeve length), ending with a WS row, as follows:

RS ROWS: Purl to M, sm, work Mock Cables pattern to M, sm, purl to end.

WS ROWS: Knit to M, sm, work Mock Cables pattern to M, sm, knit to end.

AT THE SAME TIME, work Inc Row 2, below, every 12 (8, 12, 10, 6, 6) [4, 4, 4, 6, 6] rows 4 (3, 2, 7, 4, 14) [1, 3, 3, 11, 11] time(s) total. Then work Inc Row 2 every 14 (10, 14, 12, 8, 8) [6, 6, 6, 8, 8] rows 2 (6, 4, 2, 8, 1) [15, 14, 14, 4, 4] more time(s).

INC ROW 2 (RS): P1, M1RP, purl to M, sm, work Mock Cables pattern to M, sm, purl to last st, M1LP, p1—2 sts inc.

12 (18, 12, 18, 24, 30) [32, 34, 34, 30, 30] sts inc; 61 (67, 68, 74, 80, 93) [95, 104, 104, 107, 107] total sts.

SLEEVE CAP SHAPING

ROW 1 (RS): BO 3 (1, 3, 3, 5, 4) [5, 5, 5, 5, 5] st(s) knitwise, rm as encountered, work est patt to end of row.

ROW 2 (WS): BO 3 (1, 3, 3, 5, 4) [5, 5, 5, 5, 5] st(s) purlwise, work est patt to end of row.

6 (2, 6, 6, 10, 8) [10, 10, 10, 10, 10] sts BO; 55 (65, 62, 68, 70, 85) [85, 94, 94, 97, 97] sts rem.

ROW 3 (RS): BO 2 sts knitwise, work est patt to end of row.

ROW 4 (WS): BO 2 sts purlwise, work est patt to end of row.

Rep [Rows 3 and 4] 4 (9, 1, 6, 6, 9) [11, 13, 10, 12, 11] more time(s).

20 (40, 8, 28, 28, 40) [48, 56, 44, 52, 58] sts BO; 35 (25, 54, 40, 42, 45) [37, 38, 50, 45, 49] sts rem.

SIZE 2 ONLY:
Proceed to All Sizes.

SIZES 1 AND 3-11 ONLY:

NEXT RS ROW A: BO 1 st knitwise, work est patt to end of row.

NEXT WS ROW A: BO 1 st purlwise, work est patt to end of row.

Rep [Next RS and WS Row A] 5 (-, 7, 5, 6, 6) [1, 0, 6, 4, 6] more time(s).

12 (-, 16, 12, 14, 14) [4, 2, 14, 10, 14] sts BO; 23 (25, 38, 28, 28, 31) [33, 36, 36, 35, 35] sts rem.

ALL SIZES:

NEXT ROW (RS): BO 5 sts knitwise, work est patt to end of row.

NEXT ROW (WS): BO 5 sts purlwise, work est patt to end of row.

10 sts dec; 13 (15, 28, 18, 18, 21) [23, 26, 26, 25, 25] sts rem.

SIZE 3 ONLY:

NEXT RS ROW B: BO 3 sts knitwise, work est patt to end of row.

NEXT WS ROW B: BO 3 sts purlwise, work est patt to end of row.

Rep [Next RS and WS Row B] 1 more time.

12 sts dec; 16 sts rem.

ALL SIZES:
With RS facing, BO all sts knitwise.

FINISHING

- Weave in all ends.
- Wet block each piece per the schematic. When dry, seam shoulders using the invisible horizontal seaming method; seam the sides using mattress stitch. Seam the underside of the sleeves, then seam sleeves to armholes using mattress stitch.
- Lay the garment flat with the garter stitch front edges overlapping. Mark the button position relative to the buttonhole using a locking marker. Sew the button to the left front edge using a length of working yarn threaded into the tapestry needle.

FRIGHTENING FACT

In 2018, *Entertainment Weekly* ranked *Tim Burton's The Nightmare Before Christmas* songs in order of popularity, with "What's This?" coming in at #1, followed by "This Is Halloween" at #2, and "Sally's Song" at #3.

COLLAR

Note: The collar stitches will be picked up with the WS facing so that the picked-up ridge will be hidden behind the collar once it is folded.

Using the 40 in. / 100 cm circular needle, with the WS facing and beginning at the locking marker on the left front, join the yarn and pick up and knit 56 (59, 66, 65, 65, 67) [69, 70, 74, 75, 79] sts along the left front neckline to the shoulder seam, pick up and knit 40 (34, 34, 36, 36, 39) [35, 33, 32, 30, 29] sts across the back neck, and pick up and knit 56 (59, 66, 65, 65, 67) [69, 70, 74, 75, 79] sts down the front right neckline starting at the shoulder seam and ending at the locking marker—152 (152, 166, 166, 166, 173) [173, 173, 180, 180, 187] total sts.

You may now remove the locking markers. Turn work.

Note: The first and last 4 sts are worked in garter stitch to prevent curling of collar.

ROW 1 (WS): K4, *p4, k3; rep from * to last 8 sts, p4, k4.

ROW 2 (RS): K4, *(RT) 2 times, p3; rep from * to last 8 sts, (RT) 2 times, k4.

ROW 3: K4, *p4, k3; rep from * to last 8 sts, p4, k4.

ROW 4 (RS): K4, *k1, RT, k1, p3; rep from * to last 8 sts, k1, RT, k5.

Rep [Rows 1–4] until the collar measures approx. 3¼ in. / 8.5 cm from the picked-up edge, ending with a RS row.

With WS facing, BO all sts knitwise.

Weave in all ends. Fold the collar down so the RS is facing and steam block into position. Trim all ends.

Mock Cable Chart

Key

☐ k on RS, p on WS
⊟ p on RS, k on WS
▧ RT
☐ Pattern repeat

Jack's Tailcoat Cardigan Schematic

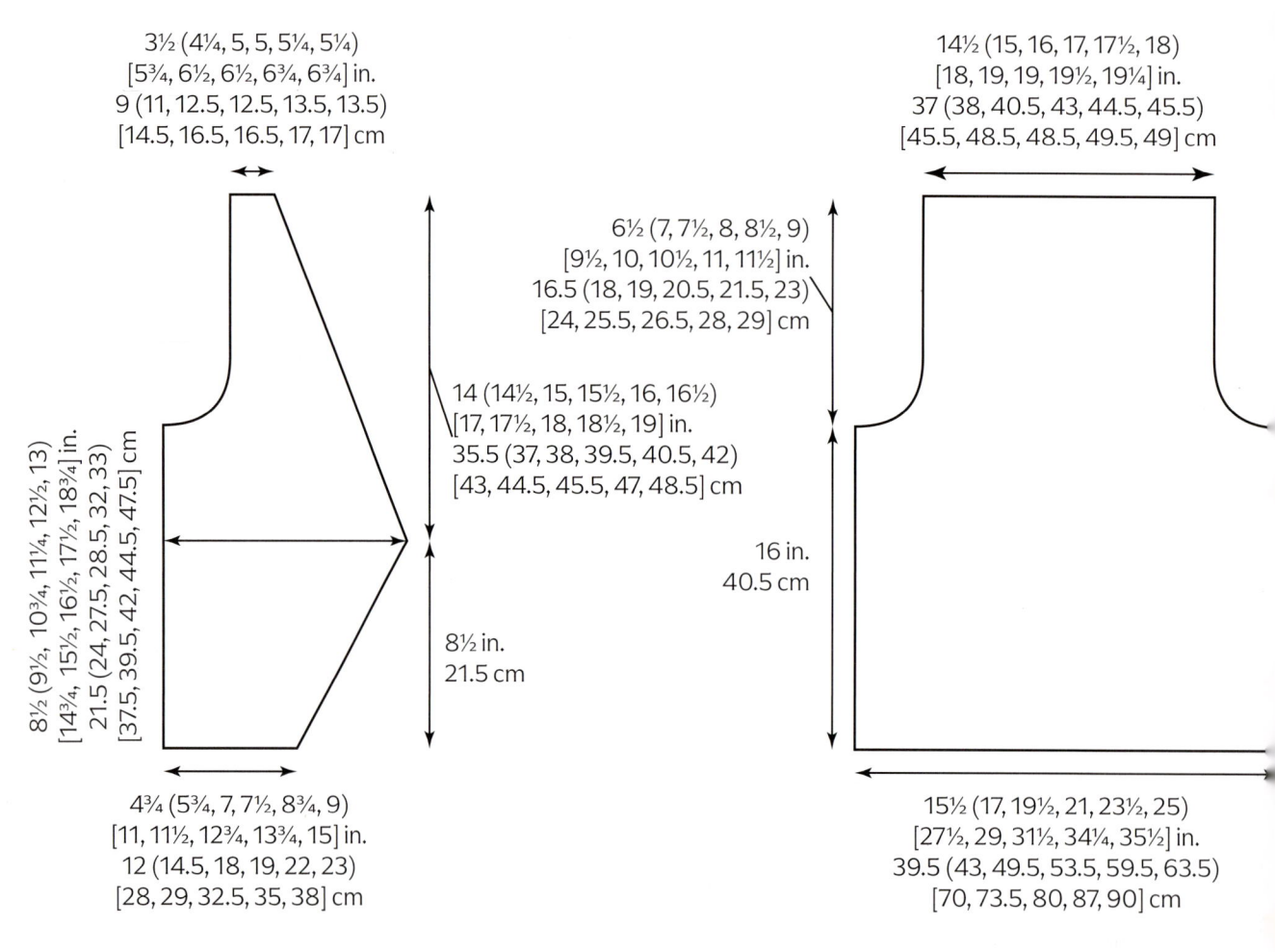

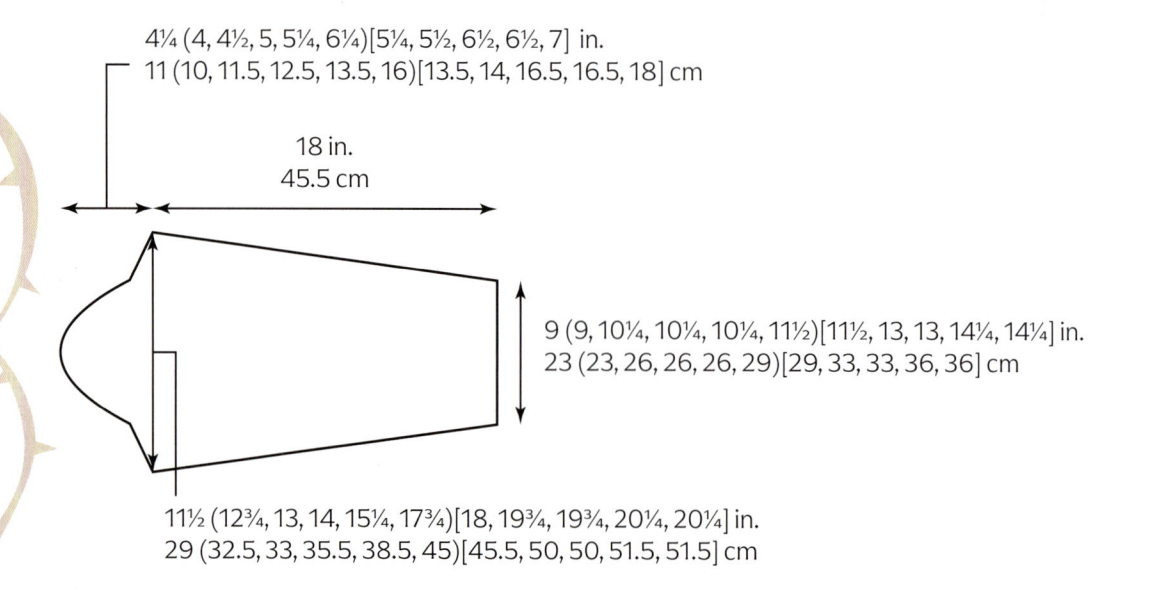

3½ (4¼, 5, 5, 5¼, 5¼)
[5¾, 6½, 6½, 6¾, 6¾] in.
9 (11, 12.5, 12.5, 13.5, 13.5)
[14.5, 16.5, 16.5, 17, 17] cm

14½ (15, 16, 17, 17½, 18)
[18, 19, 19, 19½, 19¼] in.
37 (38, 40.5, 43, 44.5, 45.5)
[45.5, 48.5, 48.5, 49.5, 49] cm

6½ (7, 7½, 8, 8½, 9)
[9½, 10, 10½, 11, 11½] in.
16.5 (18, 19, 20.5, 21.5, 23)
[24, 25.5, 26.5, 28, 29] cm

14 (14½, 15, 15½, 16, 16½)
[17, 17½, 18, 18½, 19] in.
35.5 (37, 38, 39.5, 40.5, 42)
[43, 44.5, 45.5, 47, 48.5] cm

8½ (9½, 10¾, 11¼, 12½, 13)
[14¾, 15½, 16½, 17½, 18¾] in.
21.5 (24, 27.5, 28.5, 32, 33)
[37.5, 39.5, 42, 44.5, 47.5] cm

8½ in.
21.5 cm

16 in.
40.5 cm

4¾ (5¾, 7, 7½, 8¾, 9)
[11, 11½, 12¾, 13¾, 15] in.
12 (14.5, 18, 19, 22, 23)
[28, 29, 32.5, 35, 38] cm

15½ (17, 19½, 21, 23½, 25)
[27½, 29, 31½, 34¼, 35½] in.
39.5 (43, 49.5, 53.5, 59.5, 63.5)
[70, 73.5, 80, 87, 90] cm

4¼ (4, 4½, 5, 5¼, 6¼)[5¼, 5½, 6½, 6½, 7] in.
11 (10, 11.5, 12.5, 13.5, 16)[13.5, 14, 16.5, 16.5, 18] cm

18 in.
45.5 cm

9 (9, 10¼, 10¼, 10¼, 11½)[11½, 13, 13, 14¼, 14¼] in.
23 (23, 26, 26, 26, 29)[29, 33, 33, 36, 36] cm

11½ (12¾, 13, 14, 15¼, 17¾)[18, 19¾, 19¾, 20¼, 20¼] in.
29 (32.5, 33, 35.5, 38.5, 45)[45.5, 50, 50, 51.5, 51.5] cm

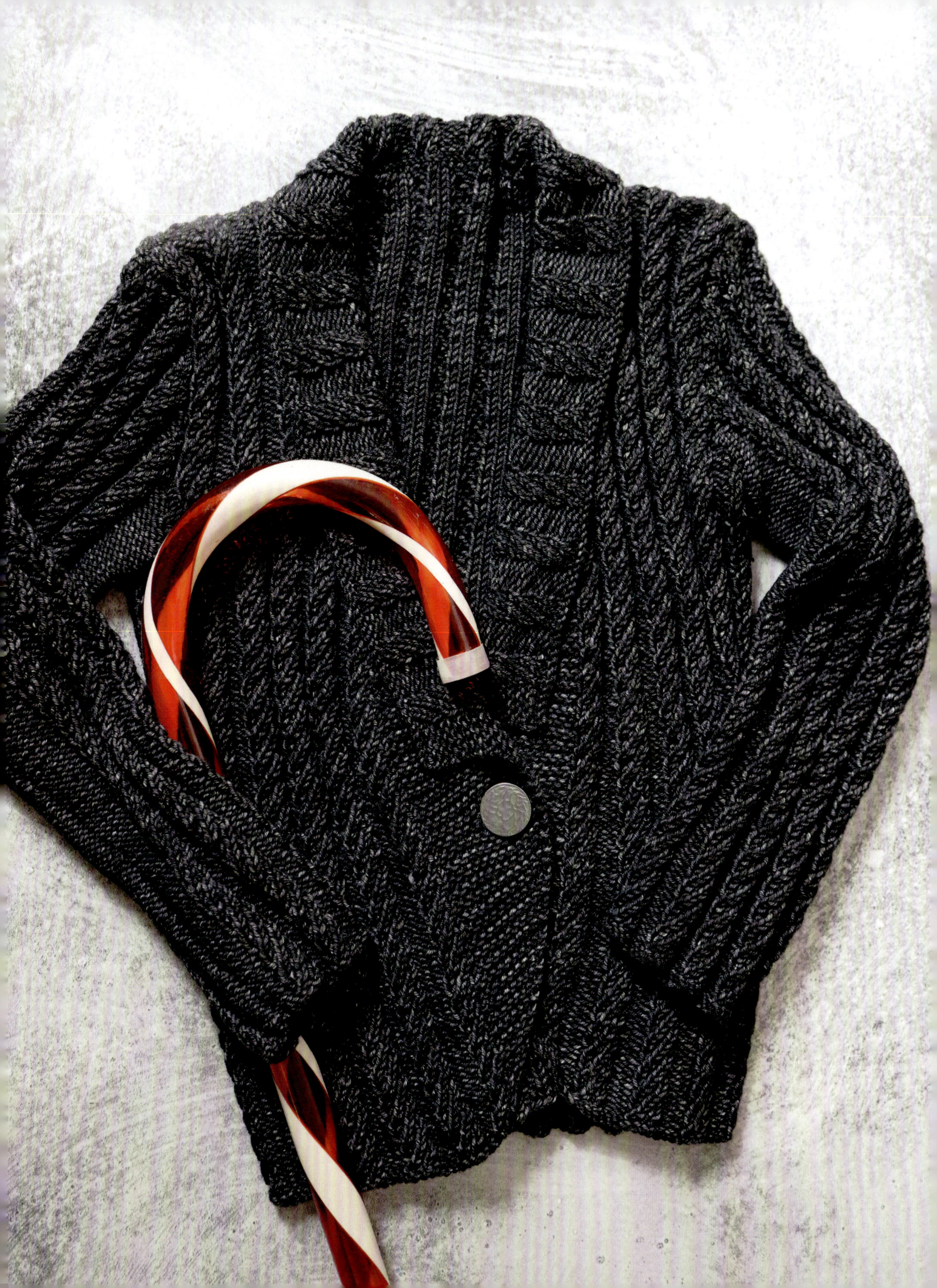

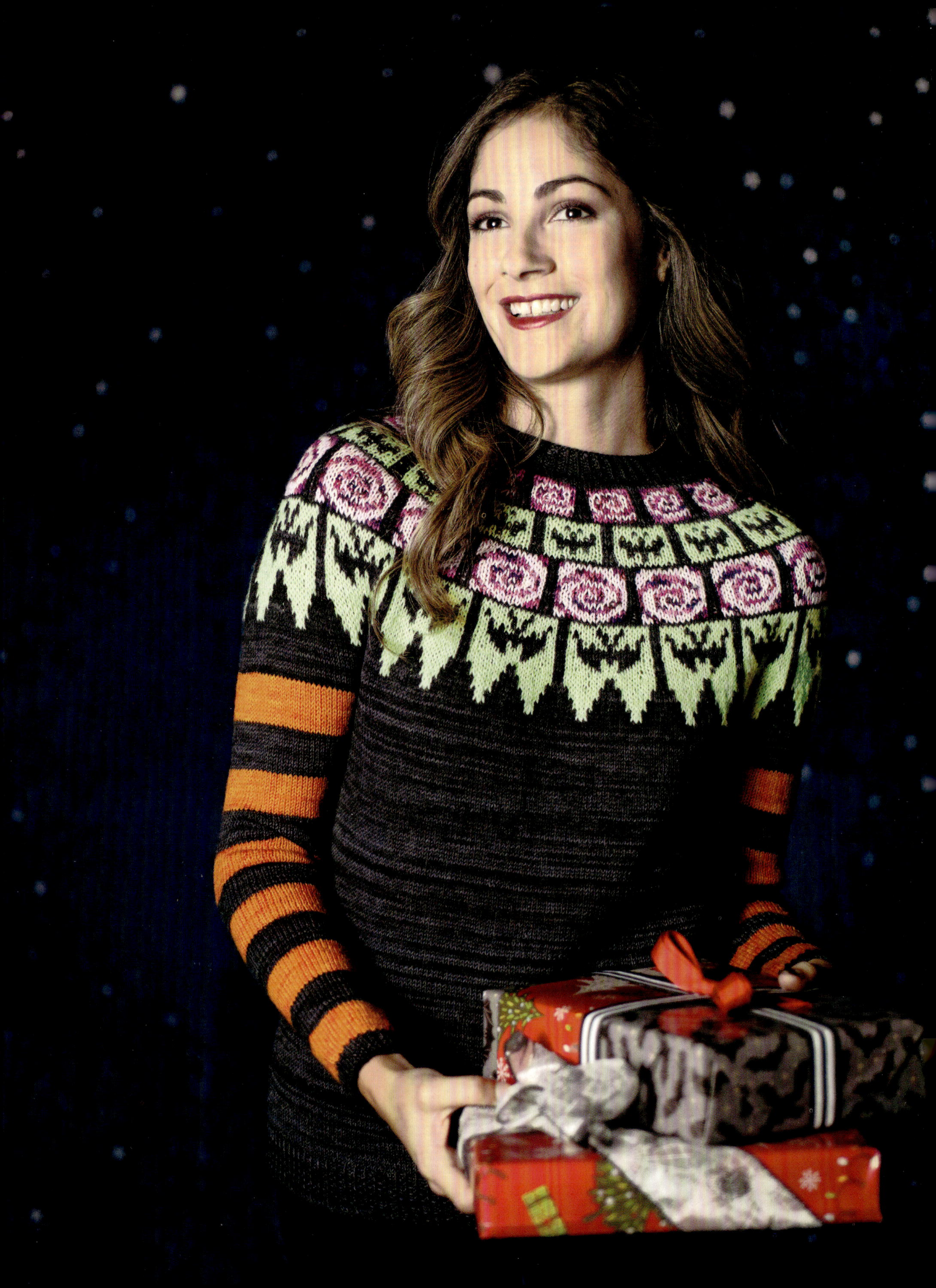

Halloween Town Pullover

Designed by
Dragon Hoard Designs

"Curiosity killed the cat, you know."
—Dr. Finkelstein

SKILL LEVEL
💀 💀 💀

One of the most difficult scenes for the stop-motion animators to execute was when Jack leaves Halloween Town, finds the doors in the forest, and reaches for the doorknob that leads him to Christmas Town. As he is drawn to the bright and jolly door with a Christmas tree, the audience sees Jack's hand moving toward the knob, along with the reflection of his face, hand, and the forest. Director Henry Selick explains, "The crew had to work inside an eight-by-eight-by-eight-foot box for two weeks, creating a forced perspective image of what Jack sees in the doorknob. We literally built a set to the view in the doorknob, then custom-built the set backward from that view." Although it appears onscreen for just a few seconds, it's a visually stunning and important scene where Jack is between two worlds.

An advanced adventure into Halloween Town, this top-down pullover, worked in the round, is sure to be your go-to for autumn excursions. Below the 1x1 twisted rib collar, stranded colorwork motifs featuring mysterious swirls and flying bats dance across the yoke. German short rows are added for a better fit, then stitches are put on hold for the sleeves to be worked later. A stockinette torso is worked until the bottom twisted ribbing, then the held stitches are picked up and worked in the round in Halloween-colored jogless stripes. You can be scary and cozy at the same time!

SIZES
1 (2, 3, 4, 5) [6, 7, 8, 9, 10, 11]

FINISHED MEASUREMENTS
Bust Circumference: 29½ (33½, 37½, 41¼, 45¼) [49¼, 53½, 57, 61, 65, 68¾] in. / 75 (85, 95.5, 105, 115) [125, 136, 145, 155, 165, 174.5] cm

Garment is designed to be worn with 0 to 2 in. / 0 to 5 cm positive ease.

YARN
Fingering weight yarn, shown in Dragon Hoard Yarn *Myth Fingering* (4-ply; 75% superwash merino wool, 25% nylon; 463 yd. / 423 m per 3½ oz. / 100 g hank)

COLORWAYS:
- Main Color (MC): Midnight, 2 (2, 2, 2, 3) [3, 3, 3, 3, 3, 3] hanks
- Contrast Color 1 (CC1): Silent Fury, 1 hank
- Contrast Color 2 (CC2): Lunar Chaos, 1 hank
- Contrast Color 3 (CC3): Tink, 1 hank
- Contrast Color 4 (CC4): Pumpkin, 1 (1, 1, 1, 2) [2, 2, 2, 2, 2, 2] hank(s)

NEEDLES
US 2 / 2.75 mm set of double-pointed needles (or preferred method for small circumference knitting) and 16 in. / 40 cm and 32 to 40 in. / 80 to 100 cm long circular needles

US 4 / 3.5 mm set of double-pointed needles (or preferred method for small circumference knitting) and 16 to 40 in. / 40 to 100 cm long circular needle or size needed to obtain gauge

CONTINUED ON THE NEXT PAGE

NOTIONS

Stitch marker
Row counter (recommended)
Waste yarn or stitch holders
Tapestry needle

GAUGE

26½ sts and 32 rows = 4 in. / 10 cm worked in stockinette stitch in the round on larger needles, taken after blocking

PATTERN NOTES

- This circular yoke style sweater is worked in the round from the top down, seamlessly. When the yoke is complete, the sleeve stitches are placed on hold while the body is completed. Once the body is complete, the sleeves are worked in the round from the underarm to the cuff.
- When working the stranded colorwork in the yoke, you may need to go up 1 to 2 needle sizes to maintain the pattern gauge.
- Read all charts from right to left as for working in the round.
- When working the increase rounds between the colorwork charts in the yoke shaping, be sure to pick up the Main Color (MC) running thread between stitches when creating the M1R.
- As the circumference of the yoke increases, adjust the length of needle as needed for comfort.
- As you change colors between the CC4 and MC stripes in the sleeves, use the Jogless Stripes method to avoid jogs at the beginning of round.

PATTERN INSTRUCTIONS

CAST ON AND COLLAR

Using MC and the smaller 16 in. / 40 cm needle, CO 116 (116, 120, 120, 124) [128, 132, 136, 136, 144, 150] sts using the Twisted German Cast On method. Pm for BOR and join to work in the rnd, being careful not to twist the sts. *The BOR M is at the center back of the sweater.*

RIB RND: *K1 tbl, p1; rep from * to end of rnd.

Rep Rib Rnd until the collar measures 1 in. / 2.5 cm from the CO edge.

NEXT RND: Knit.

YOKE

Switch to larger needles.

INC RND #1

SIZE 1 ONLY:
*K11, M1R, k12, M1R; rep from * to last st, k1.

SIZE 2 ONLY:
*K6, M1R; rep from * to last 2 sts, k2.

SIZE 3 ONLY:
*K5, M1R; rep from * to end of rnd.

SIZE 4 ONLY:
*K3, M1R, (k4, M1R) 2 times; rep from * 9 more times, (k3, M1R) 3 times, k1.

SIZE 5 ONLY:
*(K3, M1R) 3 times, k4, M1R; rep from * 8 more times, k3, M1R, k4, M1R.

SIZE 6 ONLY:
*K3, M1R; rep from * to last 2 sts, k2, M1R.

SIZE 7 ONLY:
*K2, M1R, (k3, M1R) 2 times; rep from * 15 more times, k4.

SIZE 8 ONLY:
*K2, M1R, k3, M1R; rep from * 25 more times, k3, M1R, k3.

SIZE 9 ONLY:
*(K2, M1R) 10 times, k3, M1R; rep from * 4 more times, (k3, M1R) 7 times.

SIZES 10 AND 11 ONLY:
*K2, M1R; rep from * to end of rnd.
10 (19, 24, 33, 38) [43, 48, 53, 62, 72, 75] sts inc; 126 (135, 144, 153, 162) [171, 180, 189, 198, 216, 225] sts total.

SHORT ROWS

SHORT ROW 1 (RS): K34 (37, 40, 42, 44) [47, 49, 52, 54, 59, 62], turn.
SHORT ROW 2 (WS): DS, purl to M, sm, p34 (37, 40, 42, 44) [47, 49, 52, 54, 59, 62], turn.
SHORT ROW 3: DS, knit to prev DS, process DS knitwise, k6, turn.
SHORT ROW 4: DS, purl to prev DS, process DS purlwise, p6, turn.

SHORT ROWS 5 AND 6: Rep [Short Rows 3 and 4] 1 time.

SHORT ROW 7: DS, knit to BOR M.

NEXT RND (RS): Knit to end of rnd processing DS knitwise as encountered.

COLORWORK CHART A

Work Rows 1–9 of Chart A once, joining CC1 and CC2 as required—chart is repeated 14 (15, 16, 17, 18) [19, 20, 21, 22, 24, 25] times across rnd. Break all CCs when chart is complete.

INC RND #2

*K1, M1R, k8, M1R; rep from * to end of rnd—28 (30, 32, 34, 36) [38, 40, 42, 44, 48, 50] sts inc; 154 (165, 176, 187, 198) [209, 220, 231, 242, 264, 275] sts total.

COLORWORK CHART B

Work Rows 1–9 of Chart B once, joining CC3 as required—chart is repeated 14 (15, 16, 17, 18) [19, 20, 21, 22, 24, 25] times across rnd. Break CC3 when chart is complete.

INC RND #3

*K3, M1R, k2, M1R, k4, M1R, k2; rep from * to end of rnd—42 (45, 48, 51, 54) [57, 60, 63, 66, 72, 75] sts inc; 196 (210, 224, 238, 252) [266, 280, 294, 308, 336, 350] sts total.

COLORWORK CHART C

Work Rows 1–12 of Chart C once, joining CC1 and CC2 as required—chart is repeated 14 (15, 16, 17, 18) [19, 20, 21, 22, 24, 25] times across rnd. Break all CCs when chart is complete.

INC RND #4

*M1R, k10, M1R, k1, M1R, k3; rep from * to end of rnd—42 (45, 48, 51, 54) [57, 60, 63, 66, 72, 75] sts inc; 238 (255, 272, 289, 306) [323, 340, 357, 374, 408, 425] sts total.

COLORWORK CHART D

Work Rows 1–21 of Chart D once, joining CC3 as required—chart is repeated 14 (15, 16, 17, 18) [19, 20, 21, 22, 24, 25] times across rnd. Break all CCs when chart is complete.

70 (75, 80, 85, 90) [95, 100, 105, 110, 120, 125] sts inc; 308 (330, 352, 374, 396) [418, 440, 462, 484, 528, 550] sts total.

The remainder of the body of the sweater is worked in MC only.

Knit 1 (2, 2, 3, 7) [8, 9, 11, 13, 15, 16] rnd(s) even.

INC RND #5

SIZE 1 ONLY:
*M1R, k38; rep from * to last 4 sts, k4.

SIZE 2 ONLY:
*M1R, k27, M1R, k28; rep from * to end of rnd.

SIZE 3 ONLY:
*M1R, k22; rep from * to end of rnd.

SIZE 4 ONLY:
*M1R, k15, M1R, k16; rep from * to last 2 sts, k2.

SIZE 5 ONLY:
*M1R, k9, (M1R, k10) 9 times; rep from * to end of rnd.

SIZE 6 ONLY:
*(M1R, k7) 17 times, (M1R, k6) 15 times; rep from * to end of rnd.

SIZE 7 ONLY:
*(M1R, k7) 2 times, (M1R, k6) 5 times; rep from * to end of rnd.

SIZE 8 ONLY:
(M1R, k6) 31 times, (M1R, k5) 18 times, (M1R, k6) 31 times.

SIZE 9 ONLY:
*(M1R, k5) 17 times, (M1R, k4) 9 times; rep from * to end of rnd.

SIZE 10 ONLY:
(M1R, k5) 18 times, (M1R, k6) 58 times, (M1R, k5) 18 times.

SIZE 11 ONLY:
(M1R, k4) 30 times, (M1R, k5) 62 times, (M1R, k4) 30 times.

8 (12, 16, 24, 40) [64, 70, 80, 104, 94, 122] sts inc; 316 (342, 368, 398, 436) [482, 510, 542, 588, 622, 672] sts total.

Cont in St st until the yoke measures 8½ (9, 9½, 9¾, 10) [10¼, 10½, 11, 11½, 12, 12½] in. / 21.5 (23, 24, 24.5, 25.5) [26, 26.5, 28, 29, 30.5, 32] cm from the cast on edge at the center front of the sweater.

SEPARATE BODY & SLEEVES

Remove BOR M, k47 (53, 58, 64, 69) [75, 80, 85, 91, 98, 104], place the next 64 (66, 68, 72, 80) [92, 96, 102, 112, 116, 128] sts on waste yarn or stitch holder for the right sleeve, CO 2 (3, 4, 5, 6) [7, 9, 10, 10, 10, 10] sts using the Backward Loop Cast On method, pm for new BOR, CO 2 (3, 4, 5, 6) [7, 9, 10, 10, 10, 10] more sts, k94 (105, 116, 127, 138) [149, 159, 169, 182, 195, 208], place the next 64 (66, 68, 72, 80) [92, 96, 102, 112, 116, 128] sts on waste yarn or stitch holder for the left sleeve, CO 4 (6, 8, 10, 12) [14, 18, 20, 20, 20, 20] sts using the Backward Loop method, knit to new BOR—196 (222, 248, 274, 300) [326, 354, 378, 404, 430, 456] sts rem. *The BOR M is now at the right underarm.*

BODY

Cont in St st until the body measures approx. 12¾ in. / 32.5 cm from the underarm (or 2 in. / 5 cm less than total desired body length).

HEM

Switch to smaller needles.

RIB RND: *K1 tbl, p1; rep from * to end of rnd.

Rep Rib Rnd until the hem measures 2 in. / 5 cm.

Bind off all sts in pattern using Jeny's Surprisingly Stretchy Bind Off.

SLEEVES (MAKE 2 THE SAME)

Read carefully through the following instructions before beginning to correctly work the striping pattern in tandem with the sleeve shaping.

Place the 64 (66, 68, 72, 80) [92, 96, 102, 112, 116, 128] sts of one sleeve onto the set of larger dpns and distribute evenly (or onto the larger needle in your preferred method of small circumference knitting).

Starting at the center of the underarm CO sts, join CC4 and pick up and knit 2 (3, 4, 5, 6) [7, 9, 10, 10, 10, 10] sts, pick up and knit 1 st to close the gap, knit across the live 64 (66, 68, 72, 80) [92, 96, 102, 112, 116, 128] sts, pick up and knit 1 st to close the gap, then pick up and knit 2 (3, 4, 5, 6) [7, 9, 10, 10, 10, 10] more sts, pm for BOR and join to work in the rnd—70 (74, 78, 84, 94) [108, 116, 124, 134, 138, 150] sts total.

SETUP RND: Knit.
DEC RND: K1, k2tog, knit to last 3 sts, ssk, k1—2 sts dec.

Cont in St st until the sleeve measures 15 in. / 38 cm (or 1 in. / 2.5 cm short of the desired total length), repeating the Dec Rnd every 13 (13, 10, 10, 8) [5, 5, 4, 3, 3, 3] rnds 8 (8, 10, 11, 14) [21, 23, 27, 30, 32, 37] more times.

AT THE SAME TIME, join MC after 12 rnds; alternate 12-round stripes between CC4 and MC until the sleeve reaches the target length.

18 (18, 22, 24, 30) [44, 48, 56, 62, 66, 76] sts dec; 52 (56, 56, 60, 64) [64, 68, 68, 72, 72, 74] sts rem.

CUFF

Break CC4; work the cuff with MC only. Switch to smaller needles.
SETUP RND: Knit.
RIB RND: *K1 tbl, p1; rep from * to end of rnd.
Rep Rib Rnd until the cuff measures 1 in. / 2.5 cm.
Bind off all sts using Jeny's Surprisingly Stretchy Bind Off.

FINISHING

Weave in all ends. Wet block to dimensions. Once dry, trim all ends.

FRIGHTENING FACT

The Haunted Mansion rides in both Disneyland in California and in Tokyo Disneyland get *Tim Burton's The Nightmare Before Christmas* overlays during the autumn season complete with *Nightmare*-inspired chilling narration and music, characters from the film sprinkled throughout the ride, interior and exterior *Nightmare* décor, and a fun mash-up of Christmas, Halloween, and the classic ride.

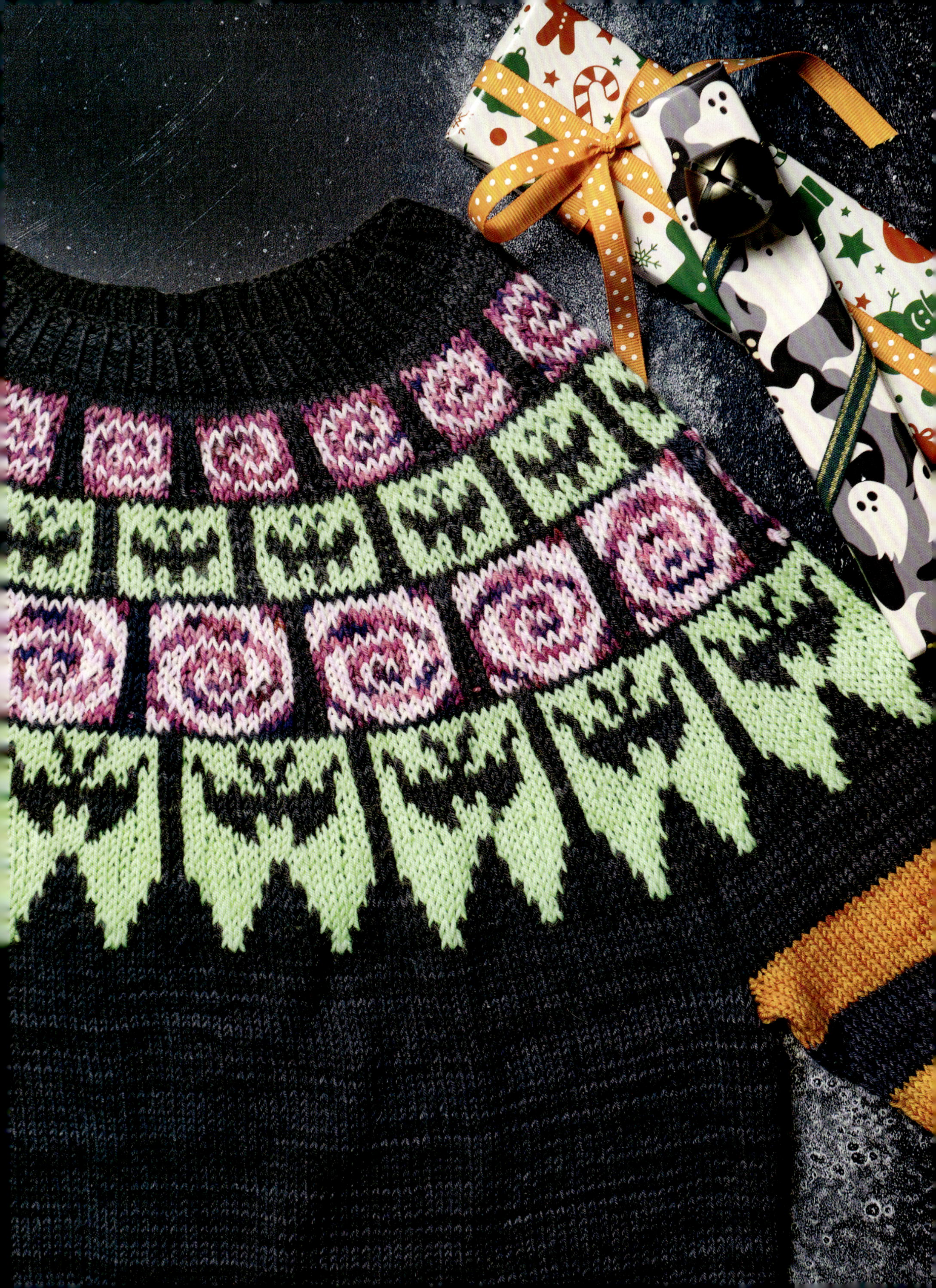

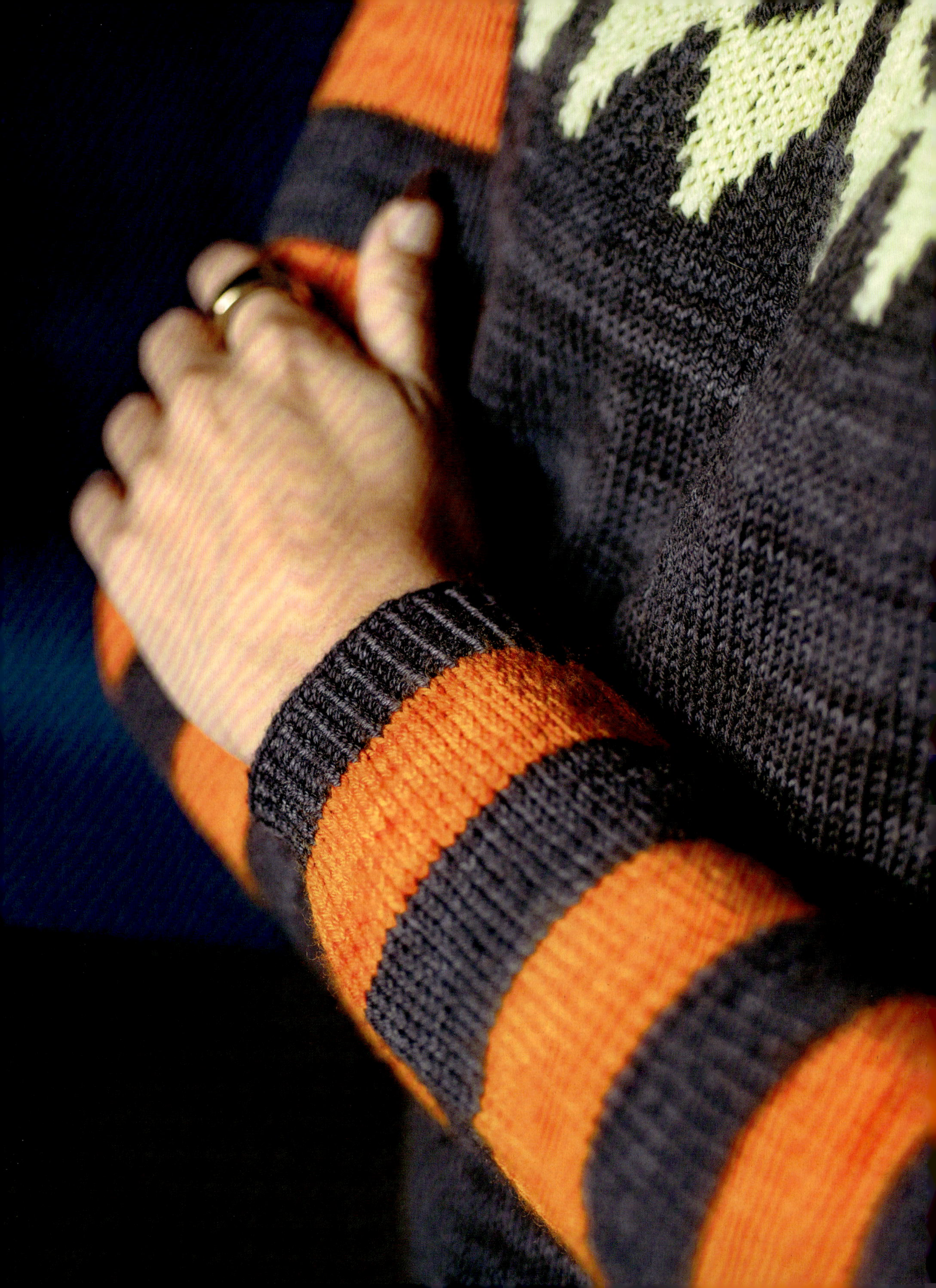

Key

- No stitch
- Knit
- MC
- CC1
- CC2
- CC3
- M1F
- Pattern repeat

Chart A

Chart B

Chart C

Chart D

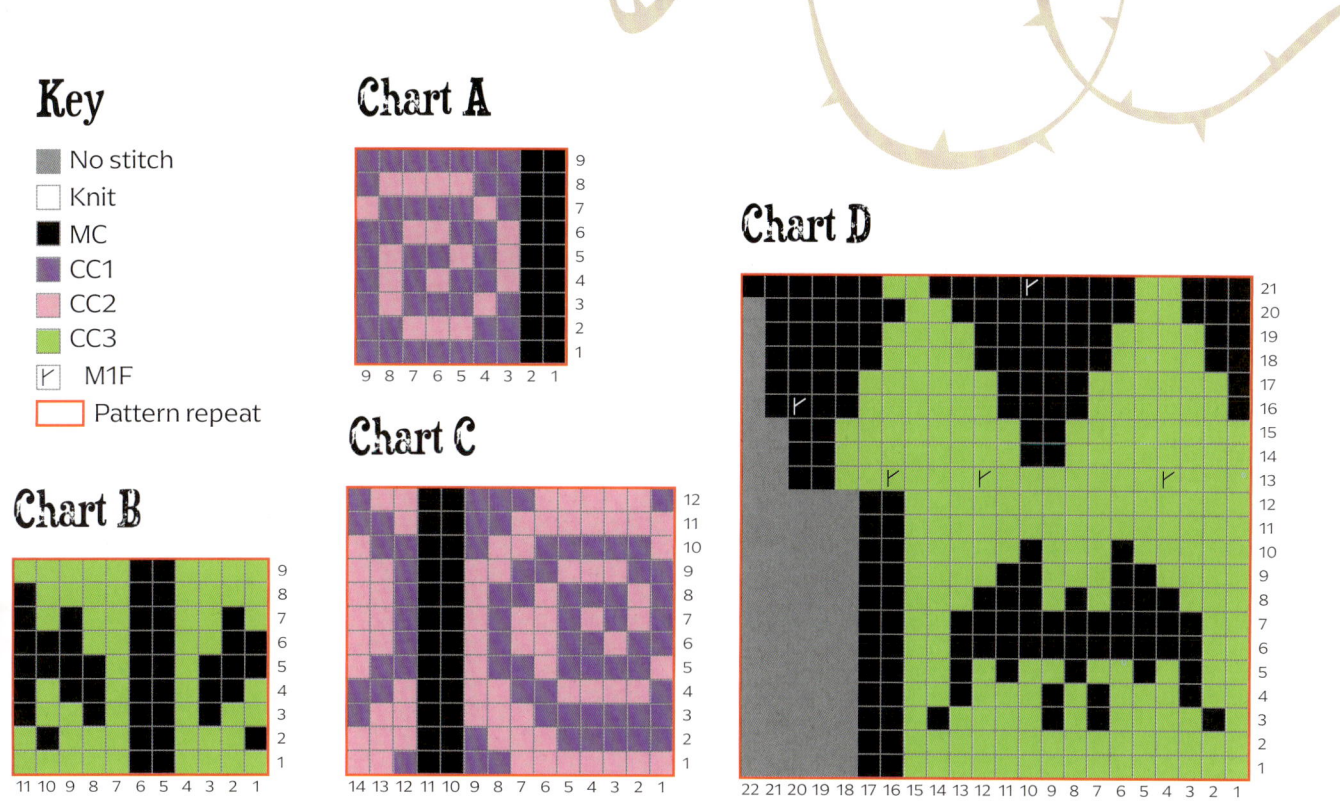

Halloweentown Town Pullover Schematic

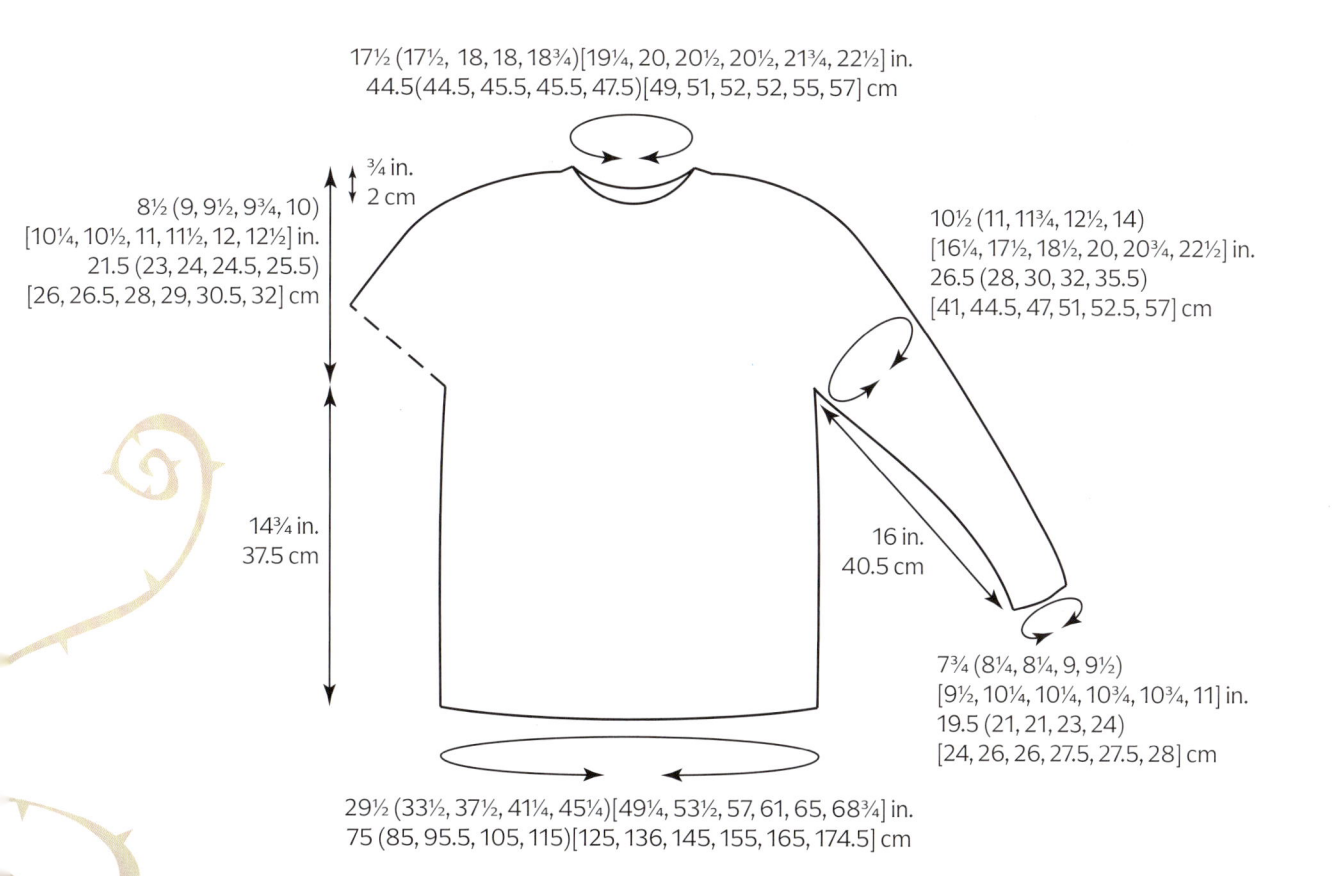

17½ (17½, 18, 18, 18¾)[19¼, 20, 20½, 20½, 21¾, 22½] in.
44.5 (44.5, 45.5, 45.5, 47.5)[49, 51, 52, 52, 55, 57] cm

¾ in.
2 cm

8½ (9, 9½, 9¾, 10)
[10¼, 10½, 11, 11½, 12, 12½] in.
21.5 (23, 24, 24.5, 25.5)
[26, 26.5, 28, 29, 30.5, 32] cm

10½ (11, 11¾, 12½, 14)
[16¼, 17½, 18½, 20, 20¾, 22½] in.
26.5 (28, 30, 32, 35.5)
[41, 44.5, 47, 51, 52.5, 57] cm

14¾ in.
37.5 cm

16 in.
40.5 cm

7¾ (8¼, 8¼, 9, 9½)
[9½, 10¼, 10¼, 10¾, 10¾, 11] in.
19.5 (21, 21, 23, 24)
[24, 26, 26, 27.5, 27.5, 28] cm

29½ (33½, 37½, 41¼, 45¼)[49¼, 53½, 57, 61, 65, 68¾] in.
75 (85, 95.5, 105, 115)[125, 136, 145, 155, 165, 174.5] cm

145

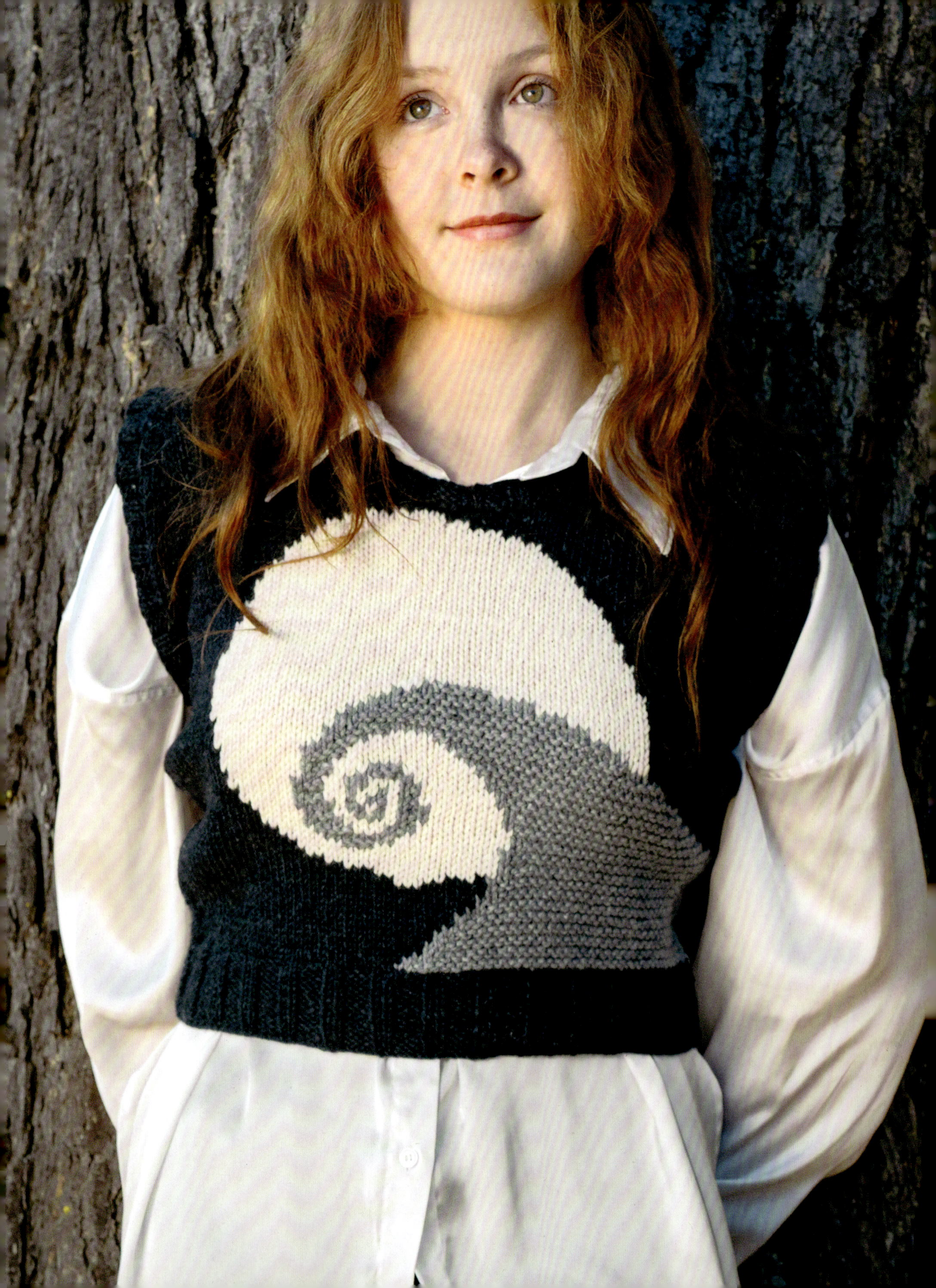

Spiral Hill Sweater Vest

Designed by
Heidi Gustad

"Well, I may as well give them what they want."
—Jack Skellington

SKILL LEVEL
💀 💀 💀

In one of the film's most iconic scenes, Jack meanders through the gravestones and mausoleums in the cemetery with his ghostly dog Zero. Spiral Hill unfurls below him as he sings about his heart's greatest desires and heads out to the Hinterlands. Spiral Hill is also home to henbane, witch hazel, pumpkins, and Sally's favorite, deadly nightshade. It is here that Sally hides and sings about her love for Jack, and where the two finally reunite at the end, accepting each other as friends and forming a romantic attachment.

Recreate the *Tim Burton's The Nightmare Before Christmas*'s iconic landmark in garment form! Knit flat from the bottom up in two panels with armhole shaping and then seamed together with mattress stitch, this vest uses intarsia colorwork and an intentional combination of stockinette and garter stitch to set the scene. Once the pieces are joined, stitches are picked up around the armholes and neckline to knit the ribbed trim. Don't wait for the next full moon to cast on!

FRIGHTENING FACT

Deadly nightshade, or *Atropa belladonna*, is one of the most toxic plants in the world. While the entire plant is toxic, the roots are the deadliest part, causing hallucinations and delirium to those who ingest it.

SIZES

1 (2, 3, 4, 5) [6, 7, 8, 9] {10, 11}

FINISHED MEASUREMENTS

Bust Circumference: 36¼ (39½, 42, 44½, 47) [50½, 53, 55½, 59] {61½, 64¾} in. / 92 (100.5, 106.5, 113, 119.5) [128.5, 134.5, 141, 150] {156, 164.5} cm

Designed to be worn with 1 to 2 in. / 2½ to 5 cm positive ease.

YARN

Worsted weight yarn, shown in Brooklyn Tweed *Imbue* (5-ply; 100% American merino wool; 104 yd. / 95 m per 1¾ oz. / 50 g hank)

COLORWAYS:

- Main Color (MC): Carbon, 5 (5, 5, 6, 6) [7, 7, 8, 8] {8, 9} hanks
- Contrast Color 1 (CC1): Ash, 1 (1, 1, 1, 1) [1, 1, 1, 1] {2, 2} hank(s)
- Contrast Color 2 (CC2): Crepe, 1 hank

NEEDLES

US 5 / 3.75 mm, 16 to 32 in. / 40 to 80 cm circular needle and set of 5 dpns

US 6 / 4 mm, 16 to 32 in. / 40 to 80 cm circular needle or size needed to obtain gauge

NOTIONS

Stitch markers

Waste yarn

Tapestry needle

GAUGE

19 sts and 28 rows = 4 in. / 10 cm in stockinette stitch worked flat on larger needle, taken after blocking

PATTERN NOTES

- This sweater vest is worked flat from the bottom up, using the smaller needle for all ribbing, changing to the larger needle for the body.
- The front and back are seamed together at the shoulders and sides before picking up neck and armhole stitches.
- The armhole and neck stitches are picked up and knit along the edges of the seamed body and worked outward in the round.
- Written instructions are provided for the construction of the garment with a chart for the Vest Front intarsia colorwork section. Written instructions are not provided for the charted front of the vest.
- Instructions for size 1 are provided first with additional sizes in parentheses, brackets, and braces. When only one set of numbers is provided, it applies to all sizes.
- The charts are designed to encompass all 11 sizes. To work the chart for your size, find the color designation for the size you are making from the chart key; a size outline is created for all sizes (except for size 11 which will use the entire width of all charts). Work only the stitches between the outline for your size. If you encounter a symbol square in a color other than your size color, treat this square as a non-increase stitch and knit it in the color surrounding it. For example, if you are working size 3, which has a light green color designation, and you encounter a pink square (the designated color for size 2), do not work the pink square as an increase or a decrease, but knit the square using MC or CC1.

PATTERN STITCHES

Stockinette St Flat (worked over any number of sts)

Row 1 (RS): Knit.

Row 2 (WS): Purl.

Rep Rows 1 and 2 for patt.

PATTERN INSTRUCTIONS

VEST BACK

CAST ON & RIBBING

Using smaller needle in 24 or 32 in. / 40 or 60 cm length for comfort and MC, CO 72 (77, 87 92, 107) [112, 122, 127, 137] {142, 152} sts using the Twisted German Cast On method. Do not join to work in the rnd.

ROW 1 (RS): K2, *p3, k2; rep from * to end of row.

ROW 2 (WS): P2, *k3, p2; rep from * to end of row.

Rep Rows 1 and 2 until ribbing measures 2 in. / 5 cm from CO edge, ending with a WS row.

BODY

Switch to larger needles.

SIZES 1, 4, 6, 7, 10, AND 11 ONLY:

ROW 1 (RS, INC): K2, M1R, knit to last 3 sts, M1L, k2—74 (-, -, 94, -) [114, 124, -, -] {144, 154} sts.

SIZES 2, 3, 5, 8, AND 9 ONLY:

ROW 1 (RS, INC): K2, M1R, knit to end of row— - (78, 88, -, 108) [-, -, 128, 138] {-, -} sts.

ALL SIZES:

*Beginning with a WS row, work 7 (5, 7, 7, 17) [13, 27, 17, 25] {25, 25} rows even in St st.

NEXT ROW (RS, INC): K2, M1R, knit to last 3 sts, M1L, k2—2 sts inc.

Rep from * 6 (8, 6, 6, 2) [3, 1, 2, 1] {1, 0} more time(s).

14 (18, 14, 14, 6) [8, 4, 6, 4] {4, 2} sts inc; 88 (96, 102, 108, 114) [122, 128, 134, 142] {148, 156} sts total. Beginning with a WS row, work 1 (3, 1, 1, 3) [1, 1, 3, 5] {5, 31} more row(s) even in St st (58 total body rows worked).

BACK ARMHOLE SHAPING

BIND OFF ROW A (RS, BIND OFF ROW): BO 3 sts knitwise, knit to end of row—85 (93, 99, 105, 111) [119, 125, 131, 139] {145, 153} sts rem.

BIND OFF ROW B (WS, BIND OFF ROW): BO 3 sts purlwise, purl to end of row—82 (90, 96, 102, 108) [116, 122, 128, 136] {142, 150} sts rem.

SIZES 1–6 ONLY: Proceed to ** below (All Sizes).

SIZES 7–11 ONLY:

ROW 1 (RS, DEC): (K2, ssk) 2 times, knit to last 8 sts, (k2tog, k2) 2 times—4 sts dec.

ROW 2 (WS): Purl to end of row.

Rep [Rows 1 and 2] - (-, -, -, -) [-, 0, 0, 1] {3, 5} more time(s).

- (-, -, -, -) [-, 4, 4, 8] {16, 24} sts dec; - (-, -, -, -) [-, 118, 124, 128] {126, 126} sts rem.

ALL SIZES:

****NEXT ROW (RS, DEC):** K2, ssk, knit to last 4 sts, k2tog, k2—2 sts dec.

Beginning with a WS row, work 5 (3, 1, 1, 1) [1, 1, 1, 1] {1, 1} row(s) even in St st.

Rep from ** 4 (8, 1, 6, 12) [15, 18, 21, 24] {23, 23} more time(s).

10 (18, 4, 14, 26) [32, 38, 44, 50] {48, 48} sts dec; 72 (72, 92, 88, 82) [84, 80, 80, 78] {78, 78} sts rem.

*****NEXT ROW (RS, DEC):** K2, ssk, knit to last 4 sts, k2tog, k2—2 sts dec.

Beginning with a WS row, work 7 (5, 3, 3, 3) [3, 3, 3, 3] {3, 3} rows even in St st.

Rep from *** 1 (1, 10, 8, 5) [4, 2, 2, 0] {0, 0} more time(s).

4 (4, 22, 18, 12) [10, 6, 6, 2] {2, 2} sts dec; 68 (68, 70, 70, 70) [74, 74, 74, 76] {76, 76} sts rem.

Beginning with a RS row, work 2 rows even in St st; 48 (50, 50, 52, 52) [54, 54, 60, 60] {62, 66} total armhole shaping rows worked (not including bind off rows).

With the RS facing, BO all sts knitwise.

VEST FRONT

CAST ON & RIBBING

Work as for the Vest Back.

BODY

Switch to larger needles.

Begin working from the Front charts (pages 156 and 158–159), reading all odd-numbered (RS) rows from right to left and all even-numbered (WS) rows from left to right, joining CC1 and CC2 as needed, as follows:

ROW 1 (RS): Following instructions for your size, work Front Left chart, pm, work Front Center chart, pm, work Front Right chart.

ROW 2 (WS): Following instructions for your size, work Front Right chart, sm, work Front Center chart, sm, work Front Left chart.

Beginning with Row 3, work charted Rows 3–58 once, sm as encountered. When completed, return to the written instructions to shape the armholes. 88 (96, 102, 108, 114) [122, 128, 134, 142] {148, 156} sts total. The Front Left and Right charts are now complete.

FRONT ARMHOLE AND RIGHT SHOULDER SHAPING

BIND OFF ROW A (RS, BIND OFF ROW): Using MC, BO 3 sts knitwise, knit to M, sm, work Row 59 of Front Center chart to next M, sm, knit to end of row with MC—85 (93, 99, 105, 111) [119, 125, 131, 139] {145, 153} sts rem.

BIND OFF ROW B (WS, BIND OFF ROW): Using MC, BO 3 sts purlwise, purl to M, sm, work Row 60 of Front Center chart to next M, sm, purl to end of row with MC—82 (90, 96, 102, 108) [116, 122, 128, 136] {142, 150} sts rem.

As the following armhole and shoulder/neckline shaping rows are worked, continue to work the Front Center chart between the markers until the Front Center chart is complete. When the chart is complete, break the CCs and remove the markers on each side of the 68 st center panel. The remainder of the front will be worked in St st using MC only.

SIZE 1 ONLY

ROW 1 (RS, DEC): K2, ssk, work est patt to last 4 sts, k2tog, k2—2 sts dec.

ROWS 2–6: Work 5 rows even in est patt.

ROWS 7–12: Rep Rows 1–6 once—78 sts rem.

ROW 13 (RS, DEC): K2, ssk, knit to last 4 sts, k2tog, k2—76 sts rem.

ROWS 14–16: Work 3 rows even in est patt. The Front Center chart is now complete.

ROW 17 (RS, BIND OFF ROW): K29, place these 29 sts on waste yarn or stitch holder for the left shoulder, bind off 18 sts knitwise, knit to end of row—29 sts rem for right shoulder.

ROW 18 (WS): Purl to end of row.

ROW 19 (DEC): Knit to last 4 sts, k2tog, k2—28 sts rem.

ROW 20: Purl to end of row.

ROW 21 (DEC): K2, ssk, knit to end of row—27 sts rem.

ROWS 22–24: Work 3 rows even in St st.

ROW 25 (DEC): K2, ssk, knit to last 4 sts, k2tog, k2—25 sts rem.

ROWS 26–28: Work 3 rows even in St st.

ROWS 29 AND 30: Rep Rows 21 and 22 once—24 sts rem.

ROW 31 (DEC): Knit to last 4 sts, k2tog, k2—23 sts rem.

ROWS 32–34: Work 3 rows even in St st.

ROWS 35–38: Rep Rows 21–24 once—22 sts rem.

ROWS 39 AND 40: Rep Rows 19 and 20 once—21 sts rem.

ROW 41 (DEC): K2, ssk, knit to end of row—20 sts rem.

ROWS 42–46: Work 5 rows even in St st.

ROW 47 (DEC): K2, ssk, knit to end of row—19 sts rem.

ROW 48: Purl to end of row.

With RS facing, BO all sts knitwise.

SIZE 2 ONLY

ROW 1 (RS, DEC): K2, ssk, work est patt to last 4 sts, k2tog, k2—2 sts dec.

ROWS 2–4: Work 3 rows even in est patt.
ROWS 5–16: Rep [Rows 1–4] 3 more times—82 sts rem. The Front Center chart is now complete.
ROW 17 (RS, DEC): K2, ssk, knit to last 4 sts, k2tog, k2—80 sts rem.
ROW 18: Purl to end of row.
ROW 19 (RS, BIND OFF ROW): K31, place these 31 sts on waste yarn or stitch holder for the left shoulder, bind off 18 sts knitwise, knit to end of row—31 sts rem for right shoulder.
ROW 20 (WS): Purl to end of row.
ROW 21 (DEC): Knit to last 4 sts, k2tog, k2—1 st dec.
ROW 22: Purl to end of row.
ROW 23 (DEC): K2, ssk, knit to end of row—1 st dec.
ROW 24: Purl to end of row.
ROWS 25–32: Rep [Rows 21–24] 2 more times—25 sts rem.
ROW 33 (DEC): Knit to last 4 sts, k2tog, k2—24 sts rem.
ROWS 34–36: Work 3 rows even in St st.
ROW 37 (DEC): K2, ssk, knit to last 4 sts, k2tog, k2—2 sts dec.
ROWS 38–42: Work 5 rows even in St st.
ROWS 43–48: Rep Rows 37–42 once—20 sts rem.
ROW 49 (DEC): K2, ssk, knit to end of row—19 sts rem.
ROW 50: Purl to end of row.
With RS facing, BO all sts knitwise.

SIZE 3 ONLY
ROW 1 (RS, DEC): K2, ssk, work est patt to last 4 sts, k2tog, k2—2 sts dec.
ROW 2 (WS): Work est patt to end of row.
ROWS 3 AND 4: Rep Rows 1 and 2 once—92 sts rem.
ROW 5 (RS, DEC): K2, ssk, work est patt to last 4 sts, k2tog, k2—2 sts dec.
ROWS 6–8: Work 3 rows even in est patt.
ROWS 9–16: Rep [Rows 5–8] 2 more times—86 sts rem. The Front Center chart is now complete.
ROW 17 (RS, DEC): K2, ssk, knit to last 4 sts, k2tog, k2—84 sts rem.
ROW 18: Purl to end of row.
ROW 19 (RS, BIND OFF ROW): K33, place these 33 sts on waste yarn or stitch holder for the left shoulder, bind off 18 sts knitwise, knit to end of row—33 sts rem for right shoulder.
ROW 20 (WS): Purl to end of row.
ROW 21 (DEC): Knit to last 4 sts, k2tog, k2—1 st dec.
ROW 22: Purl to end of row.
ROW 23 (DEC): K2, ssk, knit to end of row—1 st dec.
ROW 24: Purl to end of row.
ROWS 25–32: Rep [Rows 21–24] 2 more times—27 sts rem.
ROW 33 (DEC): Knit to last 4 sts, k2tog, k2—26 sts rem.
ROWS 34–36: Work 3 rows even in St st.
ROW 37 (DEC): K2, ssk, knit to last 4 sts, k2tog, k2—24 sts dec.
ROWS 38–40: Work 3 rows even in St st.
ROWS 41–44: Rep Rows 21–24 once—22 sts rem.
ROW 45 (DEC): Knit to last 4 sts, k2tog, k2—21 sts rem.
ROWS 46–48: Work 3 rows in St st.
ROW 49 (DEC): K2, ssk, knit to end of row—20 sts rem.
ROW 50: Purl to end of row.
With RS facing, BO all sts knitwise.

SIZE 4 ONLY
ROW 1 (RS, DEC): K2, ssk, work est patt to last 4 sts, k2tog, k2—2 sts dec.
ROW 2 (WS): Work est patt to end of row.
ROWS 3–16: Rep [Rows 1 and 2] 7 more times—86 sts rem. The Front Center chart is now complete.
ROWS 17 AND 18: Work 2 rows in St st.
ROW 19 (DEC): K2, ssk, knit to last 4 sts, k2tog, k2—84 sts rem.
ROW 20: Purl to end of row.
ROW 21 (RS, BIND OFF ROW): K33, place these 33 sts on waste yarn or stitch holder for the left shoulder, bind off 18 sts knitwise, knit to end of row—33 sts rem for right shoulder.
ROW 22 (WS): Purl to end of row.
ROW 23 (DEC): Knit to last 4 sts, k2tog, k2—1 st dec.
ROW 24: Purl to end of row.
ROW 25 (DEC): K2, ssk, knit to end of row—1 st dec.
ROW 26: Purl to end of row.
ROWS 27–34: Rep [Rows 21–24] 2 more times—27 sts rem.
ROW 35 (DEC): Knit to last 4 sts, k2tog, k2—26 sts rem.
ROWS 36–38: Work 3 rows even in St st.
ROW 39 (DEC): K2, ssk, knit to last 4 sts, k2tog, k2—24 sts rem.
ROWS 40–42: Work 3 rows even in St st.
ROWS 43–46: Rep Rows 23–26 once—22 sts rem.
ROW 47 (DEC): Knit to last 4 sts, k2tog, k2—21 sts rem.
ROWS 48–50: Work 3 rows even in St st.
ROW 51 (DEC): K2, ssk, knit to end of row—20 sts rem.
ROW 52: Purl to end of row.
With RS facing, BO all sts knitwise.

SIZE 5 ONLY
ROW 1 (RS, DEC): K2, ssk, work est patt to last 4 sts, k2tog, k2—2 sts dec.
ROW 2 (WS): Work est patt to end of row.
ROWS 3–16: Rep [Rows 1 and 2] 7 more times—92 sts rem. The Front Center chart is now complete.
ROW 17 (DEC): K2, ssk, knit to last 4 sts, k2tog, k2—2 sts dec.
ROW 18: Purl to end of row.
ROWS 19 AND 20: Rep Rows 17 and 18 once—88 sts rem.
ROW 21 (RS, BIND OFF ROW): K2, ssk, k31, place these 34 sts on waste yarn or stitch holder for the left shoulder, bind off 18 sts knitwise, knit to last 4 sts, k2tog, k2—34 sts rem for right shoulder.
ROW 22 (WS): Purl to end of row.
ROW 23 (DEC): Knit to last 4 sts, k2tog, k2—33 sts rem.
ROW 24: Purl to end of row.
ROW 25 (DEC): K2, ssk, knit to last 4 sts, k2tog, k2—31 sts rem.
ROW 26: Purl to end of row.

ROW 27 (DEC): Knit to last 4 sts, k2tog, k2—1 st dec.
ROW 28: Purl to end of row.
ROW 29 (DEC): K2, ssk, knit to end of row—1 st dec.
ROW 30: Purl to end of row.
ROWS 31–34: Rep Rows 27–30 once—27 sts rem.
ROW 35 (DEC): Knit to last 4 sts, k2tog, k2—26 sts rem.
ROWS 36–38: Work 3 rows even in St st.
ROW 39 (DEC): K2, ssk, knit to last 4 sts, k2tog, k2—24 sts rem.
ROWS 40–42: Work 3 rows even in St st.
ROWS 43–46: Rep Rows 27–30 once—22 sts rem.
ROW 47 (DEC): Knit to last 4 sts, k2tog, k2—21 sts rem.
ROWS 48–50: Work 3 rows even in St st.
ROW 51 (DEC): K2, ssk, knit to end of row—20 sts rem.
ROW 52: Purl to end of row.
With RS facing, BO all sts knitwise.

SIZE 6 ONLY
ROW 1 (RS, DEC): K2, ssk, work est patt to last 4 sts, k2tog, k2—2 sts dec.
ROW 2 (WS): Work est patt to end of row.
ROWS 3–16: Rep [Rows 1 and 2] 7 more times—100 sts rem. The Front Center chart is now complete.
ROW 17 (DEC): K2, ssk, knit to last 4 sts, k2tog, k2—2 sts dec.
ROW 18: Purl to end of row.
ROWS 19 AND 20: Rep Rows 17 and 18 once—96 sts rem.
ROW 21 (RS, BIND OFF ROW): K2, ssk, k35, place these 38 sts on waste yarn or stitch holder for the left shoulder, bind off 18 sts knitwise, knit to last 4 sts, k2tog, k2—38 sts rem for right shoulder.
ROW 22 (WS): Purl to end of row.
ROW 23 (DEC): Knit to last 4 sts, k2tog, k2—1 st dec.
ROW 24: Purl to end of row.
ROW 25 (DEC): K2, ssk, knit to last 4 sts, k2tog, k2—2 sts dec.
ROW 26: Purl to end of row.

ROWS 27–34: Rep [Rows 23–26] 2 more times—29 sts rem.
ROWS 35 AND 36: Work 2 rows even in St st.
ROW 37 (DEC): Knit to last 4 sts, k2tog, k2—28 sts rem.
ROW 38: Purl to end of row.
ROW 39 (DEC): K2, ssk, knit to end of row—27 sts rem.
ROW 40: Purl to end of row.
ROW 41 (DEC): Knit to last 4 sts, k2tog, k2—26 sts rem.
ROWS 42–44: Work 3 rows even in St st.
ROW 45 (DEC): K2, ssk, knit to last 4 sts, k2tog, k2—24 sts rem.
ROWS 46–48: Work 3 rows even in St st.
ROW 49 (DEC): Knit to last 4 sts, k2tog, k2—23 sts rem.
ROW 50: Purl to end of row.
ROW 51 (DEC): K2, ssk, knit to end of row—22 sts rem.
ROWS 52–54: Work 3 rows even in St st.
With RS facing, BO all sts knitwise.

SIZE 7 ONLY
ROW 1 (RS, DEC): (K2, ssk) 2 times, work est patt to last 8 sts, (k2tog, k2) 2 times—118 sts rem.
ROW 2 (WS): Work est patt to end of row.
ROW 3 (DEC): K2, ssk, work est patt to last 4 sts, k2tog, k2—2 sts dec.
ROW 4: Work est patt to end of row.
ROWS 5–16: Rep [Rows 3 and 4] 6 more times—104 sts rem. The Front Center chart is now complete.
ROW 17 (DEC): K2, ssk, knit to last 4 sts, k2tog, k2—2 sts dec.
ROW 18: Purl to end of row.
ROWS 19 AND 20: Rep Rows 17 and 18 once—100 sts rem.
ROW 21 (RS, BIND OFF ROW): K2, ssk, k37, place these 40 sts on waste yarn or stitch holder for the left shoulder, bind off 18 sts knitwise, knit to last 4 sts, k2tog, k2—40 sts rem for right shoulder.
ROW 22 (WS): Purl to end of row.
ROW 23 (DEC): Knit to last 4 sts, k2tog, k2—1 st dec.

ROW 24: Purl to end of row.
ROW 25 (DEC): K2, ssk, knit to last 4 sts, k2tog, k2—2 sts dec.
ROW 26: Purl to end of row.
ROWS 27–34: Rep [Rows 23–26] 2 more times—31 sts rem.
ROWS 35–38: Work [Rows 23 and 24] 2 times—29 sts rem.
ROW 39 (DEC): K2, ssk, knit to last 4 sts, k2tog, k2—27 sts rem.
ROWS 40–42: Work 3 rows even in St st.
ROW 43 (DEC): Knit to last 4 sts, k2tog, k2—26 sts rem.
ROW 44: Purl to end of row.
ROW 45 (DEC): K2, ssk, knit to end of row—25 sts rem.
ROW 46: Purl to end of row.
ROW 47 (DEC): Knit to last 4 sts, k2tog, k2—24 sts rem.
ROWS 48–50: Work 3 rows even in St st.
ROW 51 (DEC): K2, ssk, knit to last 4 sts, k2tog, k2—22 sts rem.
ROWS 52–54: Work 3 rows even in St st.
With RS facing, BO all sts knitwise.

SIZE 8 ONLY
ROW 1 (RS, DEC): (K2, ssk) 2 times, work est patt to last 8 sts, (k2tog, k2) 2 times—124 sts rem.
ROW 2 (WS): Work est patt to end of row.
ROW 3 (DEC): K2, ssk, work est patt to last 4 sts, k2tog, k2—2 sts dec.
ROW 4: Work est patt to end of row.
ROWS 5–16: Rep [Rows 3 and 4] 6 more times—110 sts rem. The Front Center chart is now complete.
ROW 17 (DEC): K2, ssk, knit to last 4 sts, k2tog, k2—2 sts dec.
ROW 18: Purl to end of row.
ROWS 19–24: Rep [Rows 17 and 18] 3 more times—102 sts rem.
ROW 25 (RS, BIND OFF ROW): K2, ssk, k38, place these 41 sts on waste yarn or stitch holder for the left shoulder, bind off 18 sts knitwise, knit to last 4 sts, k2tog, k2—41 sts rem for right shoulder.
ROW 26 (WS): Purl to end of row.

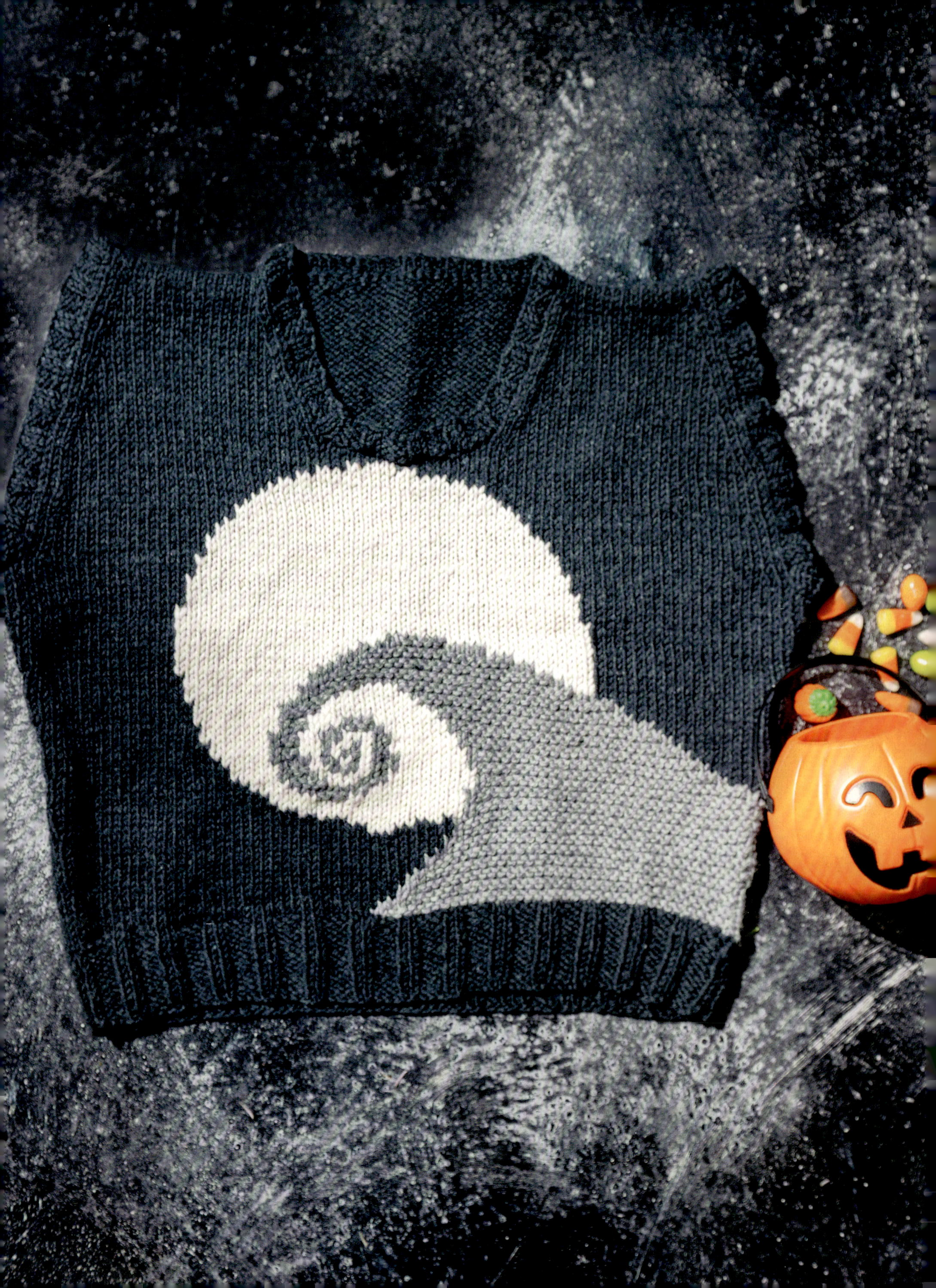

ROW 27 (DEC): Knit to last 4 sts, k2tog, k2—1 st dec.
ROW 28: Purl to end of row.
ROW 29 (DEC): K2, ssk, knit to last 4 sts, k2tog, k2—2 sts dec.
ROW 30: Purl to end of row.
ROWS 31–42: Rep [Rows 27–30] 3 more times—29 sts rem.
ROWS 43–46: Work [Rows 27 and 28] 2 times—27 sts rem.
ROW 47 (DEC): K2, ssk, knit to last 4 sts, k2tog, k2—25 sts rem.
ROWS 48–50: Work 3 rows even in St st.
ROW 51 (DEC): Knit to last 4 sts, k2tog, k2—24 sts rem.
ROW 52: Purl to end of row.
ROW 53 (DEC): K2, ssk, knit to end of row—23 sts rem.
ROW 54: Purl to end of row.
ROW 55 (DEC): Knit to last 4 sts, k2tog, k2—22 sts rem.
ROWS 56–58: Work 3 rows even in St st.
ROW 59 (DEC): K2, ssk, knit to end of row—21 sts rem.
ROW 60: Purl to end of row.
With RS facing, BO all sts knitwise.

SIZE 9 ONLY

ROW 1 (RS, DEC): (K2, ssk) 2 times, work est patt to last 8 sts, (k2tog, k2) 2 times—4 sts dec.
ROW 2 (WS): Work est patt to end of row.
ROWS 3 AND 4: Rep Rows 1 and 2 once—128 sts rem.
ROW 5 (DEC): K2, ssk, work est patt to last 4 sts, k2tog, k2—2 sts dec.
ROW 6: Work est patt to end of row.
ROWS 7–16: Rep [Rows 5 and 6] 5 more times—116 sts rem. The Front Center chart is now complete.
ROW 17 (DEC): K2, ssk, knit to last 4 sts, k2tog, k2—2 sts dec.
ROW 18: Purl to end of row.
ROWS 19–24: Rep [Rows 17 and 18] 3 more times—108 sts rem.
ROW 25 (RS, BIND OFF ROW): K2, ssk, k41, place these 44 sts on waste yarn or stitch holder for the left shoulder, bind off 18 sts knitwise, knit to last 4 sts, k2tog, k2—44 sts rem for right shoulder.

ROW 26 (WS): Purl to end of row.
ROW 27 (DEC): Knit to last 4 sts, k2tog, k2—1 st dec.
ROW 28: Purl to end of row.
ROW 29 (DEC): K2, ssk, knit to last 4 sts, k2tog, k2—2 sts dec.
ROW 30: Purl to end of row.
ROWS 31–42: Rep [Rows 27–30] 3 more times—32 sts rem.
ROWS 43–46: Work [Rows 27 and 28] 2 times—2 sts dec.
ROW 47 (DEC): K2, ssk, knit to last 4 sts, k2tog, k2—2 sts dec.
ROW 48: Purl to end of row.
ROWS 49–54: Work Rows 43–48 once—24 sts rem.
ROW 55 (DEC): Knit to last 4 sts, k2tog, k2—23 sts rem.
ROWS 56–58: Work 3 rows even in St st.
ROW 59 (DEC): K2, ssk, knit to end of row—22 sts rem.
ROW 60: Purl to end of row.
With RS facing, BO all sts knitwise.

SIZE 10 ONLY

ROW 1 (RS, DEC): (K2, ssk) 2 times, work est patt to last 8 sts, (k2tog, k2) 2 times—4 sts dec.
ROW 2 (WS): Work est patt to end of row.
ROWS 3–8: Rep [Rows 1 and 2] 3 more times—126 sts rem.
ROW 9 (DEC): K2, ssk, work est patt to last 4 sts, k2tog, k2—2 sts dec.
ROW 10: Work est patt to end of row.
ROWS 11–16: Rep [Rows 9 and 10] 3 more times—118 sts rem. The Front Center chart is now complete.
ROW 17 (DEC): K2, ssk, knit to last 4 sts, k2tog, k2—2 sts dec.
ROW 18: Purl to end of row.
ROWS 19 AND 20: Rep Rows 17 and 18 once—114 sts rem.
ROW 21 (RS, BIND OFF ROW): K2, ssk, k44, place these 47 sts on waste yarn or stitch holder for the left shoulder, bind off 18 sts knitwise, knit to last 4 sts, k2tog, k2—47 sts rem for right shoulder.
ROW 22 (WS): Purl to end of row.
ROW 23 (DEC): Knit to last 4 sts, k2tog, k2—1 st dec.

ROW 24: Purl to end of row.
ROW 25 (DEC): K2, ssk, knit to last 4 sts, k2tog, k2—2 sts dec.
ROW 26: Purl to end of row.
ROWS 27–42: Rep [Rows 23–26] 4 more times—32 sts rem.
ROWS 43–46: Work [Rows 23 and 24] 2 times—2 sts dec.
ROW 47 (DEC): K2, ssk, knit to last 4 sts, k2tog, k2—2 sts dec.
ROW 48: Purl to end of row.
ROWS 49–54: Work Rows 43–48 once—24 sts rem.
ROWS 55–58: Work [Rows 23 and 24] 2 times—22 sts rem.
ROW 59 (DEC): K2, ssk, knit to end of row—21 sts rem.
ROWS 60–62: Work 3 rows even in St st.
With RS facing, BO all sts knitwise.

SIZE 11 ONLY

ROW 1 (RS, DEC): (K2, ssk) 2 times, work est patt to last 8 sts, (k2tog, k2) 2 times—4 sts dec.
ROW 2 (WS): Work est patt to end of row.
ROWS 3–12: Rep [Rows 1 and 2] 5 more times—126 sts rem.
ROW 13 (DEC): K2, ssk, work est patt to last 4 sts, k2tog, k2—2 sts dec.
ROW 14: Work est patt to end of row.
ROWS 15 AND 16: Rep Rows 13 and 14 once—122 sts rem. The Front Center chart is now complete.
ROW 17 (DEC): K2, ssk, knit to last 4 sts, k2tog, k2—2 sts dec.
ROW 18: Purl to end of row.
ROWS 19–26: Rep [Rows 17 and 18] 4 more times—112 sts rem.
ROW 27 (RS, BIND OFF ROW): K2, ssk, k43, place these 46 sts on waste yarn or stitch holder for the left shoulder, bind off 18 sts knitwise, knit to last 4 sts, k2tog, k2—46 sts rem for right shoulder.
ROW 28 (WS): Purl to end of row.
ROW 29 (DEC): Knit to last 4 sts, k2tog, k2—1 st dec.
ROW 30: Purl to end of row.
ROW 31 (DEC): K2, ssk, knit to last 4 sts, k2tog, k2—2 sts dec.
ROW 32: Purl to end of row.
ROWS 33–48: Rep [Rows 29–32] 4 more times—31 sts rem.

ROWS 49–52: Work [Rows 29 and 30] 2 times—2 sts dec.
ROW 53 (DEC): K2, ssk, knit to last 4 sts, k2tog, k2—2 sts dec.
ROW 54: Purl to end of row.
ROWS 55–60: Work Rows 43–48 once—23 sts rem.
ROW 61 (DEC): Knit to last 4 sts, k2tog, k2—22 sts rem.
ROWS 62–64: Work 3 rows even in St st.
ROW 65 (DEC): K2, ssk, knit to end of row—21 sts rem.
ROW 66: Purl to end of row.
With RS facing, BO all sts knitwise.

LEFT SHOULDER SHAPING

Place the 29 (31, 33, 33, 34) [38, 40, 41, 44] {47, 46} sts for the left shoulder back onto the larger needle. Rejoin MC yarn with the WS facing.

SIZE 1 ONLY

ROW 18 (WS): Purl to end of row.
ROW 19 (DEC): K2, ssk knit to end of row—28 sts rem.
ROW 20: Purl to end of row.
ROW 21 (DEC): Knit to last 4 sts, k2tog, k2—27 sts rem.
ROWS 22–24: Work 3 rows even in St st.
ROW 25 (DEC): K2, ssk, knit to last 4 sts, k2tog, k2—25 sts rem.
ROWS 26–28: Work 3 rows even in St st.
ROWS 29 AND 30: Rep Rows 21 and 22 once—24 sts rem.
ROW 31 (DEC): K2, ssk, knit to end of row—23 sts rem.
ROWS 32–34: Work 3 rows even in St st.
ROWS 35–38: Rep Rows 21–24 once—22 sts rem.
ROWS 39 AND 40: Rep Rows 19 and 20 once—21 sts rem.
ROW 41 (DEC): Knit to last 4 sts, k2tog, k2—20 sts rem.
ROWS 42–46: Work 5 rows even in St st.
ROW 47 (DEC): Knit to last 4 sts, k2tog, k2—19 sts rem.
ROW 48: Purl to end of row.
With RS facing, BO all sts knitwise.

SIZE 2 ONLY

ROW 20 (WS): Purl to end of row.
ROW 21 (DEC): K2, ssk, knit to end of row—1 st dec.
ROW 22: Purl to end of row.
ROW 23 (DEC): Knit to last 4 sts, k2tog, k2—1 st dec.
ROW 24: Purl to end of row.
ROWS 25–32: Rep [Rows 21–24] 2 more times—25 sts rem.
ROW 33 (DEC): K2, ssk, knit to end of row—24 sts rem.
ROWS 34–36: Work 3 rows even in St st.
ROW 37 (DEC): K2, ssk, knit to last 4 sts, k2tog, k2—2 sts dec.
ROWS 38–42: Work 5 rows even in St st.
ROWS 43–48: Rep Rows 37–42 once—20 sts rem.
ROW 49 (DEC): Knit to last 4 sts, k2tog, k2—19 sts rem.
ROW 50: Purl to end of row.
With RS facing, BO all sts knitwise.

SIZE 3 ONLY

ROW 20 (WS): Purl to end of row.
ROW 21 (DEC): K2, ssk, knit to end of row—1 st dec.
ROW 22: Purl to end of row.
ROW 23 (DEC): Knit to last 4 sts, k2tog, k2—1 st dec.
ROW 24: Purl to end of row.
ROWS 25–32: Rep [Rows 21–24] 2 more times—27 sts rem.
ROW 33 (DEC): K2, ssk, knit to end of row—26 sts rem.
ROWS 34–36: Work 3 rows even in St st.
ROW 37 (DEC): K2, ssk, knit to last 4 sts, k2tog, k2—24 sts dec.
ROWS 38–40: Work 3 rows even in St st.
ROWS 41–44: Rep Rows 21–24 once—22 sts rem.
ROW 45 (DEC): K2, ssk, knit to end of row—21 sts rem.
ROWS 46–48: Work 3 rows in St st.
ROW 49 (DEC): Knit to last 4 sts, k2tog, k2—20 sts rem.
ROW 50: Purl to end of row.
With RS facing, BO all sts knitwise.

SIZE 4 ONLY

ROW 22 (WS): Purl to end of row.
ROW 23 (DEC): K2, ssk, knit to end of row—1 st dec.
ROW 24: Purl to end of row.
ROW 25 (DEC): Knit to last 4 sts, k2tog, k2—1 st dec.
ROW 26: Purl to end of row.
ROWS 27–34: Rep [Rows 21–24] 2 more times—27 sts rem.
ROW 35 (DEC): K2, ssk, knit to end of row—26 sts rem.
ROWS 36–38: Work 3 rows even in St st.
ROW 39 (DEC): K2, ssk, knit to last 4 sts, k2tog, k2—24 sts rem.
ROWS 40–42: Work 3 rows even in St st.
ROWS 43–46: Rep Rows 23–26 once—22 sts rem.
ROW 47 (DEC): K2, ssk, knit to end of row—21 sts rem.
ROWS 48–50: Work 3 rows even in St st.
ROW 51 (DEC): Knit to last 4 sts, k2tog, k2—20 sts rem.
ROW 52: Purl to end of row.

SIZE 5 ONLY

ROW 22 (WS): Purl to end of row.
ROW 23 (DEC): K2, ssk, knit to end of row—33 sts rem.
ROW 24: Purl to end of row.
ROW 25 (DEC): K2, ssk, knit to last 4 sts, k2tog, k2—31 sts rem.
ROW 26: Purl to end of row.
ROW 27 (DEC): K2, ssk, knit to end of row—1 st dec.
ROW 28: Purl to end of row.
ROW 29 (DEC): Knit to last 4 sts, k2tog, k2—1 st dec.
ROW 30: Purl to end of row.
ROWS 31–34: Rep Rows 27–30 once—27 sts rem.
ROW 35 (DEC): K2, ssk, knit to end of row—26 sts rem.
ROWS 36–38: Work 3 rows even in St st.
ROW 39 (DEC): K2, ssk, knit to last 4 sts, k2tog, k2—24 sts rem.
ROWS 40–42: Work 3 rows even in St st.
ROWS 43–46: Rep Rows 27–30 once—22 sts rem.

ROW 47 (DEC): K2, ssk, knit to end of row—21 sts rem.
ROWS 48–50: Work 3 rows even in St st.
ROW 51 (DEC): Knit to last 4 sts, k2tog, k2—20 sts rem.
ROW 52: Purl to end of row.
With RS facing, BO all sts knitwise.

SIZE 6 ONLY
ROW 22 (WS): Purl to end of row.
ROW 23 (DEC): K2, ssk, knit to end of row—1 st dec.
ROW 24: Purl to end of row.
ROW 25 (DEC): K2, ssk, knit to last 4 sts, k2tog, k2—2 sts dec.
ROW 26: Purl to end of row.
ROWS 27–34: Rep [Rows 23–26] 2 more times—29 sts rem.
ROWS 35 AND 36: Work 2 rows even in St st.
ROW 37 (DEC): K2, ssk, knit to end of row—28 sts rem.
ROW 38: Purl to end of row.
ROW 39 (DEC): Knit to last 4 sts, k2tog, k2—27 sts rem.
ROW 40: Purl to end of row.
ROW 41 (DEC): K2, ssk, knit to end of row—26 sts rem.
ROWS 42–44: Work 3 rows even in St st.
ROW 45 (DEC): K2, ssk, knit to last 4 sts, k2tog, k2—24 sts rem.
ROWS 46–48: Work 3 rows even in St st.
ROW 49 (DEC): K2, ssk, knit to end of row—23 sts rem.
ROW 50: Purl to end of row.
ROW 51 (DEC): Knit to last 4 sts, k2tog, k2—22 sts rem.
ROWS 52–54: Work 3 rows even in St st.
With RS facing, BO all sts knitwise.

SIZE 7 ONLY
ROW 22 (WS): Purl to end of row.
ROW 23 (DEC): K2, ssk, knit to end of row—1 st dec.
ROW 24: Purl to end of row.
ROW 25 (DEC): K2, ssk, knit to last 4 sts, k2tog, k2—2 sts dec.
ROW 26: Purl to end of row.
ROWS 27–34: Rep [Rows 23–26] 2 more times—31 sts rem.
ROWS 35–38: Work [Rows 23 and 24] 2 times—29 sts rem.
ROW 39 (DEC): K2, ssk, knit to last 4 sts, k2tog, k2—27 sts rem.
ROWS 40–42: Work 3 rows even in St st.
ROW 43 (DEC): K2, ssk, knit to end of row—26 sts rem.
ROW 44: Purl to end of row.
ROW 45 (DEC): Knit to last 4 sts, k2tog, k2—25 sts rem.
ROW 46: Purl to end of row.
ROW 47 (DEC): K2, ssk, knit to end of row—24 sts rem.
ROWS 48–50: Work 3 rows even in St st.
ROW 51 (DEC): K2, ssk, knit to last 4 sts, k2tog, k2—22 sts rem.
ROWS 52–54: Work 3 rows even in St st.
With RS facing, BO all sts knitwise.

SIZE 8 ONLY
ROW 26 (WS): Purl to end of row.
ROW 27 (DEC): K2, ssk, knit to end of row—1 st dec.
ROW 28: Purl to end of row.
ROW 29 (DEC): K2, ssk, knit to last 4 sts, k2tog, k2—2 sts dec.
ROW 30: Purl to end of row.
ROWS 31–42: Rep [Rows 27–30] 3 more times—29 sts rem.
ROWS 43–46: Work [Rows 27 and 28] 2 times—27 sts rem.
ROW 47 (DEC): K2, ssk, knit to last 4 sts, k2tog, k2—25 sts rem.
ROWS 48–50: Work 3 rows even in St st.
ROW 51 (DEC): K2, ssk, knit to end of row—24 sts rem.
ROW 52: Purl to end of row.
ROW 53 (DEC): Knit to last 4 sts, k2tog, k2—23 sts rem.
ROW 54: Purl to end of row.
ROW 55 (DEC): K2, ssk, knit to end of row—22 sts rem.
ROWS 56–58: Work 3 rows even in St st.
ROW 59 (DEC): Knit to last 4 sts, k2tog, k2—21 sts rem.
ROW 60: Purl to end of row.
With RS facing, BO all sts knitwise.

SIZE 9 ONLY
ROW 26 (WS): Purl to end of row.
ROW 27 (DEC): K2, ssk, knit to end of row—1 st dec.
ROW 28: Purl to end of row.
ROW 29 (DEC): K2, ssk, knit to last 4 sts, k2tog, k2—2 sts dec.
ROW 30: Purl to end of row.
ROWS 31–42: Rep [Rows 27–30] 3 more times—32 sts rem.
ROWS 43–46: Work [Rows 27 and 28] 2 times—2 sts dec.
ROW 47 (DEC): K2, ssk, knit to last 4 sts, k2tog, k2—2 sts dec.
ROW 48: Purl to end of row.
ROWS 49–54: Work Rows 43–48 once—24 sts rem.
ROW 55 (DEC): K2, ssk, knit to end of row—23 sts rem.
ROWS 56–58: Work 3 rows even in St st.
ROW 59 (DEC): Knit to last 4 sts, k2tog, k2—22 sts rem.
ROW 60: Purl to end of row.
With RS facing, BO all sts knitwise.

SIZE 10 ONLY
ROW 22 (WS): Purl to end of row.
ROW 23 (DEC): K2, ssk, knit to end of row—1 st dec.
ROW 24: Purl to end of row.
ROW 25 (DEC): K2, ssk, knit to last 4 sts, k2tog, k2—2 sts dec.
ROW 26: Purl to end of row.
ROWS 27–42: Rep [Rows 23–26] 4 more times—32 sts rem.
ROWS 43–46: Work [Rows 23 and 24] 2 times—2 sts dec.
ROW 47 (DEC): K2, ssk, knit to last 4 sts, k2tog, k2—2 sts dec.
ROW 48: Purl to end of row.
ROWS 49–54: Work Rows 43–48 once—24 sts rem.
ROWS 55–58: Work [Rows 23 and 24] 2 times—22 sts rem.
ROW 59 (DEC): Knit to last 4 sts, k2tog, k2—21 sts rem.
ROWS 60–62: Work 3 rows even in St st.
With RS facing, BO all sts knitwise.

Front Center Chart

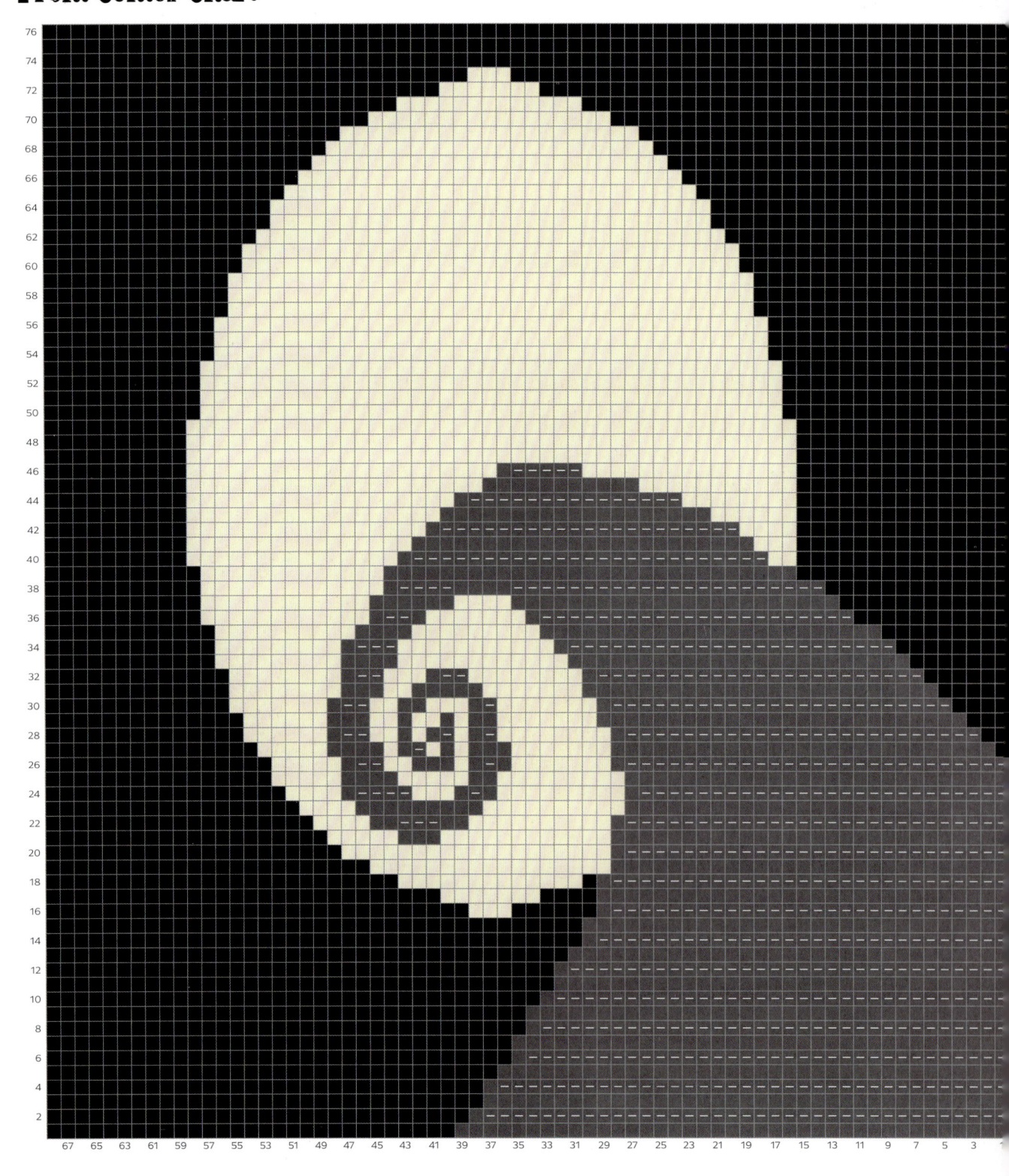

156

SIZE 11 ONLY

ROW 28 (WS): Purl to end of row.
ROW 29 (DEC): K2, ssk, knit to end of row—1 st dec.
ROW 30: Purl to end of row.
ROW 31 (DEC): K2, ssk, knit to last 4 sts, k2tog, k2—2 sts dec.
ROW 32: Purl to end of row.
ROWS 33–48: Rep [Rows 29–32] 4 more times—31 sts rem.
ROWS 49–52: Work [Rows 29 and 30] 2 times—2 sts dec.
ROW 53 (DEC): K2, ssk, knit to last 4 sts, k2tog, k2—2 sts dec.
ROW 54: Purl to end of row.
ROWS 55–60: Work Rows 43–48 once—23 sts rem.
ROW 61 (DEC): K2, ssk, knit to end of row—22 sts rem.
ROWS 62–64: Work 3 rows even in St st.
ROW 65 (DEC): Knit to last 4 sts, k2tog, k2—21 sts rem.
ROW 66: Purl to end of row.
With RS facing, BO all sts knitwise. Weave in all ends and wet block.

SEAMING

Using MC, seam vest front and back together with RS facing out (WS together). Use the invisible horizontal seaming method to join the shoulders and the mattress stitch seaming method to join the side seams.

ARMHOLE RIBBING

Using the smaller 16 in. / 40 cm needle or dpns, rejoin MC at the center of the underarm and pick up and knit 95 (100, 100, 105, 105) [110, 110, 115, 115] {120, 125} sts evenly along the armhole edge. Pm for BOR and join to work in the rnd.
RND 1: *K2, p3; rep from * to end of rnd.
RNDS 2 AND 3: Rep [Rnd 1] 2 times. Bind off all sts loosely in pattern. Repeat for second armhole.

NECKLINE RIBBING

Using the smaller 16 in. / 40 cm circular needle, rejoin MC at one of the shoulder seams and pick up and knit 120 (120, 120, 120, 120) [120, 120, 120, 130] {140, 140} sts along the neckline edge. Pm for BOR and join to work in the rnd.
RND 1: *K2, p3; rep from * to end of rnd.
RNDS 2 AND 3: Rep [Rnd 1] 2 times. Bind off all sts loosely in pattern.

FINISHING

Weave in all ends and wet block to finish. Once dry, trim all ends.

Key

- ☐ Knit on RS, purl on WS
- ⊟ Purl on RS, knit on WS
- M1L
- M1R
- ■ MC - All Sizes
- ■ CC1 - All Sizes
- ☐ CC2 - All Sizes
- ■ Size 1 Only
- ■ Size 2 Only
- ■ Size 3 Only
- ■ Size 4 Only
- ■ Size 5 Only
- ■ Size 6 Only
- ■ Size 7 Only
- ■ Size 8 Only
- ■ Size 9 Only
- ■ Size 10 Only
- ■ Size 11 Only

Front Right Chart

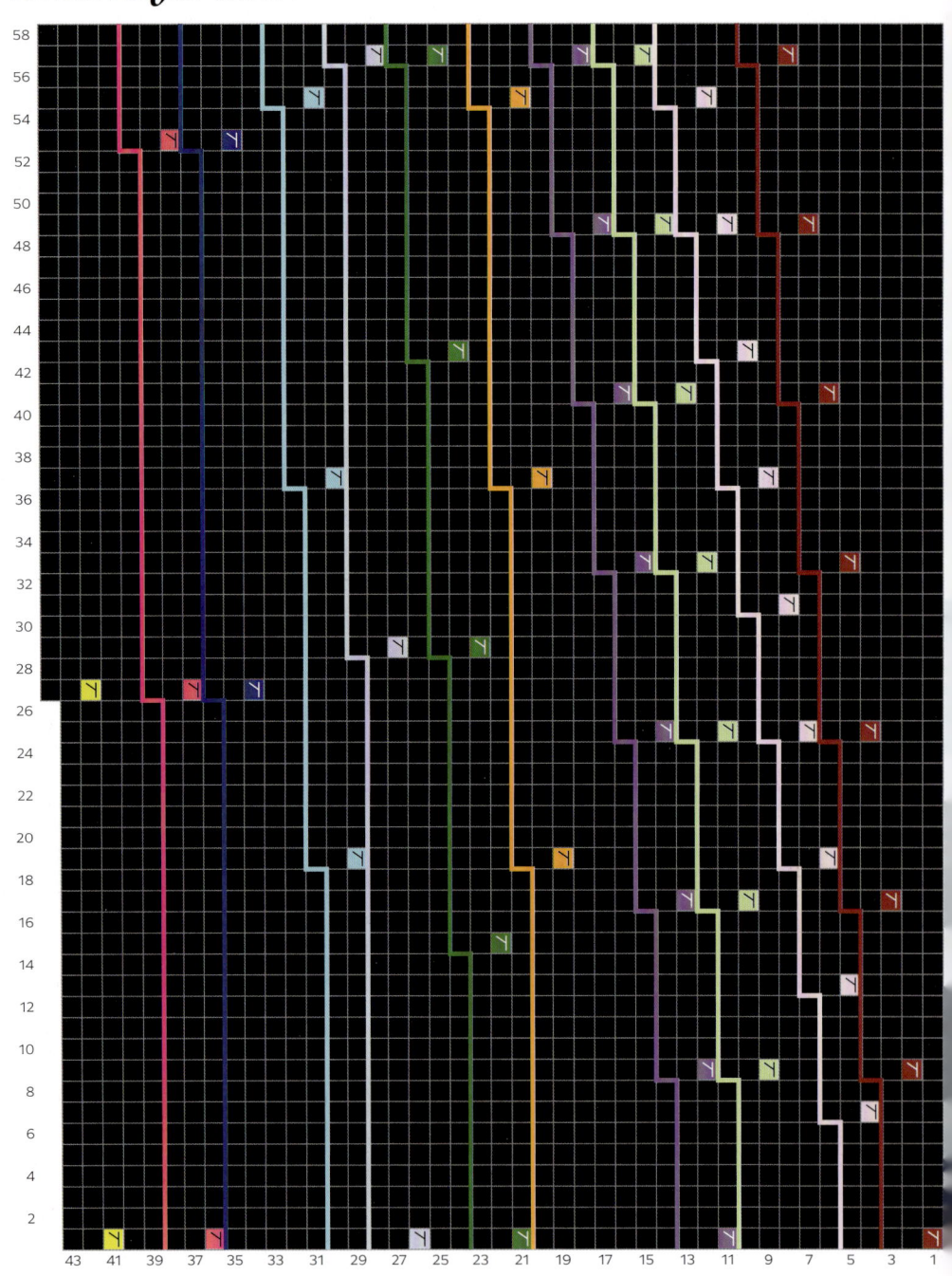

Front Left Chart

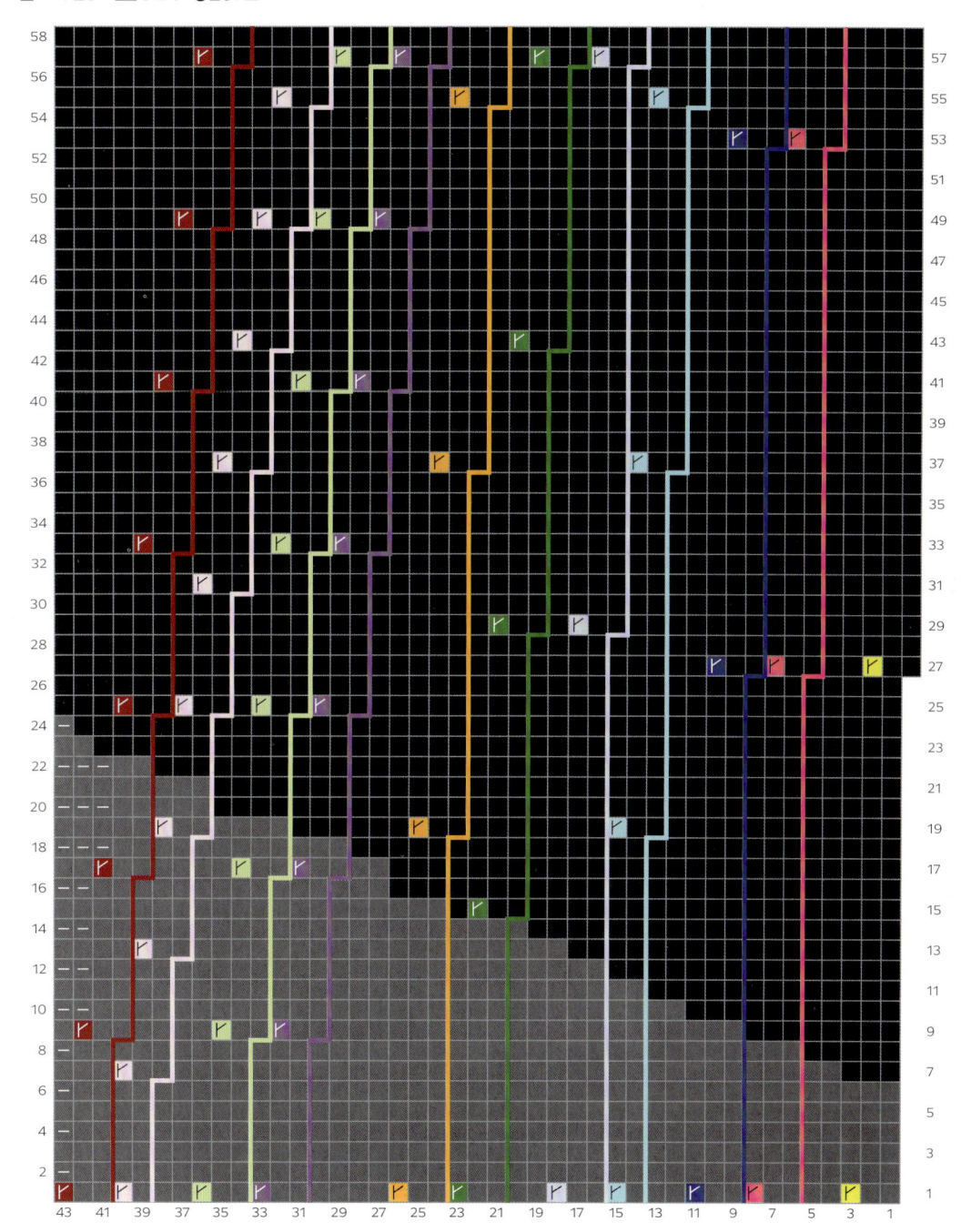

Spiral Hill Vest Schematic

**Dimensions provided for seamed Front and Back; measurements do not include ribbing widths at armholes.

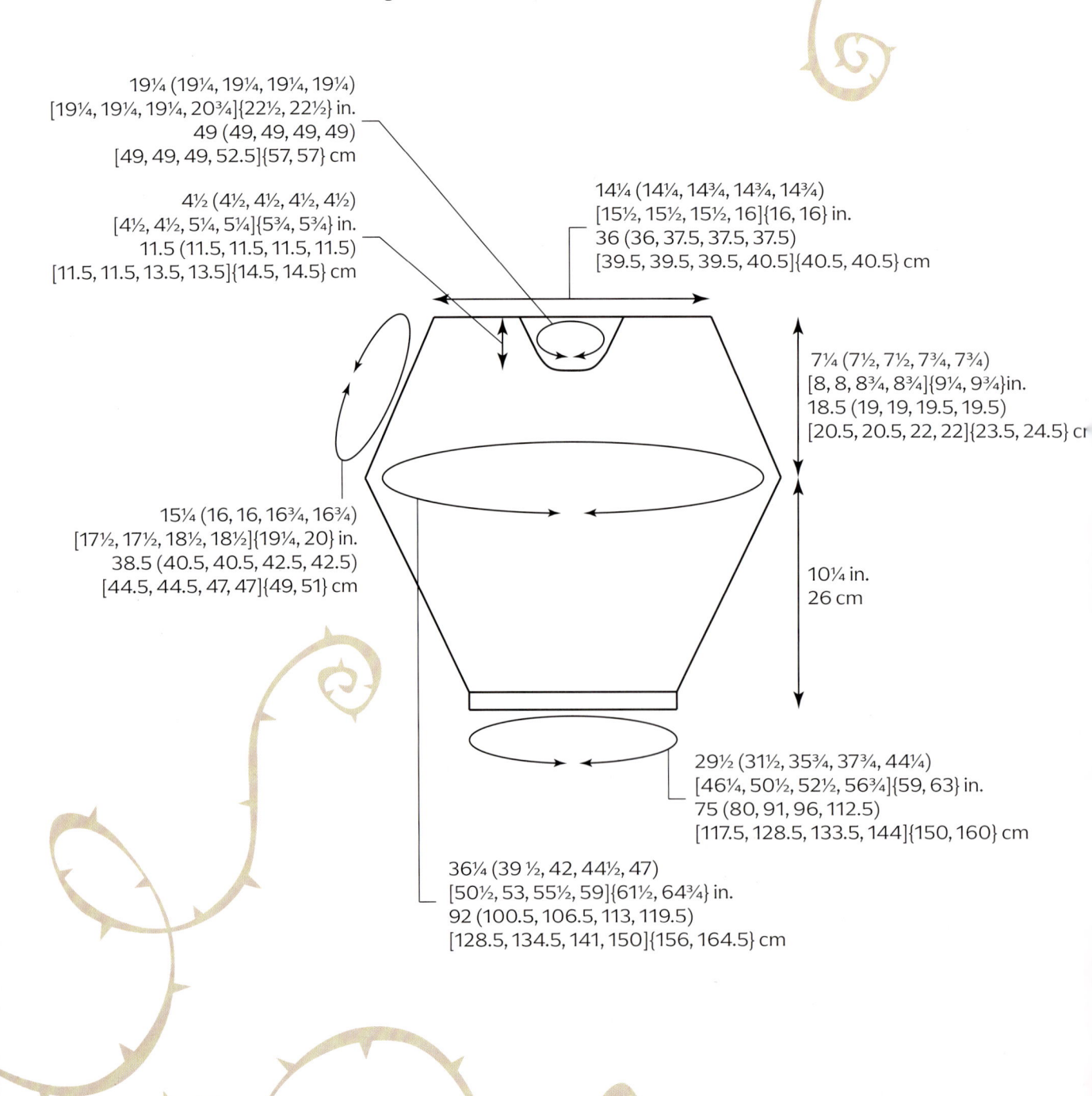

19¼ (19¼, 19¼, 19¼, 19¼)
[19¼, 19¼, 19¼, 20¾]{22½, 22½} in.
49 (49, 49, 49, 49)
[49, 49, 49, 52.5]{57, 57} cm

4½ (4½, 4½, 4½, 4½)
[4½, 4½, 5¼, 5¼]{5¾, 5¾} in.
11.5 (11.5, 11.5, 11.5, 11.5)
[11.5, 11.5, 13.5, 13.5]{14.5, 14.5} cm

14¼ (14¼, 14¾, 14¾, 14¾)
[15½, 15½, 15½, 16]{16, 16} in.
36 (36, 37.5, 37.5, 37.5)
[39.5, 39.5, 39.5, 40.5]{40.5, 40.5} cm

7¼ (7½, 7½, 7¾, 7¾)
[8, 8, 8¾, 8¾]{9¼, 9¾} in.
18.5 (19, 19, 19.5, 19.5)
[20.5, 20.5, 22, 22]{23.5, 24.5} cm

15¼ (16, 16, 16¾, 16¾)
[17½, 17½, 18½, 18½]{19¼, 20} in.
38.5 (40.5, 40.5, 42.5, 42.5)
[44.5, 44.5, 47, 47]{49, 51} cm

10¼ in.
26 cm

29½ (31½, 35¾, 37¾, 44¼)
[46¼, 50½, 52½, 56¾]{59, 63} in.
75 (80, 91, 96, 112.5)
[117.5, 128.5, 133.5, 144]{150, 160} cm

36¼ (39½, 42, 44½, 47)
[50½, 53, 55½, 59]{61½, 64¾} in.
92 (100.5, 106.5, 113, 119.5)
[128.5, 134.5, 141, 150]{156, 164.5} cm

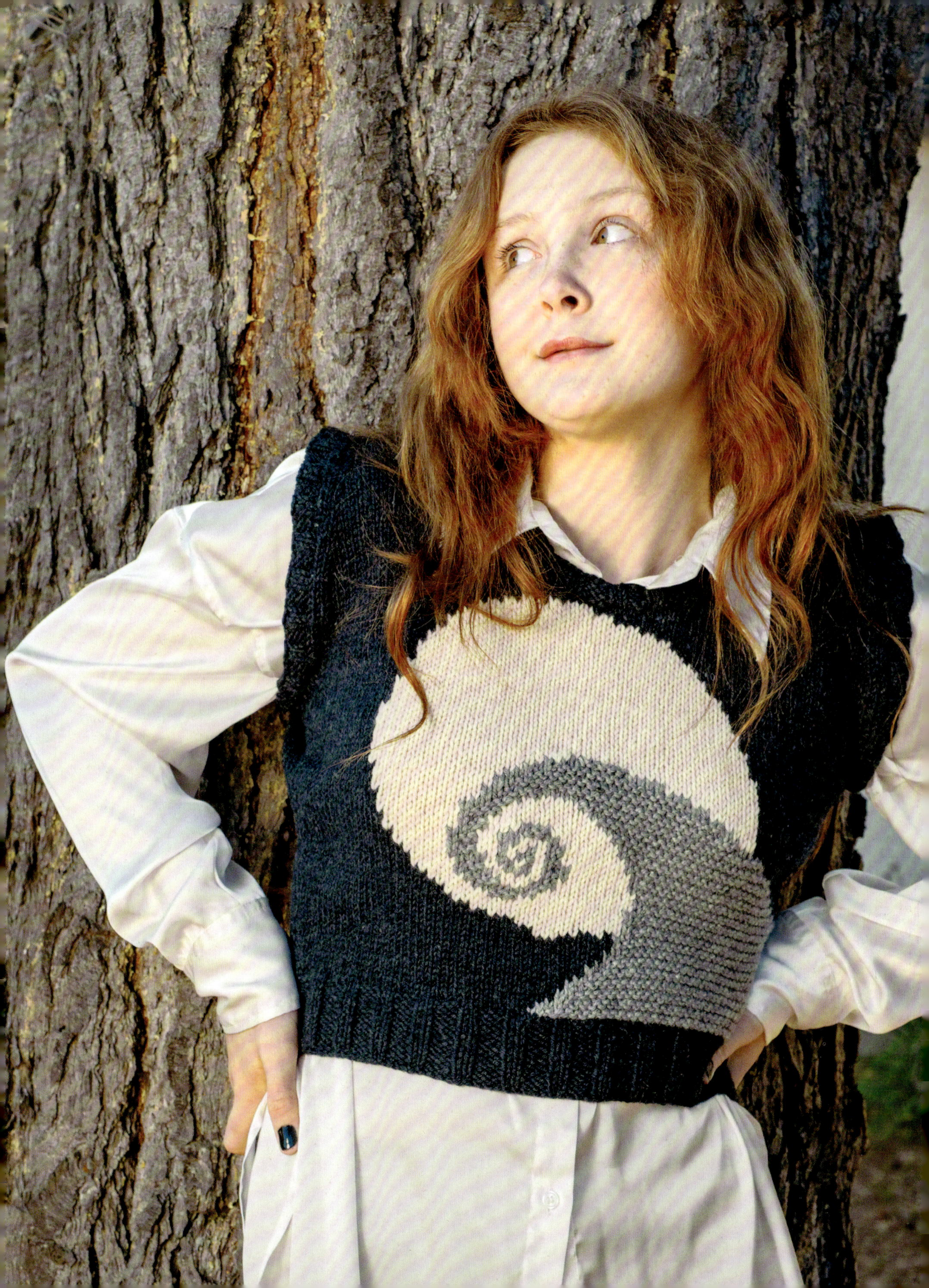

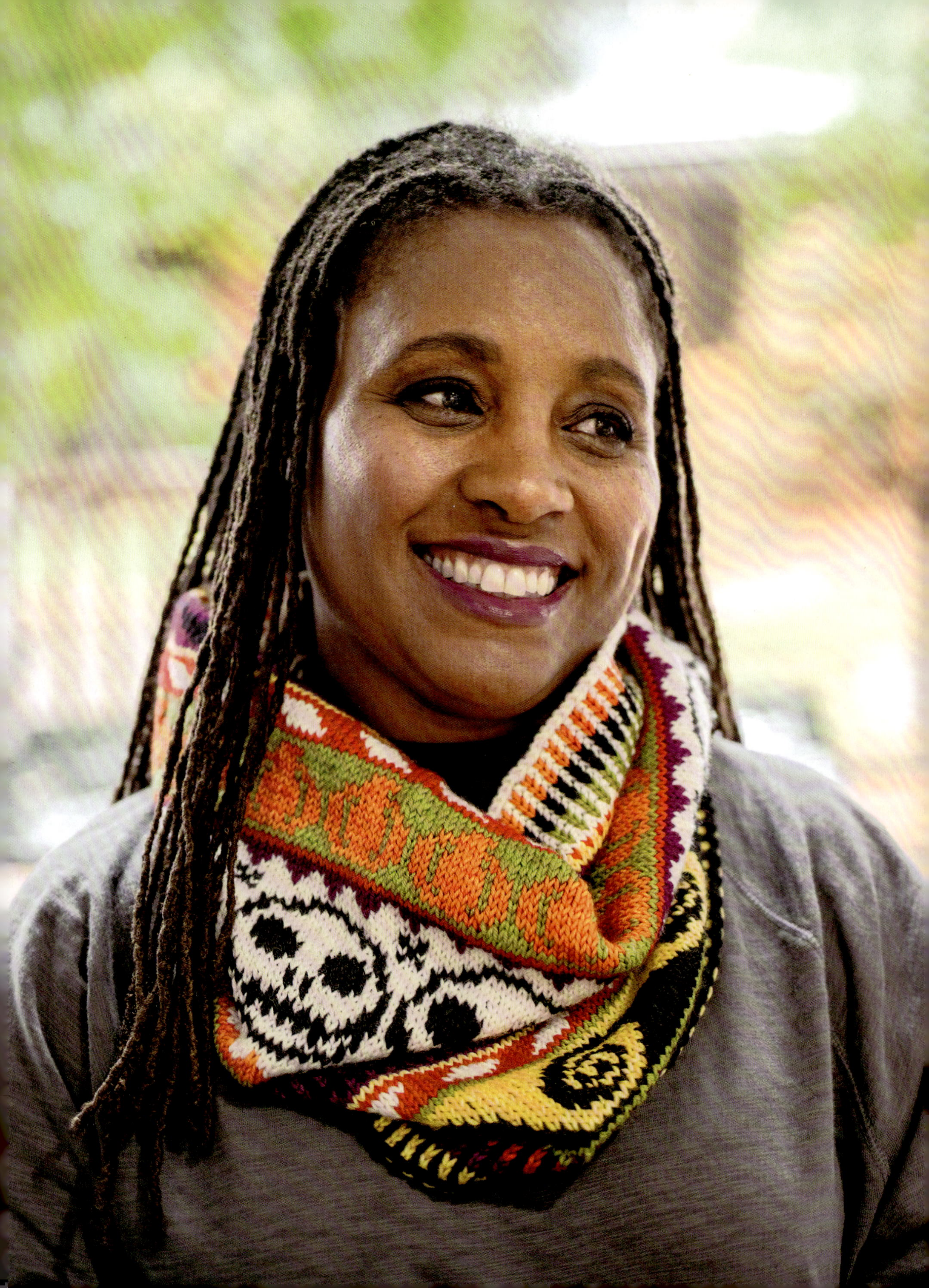

The Nightmare Before Christmas Cowl

Designed by Tanis Gray

"Jack! I've got the plans for next Halloween! I need to go over them with you so we can get started!"
—The Mayor

SKILL LEVEL

It's been said that the filmmakers were inspired by watching stores in southern California change their displays over seasonally from Halloween to Christmas merchandise. In the process of seeing the two holidays collide, fans often ask whether *Tim Burton's The Nightmare Before Christmas* is a Halloween film or a Christmas film. The voice actor of Jack Skellington, Chris Sarandon, has shared that this is the question he gets asked the most and diplomatically answers, "It's a little bit of everything." Meanwhile, both songwriter and Jack's singing voice Danny Elfman and director Henry Selick state, "It's a Halloween movie." Creator Tim Burton recalls, "Anytime there was Christmas or Halloween, it was great. It gave you some sort of texture all of a sudden that wasn't there before. . . . *Nightmare* is both, I guess, but for me, it's all about Halloween, it's Halloween Town, Halloween creatures. . . . But either one is fine, it just depends on your perspective."

This is certainly Halloween! Show your love for Jack's hometown in this colorful cowl. Worked in the round from the bottom up and flanked with quadricolor corrugated ribbing done on smaller needles, the stranded colorwork section is worked on larger needles and has Spiral Hill, candy canes, graveyard fencing, Jack's face, pumpkins, and spooky bat motifs. While the colorwork may look about as intimidating as Jack's plans to take over Christmas, no more than two colors are ever worked across one round.

SIZES
One size

FINISHED MEASUREMENTS
Height: 15½ in. / 39.5 cm
Circumference: 30 in. / 76.2 cm

YARN
DK weight yarn, shown in Hazel Knits *Lively DK* (90% superwash merino, 10% nylon; 275 yd. / 252 m per 4½ oz. / 130 g hank)

COLORWAYS:
- Color A: Signature Black, 1 hank
- Color B: Stick O' Butter, 1 hank
- Color C: Lipstick, 1984, 1 hank
- Color D: City Lights, 1 hank
- Color E: Nekkid, 1 hank
- Color F: Guac, 1 hank
- Color G: Sundazed, 1 hank

NEEDLES
US 5 / 3.75 mm, 24 in. / 61 cm long circular needle

US 6 / 4 mm, 24 in. / 61 cm long circular needle or size needed to obtain gauge

NOTIONS
Stitch markers (3; 1 unique for BOR, 2 optional for tracking repeats)

Tapestry needle

GAUGE
24 sts and 28 rnds = 4 in. / 10 cm over stranded colorwork on larger needle, taken after blocking

Make sure to check your gauge.

PATTERN NOTES

- The cowl is worked seamlessly in the round from the bottom up.
- The corrugated rib edges are worked on the smaller circular needle (1 needle size below the gauge-size needle) with the stranded colorwork portion worked on the gauge-size needle.
- When working the corrugated ribbing, be sure to move the working yarn to the back between the needles after each purl stitch is complete to ensure the floats run on the inside of the cowl.
- You may carry the colors loosely up the inside of the cowl when not being used to save on yardage and ends to weave in. Alternatively, cut the unused yarns in cases where they will not be used for more than 6 rnds.
- It may be helpful to place a marker between each chart repeat.

PATTERN INSTRUCTIONS

BOTTOM EDGING

Using the smaller needle and Color A, CO 180 sts using the Long Tail Cast On method. Place unique M for BOR and join to work in the rnd, being careful not to twist the sts.
Join Color B.
RNDS 1–3: [K1 with Color B, p1 with Color A] to end of rnd.
Join Color C.
RNDS 4–6: [K1 with Color C, p1 with Color A] to end of rnd.
Join Color D.
RNDS 7–9: [K1 with Color D, p1 with Color A] to end of rnd.

BODY OF COWL

Switch to larger needle.
Begin Chart A (pages 166 and 167), reading all rows from right to left as for working in the rnd, and join Colors E, F, and G as required. Work Rows 1–90 once (chart is worked 3 times across each rnd).
Once the chart is complete, break colors B, C, and D.

TOP EDGING AND BIND OFF

Switch to smaller needles.
RNDS 1–3: [K1 with Color F, p1 with Color E] to end of rnd.
Break Color F.
RNDS 4–6: [K1 with Color A, p1 with Color E] to end of rnd.
Break Color A.
RNDS 7–9: [K1 with Color G, p1 with Color E] to end of rnd.
Break Color G.
BO all sts knitwise with Color E.

FINISHING

Weave in all loose ends with tapestry needle to the WS.
Wet block the cowl to allow the sts to relax. Once dry, trim all ends.

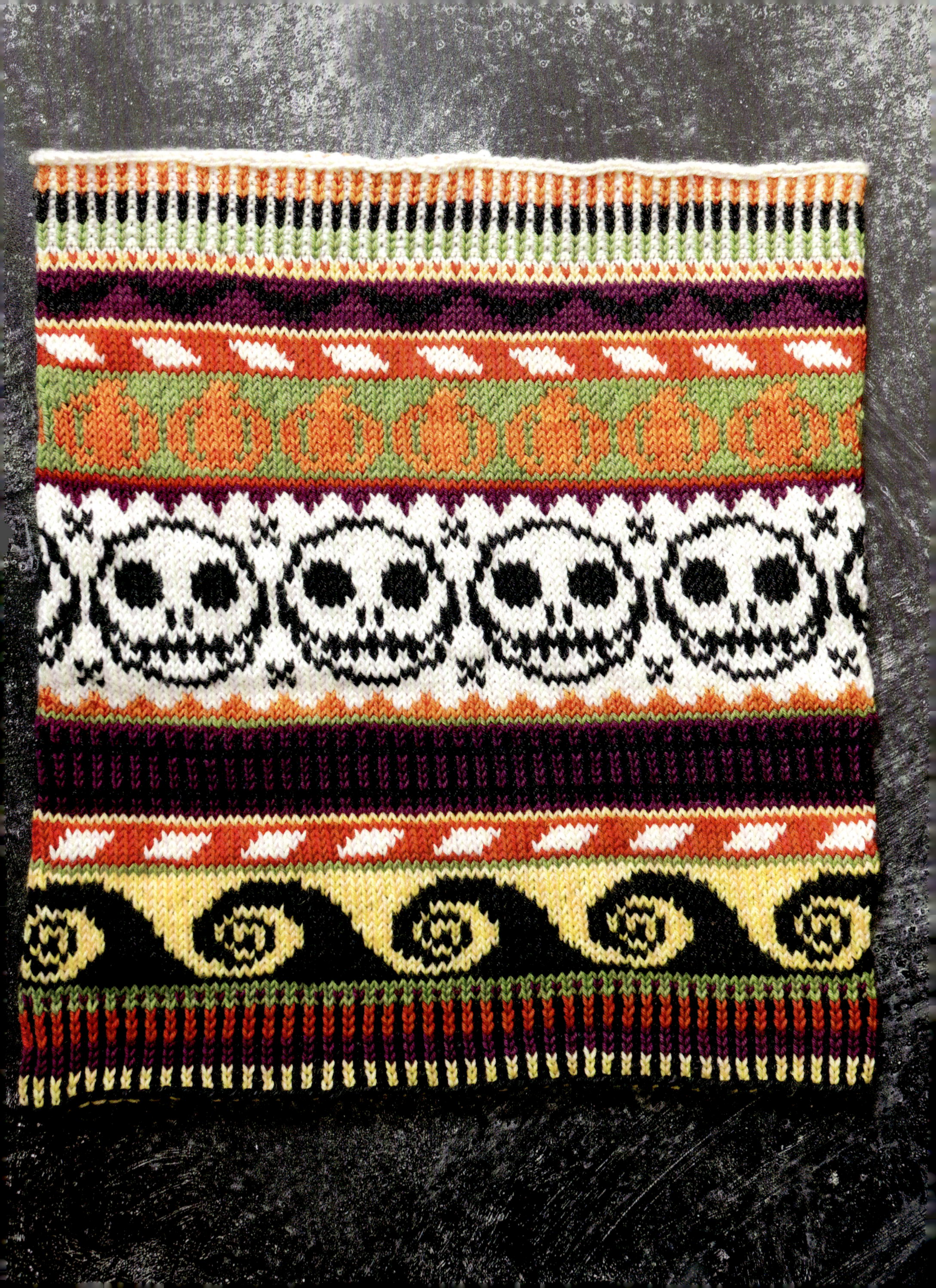

Chart A

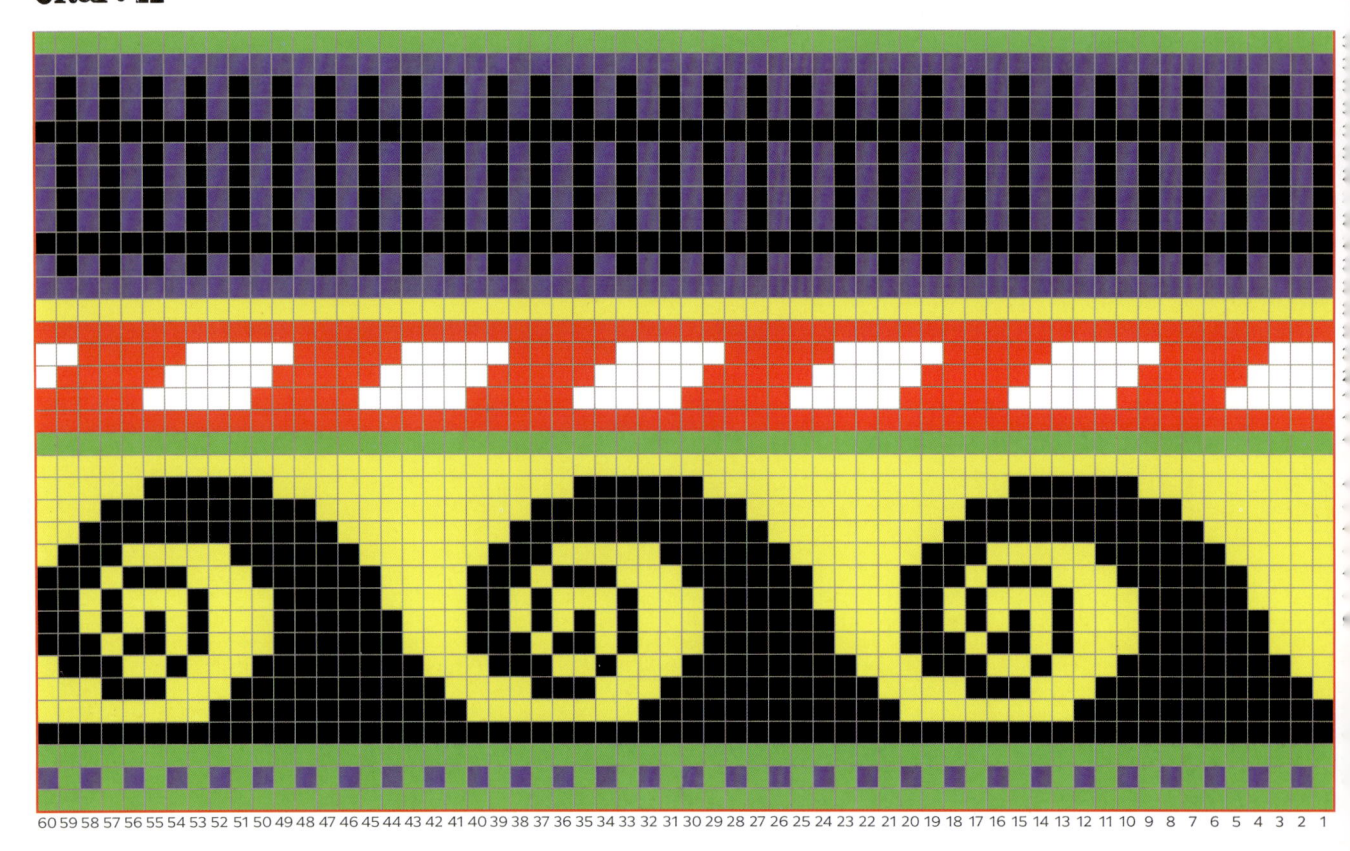

Key

- ☐ Knit
- ■ Color A
- ■ Color B
- ■ Color C
- ■ Color D
- ☐ Color E
- ■ Color F
- ■ Color G
- ▭ Pattern repeat

FRIGHTENING FACT

Alongside the door to Christmas Town are other doors that lead to other holiday lands, such as Independence Day, Valentine's Day, St. Patrick's Day, Easter, and Thanksgiving.

Chart A

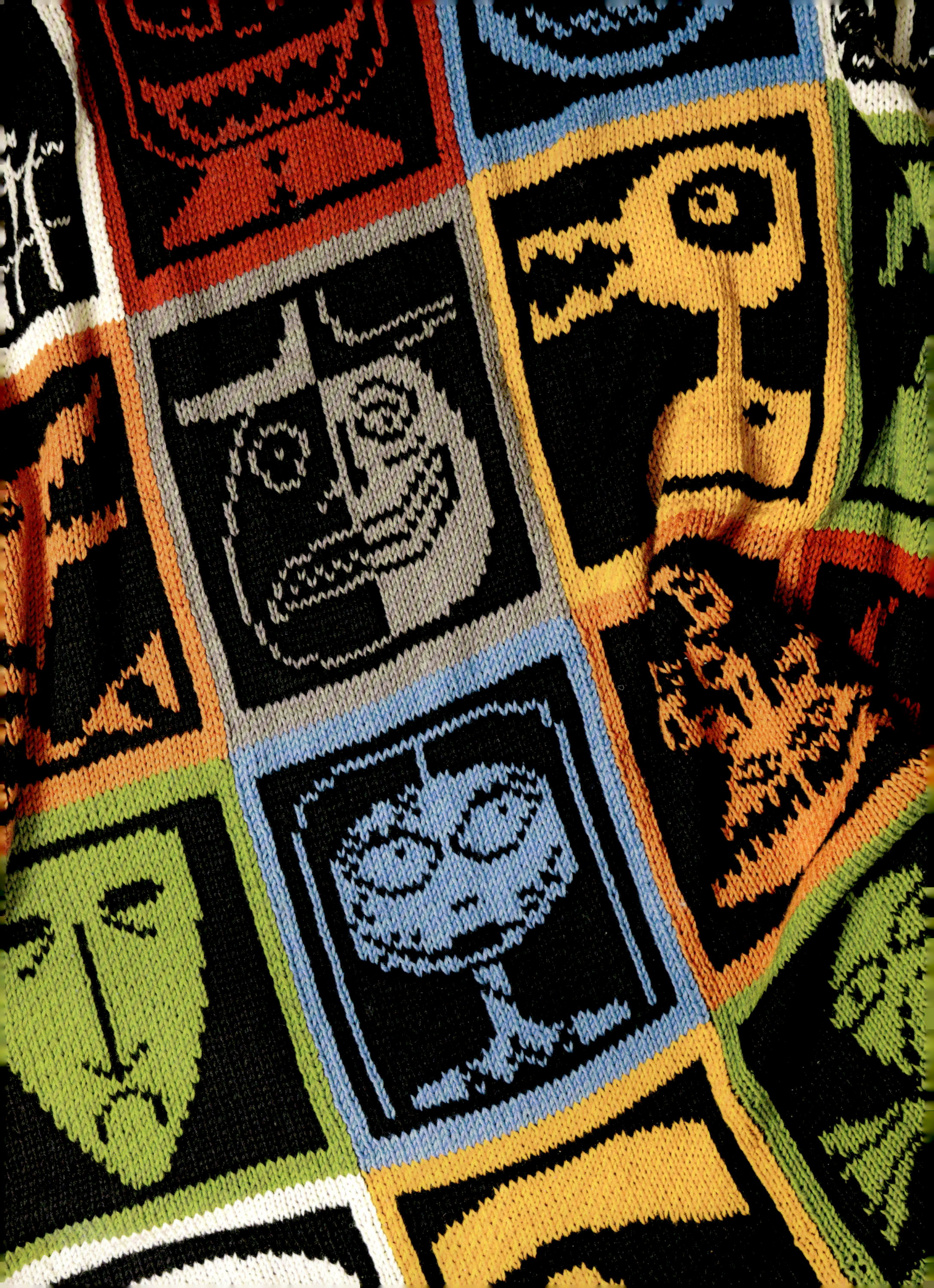

Horrifying Home Décor

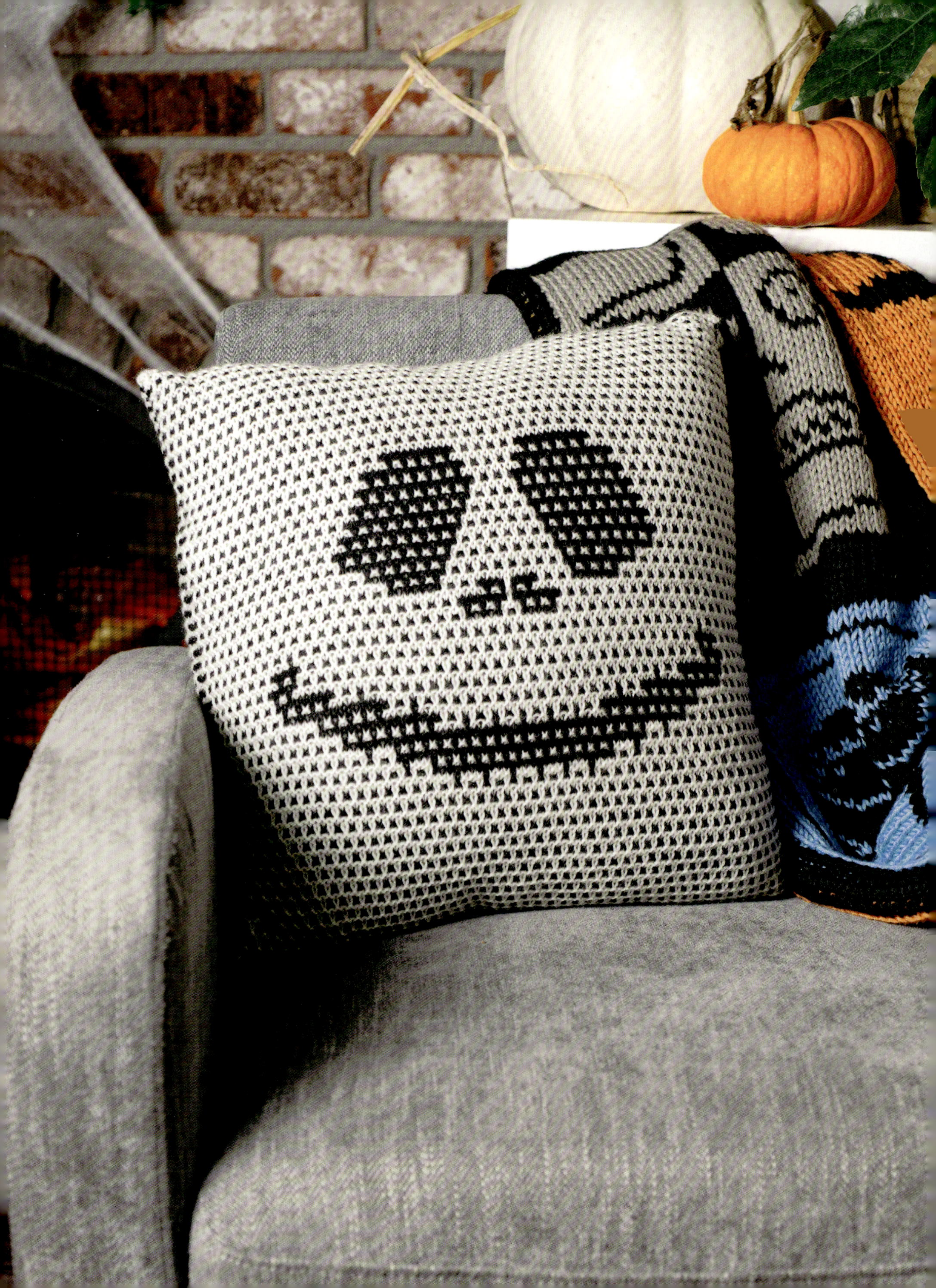

Jack Skellington Pillow

Designed by Alina Appasova

"My skull's so full, it's tearing me apart."
—Jack Skellington

SKILL LEVEL

Tim Burton broke the rules when he created his iconic protagonist Jack, voiced in the film by Chris Sarandon with the singing voice of composer Danny Elfman. Burton explains, "The first rule of drawn animation is that you have to have eyes for expression. I thought it would be great to give life to these characters that have no eyes." After convincing the studio that animators could convey Jack's soul, personality, and emotions without giving him eyeballs, puppet makers created over four hundred replacement heads with different expressions and mouth shapes to allow him to speak and sing realistically. Track reader Dan Mason matched each syllable and expression with one of the heads and synced it with the dialogue or singing soundtrack so animators knew which head to use during filming. In contrast to Jack, many of the other main characters have eyes—and they also have multiple sets of eyelids, allowing them to appear to blink on film, adding even more realism and relatability to the characters.

Who said Jack can't be snuggly? Cuddle up with Jack's quintessential skeleton grin in this mosaic colorwork pillow cover, a superb gift for any *Tim Burton's The Nightmare Before Christmas* fan. Knit flat back and forth, the cover is started with a provisional or temporary cast on. Once the knitting is complete, the cast on is removed and the stitches are grafted together with the live edge for a seamless join. The side seams are sealed up with mattress stitching around a 16-by-16-inch (40.5-by-40.5-centimeter) pillow form, making it the ideal size for hugging.

SIZES
One size

FINISHED MEASUREMENTS
Width: 16 in. / 40.5 cm

Height: 16 in. / 40.5 cm

YARN
Fingering weight yarn, shown in Berroco *Ultra Wool Fine* (100% superwash wool; 400 yd. / 366 m per 3½ oz. / 100 g skein)

COLORWAYS:
- Main Color (MC): #5301 Cream, 1 skein
- Contrast Color (CC): #5334 Cast Iron, 1 skein

NEEDLES
Two US 4 / 3.5 mm, 24 in. / 60 cm long circular needles or size needed to obtain gauge

NOTIONS
Waste yarn

US G-6 / 4 mm crochet hook

Tapestry needle

One 16 by 16 in. / 40.5 by 40.5 cm pillow form

GAUGE
25 sts and 45 rows = 4 in. / 10 cm worked flat in 2-color mosaic st, taken after blocking

Make sure to check your gauge.

PATTERN NOTES

- The pillow is worked flat and seamed. The color pattern is created using the mosaic knitting method; only one color is used per row.

- A provisional cast on is used so the bottom edges of the pillow can be seamlessly joined using Kitchener stitch.

- Waste yarn is used for the provisional cast on as well as when placing live stitches on hold for blocking the pillow before seaming. A smooth waste yarn in fingering weight is recommended to avoid felting during the blocking and to make unraveling the cast on easier.

- Carry unused yarns up the edge rather than cutting between each row used. Color changes always occur at the beginning of the right-side rows. To change colors, pick up new yarn from the back without twisting.

- Written instructions are provided for the entirety of the pattern. Optional charts are provided. Read carefully through all written instructions before working from the charts to ensure no instructions get missed.

- To work from the charts, read all RS (odd-numbered) rows from right to left. The WS rows are not charted except for the final row to ensure that the pattern is ended with a WS row; read this WS row from left to right.

- To work the WS rows from the charts, using the yarn from the previous RS row, knit the knit sts and slip the slipped sts purlwise wyif.

PATTERN STITCHES

Slip Stitch Pattern (worked over an odd number of sts)

Row 1 (RS): With CC, k3, (sl1 wyib, k1) to last 2 sts, k2.

Row 2 (WS, and all WS rows): With yarn used on previous RS row, knit the knit sts and slip the slipped sts purlwise wyif.

Row 3: With MC, knit.

Row 5: With CC, k2, (sl1 wyib, k1) to last st, k1.

Row 7: With MC, knit.

Row 8: With MC, knit.

Rep Rows 1–8 for pattern.

Jack's Face Pattern (worked over 101 sts)

Row 1 (RS): With CC, k3, (sl1 wyib, k1) to last 2 sts, k2.

Row 2 (WS, and all WS rows): With yarn used on previous RS row, knit the knit sts and slip the slipped sts purlwise wyif.

Row 3: With MC, k40, (sl1 wyib, k3) 5 times, sl1 wyib, k40.

Row 5: With CC, k2, (sl1 wyib, k1) 17 times, sl1 wyib, k27, (sl1 wyib, k1) 17 times, sl1 wyib, k2.

Row 7: With MC, k33, sl1 wyib, k3, (sl1 wyib, k1) 13 times, sl1 wyib, k3, sl1 wyib, k33.

Row 9: With CC, k3, (sl1 wyib, k1) 14 times, sl1 wyib, k37, (sl1 wyib, k1) 14 times, sl1 wyib, k3.

Row 11: With MC, k28, sl1 wyib, k3, (sl1 wyib, k1) 18 times, sl1 wyib, k3, sl1 wyib, k28.

Row 13: With CC, k2, (sl1 wyib, k1) 11 times, sl1 wyib, k51, (sl1 wyib, k1) 11 times, sl1 wyib, k2.

Row 15: With MC, k25, (sl1 wyib, k1) 6 times, sl1 wyib, k4, (sl1 wyib, k3) 4 times, sl1 wyib, k4, (sl1 wyib, k1) 6 times, sl1 wyib, k25.

Row 17: With CC, k3, (sl1 wyib, k1) 9 times, sl1 wyib, k17, (sl1 wyib, k1) 11 times, sl1 wyib, k17, (sl1 wyib, k1) 9 times, sl1 wyib, k3.

Row 19: With MC, k22, (sl1 wyib, k1) 4 times, sl1 wyib, k4, sl1 wyib, k29, sl1 wyib, k4, (sl1 wyib, k1) 4 times, sl1 wyib, k22.

Row 21: With CC, k2, (sl1 wyib, k1) 7 times, sl1 wyib, k15, (sl1 wyib, k1) 18 times, sl1 wyib, k15, (sl1 wyib, k1) 7 times, sl1 wyib, k2.

Row 23: With MC, k17, (sl1 wyib, k1) 3 times, sl1 wyib, k4, sl1 wyib, k48, (sl1 wyib, k1) 3 times, sl1 wyib, k17.

Row 25: With CC, k3, (sl1 wyib, k1) 6 times, sl1 wyib, k9, (sl1 wyib, k1) 25 times, sl1 wyib, k9, (sl1 wyib, k1) 6 times, sl1 wyib, k3.

Row 27: With MC, k16, sl1 wyib, k1, sl1 wyib, k63, sl1 wyib, k1, sl1 wyib, k16.

Row 29: With CC, k2, (sl1 wyib, k1) 6 times, sl1 wyib, k5, (sl1 wyib, k1) 30 times, sl1 wyib, k5, (sl1 wyib, k1) 6 times, sl1 wyib, k2.

Row 31: With MC, k17, sl1 wyib, k1, sl1 wyib, k61, sl1 wyib, k1, sl1 wyib, k17.

Row 33: With CC, k3, (sl1 wyib, k1) 6 times, sl1 wyib, k5, (sl1 wyib, k1) 29 times, sl1 wyib, k5, (sl1 wyib, k1) 6 times, sl1 wyib, k3.

Row 35: With MC, k19, sl1 wyib, k61, sl1 wyib, k19.

Row 37: With CC, k2, (sl1 wyib, k1) to last 3 sts, sl1 wyib, k2.

Row 39: With MC, knit.

Row 41: With CC, k3, (sl1 wyib, k1) 20 times, sl1 wyib, k5, sl1 wyib, k1, sl1 wyib, k5, (sl1 wyib, k1) 20 times, sl1 wyib, k3.

Row 43: With MC, k44, (sl1 wyib, k1) 2 times, sl1 wyib, k3, (sl1 wyib, k1) 2 times, sl1 wyib, k44.

Row 45: With CC, k2, (sl1 wyib, k1) 20 times, (sl1 wyib, k7) 2 times, (sl1 wyib, k1) 20 times, sl1 wyib, k2.

Row 47: With MC, k47, (sl1 wyib, k1) 3 times, sl1 wyib, k47.

Row 49: With CC, k3, (sl1 wyib, k1) 15 times, sl1 wyib, k7, (sl1 wyib, k1) 2 times, (sl1 wyib, k4) 2 times, (sl1 wyib, k1) 2 times, sl1 wyib, k7, (sl1 wyib, k1) 15 times, sl1 wyib, k3.

Row 51: With MC, k34, (sl1 wyib, k1) 3 times, sl1 wyib, k19, (sl1 wyib, k1) 3 times, sl1 wyib, k34.

Row 53: With CC, k2, (sl1 wyib, k1) 14 times, sl1 wyib, k11, (sl1 wyib, k1) 8 times, sl1 wyib, k11, (sl1 wyib, k1) 14 times, sl1 wyib, k2.

Row 55: With MC, k31, (sl1 wyib, k1) 5 times, sl1 wyib, k17, (sl1 wyib, k1) 5 times, sl1 wyib, k31.

Row 57: With CC, k3, (sl1 wyib, k1) 12 times, sl1 wyib, k15, (sl1 wyib, k1) 7 times, sl1 wyib, k15, (sl1 wyib, k1) 12 times, sl1 wyib, k3.

Row 59: With MC, k28, (sl1 wyib, k1) 7 times, sl1 wyib, k15, (sl1 wyib, k1) 7 times, sl1 wyib, k28.

Row 61: With CC, k2, (sl1 wyib, k1) 12 times, sl1 wyib, k17, (sl1 wyib, k1) 6 times, sl1 wyib, k17, (sl1 wyib, k1) 12 times, sl1 wyib, k2.

Row 63: With MC, k29, (sl1 wyib, k1) 7 times, sl1 wyib, k13, (sl1 wyib, k1) 7 times, sl1 wyib, k29.

Row 65: With CC, k3, (sl1 wyib, k1) 12 times, sl1 wyib, k17, (sl1 wyib, k1) 5 times, sl1 wyib, k17, (sl1 wyib, k1) 12 times, sl1 wyib, k3.

Row 67: With MC, k30, (sl1 wyib, k1) 7 times, sl1 wyib, k11, (sl1 wyib, k1) 7 times, sl1 wyib, k30.

Row 69: With CC, k2, (sl1 wyib, k1) 13 times, sl1 wyib, k17, (sl1 wyib, k1) 4 times, sl1 wyib, k17, (sl1 wyib, k1) 13 times, sl1 wyib, k2.

Row 71: With MC, k31, (sl1 wyib, k1) 7 times, sl1 wyib, k9, (sl1 wyib, k1) 7 times, sl1 wyib, k31.

Row 73: With CC, k3, (sl1 wyib, k1) 13 times, sl1 wyib, k17, (sl1 wyib, k1) 3 times, sl1 wyib, k17, (sl1 wyib, k1) 13 times, sl1 wyib, k3.

Row 75: With MC, k32, (sl1 wyib, k1) 7 times, sl1 wyib, k7, (sl1 wyib, k1) 7 times, sl1 wyib, k32.

Row 77: With CC, k2, (sl1 wyib, k1) 14 times, sl1 wyib, k17, (sl1 wyib, k1) 2 times, sl1 wyib, k17, (sl1 wyib, k1) 14 times, sl1 wyib, k2.

Row 79: With MC, k33, (sl1 wyib, k1) 6 times, sl1 wyib, k9, (sl1 wyib, k1) 6 times, sl1 wyib, k33.

Row 81: With CC, k3, (sl1 wyib, k1) 14 times, sl1 wyib, k15, (sl1 wyib, k1) 3 times, sl1 wyib, k15, (sl1 wyib, k1) 14 times, sl1 wyib, k3.

Row 83: With MC, k34, (sl1 wyib, k1) 5 times, sl1 wyib, k11, (sl1 wyib, k1) 5 times, sl1 wyib, k34.

Row 85: With CC, k2, (sl1 wyib, k1) 15 times, sl1 wyib, k13, (sl1 wyib, k1) 4 times, sl1 wyib, k13, (sl1 wyib, k1) 15 times, sl1 wyib, k2.

Row 87: With MC, knit.

Row 88: With MC, knit.

PATTERN INSTRUCTIONS

PILLOW

With waste yarn and crochet hook CO 101 sts using the Crochet Provisional Cast On method. Do not join to work in the rnd.
Join MC.
SETUP ROW (WS): Knit.
Join CC.
Work Rows 1–8 of Slip Stitch Pattern, using the written instructions or Slip Stitch chart (page 174), 6 times (48 pattern rows worked).
Work Rows 1–88 of Jack's Face Pattern, using the written instructions or Face chart (pages 174 and 175), 1 time (136 pattern rows worked).
Work Rows 1–8 of Slip Stitch Pattern, using the written instructions or Slip Stitch chart, 6 times (184 pattern rows worked; front of pillow complete).
Knit 2 rows in MC (top "seam" is complete).
Work Rows 1–8 of Slip Stitch Pattern, using the written instructions or Slip Stitch chart, 23 times (184 pattern rows worked; back of pillow is complete).
Break CC.
Knit 1 row in MC (a RS row).
Break yarn and place live sts on long piece of waste yarn for blocking.

FINISHING

Wet block gently.
Once dry, place the live sts from the waste yarn back onto one circular needle.
Carefully unravel the provisional CO and place the live sts on a second circular needle.
Thread a tapestry needle with a length of MC yarn approx. 3 times the length of the live edge.
With RS facing, graft the two sets of live sts together using Kitchener stitch.
Thread a tapestry needle with a length of CC yarn approx. 2 times the length of the side edge.
With RS facing, seam one side edge of the pillow using mattress stitch. Weave in any ends to the WS.
Insert the pillow form.
Repeat the side seaming process using CC and mattress stitch along the second side edge of the pillow. Weave the tails from the seam to the inside of the pillow.

Key

☐ Knit on RS, purl on WS
− Purl on RS, knit on WS
V Slip st purlwise: wyib on RS, wyif on WS
☐ MC
■ CC
▢ Pattern repeat

Slip Stitch Pattern Chart

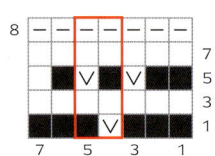

Jack's Face Pattern Chart - Left

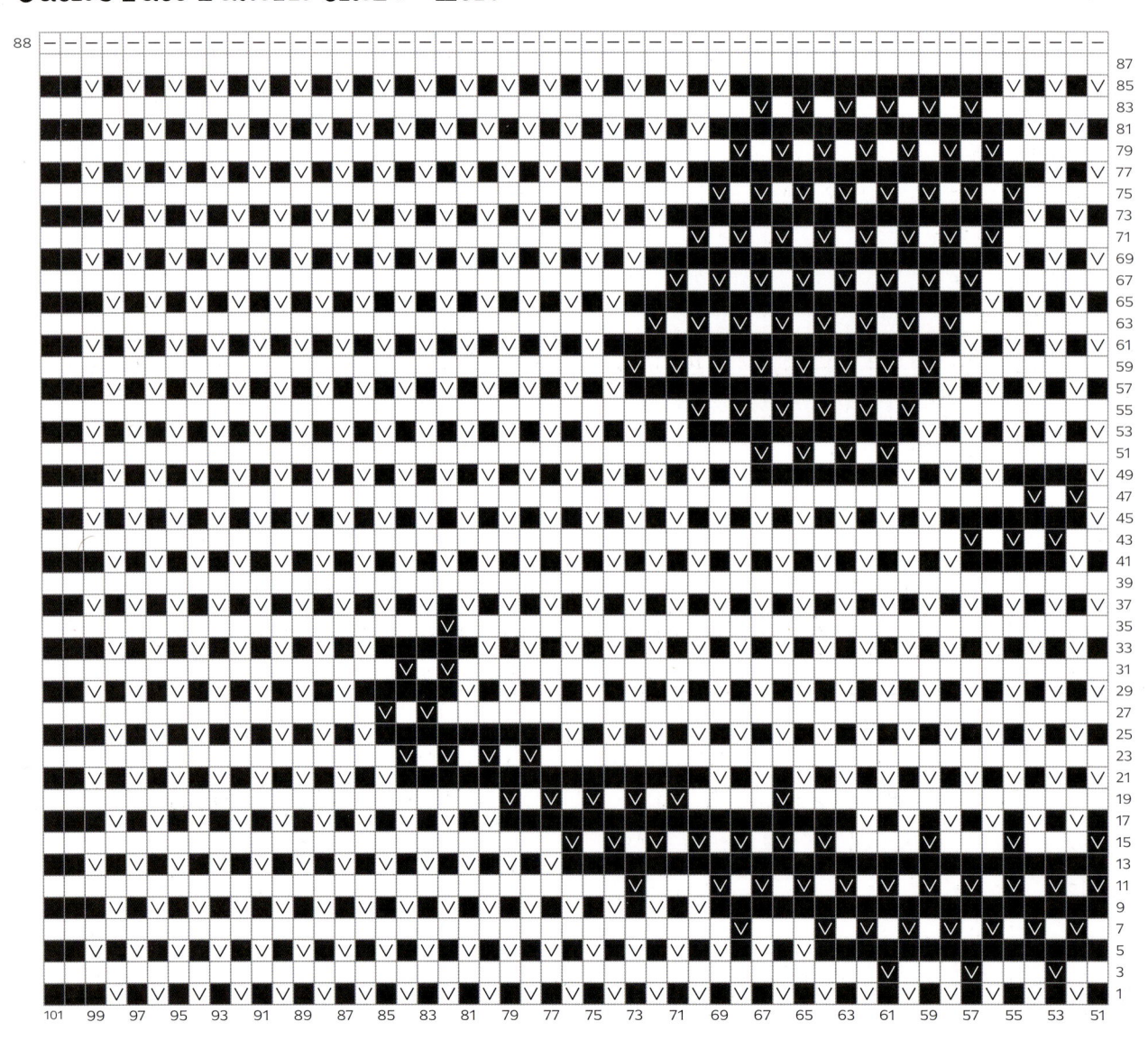

FRIGHTENING FACT

Director Henry Selick likened the production design to making a pop-up book, saying, "When we reach Halloween Town, it's entirely German Expressionism. When Jack enters Christmas Town, it's an outrageous Dr. Seussesque setpiece. Finally, when Jack is delivering presents in the 'Real World,' everything is plain, simple, and perfectly aligned."

Jack's Face Pattern Chart - Right

175

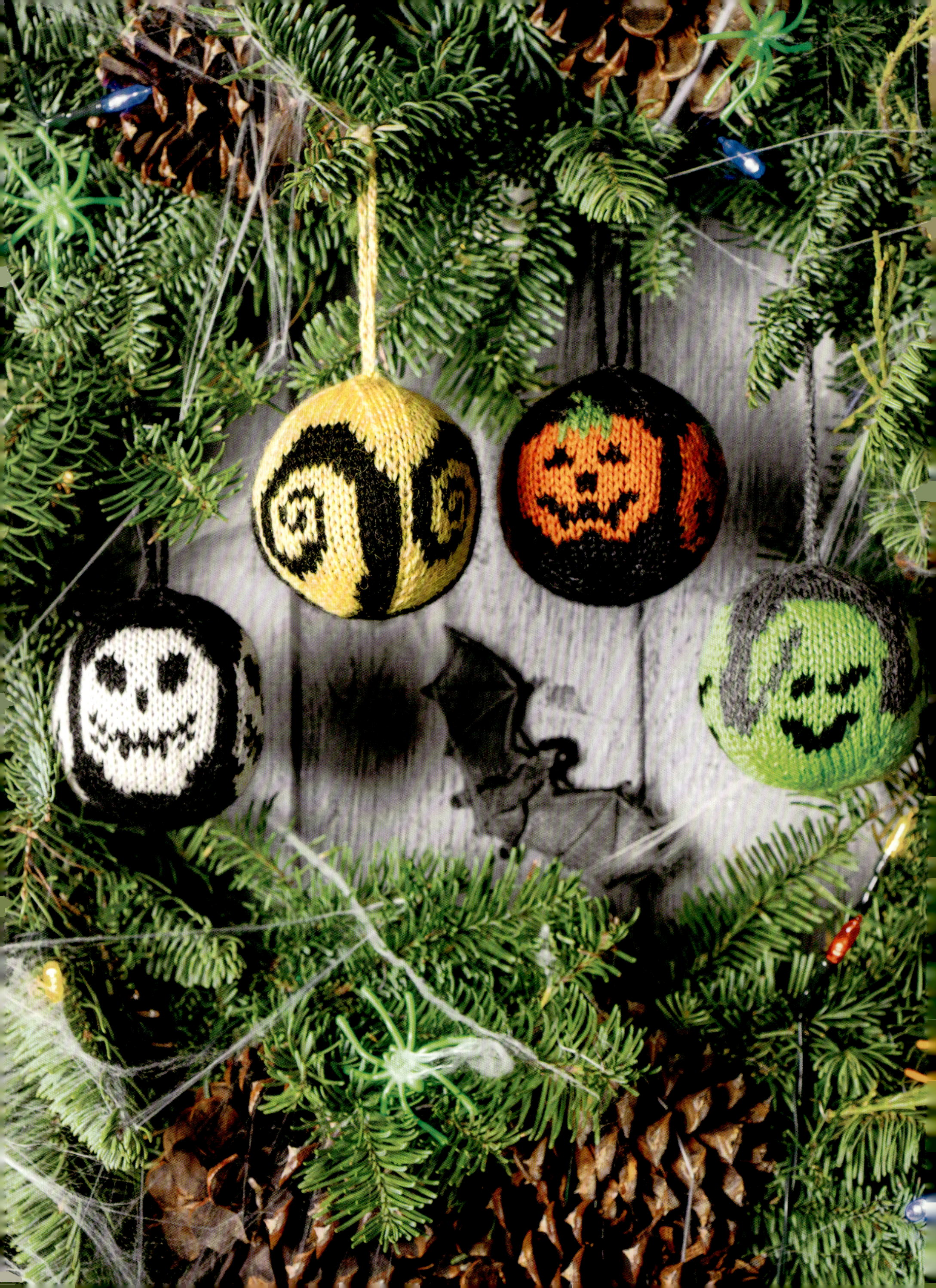

Halloween Town Ornaments

Designed by
Kristin Örnólfsdóttir

"Eureka! This year Christmas will be ours!"
– Jack Skellington

SKILL LEVEL

Once filming is completed on a live-action movie, there's still quite a bit of work to be done in postproduction. A lot of time is spent editing and cutting together the same scene shot from multiple angles, in addition to adding sound effects, special effects, the musical score, overlaid songs, and rerecording dialogue. In stop-motion, much of this work is done at the beginning during the storyboarding process. There is no cuing actors or any "Quiet on the set!" needed, and dialogue and songs are recorded beforehand. Director Henry Selick went over the script of *Tim Burton's The Nightmare Before Christmas* with the story department, painstakingly drawing out each scene. He says, "Very often I'd have people do fifty or a hundred drawings of a sequence. Then I'd go back, rework it, pull shots, shift them around. When I agreed on the sequence, we'd shoot the drawings on film and edit those. Then we'd redraw and rework the sequence and start all over again." By choreographing the animation and camera angles up front, animators would save time in the long run during the slow process of filming.

Inspired by recognizable motifs and characters from *Tim Burton's The Nightmare Before Christmas* like Jack Skellington, Spiral Hill, a pumpkin, and Oogie Boogie, these charming ornaments are the perfect complement to your Halloween décor. Keep them out and transfer them to the Christmas tree, or better yet, leave them out all year long! Worked in the round from the bottom up on dpns and rounded out with craft stuffing, each ornament is topped with a crochet chain hanging loop. Want a bigger bauble? Simply size up the yarn and needles!

SIZES
One size

FINISHED MEASUREMENTS
Circumference: approx. 8 in. / 20.5 cm

YARN
Fingering weight yarn, shown in Cascade Yarns *Cascade 220 Fingering* (100% Peruvian Highland wool; 273 yd. / 250 m per 1¾ oz. / 50 g hank)

COLORWAYS:
- Color A: #8010 Natural, 1 hank
- Color B: #7824 Jack O' Lantern, 1 hank
- Color C: #9623 Jasmine Green, 1 hank
- Color D: #4147 Lemon Yellow, 1 hank
- Color E: #8400 Charcoal, 1 hank
- Color F: #8555 Black, 1 hank
- Color G: #9430 Highland Green, 1 hank

NEEDLES
US 1.5 / 2.5 mm set of 5 double-pointed needles or size needed to obtain gauge

NOTIONS
Stitch marker (optional)

Tapestry needle

3 mm crochet hook

Polyester stuffing (approx. ⅓ oz. / 8 g per ornament)

GAUGE
32 sts and 32 rnds = 4 in. / 10 cm over stranded colorwork in the round, taken without blocking.

Gauge is not critical for the ornaments; just make sure the stitches are tight enough so the stuffing will not show through them.

PATTERN NOTES

- The ornaments are worked in the round, from bottom to top. The ornament is finished by crocheting a loop to hang the ornaments.

- When working with two (or more) colors, carry the yarns very loosely on the inside of the ornament to allow it to stretch when filled with the stuffing.

PATTERN INSTRUCTIONS

ORNAMENTS

Using Color C for Oogie Boogie or Color F for Swirl, Jack, or the Pumpkin, CO 12 sts using the Long Tail Cast On method, leaving a 12 in. / 30.5 cm tail. Distribute sts evenly over 4 dpns (3 sts per needle). Pm for BOR (if desired) and join to work in the rnd, being careful not to twist the sts.

Begin working from the chart of desired design, reading all rows from right to left as for working in the rnd, and joining additional color(s) as necessary. Work Rows 1–39 once (chart is worked 4 times across each rnd), catching floats as needed. *AT THE SAME TIME*, when Row 32 is complete, return to the Close Cast On Edge instructions for construction details. Again, after Row 36 is complete, return to the Fill Ornament instructions for construction details.

CLOSE CAST ON EDGE

Break any yarns not being used past Row 32 of the chart. Without breaking the working yarn or removing sts from the working needles, carefully turn the ornament inside out. Using the tail from your CO, thread the tapestry needle and sew the bottom of the ornament closed; weave in any ends to the WS.

Key

- ■ No stitch
- □ Knit
- □ Color A
- ■ Color B
- ■ Color C
- ■ Color D
- ■ Color E
- ■ Color F
- ■ Color G
- M1L
- M1R
- k2tog
- skp
- Pattern repeat

Spiral Hill

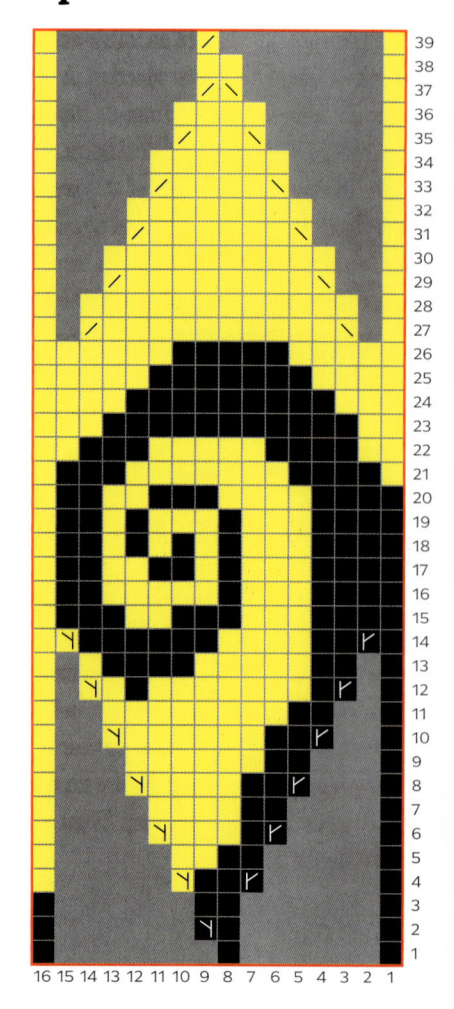

FRIGHTENING FACT

Ghostly décor is all over Halloween Town! There are so many creepy items to explore such as Jack's screaming doorbell, his dead spider pulley, eyeball knob, coffin podium, wrought iron pumpkin gates, and bat-shaped window frames.

Turn the ornament RS out again and resume the chart beginning on Row 33 with the working yarn.

FILL ORNAMENT

Without breaking the working yarn or removing sts from the working needles, carefully stuff the ornament to your desired size/density. Then resume the chart beginning on Row 37.

FINISH ORNAMENT

Leave a tail approx. 47 in. / 120 cm long.

Thread the tapestry needle with the long tail and weave through the live sts 2 times. Pull tight to secure. Do not break yarn but remove from the tapestry needle.

CREATE HANGING LOOP

Insert the crochet hook under the cinched edge of the top of the ornament, hook the long tail of the yarn, and pull through to place 1 st on your crochet hook (draw up a loop). Chain st for 8 in. / 20.5 cm. Pull tail through remaining st to secure chain. Fold the chain in half and sew the loose end to the top of the ornament with the tapestry needle to complete the loop. Weave in the yarn tail to the inside of the ornament.

FINISHING

Very gently steam block the ornament at the top, bottom, and sides with a hot iron and wet cloth.

Oogie Boogie

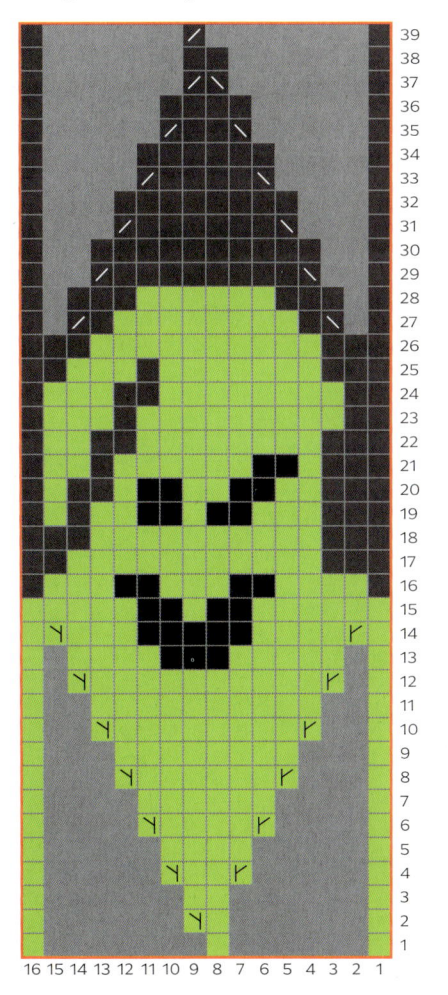

Jack

Pumpkin

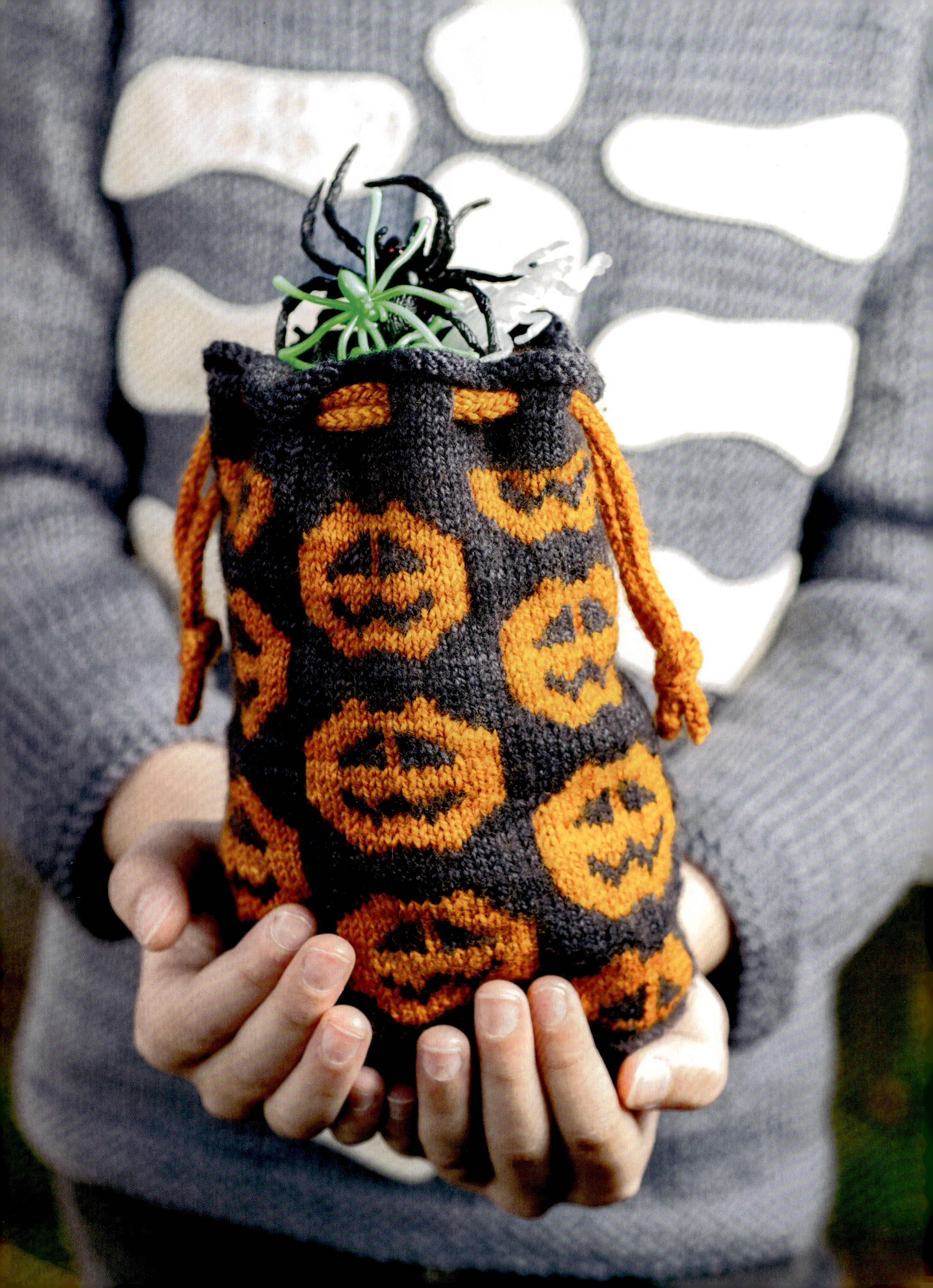

Oogie Boogie Dice Bag

Designed by Knitting Daddy Greg

*"Ashes to ashes and dust to dust!
Ooh, I'm feelin' weak . . . with hunger!
One more roll of the dice oughta do it!"*
—Oogie Boogie

SKILL LEVEL

Tim Burton's The Nightmare Before Christmas's art department based the look of Oogie Boogie on a character Tim Burton drew—it was a potato-sack-like creature filled with horrible things like insects and spiders. Oogie Boogie's sound was loosely inspired by talented African American singer, songwriter, dancer, and bandleader Cab Calloway, who was featured in multiple Betty Boop cartoons in the 1930s. Burton asked composer Danny Elfman to look to the songs "Minnie the Moocher" and "The Old Man of the Mountain" for inspiration when writing Oogie Boogie's song in the film. Animators went even further by looking at Calloway recordings to use his mannerisms and dancing as inspiration for Oogie Boogie's movements in his showstopping song.

Worked in the round from the bottom up, this little bag of tricks is dotted with grinning stranded colorwork jack-o'-lantern motifs. The real surprise is on the bottom of the bag, where raised purl stitches and balanced increases create a spiderweb effect! A round of double yarn over eyelets is added toward the top to create a place for an i-cord drawstring closure, allowing the bag to cinch shut. Keep your dice or game pieces in it, or hide your secret treasures away from the monsters that live under your stairs.

SIZES
One size

FINISHED MEASUREMENTS
Height: 8 in. / 20.5 cm
Circumference: 11 in. / 28 cm

YARN
Fingering weight yarn, shown in Kim Dyes Yarn *Sourdough Sock* (80% superwash merino wool, 20% nylon; 400 yd. / 366 m per 3½ oz. / 100 g hank)

COLORWAYS:
- Main Color (MC): Black, 1 hank
- Contrast Color (CC): Warmth, 1 hank

NEEDLES
US 1 / 2.25 mm set of 4 double-pointed needles or size needed to obtain gauge

NOTIONS
Stitch marker (optional)
Row counter (optional)
Tapestry needle

GAUGE
37 sts and 50 rnds = 4 in. / 10 cm over stranded colorwork worked in the round, taken after blocking

Make sure to check your gauge.

PATTERN NOTES

- This dice bag is worked in the round from the bottom up. Increases and decreases for the shaping of the bag are relative to the stitches on each dpn; we recommend using the number of dpns specified.
- The drawstring for this dice bag is constructed with two i-cords.
- The eyelets at the top of the bag are formed with double yarn overs. On the round following the creation of the double yarn overs, knit into the first yarn over and drop the second yarn over off the needle. This will create a slightly larger eyelet that will be easier to run the i-cords through.

PATTERN INSTRUCTIONS

SPIDERWEB BOTTOM OF BAG

Using MC, CO 6 sts using the Long Tail Cast On method. Distribute sts evenly over 3 dpns (2 sts per needle). Pm for BOR (if desired) and join to work in the rnd.
RND 1: Knit.
RND 2 (INC): *Kfb; rep from * to end of rnd—12 sts.
RND 3: Knit.
RND 4 (INC): *K1, M1L, purl to last st of dpn, M1R, k1; rep from * to end of rnd—18 sts.
RND 5 (INC): *K1, M1L, knit to last st of dpn, M1R, k1; rep from * to end of rnd—24 sts.
RND 6 (INC): Work as for Rnd 5—30 sts.
RND 7 (INC): Work as for Rnd 4—36 sts.
RND 8 (INC): Work as for Rnd 5—42 sts.
RND 9 (INC): Work as for Rnd 5—48 sts.
RND 10: Knit.
RND 11 (INC): Work as for Rnd 4—54 sts.
RND 12: Knit.
RND 13 (INC): Work as for Rnd 5—60 sts.
RND 14: Knit.
RND 15 (INC): Work as for Rnd 5—66 sts.
RND 16: *K1, purl to last st of dpn, k1; rep from * to end of rnd.
RND 17 (INC): Work as for Rnd 5—72 sts.
RND 18: Knit.
RND 19 (INC): Work as for Rnd 5—78 sts.
RND 20: Knit.
RND 21 (INC): Work as for Rnd 5—84 sts.
RND 22: *K1, purl to last st of dpn, k1; rep from * to end of rnd.
RND 23 (INC): Work as for Rnd 5—90 sts.
RND 24: Knit.
RND 25 (INC): Work as for Rnd 5—96 sts.
RND 26: Knit.
RND 27 (INC): Work as for Rnd 5—102 sts.
RND 28: Knit.
RND 29: *K1, purl to last st of dpn, k1; rep from * to end of rnd.
RND 30: Knit.

JACK-O'-LANTERN BODY OF BAG

Begin Chart A, reading all rows from right to left as for working in the rnd, joining CC as required. Work Rnds 1–20 three times total (chart is repeated 3 times across the rnd), or to desired length, ending with Rnd 10 or 20. When complete, break CC. The Top of Bag will be worked with MC only.

TOP OF BAG

RND 1: Knit.
RND 2 (DEC): *Ssk, knit to last 2 sts on dpn, k2tog; rep from * to end of rnd—96 sts.
RND 3: Knit.
RND 4 (DEC): Work as for Rnd 2—90 sts.
RND 5: Knit.
RND 6 (DEC): Work as for Rnd 2—84 sts.
RND 7: Knit.
RND 8 (INC): *K2, yo twice, k2tog, k2; rep from * to end of rnd—98 sts.
RND 9 (DEC): *K2, knit into first yo, drop second yo, k3; rep from * to end of rnd—84 sts (ensure 28 sts are on each dpn when finished).
RND 10 (INC): *K1, M1L, knit to last st of dpn, M1R, k1; rep from * to end of rnd—90 sts.
RND 11 (INC): Work as for Rnd 10—96 sts.
RND 12 (INC): Work as for Rnd 10—102 sts.
RND 13: Knit.
Bind off all sts loosely knitwise.
Weave in ends and wet block the bag. Allow to dry and trim ends.

I-CORD DRAWSTRINGS

**Using CC, CO 3 sts using the Long Tail Cast On method. Work a 3-stitch i-cord for 17 in. / 43 cm. Bind off all sts knitwise.
Repeat from ** to make a second drawstring identical to the first.
Weave in tails from i-cords to the inside of the tube. Do not block.

FINISHING

Once the bag is dry, weave each i-cord through all the eyelets at the top of the bag so that each i-cord forms a U shape on opposite sides of the bag. Knot the ends of each i-cord together.

Chart A

Key

- ☐ Knit
- ■ MC
- ▨ CC
- ▢ Pattern repeat

Oogie Boogie Dice Bag Schematic

8 in. / 0.5 cm

11 in. / 28 cm

FRIGHTENING FACT

Oogie Boogie voice actor Ken Page and composer Danny Elfman shared the same lawyer, who connected the two.

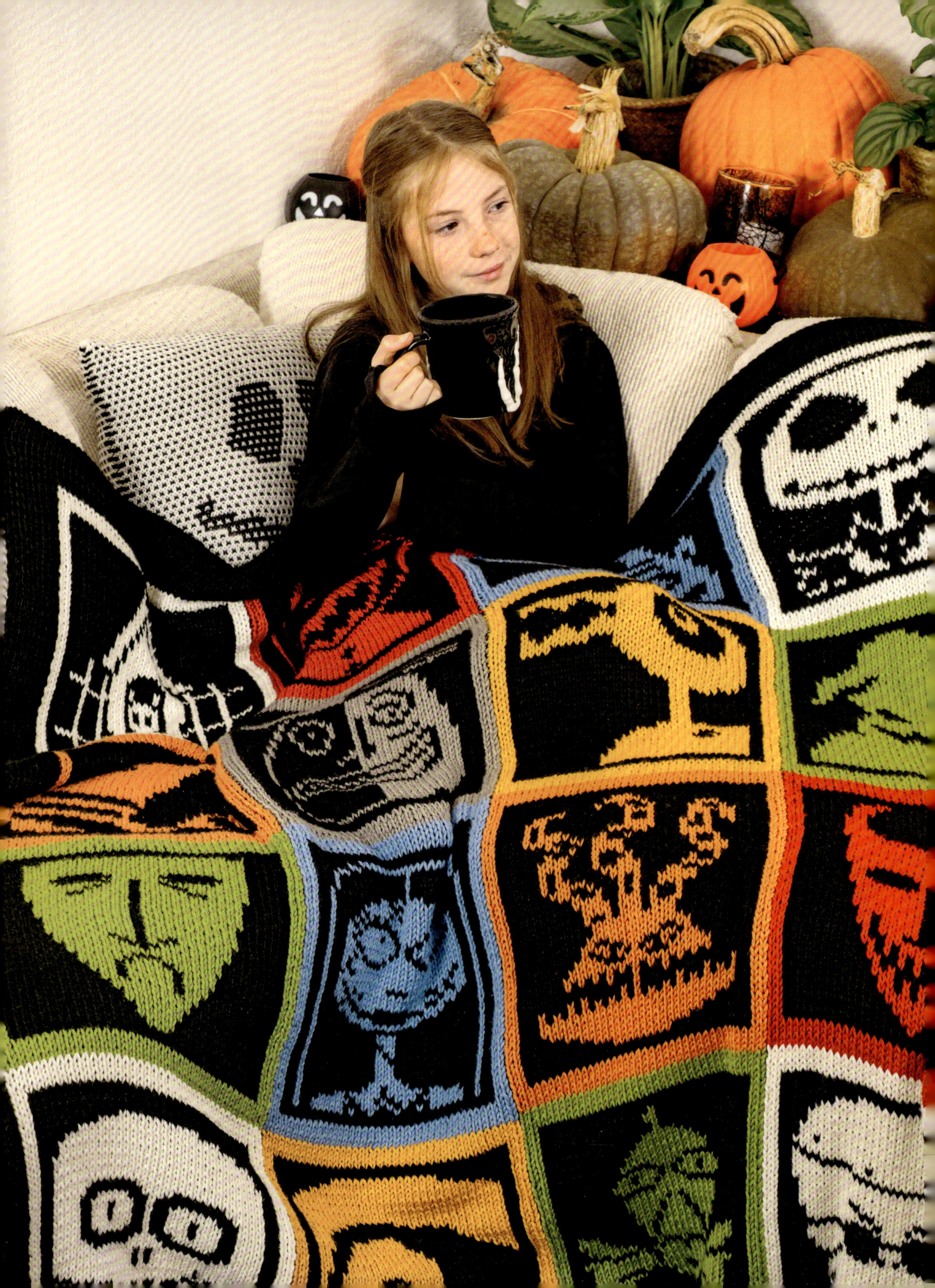

The Nightmare Before Christmas Throw

Designed by
Jennifer Lori

*"'Twas a long time ago, longer now than it seems,
in a place that perhaps you've seen in your dreams.
For the story that you are about to be told
took place in the holiday worlds of old.
Now, you've probably wondered where holidays come from.
If you haven't, I'd say it's time you began."*

—Santa Claus

SKILL LEVEL

Tim Burton's *The Nightmare Before Christmas* original story was based on a poem creator Tim Burton wrote long before production began, when he was an animator at Walt Disney Studios in the 1980s. Three pages long, written in a style similar to Dr. Seuss, and accompanied by sketches and notes, the poem didn't become something more until a decade later. Although the original concept was for a thirty-minute holiday TV special—like those from his childhood—or a children's book, Burton looked to stop-motion animator Henry Selick to direct a full-length feature film. Burton says, "I love stop-motion. There's always a certain beauty to it, yet it's unusual at the same time. It has reality. Especially on a project like *Nightmare*, where the characters are so unreal, it makes them more believable, more solid." After a production company was started from scratch, it took 15 animators and more than 100 puppet, prop, and set makers—working across 19 soundstages with 230 sets—over three years to complete the film.

The gang's all here! Enjoy your very own trip to Halloween Town without ever leaving your couch with this colorful cast of characters wrapped around you. Sixteen charts represent Jack, the Clown with the Tear-Away Face, the Vampire Teddy, Zero in his doghouse, Oogie Boogie, the Killer Duck, the Mayor, the Striped Snake, Lock, Harlequin, Sally, Shock, Dr. Finkelstein, Undersea Gal, Spiral Hill, and Barrel. This throw is worked in one piece using a combination of double knitting and intarsia to create a fully reversible color-block blanket with the inverse of each character on the back. Slip-stitch edges create a tidy finish on this squishy masterpiece.

SIZES
One size

FINISHED MEASUREMENTS
Width: 56 in. / 142 cm
Length: 53 in. / 134.5 cm

YARN
Bulky weight yarn, shown in Berroco *Comfort Chunky* (50% superfine nylon, 50% superfine acrylic; 150 yd. / 138 m per 3½ oz. / 100 g skein)

COLORWAYS:
- Main Color (MC): #5734 Liquorice, 13 skeins
- Contrast Color 1 (CC1): #5701 Ivory, 3 skeins
- Contrast Color 2 (CC2): #5740 Seedling, 3 skeins
- Contrast Color 3 (CC3): #5743 Goldenrod, 2 skeins
- Contrast Color 4 (CC4): #5750 Primary Red, 2 skeins
- Contrast Color 5 (CC5): #5724 Pumpkin, 2 skeins
- Contrast Color 6 (CC6): #5726 Cornflower, 2 skeins
- Contrast Color 7 (CC7): #5771 Driftwood Heather, 1 skein

NEEDLES
US 10 / 6 mm, 47 in. / 120 cm circular needle or size needed to obtain gauge

NOTIONS
Row counter (optional)

Elastic band (optional, see Pattern Notes)

Tapestry needle

GAUGE
13½ sts and 19 rows = 4 in. / 10 cm in 2-color double knitting worked flat, taken after blocking

PATTERN NOTES

- This blanket is worked flat, from bottom to top, using the Double Knitting method. Charts are provided for the 2-color double-knit motifs.
- Double knitting is a technique that produces a double thickness of fabric that looks like right-side stockinette stitch on both sides. The reverse sides of the 2-color motifs are inverse colors.
- Two stitches worked are counted as 1 chart stitch worked. As such the charts are numbered as having 39 knit-facing stitches but are worked across 78 blanket stitches.
- Always bring both working yarns to front or back between the needles before working the next stitch with the appropriate color.
- The blanket borders are worked in double knitting from two balls of MC to ensure they have the same tension and thickness as the blanket's center where the 2-color motifs are worked. These skeins will be designated as MCA (Main Color Yarn A) and MCB (Main Color Yarn B) to avoid mixing them up.
- Every row is worked in double knitting, beginning with a selvedge stitch. The RS chart rows are worked from right to left with the colors indicated; the WS rows are worked from left to right with MC and CC reversed.
- Optional instructions are provided for hiding the WS intarsia color change twists between the charts.
- The cast on edge is the longest row as the stitches have not yet doubled up. The overall width of the cast on edge will decrease by approximately half once the double knitting begins. You may find it helpful to wrap an elastic band a few times around the far end of your knitting needle during the cast on to act as a stopper. This elastic band can be removed after the stitches are cast on and the double knitting begins.

SPECIAL TECHNIQUES

Intarsia Color Change:

The following steps ensure the color changes remain on the WS of the work, where they will be hidden during Finishing.

RS Rows: With old and new CCs and MC held to the back of the work (the WS), move the old CC to the left and pick up the new CC from underneath to work the next stitch with the new CC.

WS Rows: With old and new CCs and MC held to the front of the work (the WS), move the old CC to the left and pick up the new CC from underneath. Move the new CC and MC together to the back (the RS) between the needles before knitting the next stitch with the new CC.

PATTERN INSTRUCTIONS

CAST ON & BOTTOM BORDER

Using 2 skeins of MC, designating one as Yarn A (MCA) and one as Yarn B (MCB), cast on 348 sts using the Two-Color Long Tail Cast On method. Do not join to work in the rnd.

Note: The 2 loops from the cast on slipknot will count as 2 stitches. The 2 loops remaining from the p2tog at the end of each row will count as 2 stitches. These 2 stitches will be slipped together, knitwise, at the start of each row and make up the selvedge stitch.

ROW 1 (WS): Sl2 sts together knitwise, *k1 with MCA, p1 with MCB; rep from * to last 2 sts, p2tog with MCA and MCB held together.

ROW 2 (RS): Sl2 sts together knitwise, *k1 with MCB, p1 with MCA; rep from * to last 2 sts, p2tog with MCA and MCB held together.

Rep [Rows 1 and 2] 5 more times, then Row 1 once more (14 rows worked including cast on).

BLANKET BODY

Read carefully through this section before beginning to ensure no steps get missed.

Begin 2-color motif charts (pages 190 and 191). Work Rows 1–56 of each chart once, reading all RS rows from right to left and WS rows from left to right, joining CCs as required.

The bottom row of motifs will be Charts A, B, C, and D; written instructions on establishing the placement of the charts is provided.

The second row of motifs will be Charts E, F, G, and H; the third row of motifs will be Charts I, J, K, and L; and the top row of motifs will be Charts M, N, O, and P. Each of these rows of charted motifs will be knit in the same manner as the first.

AT THE SAME TIME, at the left and right edges of the blanket, an 18-stitch border will be created using 2 skeins of MC (still designated as MCA and MCB). Do not break these yarns; they will be used throughout the body of the blanket. As the left and right borders are established, a second MCB will be designated; there will be two MCBs—one at each edge of the blanket.

Row 1 (RS): Sl2 sts together knitwise, (k1 with MCB, p1 with MCA) 8 times {right border}, drop MCB, using MCA and CC1 work Chart A over the next 78 sts, drop CC1, using MCA and CC2 work Chart B over the next 78 sts, drop CC2, using MCA and CC3 work Chart C over the next 78 sts, drop CC3, using MCA and a new skein of CC1 work Chart D over the next 78 sts, drop CC1, join a new skein of MC and designate as MCB, (k1 with MCB, p1 with MCA) 8 times, move MCA and MCB to the front between the needles and p2tog with MCA and MCB held together {left border}.

Row 2 (WS): Sl2 sts together knitwise, (k1 with MCA, p1 with MCB) 8 times {left border}, drop MCB, using MCA and CC1 work Chart D over the next 78 sts, drop CC1, using MCA and CC3 work Chart C over the next 78 sts, drop CC3, using MCA and CC2 work Chart B over the next 78 sts, drop CC2, using MCA and CC1 work Chart A over the next 78 sts, drop CC1, (k1 with MCA, p1 with MCB) 8 times, move MCA and MCB to the front between the needles and p2tog with MCA and MCB held together {right border}.

Rep [Rows 1 and 2] 27 more times to complete all 56 rows of the charts.**

Repeat from ** to ** 3 more times, substituting in the charts in the established order, using CCs as indicated by the chart key (page 190) or schematic (page 188) for each chart. A total of 224 charted rows are worked (56 rows per chart; 4 total rows of charts). Break any remaining CCs and MCB from the left border, leaving a 6 in. / 15 cm tail for weaving in. The top border will be worked with MCA and MCB (from the right border) only.

TOP BORDER

ROW 1 (RS): Sl2 sts together knitwise, *k1 with MCB, p1 with MCA; rep from * to last 2 sts, p2tog with MCA and MCB held together.

ROW 2 (WS): Sl2 sts together knitwise, *k1 with MCA, p1 with MCB; rep from * to last 2 sts, p2tog with MCA and MCB held together.

Rep [Rows 1 and 2] 5 more times, then Row 1 once more (13 rows worked).

With WS facing, bind off all sts using the Two-Color Bind Off.

FINISHING

Weave in all ends to the WS of the blanket.

OPTIONAL HIDING OF COLOR TWISTS

Thread the tapestry needle with a length of MC yarn. With the WS facing, beginning at the bottom of the blanket, insert the tapestry needle under the left leg of the leftmost MC column of stitches and under the right leg of the rightmost column of stitches at the color change between charts. Whipstitch around these two legs to hide the twist. Continue this all the way up the blanket in the same column of stitches. Repeat at each column of twists between the 4 columns of charts.

Break the MC yarn and weave in any ends to the WS.

Carefully wet block the blanket to the provided dimensions. Double knitting blocks similarly to 1x1 ribbing and will want to stretch widthwise. Be sure to support your work when moving from the water to the blocking surface to avoid overstretching. Allow to dry completely. Trim all ends.

FRIGHTENING FACT

Disney gave Skellington Productions—a company started exclusively for this film—2 years and $18 million to make the movie. It ended up taking over 3 years and came in at $24 million to make.

The Nightmare Before Christmas Throw Schematic

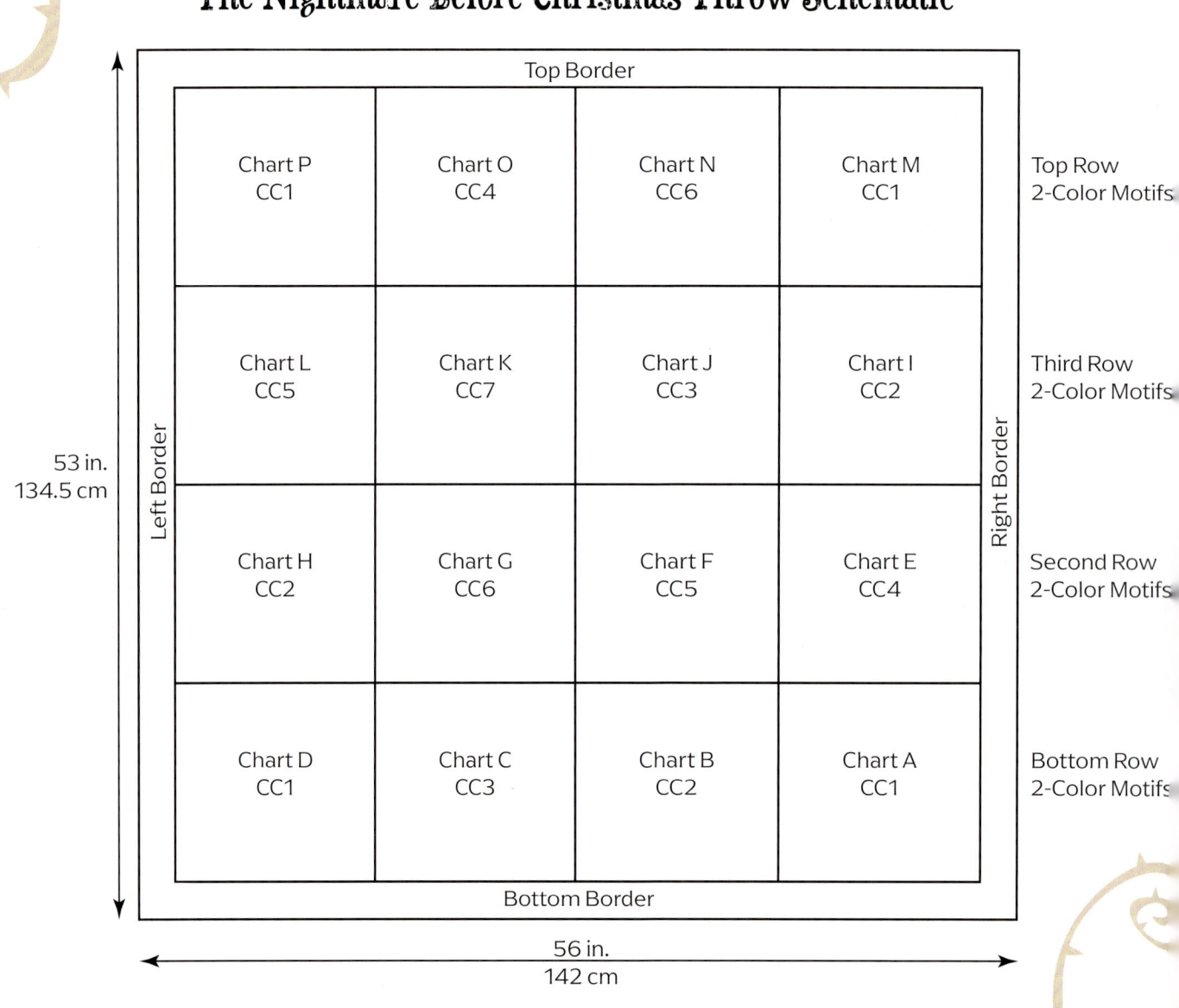

	Top Border			
Chart P CC1	Chart O CC4	Chart N CC6	Chart M CC1	Top Row 2-Color Motifs
Chart L CC5	Chart K CC7	Chart J CC3	Chart I CC2	Third Row 2-Color Motifs
Chart H CC2	Chart G CC6	Chart F CC5	Chart E CC4	Second Row 2-Color Motifs
Chart D CC1	Chart C CC3	Chart B CC2	Chart A CC1	Bottom Row 2-Color Motifs

Left Border / Right Border / Bottom Border

53 in.
134.5 cm

56 in.
142 cm

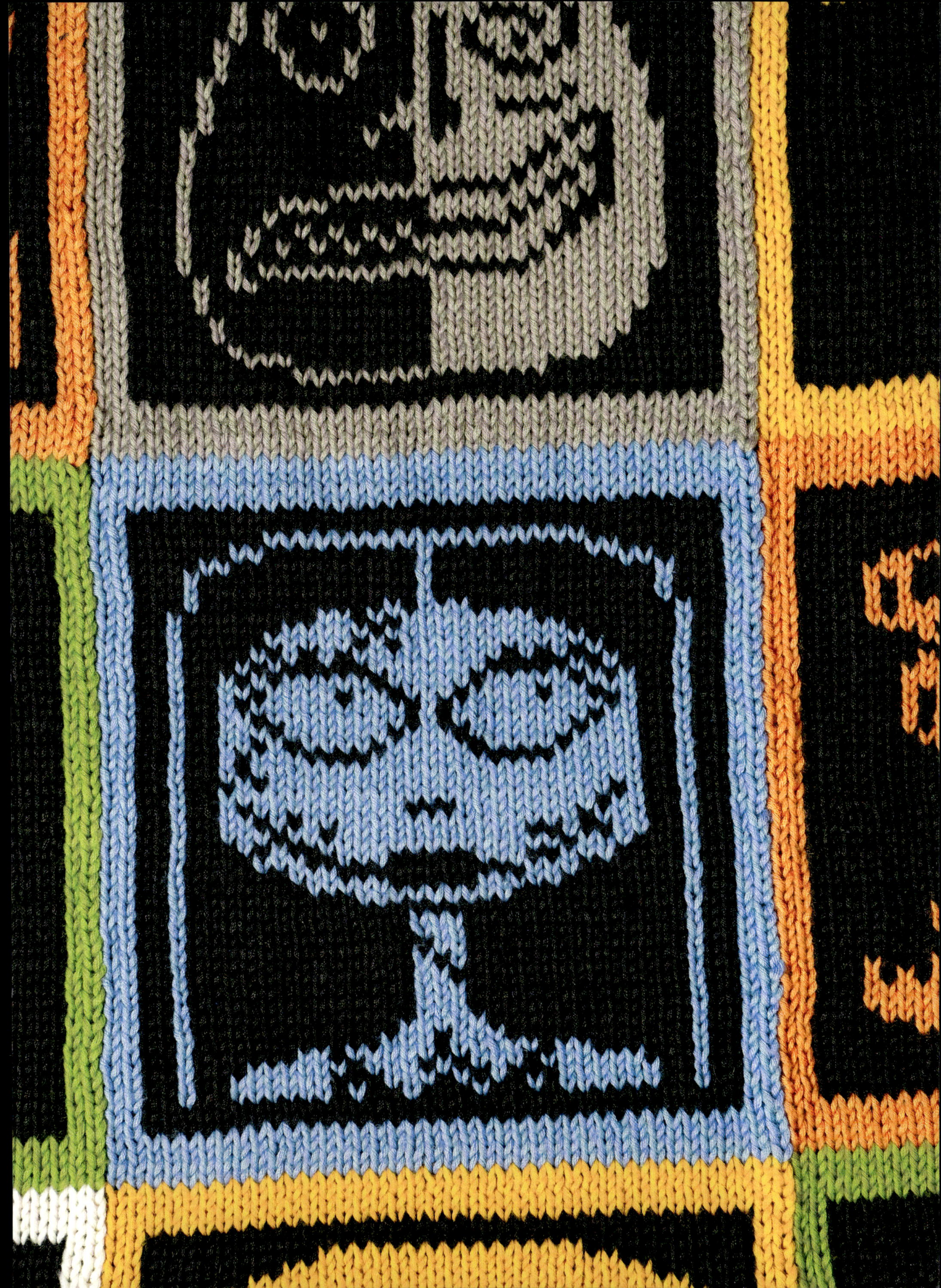

Key

- ☐ Knit
- ■ MC
- ☐ CC1
- 🟩 CC2
- 🟧 CC3
- 🟥 CC4
- 🟧 CC5
- 🟪 CC6
- ⬜ CC7

Chart A

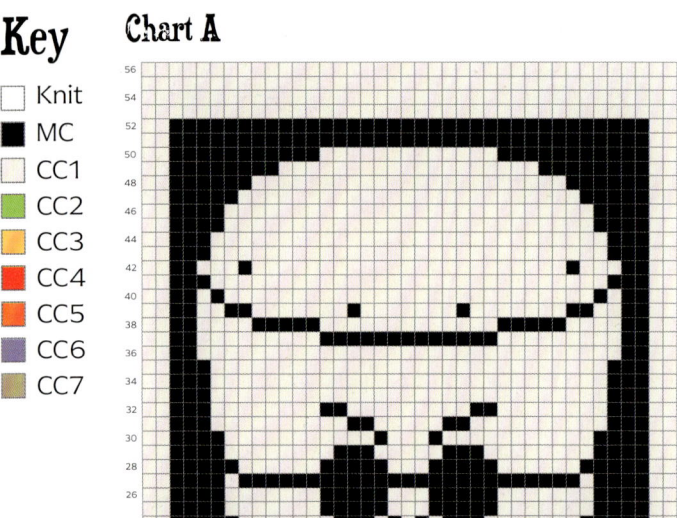

Chart B

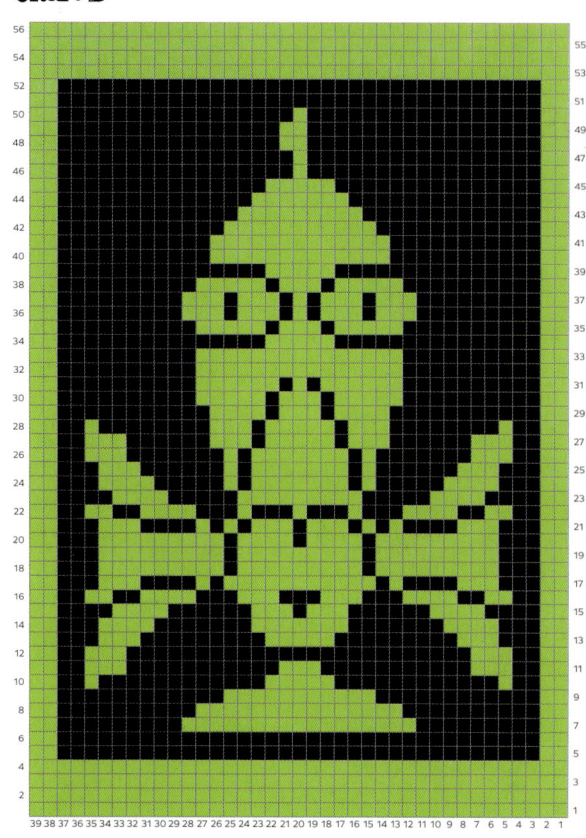

Chart C

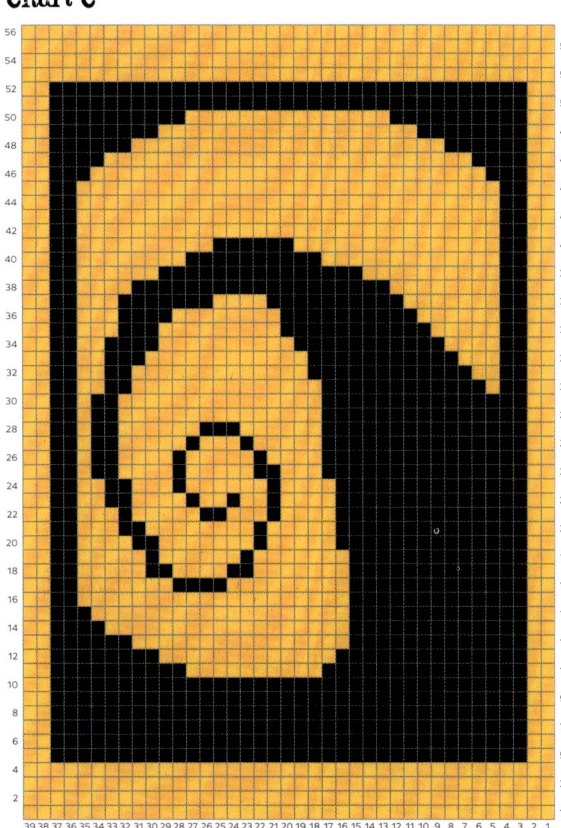

Chart D

Chart E

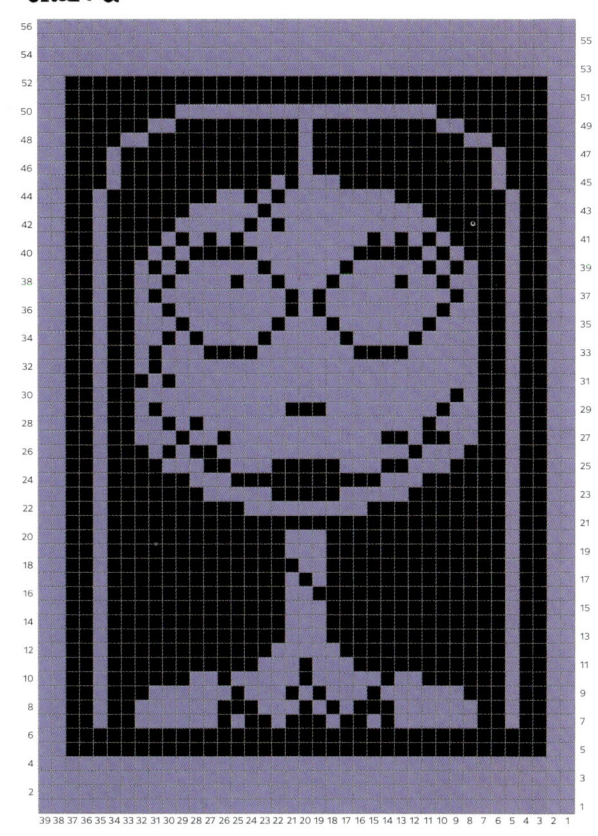

Chart F

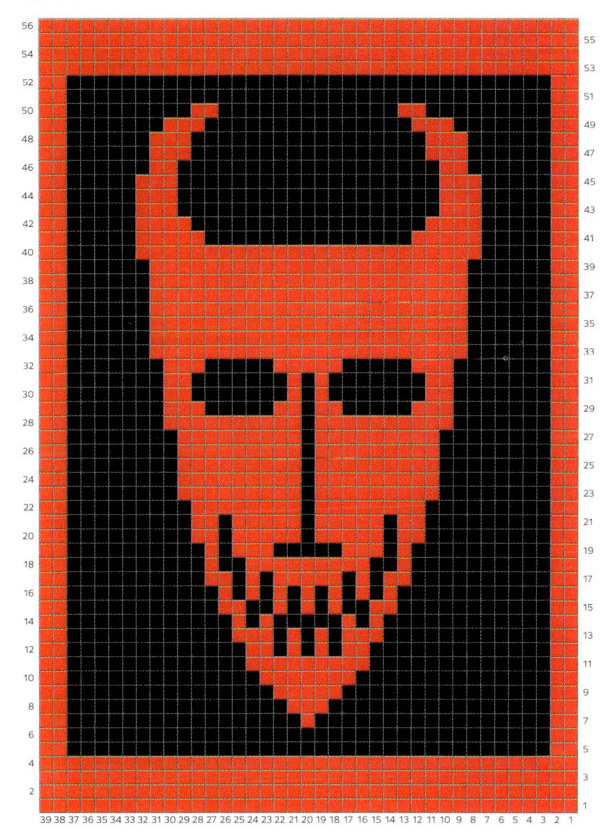

Chart G

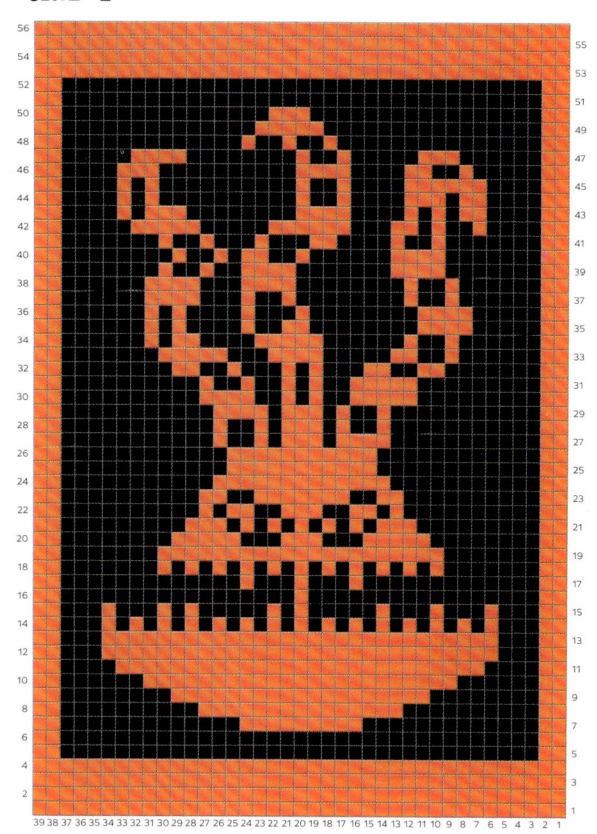

Chart H

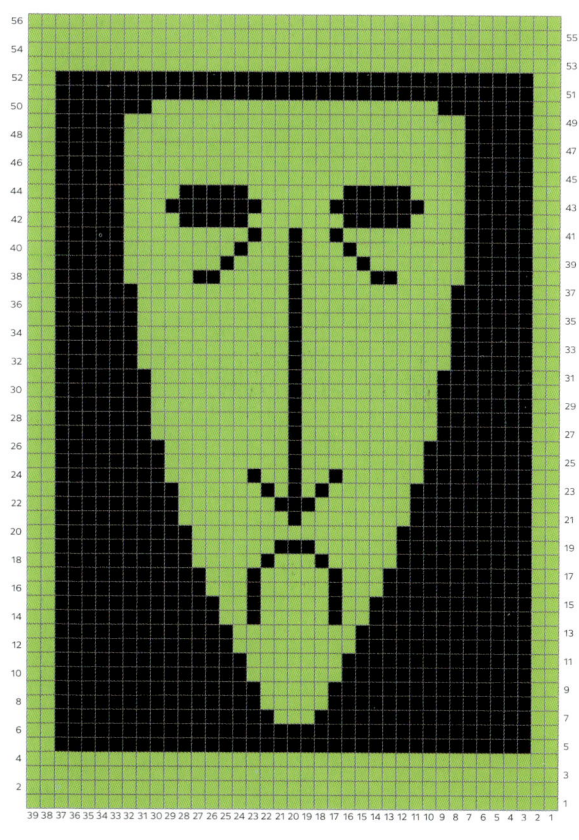

Key

- ☐ Knit
- ■ MC
- ☐ CC1
- ☐ CC2
- ☐ CC3
- ☐ CC4
- ☐ CC5
- ☐ CC6
- ☐ CC7

Chart I

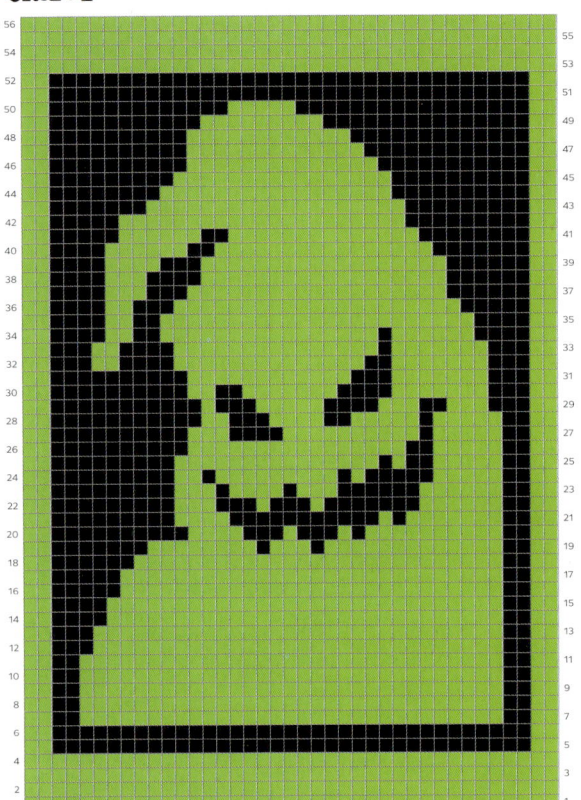

Chart J

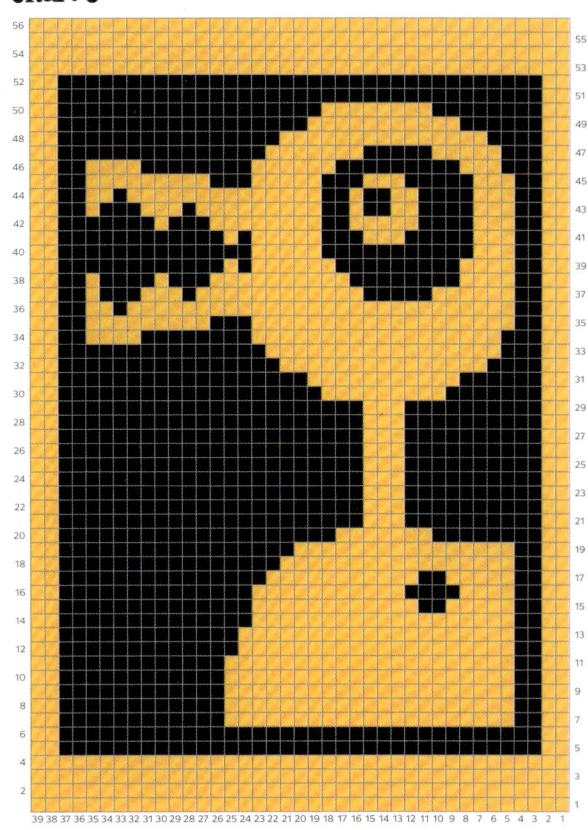

Chart K

Chart L

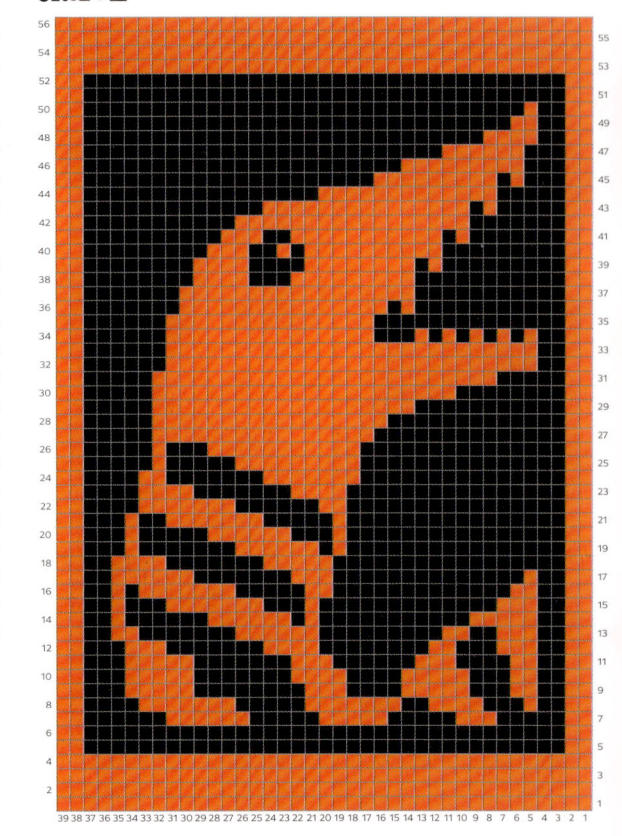

Chart M

Chart N

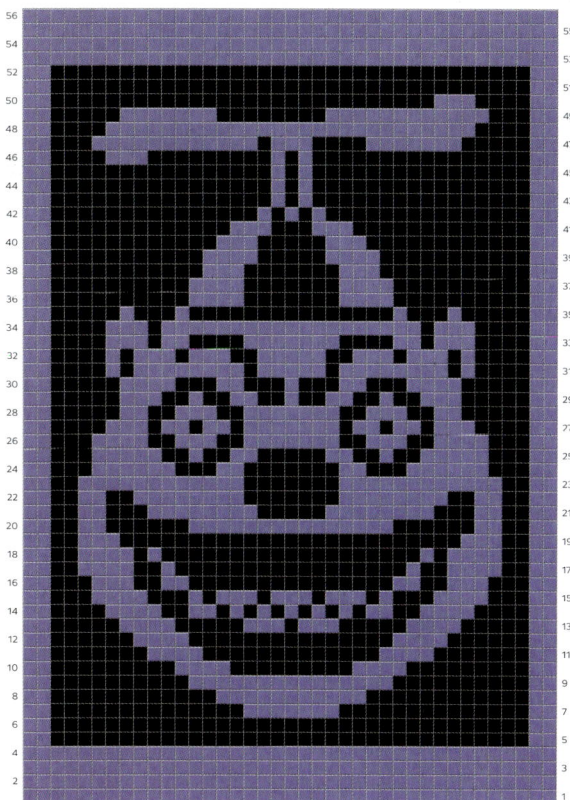

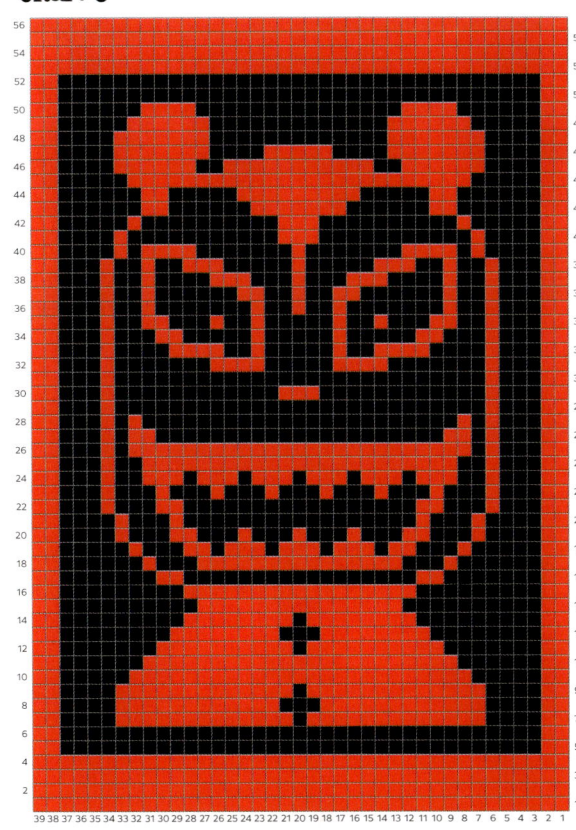

Chart O

Chart P

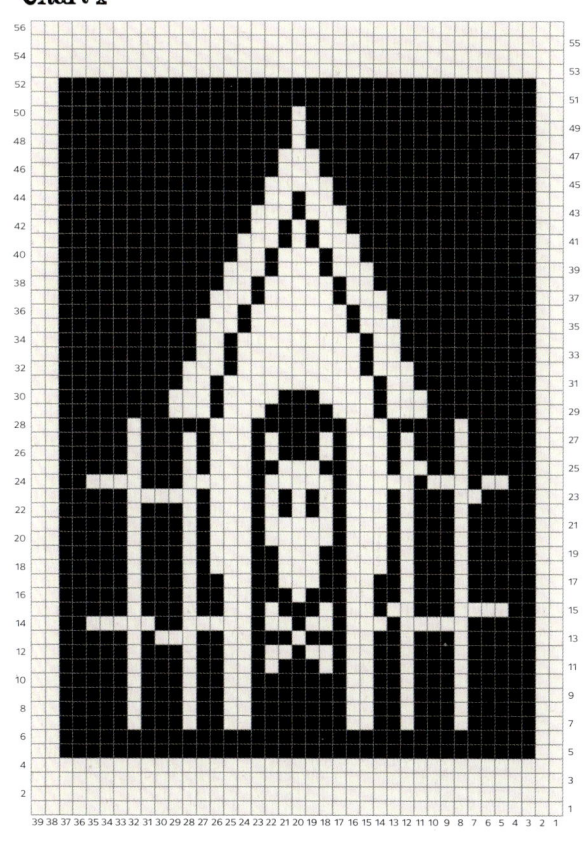

193

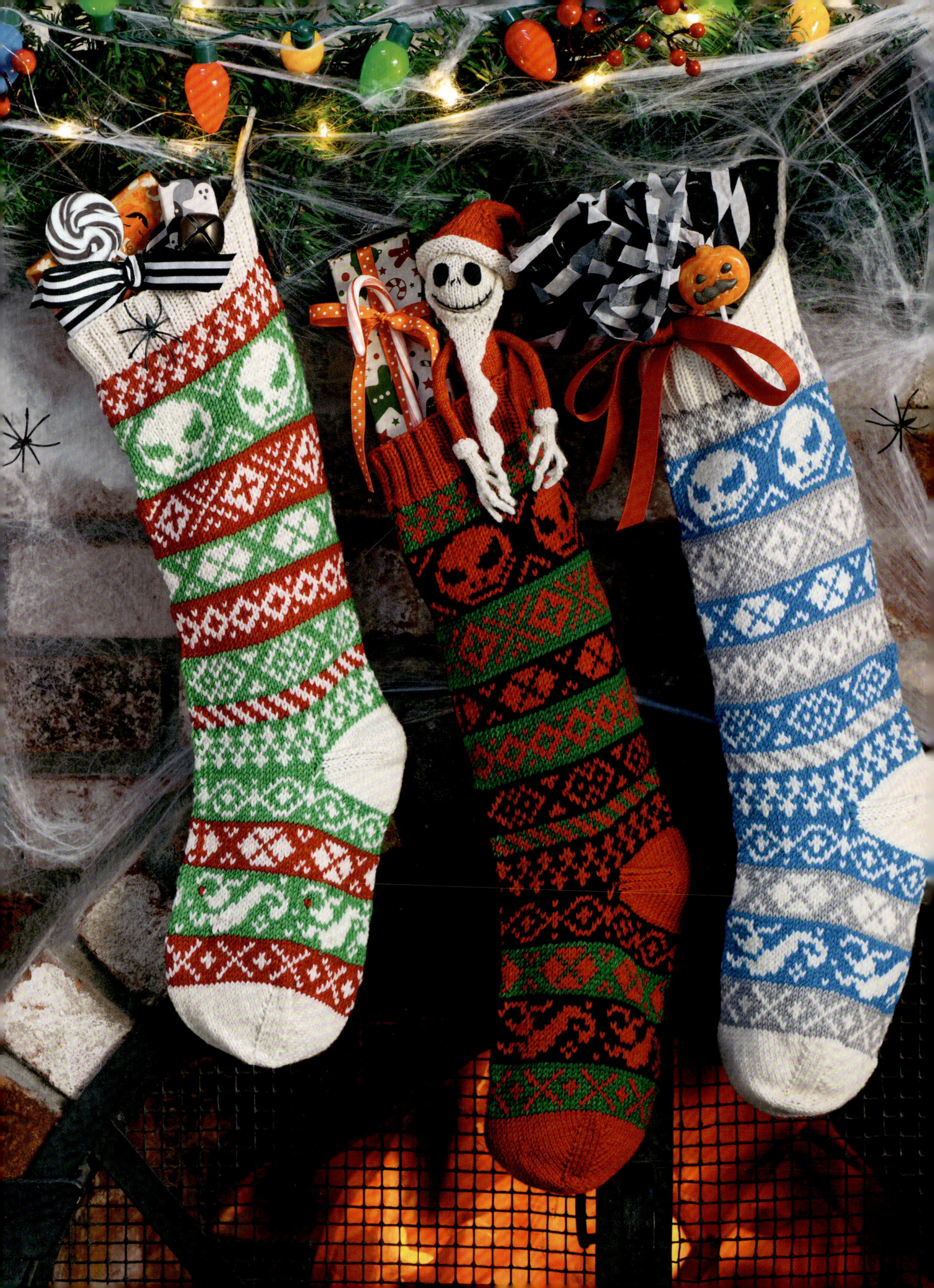

Festive Stockings

Designed by
Jesie Ostermiller

"Listen, everyone! I want to tell you about Christmas Town."
– Jack Skellington

SKILL LEVEL

Past the Hinterlands and through the door adorned with a sparkling Christmas tree lies Christmas Town, described by art director Deane Taylor as a place with "kind of an old-fashioned Christmas-card feel." Indeed, Christmas Town is vastly different from Jack's scary Halloween Town. The "What's This?" song that Jack sings upon discovering Christmas Town was composer Danny Elfman's way for Jack to stumble upon "this wonderful new place." The first completed sequence the production team animated and showed to Disney was seen by visual consultant Rick Heinrichs as "a stand-alone, if you will, part of the film." In contrast to Halloween Town with its bent perspective, Christmas Town relied on a much brighter palette, a softer, almost Dr. Seuss feel, and a forced perspective, a technique used to make objects seem closer, farther, larger, or smaller through optical illusions.

What's this? A festive stocking featuring leading man Jack Skellington and his trusty dog Zero! Striking the perfect balance between traditional knitting motifs and nightmarish characters, this is a stocking that all *Disney Tim Burton's The Nightmare Before Christmas* fans will delight in this holiday season. Worked in the round from the toe up with a forethought heel placed while working the stranded colorwork motifs and finished once the rest of the knitting is complete, it's topped with an easy 2x2 ribbed cuff to prevent rolling. An i-cord loop is added at the end for hanging. Make one in traditional holiday colors, Halloween colors, or any colors you choose!

SIZES
One size

FINISHED MEASUREMENTS
Stocking Circumference: 11½ in. / 29 cm

Length from Cuff to Toe: 21 in. / 53.5 cm

YARN
Worsted weight yarn, shown in Urth Yarns *16 Worsted* (100% extra-fine merino; 220 yd. / 200 m per 3½ oz. / 100 g hank)

COLORWAYS:

Version 1
- Color A: #N20 Natural, 1 hank
- Color B: #R70 Cherry Red, 1 hank
- Color C: #G70 Green, 1 hank

Version 2
- Color A: #R60 Red, 1 hank
- Color B: #G100 Dark Green, 1 hank
- Color C: #N30 Black, 1 hank

Version 3
- Color A: #N10 Light Natural, 1 hank
- Color B: #N90 Grey, 1 hank
- Color C: #BL80 Blue, 1 hank

NEEDLES
US 2 / 2.75 mm set of 5 dpns or size needed to obtain gauge

NOTIONS
Stitch marker

Locking stitch marker

Tapestry needle

Worsted weight smooth waste yarn

GAUGE

28 sts and 30 rows = 4 in. / 10 cm in stranded colorwork in the round, taken after blocking

Make sure to check your gauge.

PATTERN NOTES

- This stocking is worked in the round from the toe up, with a forethought heel placed while working the colorwork charts. When slipping stitches for the placement of the forethought heel, slip all stitches purlwise.
- The instructions for the stocking are written to be worked using one needle size; however you may need to adjust your needle size to maintain an even gauge over non-colorwork portions of the stocking (the heel and toe).
- When changing colors between sections of the colorwork chart, break the unused yarns, leaving a tail for weaving. Alternatively, carry the unused yarn loosely up the inside of the stocking to save on ends to weave in.
- The cuff is worked in 2x2 ribbing to prevent rolling. An i-cord hanging loop is worked seamlessly into the end of the cuff bind off to finish the stocking.
- If desired, you may duplicate stitch a red nose onto Zero (on Row 17 of the Foot chart).

PATTERN INSTRUCTIONS

CAST ON & TOE

Using Color A, CO 40 sts using Judy's Magic Cast On method. Distribute the sts evenly over 4 dpns (10 sts per needle). The first needle of the rnd will be Needle 1, and Needles 2, 3, and 4 will follow. Pm for BOR and join to work in the rnd.

SETUP RND: Knit.
RND 1 (INC): *K2, M1L, knit to end of Needle 1, knit to last 2 sts of Needle 2, M1R, k2; rep from * once more over Needles 3 and 4—4 sts inc.
RND 2: Knit.
Rep [Rnds 1 and 2] 9 more times. 40 sts inc; 80 sts total.
Remove BOR M, k20, pm for new BOR.

Note: The BOR M is now located on the bottom of the foot. The needle designations will rotate along with the BOR relocation—Needle 1 is still the first needle following the new BOR M.

FOOT

Begin Foot chart (page 198), reading all rows from right to left as for working in the rnd, joining Colors B and C as required. Work Rnds 1–39 once (chart is worked twice across each rnd).

Once the chart is complete, break all yarns. Clip a locking marker into the final stitch of Rnd 39. This indicator will be used during the heel; do not remove this marker until directed.

PLACING THE FORETHOUGHT HEEL

Without knitting any sts, and keeping the BOR M in place, slip the last 19 sts of Needle 4 onto Needle 1 (39 sts on Needle 1).
Join the waste yarn at the right edge of the just slipped sts and, using Needle 4, knit to the BOR M (20 sts on Needle 4).
Slip the BOR M and k19 (38 total sts worked with waste yarn).
Slip the last 19 sts worked with waste yarn back to Needle 1, ready to start a new round at the BOR M. There are 20 sts on each of the 4 dpns.

LEG

Begin Leg chart (page 199), reading all rows from right to left as for working in the rnd, joining Colors A, B, and C as required. Work Rnds 1–80 once (chart is worked twice across each rnd).

Once the chart is complete, break Colors B and C; the cuff is worked with Color A only.

CUFF & HANGING LOOP

SETUP RND: Knit.
RIB RND: *K2, p2; rep from * to end of rnd.
Rep Rib Rnd until the cuff measures 1½ in. / 4 cm.
BO all sts in pattern until 2 sts rem (1 st on RHN, 1 st on LHN), knit the final st on the LHN. Pick up and knit 1 st from the start of the bound off edge—3 sts total.
Work a 3-stitch i-cord for 3 in. / 7.5 cm. Bind off all sts knitwise.
Break Color A leaving a 10 in. / 25.5 cm tail. Thread the tapestry needle with the yarn tail and secure the bound off edge of the i-cord to the base of the i-cord to form a hanging loop.

FORETHOUGHT HEEL

Carefully remove the waste yarn and distribute the 38 live sts above and below the removed waste yarn evenly over 4 dpns (76 sts total; 19 sts per needle).
Rejoin Color A at the right edge of the live sts adjacent to the locking marker. The locking marker can now be removed.
RND 1: Knit.
RND 2 (DEC): *Knit to last 3 sts on Needle 1, k2tog, k1, k1, ssk, knit to end of Needle 2; rep from * once more over Needles 3 and 4—4 sts dec.

Rep [Rnd 2] 11 more times. 48 sts dec; 28 sts rem (7 sts per needle).

GRAFTING SETUP RND (PARTIAL RND): Knit to the end of Needle 1 (7 sts). Cut yarn leaving a 20 in. / 51 cm tail.

Rearrange sts onto 2 dpns as follows: Slip 7 sts from Needle 3 to Needle 2 (14 sts now on Needle 2).

Slip 7 sts from Needle 4 to Needle 1 (14 sts now on Needle 1).

Thread the tapestry needle with the remaining tail. Holding the 2 rem dpns parallel, graft the heel closed using Kitchener stitch.

FINISHING

Weave in all ends and wet block to measurements. Allow to dry completely. Trim all ends.

FRIGHTENING FACT

Every tree in Christmas Town is shaped like a pine tree and decorated for Christmas. This creates a stark contrast to the dead, bare trees in Halloween Town.

Festive Stocking Schematic

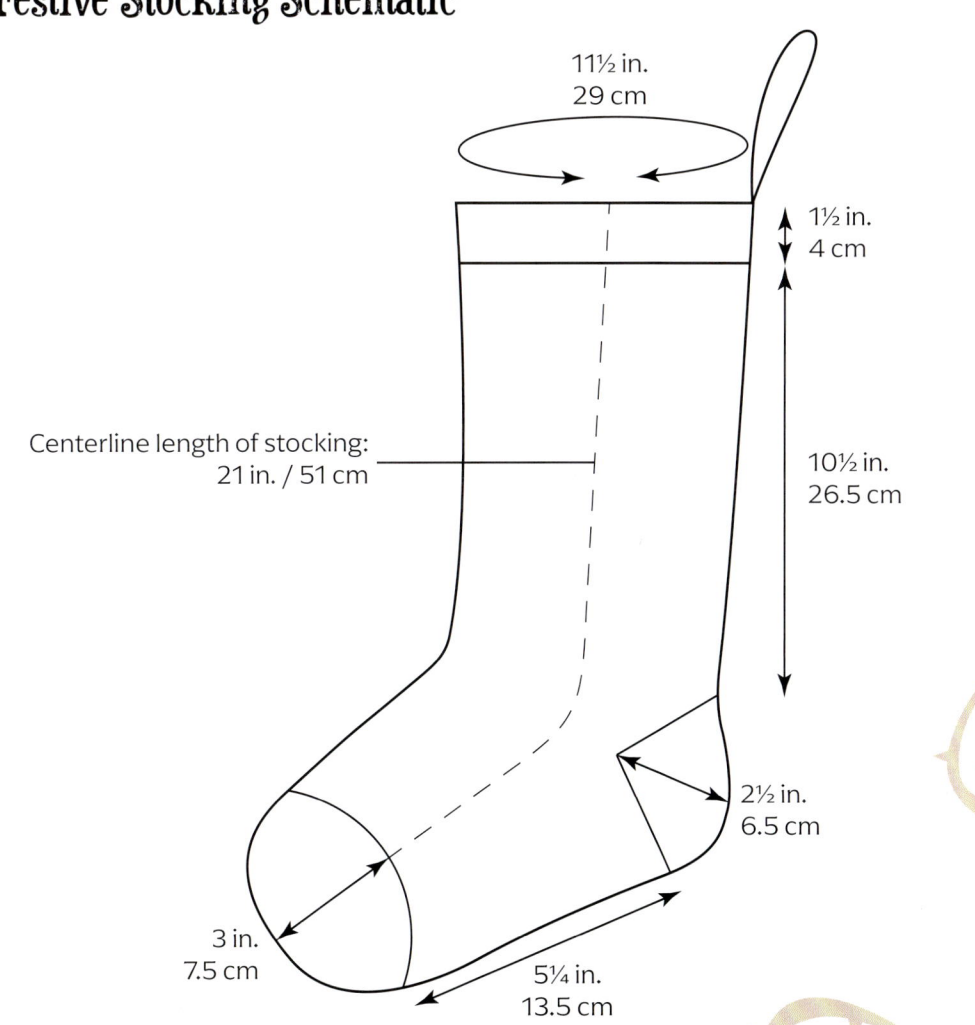

- 11½ in. / 29 cm
- 1½ in. / 4 cm
- 10½ in. / 26.5 cm
- Centerline length of stocking: 21 in. / 51 cm
- 2½ in. / 6.5 cm
- 3 in. / 7.5 cm
- 5¼ in. / 13.5 cm

Foot Chart

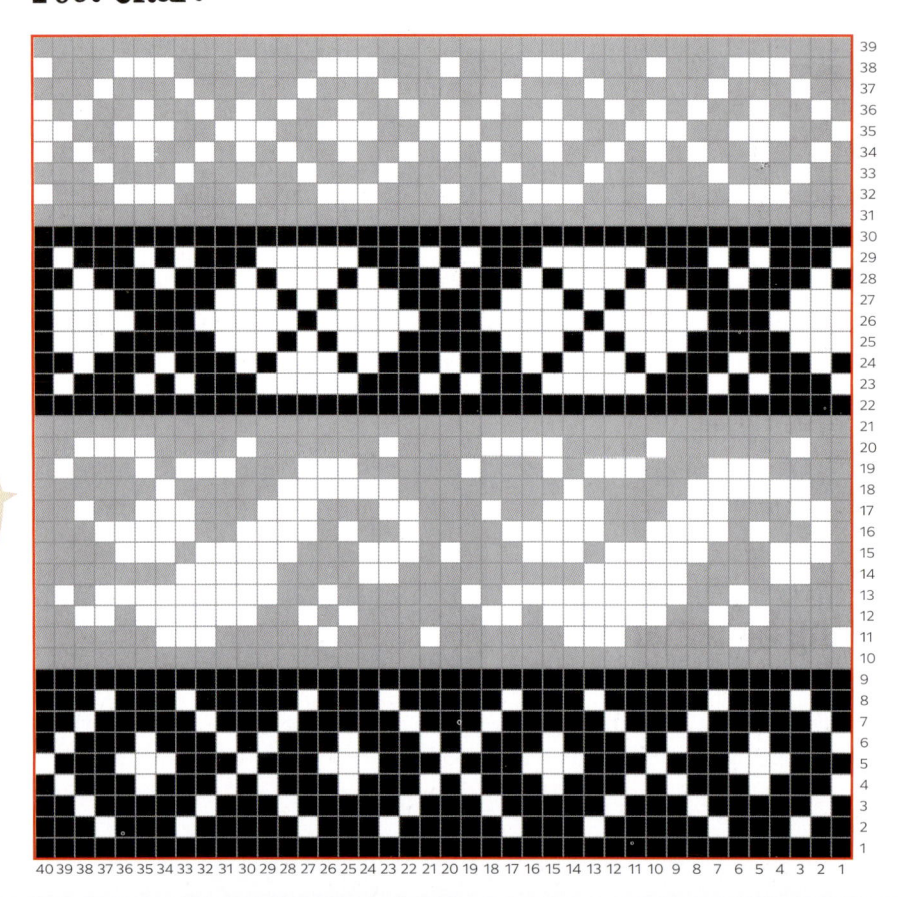

Leg Chart

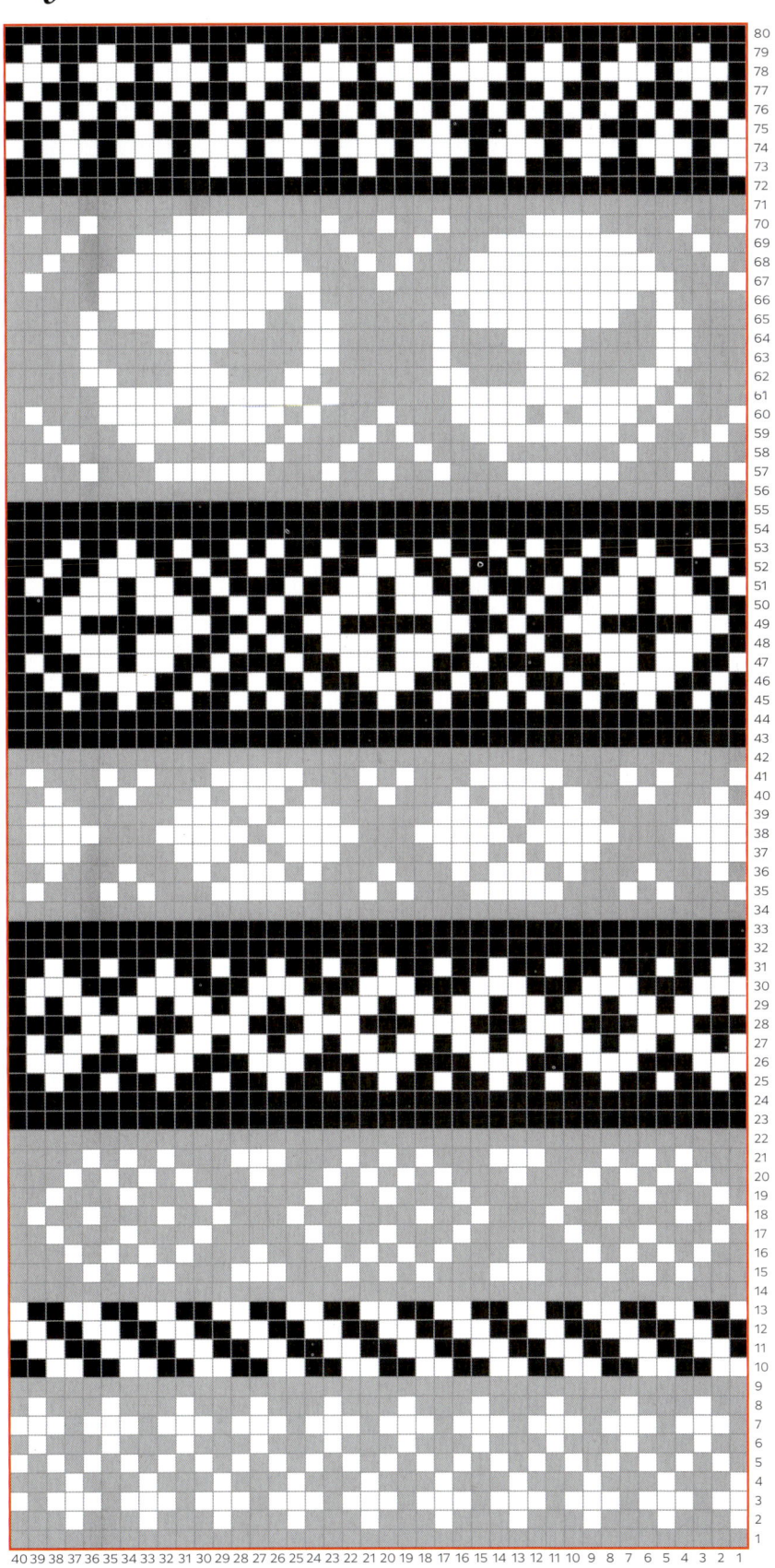

Key
- ☐ Knit
- ☐ Color A
- ■ Color B
- ▨ Color C
- ▢ Pattern repeat

Worm's Wort

Deadly Night Shade

Frog's Breath

Sally's Potion Jars

Designed by
Stephanie Dosen of
Tiny Owl Knits

"You've poisoned me for the last time, you wretched girl!"
—Dr. Finkelstein

SKILL LEVEL
💀 💀 💀

The film crew and craftspeople had to be as resourceful as Sally when creating the beloved film! Skellington Productions was formed in July 1991, with production on *Tim Burton's The Nightmare Before Christmas* starting in October of that year. With 19 soundstages, dozens of talented craftspeople, animators, puppets, and 8 separate camera crews, the 35,000-foot warehouse, located in San Francisco on 7th Street, was its own little city. Each active set was sectioned off with thick black curtains to keep light out from neighboring sets. Animator Justin Kohn says, "It was like visiting this crazy museum.... You'd part the curtain, and it was like visiting a whole new world with clouds and stars everywhere." When production began filming the "What's This?" Christmas Town scene, pile-driving from construction crews up the street caused the ground to shake and the puppets to move slightly. Animator Mike Belzer says of the problem, "I freaked out, [wondering] 'How can we make a stop-motion film with this going on?'" Crews had to carefully plan their shooting until construction finished a few weeks later.

Sally's mysterious potion jars are ready to hold all of your trinkets and knitting notions! These spellbinding jars are knit in wool and then felted—a process done with hot water and friction to shrink down protein fibers—so they can stand on their own. By inserting your hand into the bottom of the Frog's Breath jar, a surprise frog puppet will pop out with a mouth that can open and close! I thought you liked Frog's Breath?

SIZES
One size

FINISHED FELTED MEASUREMENTS
(see schematic for full measurements)

Deadly Nightshade: 7 in. / 18 cm tall (with lid)

Frog's Breath: 6½ in. / 16.5 cm tall (with lid)

Worm's Wort: 8½ in. / 21.5 cm tall

YARN
Bulky weight yarn, shown in Brown Sheep Company *Lamb's Pride Bulky* (85% wool, 15% goat mohair; 125 yd. / 114 m per 4 oz. / 113 g skein)

COLORWAYS:
- Yarn A: #M03 Grey Heather, 1 skein
- Yarn B: #M04 Charcoal Heather, 1 skein
- Yarn C: #M113 Oregano, 1 skein
- Yarn D: #M06 Deep Charcoal, 1 skein

NEEDLES
US 13 / 9 mm, 16 in. / 40 cm long circular needle and set of 4 or 5 dpns or size needed to obtain gauge

NOTIONS
Stitch markers

Waste yarn or stitch holder

Row counter (optional)

Tapestry needle

2 yd. / 1¾ m bulky weight yellow scrap yarn

Straight sewing pins

Dish or hand soap and hot water for felting

CONTINUED ON THE NEXT PAGE

- Felting needle OR black sewing thread and sewing needle
- Polyester stuffing (approx. 3 oz. / 85 g)
- Green (frog-colored) sewing thread and sewing needle
- Approx. 1 yd. of light tan quilting cotton fabric
- Fabric glue
- **Additional Notions for Label Making** (select items based on Making the Label methods; see page 206)
- Method 1: Copy machine OR computer scanner & printer, clear tape, a bright window, black fabric pen
- Method 2: Computer scanner and printer, printer paper, spray adhesive (repositionable)
- Method 3: Pencil and black fabric pen

GAUGE

12 sts and 16 rows = 4 in. / 10 cm worked in St st in the round before felting

PATTERN NOTES

- Be sure to use a natural fiber yarn that felts; 100% wool works best. Alpaca will felt but might not have a sturdy enough structure. Test your yarn first to be sure.
- All three jars and both lids are worked in stockinette stitch in the round.
- Frog's Breath jar is a puppet. It is knit as one long tube and then telescoped down inside itself at the end of the felting process. Lid is not attached.
- Deadly Nightshade and Worm's Wort jars are worked from the top down, in the round. Both jars are stuffed with polyester stuffing for structure.
- Label templates provided in book are exact size measured by border. Three label-making methods are provided. Choose the one that best suits your abilities/tools. The labels are glued onto the jars using fabric glue around the edges, and covered by a felted border, which is also glued on.

PATTERN INSTRUCTIONS

FROG'S BREATH JAR (PUPPET)

Using Yarn A and the 16 in. / 40 cm circular needle, CO 40 sts using the Long Tail Cast On method. Pm for BOR and join to work in the rnd, being careful not to twist the sts.

RNDS 1–30: Knit.

Note: When the circumference of the piece becomes too small for the circular needle in the following rnds, change to dpns.

RND 31 (DEC): (K6, k2tog) to end of rnd—35 sts.

RNDS 32–42: Knit.

Break Yarn A; join Yarn D.

RNDS 43–60: Knit.

RND 61 (DEC): (K5, k2tog) to end of rnd—30 sts.

RNDS 62 AND 63: Knit.

Break Yarn D; join Yarn C.

RND 64 (DEC): (K4, k2tog) to end of rnd—25 sts.

RNDS 65 AND 66: Knit.

RND 67 (DEC): (K3, k2tog) to end of rnd—20 sts.

RNDS 68 AND 69: Knit.

TOP OF FROG'S MOUTH

RND 70: K12, CO 12 sts using the Backward Loop Cast On method—24 sts. Place the rem 8 sts onto waste yarn or stitch holder. Divide the 24 sts evenly onto dpns for comfort and cont in the rnd.

RNDS 71–80: Knit.

RND 81 (DEC): (Ssk, k8, k2tog) to end of rnd—20 sts.

RNDS 82–84: Knit.

RND 85 (DEC): (Ssk, k6, k2tog) to end of rnd—16 sts.

RND 86: Knit.

RND 87 (DEC): (Ssk, k4, k2tog) to end of rnd—12 sts.

Break yarn leaving a 12 in. / 30.5 cm tail. Divide the rem 12 sts evenly over 2 needles: 6 sts per needle. Hold the two needles parallel. Thread tapestry needle with the tail and graft the live sts closed using Kitchener stitch.

BOTTOM OF FROG'S MOUTH

Place the 8 live sts from waste yarn or stitch holder onto a dpn.

With RS facing, join Yarn C and knit across the 8 sts, CO 8 sts using the Backward Loop Cast On method—16 sts. Divide the 16 sts evenly onto dpns for comfort; pm for BOR and join to work in the rnd.

RNDS 1–11: Knit.

RND 12 (DEC): (Ssk, k4, k2tog) to end of rnd—12 sts.

Break yarn leaving a 12 in. / 30.5 cm tail. Divide the rem 12 sts evenly over 2 needles: 6 sts per needle. Hold the two needles parallel. Thread tapestry needle with the tail and graft the live sts closed using Kitchener stitch.

SEAMING FROG MOUTH

Thread the tapestry needle with a length of Yarn C. Close the top and bottom cast on edges of the back of the mouth using whipstitch.

SHAPING THE JAR

Felt jar (see FELTING on page 205).

Note: The following shaping must be done while puppet is still damp. Finished jar has a telescoping effect with 3 layers: outer jar, inner jar, and frog in the middle. When resting, frog tucks down into jar completely with lid flat on top.

With felted jar resting flat, measure approx. 6½ in. / 16.5 cm from bottom of jar (the cast on edge). Fold at this measurement and tuck the rest of the work down into outer jar (this first fold creates the rim of the outer jar).

Insert your hand into the frog puppet and push him back up through center of jar creating another fold at bottom inside of jar. Be sure frog isn't sticking out of the jar when resting. Work the folds to create 3 evenly distributed layers with 2 folds. Leave in an arid location to dry with frog completely telescoped into the jar.

FROG'S BREATH LID

Using Yarn A and a dpn, CO 6 sts using the Long Tail Cast On method, leaving a 6 in. / 15 cm tail. Distribute sts evenly over 2 dpns (3 sts per needle). Pm for BOR and join to work in the rnd, being careful not to twist the sts.

RND 1 (INC): (Kfb) to end of rnd—12 sts.

Work in additional dpns for comfort as the circumference increases.

RND 2: Knit.

RND 3 (INC): (Kfb, k1) to end of rnd—18 sts.

RND 4: Knit.

RND 5 (INC): (K2, kfb) to end of rnd—24 sts.

RND 6: Knit.

RND 7 (INC): (K3, kfb) to end of rnd—30 sts.

RND 8: Knit.

RND 9 (INC): (K4, kfb) to end of rnd—36 sts.

RNDS 10–12: Knit.

RND 13 (DEC): (K4, k2tog) to end of rnd—30 sts.
RND 14: Knit.
RND 15 (DEC): (K3, k2tog) to end of rnd—24 sts.
RND 16: Knit.
RND 17 (DEC): (K2, k2tog) to end of rnd—18 sts.
RND 18: Knit.
RND 19 (DEC): (K1, k2tog) to end of rnd—12 sts.
RND 20: Knit.
RND 21 (DEC): (K2tog) to end of rnd—6 sts.

Break yarn leaving a 6 in. / 15 cm tail. Thread the tapestry needle with the tail, and using the tapestry needle, weave end through live sts cinching them closed.

Using the CO tail, weave 6 CO sts closed. Felt lid (see FELTING on page 205).

Press the lid flat so the cast on and bind off are in the center top and center bottom. Shape into a circle and leave in an arid location to dry flat.

EYEBALLS (MAKE 2 THE SAME)

Note: Eyes and eyelids are knitted, felted, and attached separately after jar is felted and dried.

Using the scrap bulky weight yellow yarn and a dpn, CO 5 sts using the Long Tail Cast On method.

Work a 5-stitch i-cord for 4 rnds.

Break yarn and thread through live sts, cinching them closed. Using a tapestry needle, stitch the CO and BO edges together to make a little ball. Felt eyeballs and leave to dry (see FELTING on page 205).

EYELIDS (MAKE 2 THE SAME)

Using Yarn C and a dpn, CO 12 sts using the Long Tail Cast On method. Do not join to work in the rnd.

ROW 1 (RS, DEC): (Ssk) 3 times, (k2tog) 3 times—6 sts.
ROW 2 (WS): Purl.
ROW 3 (DEC): Ssk, (k2tog) 2 times—3 sts.

Break yarn and thread through live sts from right to left cinching them closed. Felt eyelids and leave to dry flat (see FELTING on page 205).

FINISHING EYES

When the eyes and eyelids are fully felted and dried, wrap the fan-shaped eyelid around the eyeball and stitch them together using green sewing thread and sewing needle. Stitch eyelids to frog head referencing the photos as inspiration for placement.

To create the pupils, cut approx. ½ in. / 1 cm of Yarn D, un-ply it, and using your fingers, roll it into a tiny ball. Use a felting needle (or a sewing needle and black thread) to attach the pupil to the eyeball. Be sure the pupil placement is a little uneven to make the frog look a bit shocked and silly.

FINISHING

When jar is fully dry, make and attach label. See Making the Labels on page 206 for label instructions. Do not attach lid; place lid on top of jar for display when frog is tucked in.

DEADLY NIGHTSHADE JAR

Using Yarn B and set of dpns, CO 24 sts using the Long Tail Cast On method. Pm for BOR and join to work in the rnd, being careful not to twist the sts.

Note: When the circumference of the piece allows, use the circular needle for comfort. When the circumference of the piece becomes too small for the circular needle again, change back to dpns.

RNDS 1–4: Knit.
RND 5 (INC): (K2, kfb) to end of rnd—32 sts.
RNDS 6–8: Knit.
RND 9 (INC): (K1, kfb) to end of rnd—48 sts.
RNDS 10–14: Knit.
RND 15 (DEC): (K10, k2tog) to end of rnd—44 sts.
RNDS 16–18: Knit.
RND 19 (DEC): K5, (k2tog, k9) 3 times, k2tog, k4—40 sts.
RNDS 20–22: Knit.
RND 23 (DEC): (K8, k2tog) to end of rnd—36 sts.
RNDS 24–26: Knit.
RND 27 (DEC): K4, (k2tog, k7) 3 times, k2tog, k3—32 sts.
RND 28: Knit.
RND 29 (DEC): (K6, k2tog) to end of rnd—28 sts.
RND 30: Knit.
RND 31 (DEC): K3, (k2tog, k5) 3 times, k2tog, k2—24 sts.
RND 32: Knit.
RND 33 (DEC): (K2, k2tog) to end of rnd—18 sts.
RND 34 (DEC): (K1, k2tog) to end of rnd—12 sts.
RND 35 (DEC): (K2tog) to end of rnd—6 sts.

Break yarn leaving a 6 in. / 15 cm tail. Thread the tapestry needle with the tail, and using the tapestry needle, weave end through live sts cinching them closed.

SHAPING THE JAR

Felt jar (see FELTING on page 205).
Note: The following shaping must be done while the jar is still damp.

This jar has a concave dome tucked in at the bottom to create stability. Push up the dome while you are shaping. Optionally, stuff the jar lightly with polyester stuffing to help maintain shape while drying. Leave in arid location to dry. Remove stuffing when dry to store trinkets.

DEADLY NIGHTSHADE LID

Using Yarn B and a dpn, CO 6 sts using the Long Tail Cast On method, leaving a 6 in. / 15 cm tail. Distribute sts evenly over 2 dpns (3 sts per needle). Pm for BOR and join to work in the rnd, being careful not to twist the sts.

RND 1 (INC): (Kfb) to end of rnd—12 sts.

Work in additional dpns for comfort as the circumference increases.

RND 2: Knit.
RND 3 (INC): (Kfb, k1) to end of rnd—18 sts.

RND 4 (INC): (K2, kfb) to end of rnd—24 sts.
RND 5: Knit.
RND 6 (INC): (K3, kfb) to end of rnd—30 sts.
RNDS 7–9: Knit.
RND 10 (DEC): (K3, k2tog) to end of rnd—24 sts.
RND 11: Knit.
RND 12 (DEC): (K2, k2tog) to end of rnd—18 sts.
RND 13 (DEC): (K1, k2tog) to end of rnd—12 sts.
RND 14: Knit.
RND 15 (DEC): (K2tog) to end of rnd—6sts.

Break yarn leaving a 6 in. / 15 cm tail. Thread the tapestry needle with the tail, and using the tapestry needle, weave end through live sts cinching them closed.

Using the CO tail, weave 6 CO sts closed. Felt lid (see FELTING, this page).

Press the lid flat temporarily, so that the cast on and bind off edges are opposite one another, at the center front and center back outer edges (not on top and bottom). Then shape the flattened lid into a curved dome and leave in an arid location to dry.

DEADLY NIGHTSHADE BLACK LID CORDS

Using Yarn D and a dpn, CO 2 sts using the Long Tail Cast On method.

Work a 2-stitch i-cord for 30 in. / 76 cm.

Break yarn and thread through live sts, cinching them closed.

Felt cord (see FELTING, this page).

While cord is damp, cut into 2 even pieces. Wrap one cord around mouth of finished jar and trim to desired length. Stitch cord closed into a circle using a length of Yarn D. Roll cord between hands to felt the closure. Rep for the second cord.

FINISHING

When jar is fully dry, make and attach label. See Making the Labels on page 206 for label instructions.

Place black cords around mouth of jar when fully dried. Secure lid to top of jar with a few sts in the back using Yarn B and tapestry needle.

WORM'S WORT JAR

Using Yarn C and set of dpns, CO 14 sts using the Long Tail Cast On method. Pm for BOR and join to work in the rnd, being careful not to twist the sts.

Note: When the circumference of the piece allows, use the circular needle for comfort. When the circumference of the piece becomes too small for the circular needle again, change back to dpns.

RNDS 1–14: Knit.
RND 15 (INC): (Kfb, k3, kfb, k2) to end of rnd—18 sts.
RND 16: Knit.
RND 17 (INC): (Kfb, k5, kfb, k2) to end of rnd—22 sts.
RND 18 (INC): (Kfb, k7, kfb, k2) to end of rnd—26 sts.
RND 19 (INC): (Kfb, k9, kfb, k2) to end of rnd—30 sts.
RND 20 (INC): (Kfb, k11, kfb, k2) to end of rnd—34 sts.
RNDS 21–25: Knit.
RND 26 (DEC): K1, ssk, k10, k2tog, k3, k2tog, k10, k2tog, k2—30 sts.
RNDS 27–32: Knit.
RND 33 (DEC): K1, ssk, k8, k2tog, k3, k2tog, k8, k2tog, k2—26 sts.
RNDS 34–39: Knit.
RND 40 (DEC): K1, ssk, k6, k2tog, k3, k2tog, k6, k2tog, k2—22 sts.
RNDS 41–46: Knit.
RND 47 (DEC): K1, ssk, k4, k2tog, k3, k2tog, k4, k2tog, k2—18 sts.
RND 48: Knit.
RND 49 (DEC): K1, ssk, k2, k2tog, k3, k2tog, k2, k2tog, k2—14 sts.
RND 50: Knit.
RND 51 (DEC): (K2tog) to end of rnd—7 sts.

Break yarn leaving a 6 in. / 15 cm tail. Thread a tapestry needle with the tail, and using the tapestry needle, weave end through live sts cinching them closed.

SHAPING THE JAR

Felt jar (see FELTING, this page).

Note: The following shaping must be done while the jar is still damp.

This jar has a deep concave dome tucked in at the bottom to create stability. Push up the dome while you are shaping. This jar is stuffed densely with polyester stuffing while it is still wet to help with shape. Leave in arid location to dry. Remove stuffing when dry if desired.

FINISHING

When jar is fully dry, make and attach label. See Making the Labels on page 206 for label instructions.

Fold down the top lip of the neck by 1 in. / 2.5 cm to create a rim.

FELTING

In the sink, *drench knitted item in hot water and squeeze some water out. Add enough dish or hand soap to the item to work up a soapy lather. It should feel similar to hair washing. Agitate soapy wool roughly between your hands working in all directions for about 10 minutes. Rinse out soap using hot water while continuing agitation. Repeat from * until the item turns into solid felt. Rinse out soap completely. This process can take up to 45 minutes. When fabric has turned to felt, begin shaping item to resemble photos. Wet wool behaves like clay and will retain the shape it dries in.

MAKING THE LABELS

Labels printed in book are actual size.

METHOD 1: PRINT AND TRACE

Step 1: Make a paper copy of label (provided on pages 208 and 209) by using either a copy machine or a scanner and printer.

Step 2: Tape the paper copy to a bright window.

Step 3: Cut out a piece of fabric larger than the label.

Step 4: Use a fabric marker to trace letters and border.

METHOD 2: PRINTING LABELS ONTO FABRIC USING HOME PRINTER

IMPORTANT: Use this method at your own risk. There is potential for damage to printer if done incorrectly.

Step 1: Scan the labels to create a JPG file. If necessary, resize JPG to exact measurements as follows:
- Deadly Nightshade: 3½ in. / 9 cm wide by 4½ in. / 11.5 cm high
- Frog's Breath: 3½ in. / 9 cm wide by 4 in. / 10 cm high
- Worm's Wort: 3 in. / 7.5 cm wide by 4 in. / 10 cm high

Step 2: Print label directly onto fabric as follows:
- 2a: Lightly coat a piece of printer paper with repositionable adhesive spray and allow to dry. When dried it should be tacky to the touch.
- 2b: Place a piece of fabric over the sticky paper and smooth out wrinkles.
- 2c: Carefully cut fabric to the exact size of printer paper.
- 2d: Load fabric coated paper into printer tray and print label.

METHOD 3: DIRECT TRACE

If you don't have access to a printer:

Step 1: Place the cotton fabric directly on template in book and trace labels, including the border, using a pencil.

Step 2: Place fabric on a hard surface and darken letters using a black fabric pen. There is no need to darken the border; this is just a cutting reference, so can be left in pencil.

ATTACHING THE LABELS

Cut out fabric label along border. Apply thin layer of fabric glue to back side of label around edges only and secure to jar. Use sewing pins to keep it in place as it dries.

Make a felted label border as follows: Cut a strand of coordinating wool approx. 24 in. / 61 cm in length. Wet the strand of wool and roll it back and forth between your hands to make it felt while keeping it smooth and straight. Leave the strand in a straight line to dry. When dry, glue it along border of label, again using pins to secure. Cut border at corners to help it lie flat. Trim excess.

FROG'S BREATH

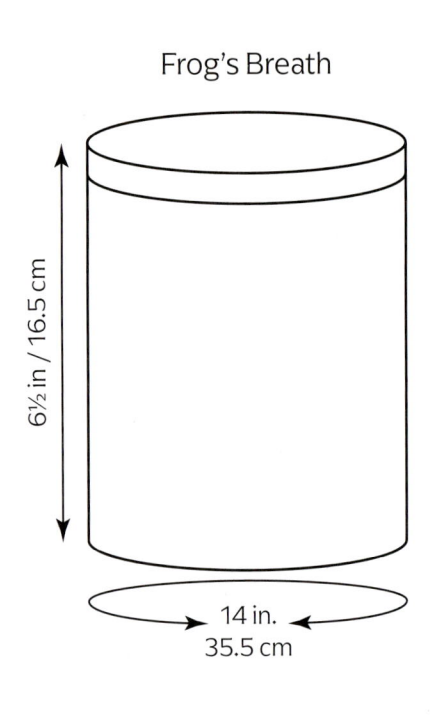

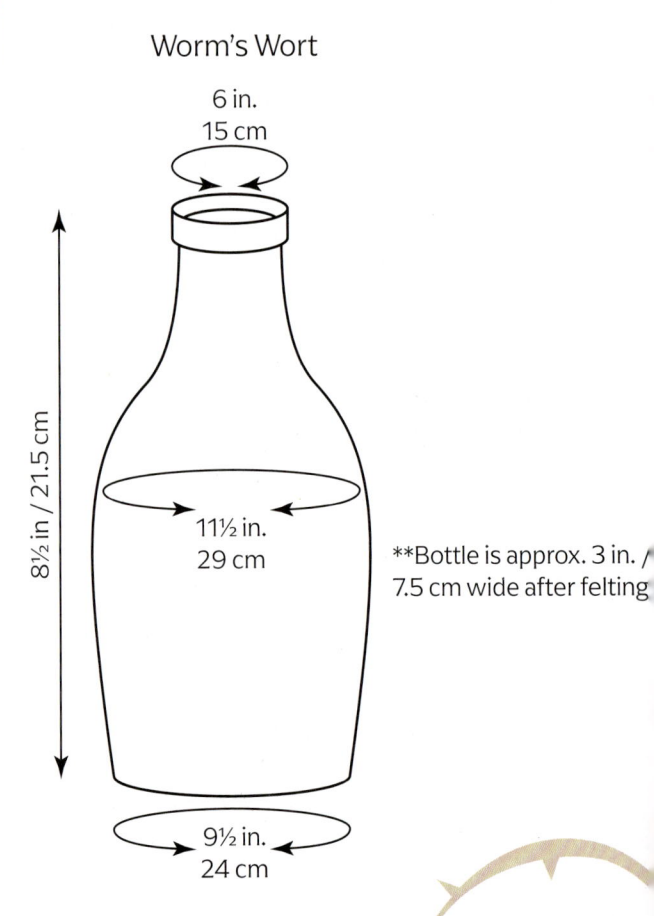

Sally's Potion Jars Labels and Schematics

FROG'S BREATH

Frog's Breath

6½ in / 16.5 cm

14 in.
35.5 cm

Worm's Wort

Worm's Wort

6 in.
15 cm

8½ in / 21.5 cm

11½ in.
29 cm

**Bottle is approx. 3 in. / 7.5 cm wide after felting

9½ in.
24 cm

Sally's Potion Jars Labels and Schematics

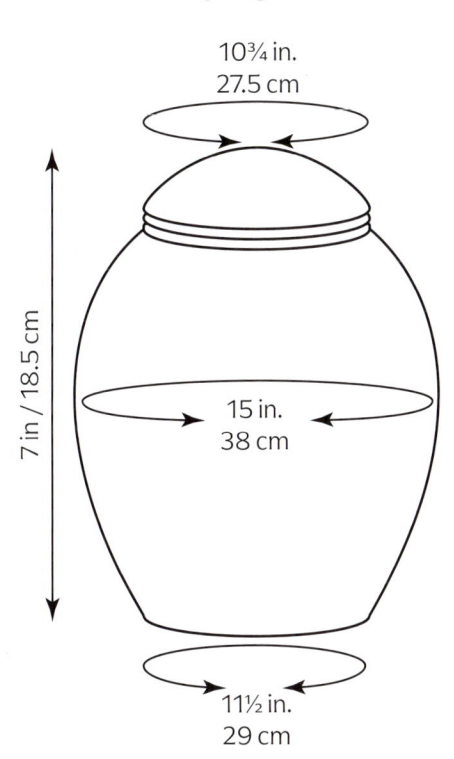

Deadly Nightshade

10¾ in.
27.5 cm

7 in / 18.5 cm

15 in.
38 cm

11½ in.
29 cm

DEADLY NIGHT SHADE

FRIGHTENING FACT

Tim Burton's The Nightmare Before Christmas was the first ever full-length stop-motion animation feature.

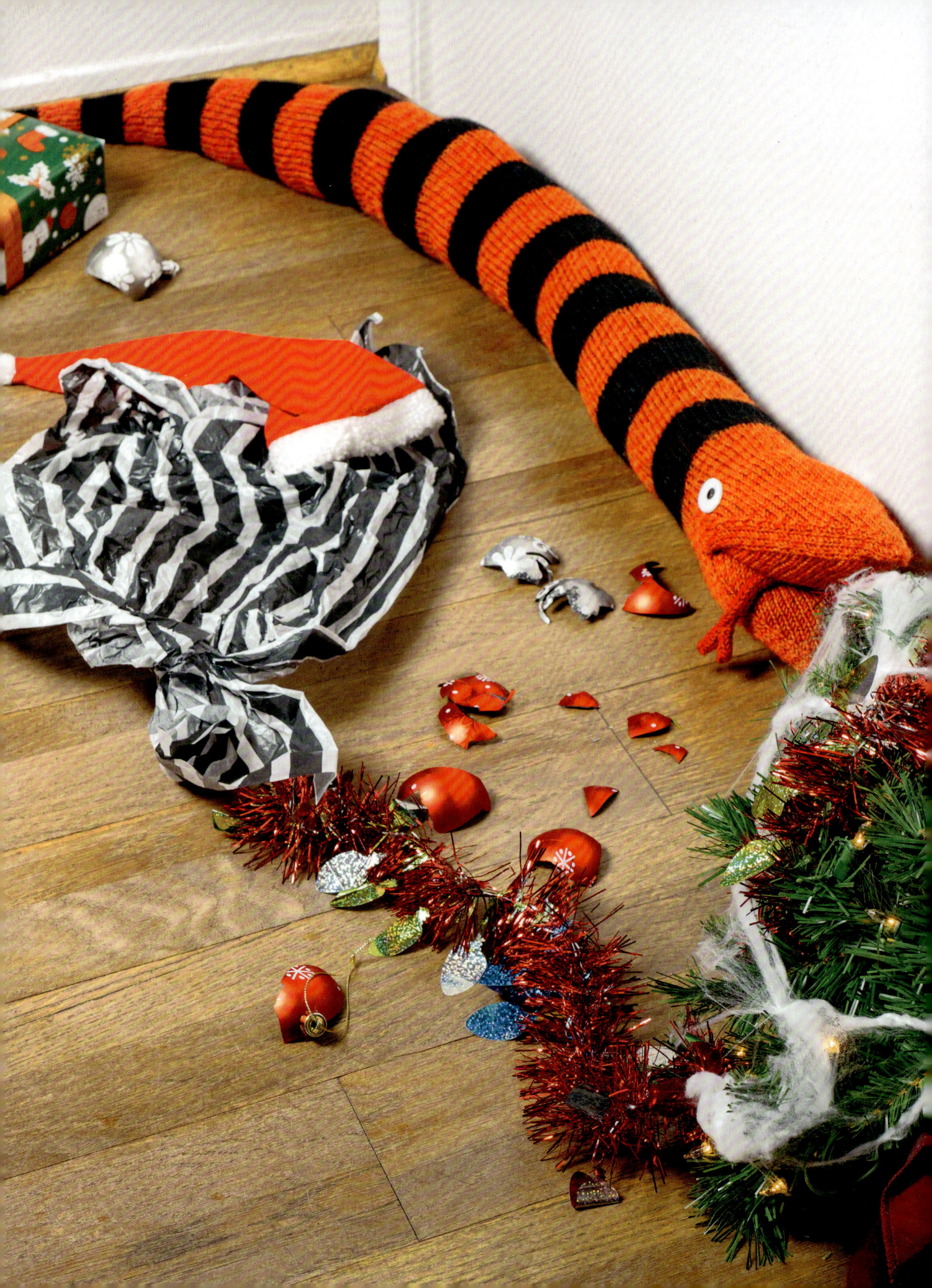

Snake Draft Blocker

Designed by
Tanis Gray

"Naughty children never get any presents!"
—Santa Claus

SKILL LEVEL
💀 💀 💀

Animators love planting "Easter eggs," hidden references to inside jokes, in their films. In this film, some of the gifts that were given to children in the Real World are nods to earlier Tim Burton films. The striped Christmas tree-eating snake is reminiscent of the sandworms in 1988's *Beetlejuice*, while the shrunken head being pulled out of the box by the little boy is from the afterlife waiting room from the same film. The flying Vampire Teddy and the evil quacking duck toy are both nods to 1992's *Batman Returns*, referencing Shreck's department store logo and the Penguin's vehicle of choice, respectively. There is even a hidden Mickey on one girl's nightgown when the toys begin to attack!

A low-maintenance pet that won't eat the Christmas tree, this striped snake can be a cozy snuggling companion or a guardian tucked at the base of a door to block wintry drafts. The snake is worked from the tail up in the round, as long or as short as desired, with simple increases and jogless stripes, stuffing as you go. The head is split into two parts and decreased similarly to basic top-down sock construction. A simple i-cord forked tongue and safety eyes are added on to give your snake some persssssssssssonality.

FRIGHTENING FACT

Another hidden Mickey can be seen on Jack's worktable among the clutter of his Christmas experiments in the form of a tiny Mickey head from the top of a mechanical pencil. Animator Anthony Scott got permission from director Henry Selick to hide it in the film as a nod to Disney.

SIZES
One size

FINISHED MEASUREMENTS
Length: 41 in. / 104 cm from nose tip to tail tip

Circumference: 10½ in. / 26.5 cm at widest part of body

YARN
Worsted weight yarn, shown in Berroco *Ultra Alpaca* (50% superfine alpaca, 50% Peruvian wool; approx. 219 yd. / 200 m per 3½ oz. / 100 g hank)

COLORWAYS:
- Color A: #6245 Pitch Black, 1 hank
- Color B: #6268 Candied Yam Mix, 1 hank

NEEDLES
US 5 / 3.75 mm set of 2 double-pointed needles

US 6 / 4 mm set of 4 double-pointed needles or size needed to obtain gauge

NOTIONS
Stitch markers

Red worsted weight yarn (approx. 3 yd. / 2.75m) for tongue

Polyester stuffing (approx. 9 oz. / 255 g)

Smooth waste yarn or stitch holder

Pair of safety eyes (approx. 30 by 20 mm)

Tapestry needle

GAUGE
20 sts and 28 rnds = 4 in. / 10 cm over St st in the round on larger needle, taken without blocking

PATTERN NOTES

- The snake is worked from the tail up and knit in the round. The head is split into two sections to create the mouth opening.
- Do not break yarns between the Color A and Color B stripes in the body of the snake. Carry the yarns loosely up the inside to save on yardage and ends to weave in.
- As you change colors between the Color A and Color B stripes in the body of the snake, use the Jogless Stripes method to avoid jogs at the beginning of round.

PATTERN INSTRUCTIONS

CAST ON—TAIL

Using Color A and gauge-size needles, CO 9 sts using the Circular Cast On method. Distribute 3 sts on each of 3 dpns. Pm for BOR (if desired) and join to work in the rnd. Increases for the shaping of the snake body are relative to the stitches on each dpn; we recommend using the number of dpns specified.
Knit 11 rnds. These 11 rnds make up the tip of the tail and are considered Stripe 1.

STRIPED BODY

Join Color B.

STRIPE 2—COLOR B
RND 1: Knit.
RND 2 (INC): *Knit to end of dpn, M1L; rep from * 2 more times—12 sts.
RNDS 3–12: Knit.

STRIPE 3—COLOR A
RND 1: Knit.
RND 2 (INC): *Knit to end of dpn, M1L; rep from * 2 more times—3 sts inc.
RNDS 3–7: Knit.
RND 8 (INC): *Knit to end of dpn, M1L; rep from * 2 more times—3 sts inc.
RNDS 9–12: Knit.

STRIPE 4—COLOR B
RND 1: Knit.
RND 2 (INC): *Knit to end of dpn, M1L; rep from * 2 more times—3 sts inc.
RNDS 3–7: Knit.
RND 8 (INC): *Knit to end of dpn, M1L; rep from * 2 more times—3 sts inc.
RNDS 9–12: Knit.

STRIPES 5-8
Rep [Stripes 3 and 4] 2 more times. There will be a total of 48 sts (16 sts per dpn).
Carefully turn the snake inside out and weave in the tail of Colors A and B to the WS before proceeding.

FINISH THE STRIPES
Turn the snake RS out.
*With Color A: Knit 12 rnds.
With Color B: Knit 12 rnds.*
Rep from * to * until work measures 33½ in. / 85 cm or until there are 21 total stripes, ending with a full Color A stripe.
AT THE SAME TIME, stuff the body of the snake with the polyester stuffing to avoid difficulties when the snake is full length.
Break Color A. The remainder of the snake is worked with Color B only.
Knit 6 rnds. After completing the 6th rnd, place the first 24 sts of the rnd on one dpn; place the remaining 24 sts on waste yarn or stitch holder.

TOP OF HEAD/MOUTH

INCREASE ROW (RS): K1, M1R, knit to last st, M1L, k1—26 sts. Cast on 26 sts to the end of the row using the Backward Loop method—52 sts total.

Join sts to work in the rnd making sure to move the newly cast-on sts across the WS (purl side) of the top of head; the opening for the mouth should be below/behind the existing working sts. Pm for BOR and place a mid-round marker between sts 26 and 27; markers will be indicators of the division between the top of the head (the first 26 sts) and the roof of the mouth (the second 26 sts). Distribute sts over additional needle as needed for comfort.

RND 1: Knit.
RND 2 (INC): *K1, M1R, knit to 1 st before M, M1L, k1, sm; rep from * once more—4 sts inc.
RNDS 3 AND 4: Rep [Rnds 1 and 2] 1 time—60 sts.
RNDS 5–24: Knit.
RND 25 (DEC): *K1, ssk, knit to 3 sts before M, k2tog, k1; rep from * once more—4 sts dec.
RND 26: Knit.
RNDS 27–30: Rep [Rnds 25 and 26] 2 times—48 sts.
RND 31 (DEC): *K1, ssk, knit to 3 sts before M, k2tog, k1; rep from * once more—4 sts dec.
RNDS 32 AND 33: Knit.

RNDS 34–63: Rep [Rnds 31–33] 10 times—4 sts rem.

RND 64 (DEC): Ssk, k2tog—2 sts rem. Break yarn, pull tail through remaining live sts, and cinch closed. Secure tail to WS.

BOTTOM OF HEAD/MOUTH

Place the live 24 sts onto a gauge-size needle. Rejoin Color B with the RS facing.

INCREASE ROW (RS): K1, M1R, k22, M1L, k1—26 sts. Cast on 26 sts to the end of the row using the Backward Loop method—52 sts total.

Join sts to work in the rnd making sure to move the newly cast-on sts across the WS (purl side) of the bottom of the head; the opening for the mouth should mirror the top of the head, below/behind the existing working sts. Pm for BOR and place a mid-round marker between sts 26 and 27; markers will be indicators of the division between the bottom of the head (the first 26 sts) and the bottom of the mouth (the second 26 sts). Distribute sts over additional needle as needed for comfort. Beginning with Rnd 1, work as for the Top of Head/Mouth.

FINISH THE HEAD

Secure the safety eyes on the top of the head using the photos as a reference for placement.

Stuff the head with stuffing.

Using Color B, thread the tapestry needle and whipstitch the opening of the mouth closed, going past each edge of the mouth by 1 in. / 2.5 cm.

TONGUE

Using the red worsted weight yarn and the smaller needles, CO 4 sts using the Long Tail Cast On method, leaving a 10 in. / 25.5 cm tail. Work a 4-stitch i-cord for 4 in. / 10 cm.

NEXT ROW (RS, INC): [Kfb] 2 times—4 sts total. Place the remaining 2 unworked sts on waste yarn.

Work a 4-stitch i-cord for 1 in. / 2.5 cm. Bind off all sts knitwise.

Place the live 2 sts onto a smaller needle. Rejoin the red yarn with the RS facing.

SETUP ROW (RS, INC): [Kfb] 2 times—4 sts total.

Work a 4-stitch i-cord for 1 in. / 2.5 cm. Bind off all sts knitwise.

FINISHING

Using the cast on tail of the tongue, attach the tongue to the center whipstitch seam at the back of the mouth.

Weave in all loose ends with tapestry needle to the WS.

Do not block.

213

Glossary and Techniques

CAST ONS

ALTERNATING CABLE CAST ON

A variation of the Cable Cast On method that is geared toward projects that begin with a ribbed edge: Stitches are cast on alternately knitwise and purlwise to mimic those of the subsequent ribbing.

Make a slipknot and place it on the needle. Holding the needle with the slipknot in your left hand, insert the right needle into the stitch. Knit but do not drop the stitch from the left needle; place this new stitch onto the left needle (1 new stitch made).

*Step 1: Insert the right needle between the first 2 stitches on the left needle from the back and purl; place the new stitch on the left needle (1 new stitch made).

Step 2: Insert the right needle between the first 2 stitches on the right needle from the front and knit; place the new stitch on the left needle (1 new stitch made).

Repeat from * until the required number of stitches is on the needle.

BACKWARD LOOP CAST ON

*Holding the yarn over your left thumb with the end coming from the ball held by your last three fingers and at the outside of the thumb, insert the needle up under the yarn next to the outside of your thumb. Remove your thumb from the loop, and pull the end to tighten the yarn slightly to snug the yarn up on the needle.

Repeat from * until the required number of stitches has been cast on.

CIRCULAR CAST ON

Stitches are cast on over/around a large loop that is subsequently pulled tight to close any gap. This is best worked over double-pointed needles.

Note: Stitches will be cast on to the needle, alternately loading the stitches with the needle above the loop and loading the stitches with the needle inside the loop. The final stitch will be cast on with the needle inside the loop.

Create a loop of yarn that is approximately 1 to 2 in. / 2.5 to 5 cm in diameter by crossing the short tail (enough to weave in at the end) in front of the working yarn (the yarn attached to the working ball) and pinching this crossing point between the thumb and middle finger of the left hand. Tension the working yarn over top of the pointer finger and under the ring finger of the left hand so that your fingers look like they are creating a lowercase b.

To begin, insert the right-hand needle through the front of the loop, and yarn over counterclockwise around the needle; pull the needle back through the loop toward you (1 stitch cast on).

*To cast on a stitch above the loop, leave the right-hand needle outside/above the loop and yarn over counterclockwise around the needle (secure the new loop by placing the pointer finger of the right hand on top of this new loop) (1 stitch cast on).

To cast on a stitch inside of the loop, insert the right-hand needle through the front of the loop (swinging the needle counterclockwise and down), and yarn over counterclockwise around the needle; pull the needle back through the loop.

Repeat from * until the required number of stitches is on the needle. Once all the stitches are cast on, pull the short tail to cinch up the loop. As the stitches are worked on the first few rounds, the loop may loosen; you can cinch the loop closed again by pulling the short tail and securing to the wrong side once enough fabric is established.

JUDY'S MAGIC CAST ON

This cast on creates a closed starting point, such as the toe of a sock. Two double-pointed needles (or two needle tips of the Magic Loop method) are held parallel in the right hand with the tips pointing to the left. The needle closer to you will be the front needle, and the needle farther from you will be the back needle.

With the left hand, drape a length of yarn over the back needle so that the tail falls between the two needles and the end attached to the ball of yarn drapes over the back needle.

Make a half twist of the strands counterclockwise so that the end attached to the ball is now in front and the tail is in back. This twist secures the first stitch on the back needle.

Split the yarn tails so that the shorter tail is over your thumb and the end attached to the ball is over your pointer finger; both tails should be caught by the last 3 fingers of your hand (similar to the setup for the Long Tail Cast On).

*Keeping the left hand stationary, swing the needles clockwise over the back tail, then down, under, and back up to catch the back tail with only the front needle—1 new stitch on the front needle.

Swing the needles counterclockwise and down over the front tail so that the front yarn moves up between the two needles and backward over the back needle—1 new stitch on the back needle.

Repeat from * until you have the total number of stitches, minus 1, on the needles (you will have 1 more stitch on the back needle than the front needle).

To complete the cast on, place the final stitch on the front needle as above. Give the yarn tails one more half twist to secure. Rotate the needles so that they are in the left hand, with the tips pointed to the right, to begin knitting.

LONG TAIL CAST ON

Make a slipknot with the yarn, leaving a tail long enough to cast on the required number of stitches (usually about 1 in. / 2.5 cm per stitch), and place the slipknot onto the needle. Holding the needle in your right hand, clasp both strands in your lower three fingers with the long tail over your thumb and the end coming from the ball over your index finger.

*Spread your thumb and index finger apart to form a V. Insert the needle tip up between the two strands on your thumb. Bring the needle tip over the top of the first strand around your index finger, then down to draw a loop between the strands on your thumb. Remove your thumb and tighten the stitch on the needle—1 stitch cast on. Place your thumb and index finger between the strands of yarn again. Repeat from * until the required number of stitches has been cast on.

TWO-COLOR LONG TAIL CAST ON

Note: As you work the steps below, periodically untwist your yarns to avoid frustration.

Make a slipknot with the tails of both yarns, leaving a tail long enough to weave in the ends, and place the slipknot onto the needle. Hold the needle in your right hand. This slipknot will count as the first 2 stitches cast on.

Step 1: With Yarn A over the thumb and Yarn B over the index finger, cast on 1 stitch per the Long Tail Cast On method as noted above—1 Yarn B stitch is cast on.

Step 2: Move Yarn B forward, to the left of Yarn A, and switch the yarn positions so Yarn A is now over the index finger and Yarn B is over the thumb. Cast on 1 stitch per the Long Tail Cast On method—1 Yarn A stitch is cast on.

Step 3: Move Yarn A forward, to the left of Yarn B, and switch the yarn positions so Yarn A is back over the thumb and Yarn B is over the index finger. Cast on 1 stitch per the Long Tail Cast On method—1 Yarn B stitch is cast on.

Repeat Steps 2 and 3 until the required number of stitches has been cast on.

TWISTED GERMAN CAST ON

Make a slipknot with the yarn leaving a tail long enough to cast on the required number of stitches (usually about 1 in. / 2.5 cm per stitch), and place the slipknot onto the needle.

*Holding the needle and yarn as for a Long Tail Cast On, bring the needle toward you, under both strands around your thumb. Swing the tip up and toward you again, then down into the loop on your thumb, then up in front of the loop on your thumb. Then swing it over the top of the loops and over the first strand on your index finger, catch that strand, and bring the needle back down through the thumb loop and to the front, turning your thumb as needed to make room for the needle to pass through. Remove your thumb from the loop, then pull the strands to tighten the stitch. Repeat from * until the required number of stitches has been cast on.

PROVISIONAL CAST ON

CROCHET PROVISIONAL CAST ON

With waste yarn, make a slipknot and place on the crochet hook. Hold the needle in your left hand, the waste yarn over your left index finger, and the crochet hook in your right hand.

*Hold the needle above the yarn coming from the hook. With the crochet hook, reach over the top of the needle and make a chain, making sure the yarn goes around the needle—1 stitch cast on. Repeat from * until the required number of stitches has been cast on. Cut the yarn and fasten off the last chain, being careful not to tighten the stitch.

Change to the working yarn, ready to work across the cast on stitches per pattern.

When going to finish the edge or pick up the stitches to continue working in the other direction, pull the waste yarn tail out of the last stitch cast on, and pull carefully to unzip the edge, placing the resulting stitches onto the needle as you go.

BIND OFFS

THREE-NEEDLE BIND OFF

The Three-Needle Bind Off is a way to join two sets of live stitches in a bound-off edge, creating a firm seam. This method of seaming is ideal for seams that need structure to support the weight of the body and sleeves of a garment.

Place each set of stitches to be joined on separate needles, making sure the needle tips are at the right-hand edge of the sts to be bound off.

Hold both needles in your left hand with needle tips pointing to the right.

With your right hand, insert a third needle knitwise into the first stitch on both needles, then knit them together—1 stitch from each needle has been joined. *Knit the next stitch on both needles together; lift the first stitch worked over the stitch just worked and off the needle—1 stitch bound off.

Repeat from * until all stitches have been worked and 1 stitch remains on the right needle. Cut yarn and fasten off the remaining stitch.

TWO-COLOR BIND OFF

This bind off is used for Double Knitting to ensure both yarns are used for the bind off.

Step 1: K2tog with Yarns A and B held together; 1 stitch of each color will now be on the right-hand needle.

Step 2: Holding Yarns A and B to the back, knit 1 stitch with Yarn A. Pass the 2 stitches of Yarns A and B from Step 1 over the stitch just knit and off the needle—1 stitch bound off. Move both yarns to the front between the needles.

Step 3: Holding Yarns A and B to the front, purl 1 stitch with Yarn B. Pass the stitch remaining from Step 2 over the stitch just purled and off the needle—1 stitch bound off. Move both yarns to the back between the needles.

Step 4: Holding Yarns A and B to the back, knit 1 stitch with Yarn A. Pass the stitch remaining from Step 3 over the stitch just knit and off the needle—1 stitch bound off. Move both yarns to the front between the needles.

Step 5: Holding Yarns A and B to the front, purl 1 stitch with Yarn B. Pass the stitch remaining from Step 4 over the stitch just purled and off the needle—1 stitch bound off. Move both yarns to the back between the needles.

Repeat Steps 4 and 5 until 2 stitches remain on the left-hand needle. K2tog with Yarns A and B held together. Pass the stitch remaining from the previous step over the k2tog just worked and off the needle—final stitch bound off. Break Yarns A and B and pull tails through the remaining stitch to secure.

MODIFIED ICELANDIC BIND OFF

The Modified Icelandic Bind Off is a stretchy bind off method that pairs nicely with garter stitch fabric.

Step 1: Knit 1 stitch loosely.

Step 2: Slip the next stitch purlwise (2 stitches on right-hand needle).

Step 3: Pass the knit stitch over the slipped stitch from right to left and off the needle—1 stitch bound off, 1 stitch remaining on the right-hand needle.

Step 4: Transfer the remaining stitch purlwise from the right-hand to left-hand needle.

Repeat Steps 1–4 until 1 stitch remains on the left-hand needle after completing Step 4.

Knit this remaining stitch. Break the working yarn and pull the tail through the remaining stitch, pulling tight to cinch closed.

JENY'S SURPISINGLY STRETCHY BIND OFF

A sufficiently stretchy bind off for the brim of a hat or the cuff of a sock, this bind off is also structural enough for a collar or button band of a sweater.

Special Technique: Yarn over backward—move the working yarn over the top of the right-hand needle from back to front (the opposite of a standard yarn over) and to the back again between the needles, creating a new stitch on the right-hand needle.

To process a knit stitch: Yarn over backward, knit 1 stitch.

To process a purl stitch: Yarn over, purl 1 stitch.

To begin binding off, knit or purl the first stitch (as it presents) without any yarn overs. *Process the second stitch with its yarn over. There will now be 3 stitches on the right-hand needle. With the left-hand needle, pull the 2 rightmost stitches (the original stitch and the yo) over the leftmost stitch and off the needle—1 stitch remains on the right-hand needle. Repeat from * until all sts are bound off.

INCREASES

KFB: Knit into the front of the next stitch but do not remove it from the left needle. Bring the right needle to the back of work and knit into the back of the same stitch, then drop the stitch from the left needle—1 stitch increased.

M1L (MAKE 1 STITCH, LEFT LEANING): Insert left needle under the strand between the stitch just worked and the next stitch from front to back; knit this through the back loop—1 stitch increased.

M1LP (MAKE 1 STITCH PURLWISE, LEFT LEANING): Insert left needle under the strand between the stitch just worked and the next stitch from front to back; purl this through the back loop—1 stitch increased.

M1LPX2 (MAKE 1 STITCH PURLWISE 2 TIMES UNDER SAME STRAND, LEFT LEANING): *Insert the left-hand needle under the running thread from front to back, and purl this new loop through the back loop; repeat from * under the same running thread—2 stitches increased.

M1R (MAKE 1 STITCH, RIGHT LEANING): Insert left needle under the strand between the stitch just worked and the next stitch from back to front; knit this through the front—1 stitch increased.

M1RP (MAKE 1 STITCH PURLWISE, RIGHT LEANING): Insert left needle under the strand between the stitch just worked and the next stitch from back to front; purl this through the front—1 stitch increased.

M1RPX2 (MAKE 1 STITCH PURLWISE 2 TIMES UNDER SAME STRAND, RIGHT LEANING): *Insert the left-hand needle under the running thread from back to front, and purl this new loop through the front; repeat from * under the same running thread—2 stitches increased.

JOGLESS STRIPES

Knitting in the round is a coil; the end of a round pushes up on top of the previous round rather than ending at the marker. As such, when you change to a new color when striping a project worked in the round, you will see a jog in the colors. This technique minimizes this jog and allows for a smoother color transition.

Knit 1 round with your new color. Move the beginning of round marker to the right needle.

Use the tip of the right needle to pick up the right leg of the stitch below the first stitch of the new round (the leg will be the color of the old yarn) from back to front; place this new stitch onto the left needle right beside the first stitch of the new round. Knit these 2 stitches together. Knit to the end of the round as normal.

I-CORD

An i-cord is a long, narrow knitted tube that mimics knitting in the round but is worked with just two needles, flat. It must be worked on double-pointed needles or a circular needle (a needle with tips at each end). A straight needle with a stopper at one end will not work.

Cast on the number of stitches listed in the pattern (usually between 2 and 4 stitches). Slide the stitches to the right end of the needle and pull the working yarn behind the back of the work ready to knit the first stitch closest to the right needle tip. This will create a tube.

Row 1: Knit, then slide stitches back to right end of needle. Do not turn; pull the working yarn behind.

Repeat Row 1 until the cord is the desired length. Finish off the cord as directed in the pattern.

I-CORD AROUND WIRE

Similar to the standard i-cord, this variation creates a tube around a fixed object (armature wire or pipe cleaner). It is best worked on double-pointed needles.

Cast on the number of stitches listed in the pattern (usually between 2 and 4 stitches). Slide the stitches to the right end of the needle. Place the armature wire perpendicular to the working needle and pull the working yarn behind the back of the work and around the armature wire ready to knit the first stitch closest to the right needle tip. This will create a tube.

Row 1: Knit, then slide stitches back to right end of needle. Do not turn; pull the working yarn behind the stitches and the armature wire.

Repeat Row 1 until the cord is the desired length. Finish off the cord as directed in the pattern.

ONE ROW BUTTONHOLE

This in-line buttonhole method allows for a buttonhole to be created mid-work, without breaking or joining new yarn. The following instructions create a 4-stitch buttonhole; adjust the numbers according to the size of buttonhole required for the pattern.

Step 1: With the right side facing, move the working yarn to the front between the needles, slip 1 stitch purlwise, move yarn to the back between the needles. Do not turn the work.

Step 2: Slip the next stitch purlwise from left-hand to right-hand needle. Pass the first slipped stitch over the second slipped stitch from right to left and off the needle (1 stitch bound off).

Step 3: Repeat [Step 2] 3 more times (4 total stitches bound off).

Step 4: Slip the last stitch from the right-hand needle purlwise to the left-hand needle; turn work.

Step 5: With the wrong side facing, cast on 5 stitches using the Cable Cast On method. On the final stitch cast on, before placing the new stitch on the left-hand needle, move the working yarn to the front between the needles. Place final stitch on left-hand needle. Turn work.

Step 6: With the right side facing, slip the first stitch on the left-hand needle knitwise to the right-hand needle. Pass the final cast on stitch over the just-slipped stitch from right to left and off the needle (1 stitch bound off).

SHORT ROWS

GERMAN SHORT ROWS

Double stitches are created by distorting the stitch at the end of the previously turned row.

On knit rows (following a turn): Move the working yarn to the front between the needles. Slip the first stitch purlwise to the right-hand needle. To create the double stitch (DS), pull the working yarn up and over the back of the right-hand needle so the stitch now looks like an upside-down V, with 2 legs. Keep the yarn in back, ready to knit the next stitch, and work across the row in pattern.

On purl rows (following a turn): With the working yarn still in front, slip the first stitch purlwise to the right-hand needle. To create the double stitch (DS), pull the working yarn up and over the back of the right-hand needle so the stitch now looks like an upside-down V, with 2 legs. Move the working yarn to the front between the needles, ready to purl the next stitch, and work across the row in pattern.

To process a double stitch on a subsequent row: Work to the double stitch and knit (or purl) the two legs together as if it were one stitch as a k2tog or p2tog.

WRAP AND TURN (W&T) SHORT ROWS

Slip all stitches purlwise in the following sequences.

On knit rows: Knit to instructed turning point. With the yarn in back, slip the next stitch to the right needle, move the yarn to the front between needles, slip the stitch back to the left needle, and move the yarn back between needles to the purl side. Turn work.

On purl rows: Purl to the instructed turning point. With the yarn in front, slip the next stitch to the right needle, move the yarn to the back between needles, slip the stitch back to the left needle, and move the yarn to the front between needles to the purl side. Turn work.

To process the wrap on a subsequent row: Work to the wrapped stitch, pick up the wrap from front to back for a knit stitch (and from back to front for a purl stitch), and place the wrap on the left needle. Work the wrap together with the stitch as a k2tog or p2tog.

STRANDED COLORWORK

Sometimes referred to as Fair Isle knitting, stranded colorwork uses two (or more) colors per round, with the color not currently in use being stranded, or carried, loosely across the wrong side of the work. Both yarns can be held in either the right or left hand, however you prefer to knit, or with one color in each hand. Whichever method you use, make sure to maintain even tension and keep the position vertically to maintain color dominance. The bottom strand carried will have more dominance than the top; it's best practice to carry the contrast colors as the dominant (or bottom) yarn.

When rounds of stranded colorwork are placed between rounds of stockinette, make sure to check both gauges before you begin; most knitters will work the stranded colorwork section more tightly than plain stockinette. Adjust your needle size when switching to the stranded section as needed to match gauge and remember to change back to the smaller needle(s) when beginning the next section of plain stockinette.

As you work across a round of the pattern, spread the stitches just worked apart slightly before knitting the next stitch with the color that has been carried across the wrong side. The float across the back should be relaxed, not sagging, but should also not be tight, so as to avoid puckering of the fabric.

If floats between color changes will be more than ¾ in. / 1 to 2 cm long, it's a good idea to catch the unused/floating color to reduce the risk of snagging the float later. The easiest way to do this is to hold the color to be "caught" in your left hand and the working color in your right hand. Insert the right needle into the next stitch and under the floated yarn, then knit as usual, allowing the floated yarn to come back down behind the needles so the working yarn will lie over the top of it on the next stitch. Catching floats more regularly than is necessary uses more yarn and can create a stiffer fabric.

DOUBLE KNITTING

Double knitting is a method of creating two-sided fabric, such as for a scarf or a coaster, without having an exposed wrong side. The front and back of the fabric are made simultaneously, knitting all stitches with one color, and purling all adjacent stitches with the opposite color, so that the front and back of the project are mirrors of one another. As such, double knitting is done in multiples of 2 stitches. The colorwork charts provided for Double Knitting indicate the color of the stitch that will be knit; the opposite color will be worked on all purl stitches and is not charted.

To work in the round:

*Move both yarns to the back between the needles as if to knit (if not already in position) and knit 1 stitch using the color indicated in the chart square. After completing the knit stitch, move both yarns to the front between the needles as if to purl and purl the next stitch with the opposite color to what is indicated for the knit stitch. Repeat from * to end of round.

To work flat:

With the RS facing: *Move both yarns to the back between the needles as if to knit (if not already in position) and knit 1 stitch using the color indicated in the chart square. After completing the knit stitch, move both yarns to the front between the needles as if to purl and purl the next stitch with the opposite color to what is indicated for the knit stitch. Repeat from * to end of row.

With the WS facing: *Move both yarns to the back between the needles as if to knit (if not already in position) and knit 1 stitch using the *opposite* color indicated in the chart square. After completing the knit stitch, move both yarns to the front between the needles as if to purl and purl the next stitch with the color indicated in the chart square. Repeat from * to end of row.

DUPLICATE STITCH

Sometimes called Swiss darning, duplicate stitch is a way of adding sections of color to a knitted piece without having to work stranded knitting or intarsia. The technique covers each stitch completely. Large areas can become thick and stiff, so it's best used in small areas.

With the color to be stitched threaded into a tapestry needle, insert the needle from wrong side to right side in the stitch below the first stitch to be covered.

*Insert the tapestry needle under both legs of the stitch in the row above the stitch to be covered, and pull the yarn through, being careful not to pull the yarn too tightly. Insert the needle back into the same spot where you initially brought it to the RS, and pull the yarn through to completely cover the first stitch. Bring the needle up through the stitch below the next stitch to be covered. Repeat from * to continue covering stitches.

APPLYING/PLACING BEADS

CROCHET HOOK METHOD

Using abbreviated letters to indicate the color of bead (e.g., G for green, R for red, or Y for yellow), AB-X indicates to apply a bead to the fabric.

Using a crochet or bead hook appropriate to the size of bead being used, insert the hook through the bead and leave the bead on the hook. With the crochet hook, pick up the loop of the stitch over which you want to place the bead and let it drop off your knitting needle. Pull this loop through the bead and place the loop back onto the left-hand needle, then remove the crochet hook. Knit this stitch in pattern to secure the bead.

KITCHENER STITCH

Often referred to as grafting, Kitchener stitch joins two sets of live stitches without a visible seam. This seaming method is not well suited for joining shoulder seams, which need to support the weight of the body and sleeves of the garment. It should be used for smaller seamed areas or for joining sections of a cowl or the toe of a sock that is expected to be stretched.

Work a few stitches at a time, pulling the yarn loosely, then adjust the length of each stitch to match the tension on each side of the join.

Place each set of stitches to be joined onto two separate needles, making sure the needle tips are at the right-hand edge of the stitches to be joined.

Hold both needles in your left hand, parallel, with needle tips pointing to the right.

Step 1: Thread the tapestry needle.

Step 2: Insert tapestry needle purlwise through first stitch on front needle and pull the yarn through, leaving stitch on front needle.

Step 3: Insert tapestry needle knitwise through first stitch on back needle and pull the yarn through, leaving stitch on back needle.

Step 4: Insert tapestry needle knitwise through first stitch on front needle, slip the stitch off front needle, and pull the yarn through.

Step 5: Insert tapestry needle purlwise through next stitch on front needle and pull the yarn through, leaving stitch on front needle.

Step 6: Insert tapestry needle purlwise through first stitch on back needle, slip the stitch off back needle, and pull the yarn through.

Step 7: Insert tapestry needle knitwise through next stitch on back needle and pull the yarn through, leaving stitch on back needle.

Repeat Steps 4-7 until the yarn has been threaded through the last stitch of each needle once. Insert tapestry needle knitwise into last stitch on front needle, slip the stitch off front needle, and pull yarn through. Then insert tapestry needle purlwise into last stitch on back needle, slip stitch from needle, and pull yarn through. Weave in ends on the wrong side to secure.

MATTRESS STITCH

Mattress stitch creates an invisible seam along two adjoining edges.

Place the pieces being sewn together side by side on a flat surface with the right sides facing you. Thread a tapestry needle with a piece of yarn about 3 times longer than the seam to be sewn.

Beginning at the bottom edge, insert the tapestry needle under one bar between the edge stitches on one piece, then under the corresponding bar on the other piece. *Insert the tapestry needle under the next two bars of the first piece, then under the next two bars of the other piece.

Repeat from *, alternating sides until the seam is complete, ending on the last bar or pair of bars on the first piece. Weave in ends on the wrong side to secure.

HORIZONTAL INVISIBLE SEAMING

A method of seaming two horizontal pieces of knit fabric together, such as a cast on edge to a bind off edge (or two cast on / two bind off edges).

Align the two edges to be seamed so that they are lined up, stitch by stitch, with the right sides facing up.

With a tapestry needle threaded with a length of yarn approximately 3 times the length of the seamed edges, insert the needle under both legs of the first stitch of one piece and pull the yarn through (leaving a tail for weaving in).

Insert the needle under both legs of the lined-up stitch on the opposite edge (the piece you are joining to) and pull the yarn through.

Repeat these two steps (without leaving a tail for weaving in on each subsequent stitch) until all the stitches are seamed. Once the seaming is complete, you may adjust the tension of the seaming yarn so the seam lies flat and the stitches appear the same size as the joined edges. Trim ends and weave in.

TWISTED HEEL FLAP PICK UP

To create a smaller internal seam and avoid holes along the edges of the heel flap, a twisted method can be used for heel flaps that have a slipped stitch edge.

With the wrong side of the flap facing, and working from the top of the heel flap toward the live stitches on the needle at the bottom of the heel flap, pick up the innermost leg (the left leg of the stitches along the right edge of the heel flap; the right leg of the stitches along the left edge of the heel flap) of each stitch with a spare dpn. You will pick up 1 leg for each slipped edge stitch.

Turn the work so the right side is facing and knit each new stitch through the back loops to twist closed.

STEM STITCH

The stem stitch is an embroidery technique used to create decorative straight lines on fabric.

Thread a tapestry needle with yarn. From the wrong side of the fabric, push the tapestry needle to the right side of the project, then insert the tapestry needle back into the fabric ¼ in. / .5 cm (or the desired total stitch length) beyond the original entry point to the wrong side.

*From the wrong side of the fabric, push the tapestry needle to the right side of the project ⅛ in. / .25 cm back (or half the desired total stitch length) from the previous entry point, then insert the tapestry needle back into the fabric ¼ in. / .5 cm (or the desired total stitch length) beyond the previous entry point to the wrong side.

Repeat from * to the end of the fabric, securing the tail to the wrong side.

RUNNING STITCH

Running stitch can be used to decorate knitted fabric, such as when adding eyes or mouths, as a visible technique, or it can be used to cinch sections of work, as a less visible technique.

DECORATIVE RUNNING STITCH

Thread the tapestry needle with the working yarn. *Starting at the bottommost point of the designated embroidery location, from the wrong side, push the tapestry needle through to the right side of the work, carry it across the front of the work over the desired number of stitches/rows, and then push it back through to the wrong side. Ensure the yarn isn't loose or saggy but isn't so tight that it puckers. Repeat from *, moving up one row / over one stitch, until the embellished work is complete. Cut yarn and weave tails to the wrong side to secure.

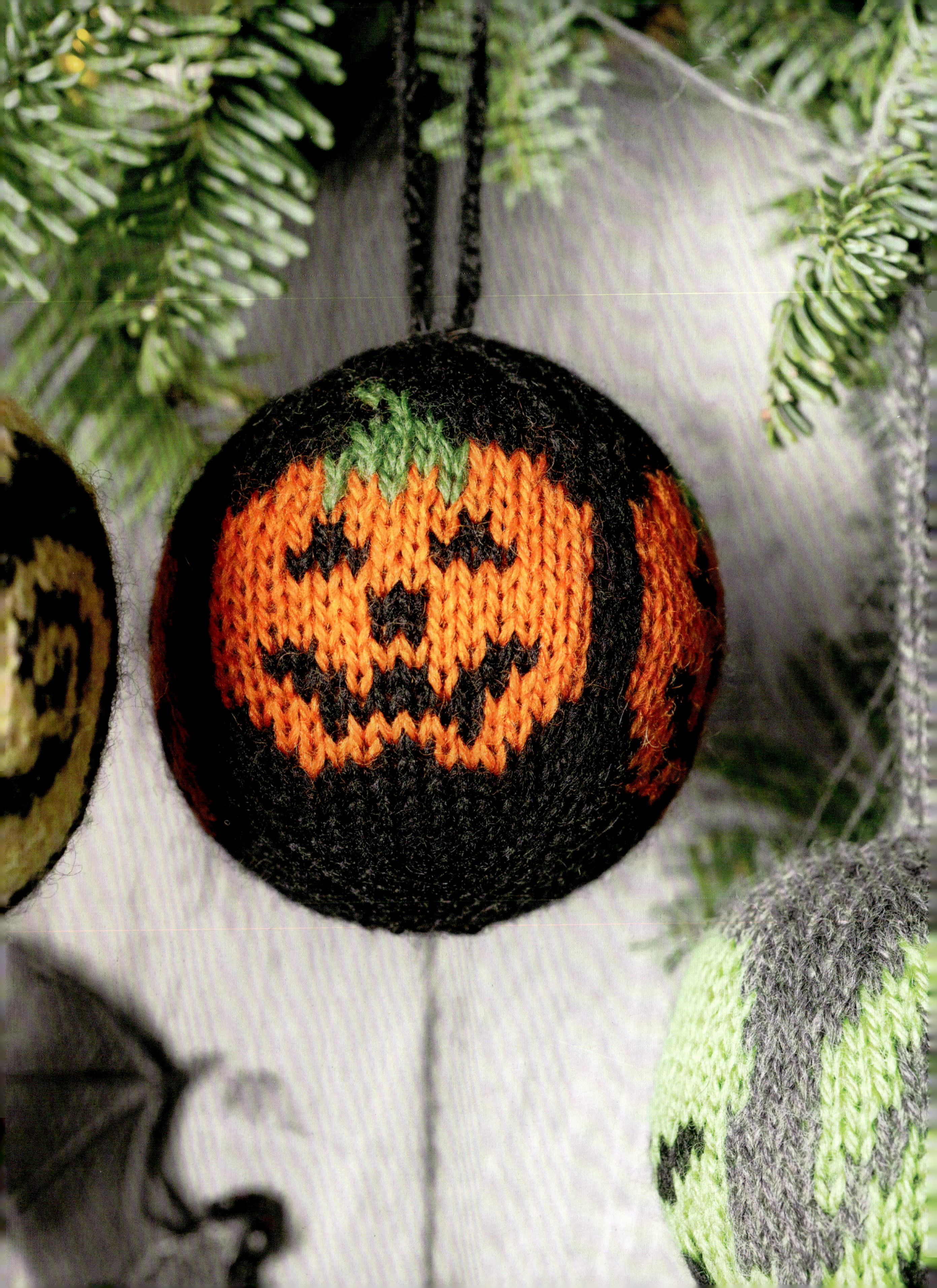

Abbreviations

2/2 LC—slip 2 stitches to cable needle and hold to front, knit 2; knit 2 stitches from cable needle
2/2 RC—slip 2 stitches to cable needle and hold to back, knit 2; knit 2 stitches from cable needle
AB—apply bead
APPROX.—approximately
BO—bind off
BOR—beginning of round/row
CC—contrast color
CM—centimeter(s)
CO—cast on
CONT—continue
DEC—decrease(s/d)
DPN(S)—double-pointed needle(s)
DS—double stitch (used in German short rows)
EST—established
G—gram(s)
IN.—inch(es)
INC—increase(s/d)
K—knit
K2TOG—knit 2 stitches together (1 stitch decreased)
K3TOG—knit 3 stitches together (2 stitches decreased)
K6BELOW—knit into the stitch 6 rows below the first stitch on the left-hand needle, dropping the stitches down above the new stitch (creating 6 ladders of the opposite color)
KFB—knit into front and back of same stitch (1 stitch increased)
LHN—left-hand needle
M—marker
m—meter(s)
M-A (B, C, ETC.)—marker A (B, C, etc.)
M1L—insert the left-hand needle under the running thread from front to back; knit this new loop through the back loop (1 stitch increased)
M1LP—insert the left-hand needle under the running thread from front to back; purl this new loop through the back loop (1 stitch increased)

M1LPX2—*insert the left-hand needle under the running thread from front to back, and purl this new loop through the back loop; repeat from * under the same running thread (2 stitches increased)
M1R—insert the left-hand needle under the running thread from back to front; knit this new loop (1 stitch increased)
M1RP—insert the left-hand needle under the running thread from back to front; purl this new loop (1 stitch increased)
M1RPX2—*insert the left-hand needle under the running thread from back to front, and purl this new loop; repeat from * under the same running thread (2 stitches increased)
MC—main color
MM—millimeter(s)
OZ.—ounce(s)
P—purl
P2TOG—purl 2 stitches together (1 stitch decreased)
PATT—pattern
PM—place marker
PM-A (B, C, ETC.)—place marker A (B, C, etc.)
PREV—previous
REM—remain(s/ing)
REP—repeat
RHN—right-hand needle
RM—remove marker
RND(S)—round(s)
RS—right side
RT—knit 2 stitches together leaving the original stitches on the left-hand needle; insert the right-hand needle tip between the needles and knit the first stitch again; drop both stitches off the left-hand needle
S2KP—slip 2 stitches knitwise, knit 1, pass slipped stitches over (2 stitches decreased)

SKP—slip 1 stitch knitwise, knit 1, pass slipped stitch over (1 stitch decreased)
SL—slip stitch purlwise (unless otherwise noted)
SL3KYOK—slip 3 stitches purlwise from left-hand needle to right-hand needle, then using the left-hand needle tip, lift the first slipped stitch up and over the second and third stitches from right to left and off the needle, move the remaining stitches purlwise back to the left-hand needle, knit 1, yarn over, knit 1
SM—slip marker
SSK—slip 1 stitch knitwise, slip second stitch knitwise, move these 2 stitches back to left-hand needle purlwise, and knit 2 together through the back loop (1 stitch decreased)
SSM—side seam marker
SSP—slip 1 stitch knitwise, slip second stitch knitwise, move these 2 stitches back to left-hand needle purlwise, and purl 2 together through the back loop (1 stitch decreased)
ST ST—stockinette stitch
ST(S)—stitch(es)
TBL—through back loop(s)
TURN—turn work so opposite side of work is facing
W&T—wrap and turn (short row method)
WS—wrong side
WYIB—with yarn in back
WYIF—with yarn in front
YD.—yard(s)
YO—yarn over (1 stitch increased)
SLASH (/)—used to separate US units from metric measurements
ASTERISK (*)—used to indicate the beginning of a length of instructions to be repeated
PARENTHESES ( ) OR BRACKETS [ ] OR BRACES { }—used to indicate a set of instructions to be repeated or to differentiate between sizes

Yarn Resource Guide

Berroco
Berroco.com

Biscotte Yarns
Biscotteyarns.com

Brooklyn Tweed
Brooklyntweed.com

Brown Sheep Company
Brownsheep.com

Cascade Yarns
Cascadeyarns.com

Dragon Hoard Yarn
Dragonhoardyarnco.com

Freia Fine Handpaint Yarns
Freiafibers.com

Hazel Knits
Hazelknits.com

Jamieson's of Shetland
Jamiesonsofshetland.co.uk

Keenan Hand Dyed Yarn
Keenanyarn.com

Kim Dyes Yarn
Kimdyesyarn.com

Lattes & Llamas
Lattesandllamas.com

Leading Men Fiber Arts
Leadingmenfiberarts.com

The Lemonade Shop
Thelemonadeshopyarns.com

LolaBean Yarn Co.
Lolabeanyarnco.com

Magpie Fibers
Magpiefibers.com

O-Wool
o-wool.com

The Plucky Knitter
Thepluckyknitter.com

Queen City Yarn
Queencityyarn.com

Seven Sisters Arts
Sevensistersarts.com

SweetGeorgia Yarns
Sweetgeorgiayarns.com

Urban Girl Yarns
urbangirlyarns.com

Urth Yarns
Urthyarns.com

A Whimsical Wood Yarn Co.
awhimsicalwoodyarnco.com

INSIGHT EDITIONS

PO Box 3088
San Rafael, CA 94912
www.insighteditions.com

Find us on Facebook: www.facebook.com/InsightEditions
Follow us on Twitter: @insighteditions
Follow us on Instagram: @insighteditions

Copyright © 2023 Disney

All rights reserved. Published by Insight Editions, San Rafael, California, in 2023.

No part of this book may be reproduced in any form without written permission from the publisher.

ISBN: 978-1-64722-928-3

Publisher: Raoul Goff
VP, Co-Publisher: Vanessa Lopez
VP, Creative: Chrissy Kwasnik
VP, Manufacturing: Alix Nicholaeff
VP, Group Managing Editor: Vicki Jaeger
Publishing Director: Jamie Thompson
Designer: Brooke McCullum
Senior Editor: Samantha Holland
Editorial Assistant: Emma Merwin
Managing Editor: Maria Spano
Senior Production Editor: Katie Rokakis
Production Manager: Deena Hashem
Senior Production Manager, Subsidiary Rights: Lina s Palma-Temena

Technical Editing by Meaghan Schmaltz

Photo Art Direction: Judy Wiatrek Trum
Photography: Paulette Phlipot
Prop Stylist Elena P. Craig
Hair and Makeup by: Hanna Costa

Special thanks to our models: Teagan, Caoimhe, Oonagh, Cassidy, Naila, Natalia, Rena, Nelson, and Sabrina

ROOTS of PEACE   REPLANTED PAPER

Insight Editions, in association with Roots of Peace, will plant two trees for each tree used in the manufacturing of this book. Roots of Peace is an internationally renowned humanitarian organization dedicated to eradicating land mines worldwide and converting war-torn lands into productive farms and wildlife habitats. Roots of Peace will plant two million fruit and nut trees in Afghanistan and provide farmers there with the skills and support necessary for sustainable land use.

Manufactured in China by Insight Editions

10 9 8 7 6 5 4 3 2 1

For Grace, the Queen of Halloween Town

ACKNOWLEDGMENTS

Like Oogie Boogie, "I'm gonna do the best I can," but that would not have been possible without so many talented and exceptional people working beside me.

Deepest gratitude to my editor, Sammy Holland, who ushered me through the door to Halloween Town. I will never slip Deadly Nightshade into your tea and am always delighted to recite Shakespearian quotations with you. You are the Sally to my Jack.

Thank you to my family, Roger, Callum, and Astrid. Your patience while I explored Jack's world, your willingness to watch the film over and over and live through Halloween for many months, your encouragement, and your love made this a family adventure. You're my favorite trio of trick-or-treaters and I'll always share my candy with you.

I'm so grateful to have parents who supported my love of animation, fiber, and art from an early age. Mom and Dad, I am thankful for you every day. I love you to Halloween Town and back.

To my spectacularly skilled tech editor, Meaghan Schmaltz, thank you for your friendship, patience, and dedication. "We're simply meant to be."

I have extreme appreciation for the wonderful designers who went down the Nightmare rabbit hole with me. Both old friends and new, my deepest thanks for your talents and inspiration. You all deserve extra presents from Sandy Claws.

Thank you to the brilliant dyers who offer yarn support and enthusiasm. You helped bring these excellent projects to life with your skill.

To my sample knitter Drew Harder, I don't know how you do it, but you're amazing! Thank you for your nimble and quick knitting hands.

Finally, to my second family at Insight Editions, thank you for joining me at my side to gaze at the stars like Sally and Jack, for continuing to write books together, and for believing in me.